U2

THE BEST OF
PROPAGANDA
20 YEARS OF THE OFFICIAL U2 MAGAZINE

CARLTON
BOOKS

CONTENTS

This is a Carlton book

First published in Great Britain by
Carlton Books Limited 2003
20 Mortimer Street
London W1T 3JW

Text & Design copyright © U2 Limited 2003

ISBN 1 84442 987 3

Project Editor: Ian Gittins
Editorial Manager: Lorna Russell
Art Director: Clare Baggaley
Design: Steve Averill
Layout Design: Bobbi at DW Design
Production: Lisa Moore

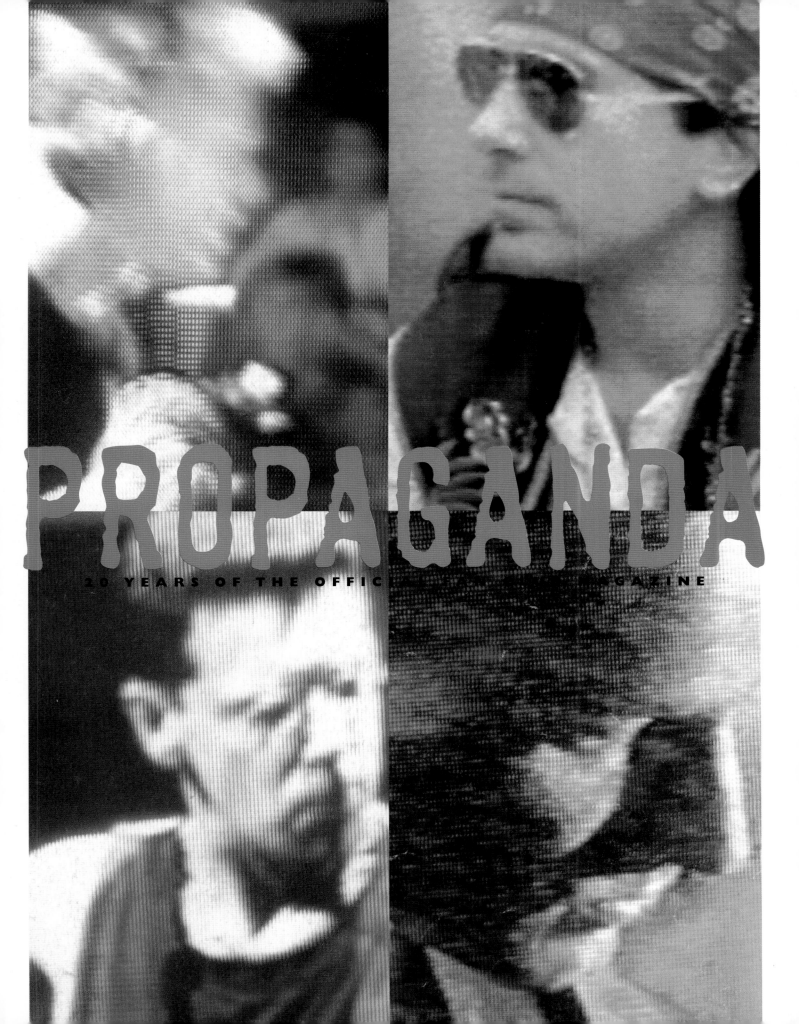

PROPAGANDA

20 YEARS OF THE OFFIC... ...GAZINE

FOREWORD

by U2 and PAUL McGUINNESS

U2 have always attracted a pretty smart following, people who managed to discover what we were up to long before we knew it. And since I am both a fan and a member of the band, *Propaganda* was essential reading. To be honest, it was never U2 propaganda as such, because although we made suggestions for stories, we had no idea what was going to be in each issue until it came through the letter box. In fact, it was actually very useful for finding out what we think of each other, particularly on the odd occasions when we stopped talking. For instance it was a revelation to discover what Larry thought of the *Passengers* album... I had no idea!

BONO

You don't want to read about yourself in your own magazine all the time, so it was great that in *Propaganda* you'd find interviews with B.B.King or Wim Wenders, or learn about a new Greenpeace project, or check out what fans wanted to swap with each other. One of the best things about *Propaganda,* from our point of view, is that we never knew what was going to be in it.

LARRY

It's amazing to think there have been over thirty issues of our own magazine. That's nearly a thousand pages. It's like a fans'-eye encyclopedia of the band over a couple of decades, a collection of grainy snapshots from defining moments down the years. Looking through its back pages now is like delving through a family album put together by fans. Fair play to the writers and editors for maintaining such enthusiasm. We lost interest in ourselves ages ago!

EDGE

Propaganda was a great way of keeping up with what our fans were into as our audience grew. We've always believed in people doing it for themselves, and at times the magazine carried information on scores of unofficial U2 'zines from all over the world... all trying to outdo our official one! Because the readers were kind of on the inside a little, it was also cool that we could put out one-off releases to them like the *Melon* or *Hasta La Vista* CDs. In the beginning we just wanted a great regular magazine about the group and what we were into. And we got that with *Propaganda*. Except for the "regular" bit!

ADAM

Fanzine culture was an integral part of the punk music environment from which U2 came in the late 70s. Those very first U2 magazines had that real D-I-Y ethos about them, and even when it became a glossy, it was edited by fans and retained the voice of fans. We'd often learn things through the magazine that were annoying fans – like the way concert tickets went on sale, always a great bone of contention. It upped the game for us, ensuring we created as fair a process as we could. Good communication with fans has always been critical for U2 and, until the arrival of the net, *Propaganda* was an essential part of our relationship with our audience. Reading this book is like seeing my life flash before me...

PAUL McGUINNESS, U2 MANAGER

U2 MAGAZINE

NOVEMBER 1981 – SUMMER 1985

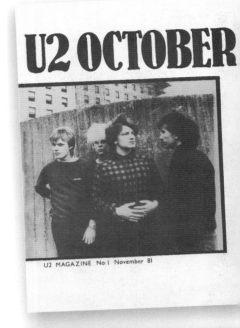

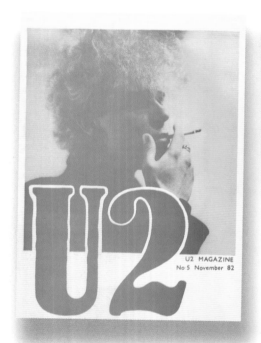

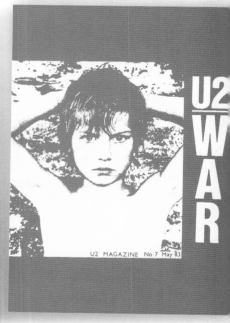

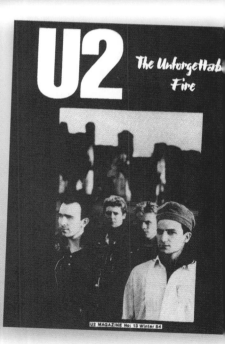

U2 MAGAZINE No 2 February 82

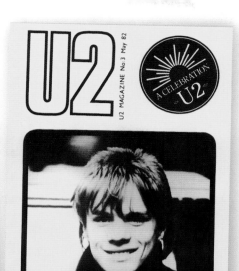

U2 MAGAZINE No 3 May 82

A CELEBRATION U2

U2 MAGAZINE No 4 August 82

U2 MAGAZINE No: 8 August 83

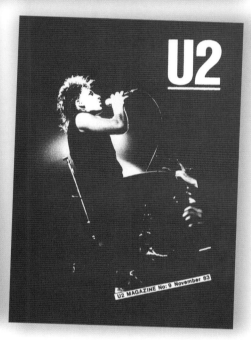

U2 MAGAZINE No: 9 November 83

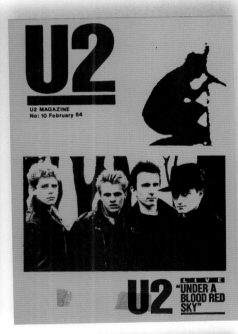

U2 MAGAZINE No: 10 February 84

U2 LIVE "UNDER A BLOOD RED SKY"

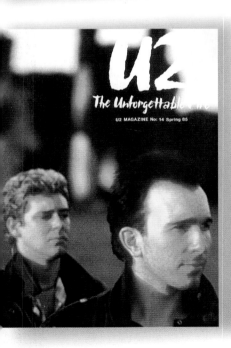

The Unforgettable Fire

U2 MAGAZINE No: 14 Spring 85

U2 MAGAZINE No: 15 Summer 85

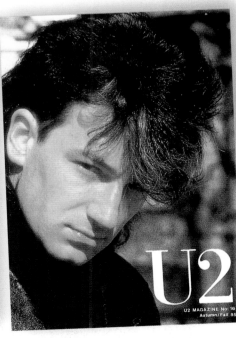

U2 MAGAZINE No: 16 Autumn/Fall 85

U2 *ISSUE 1*

U2 OCTOBER

U2 MAGAZINE No:1 November 81

U2's FIRST AMERICAN WRITE-UP!
RS 19.2.81
U2: HERE COMES THE "NEXT BIG THING"
by James Henke

Here I am, an American writer, dining with an Irish band in a Greek restaurant in the heart of England. Strange? Well, so is the scene that's unfolding in front of me. A few feet away, two musicians are seated on a platform. One is playing bazouki, a string instrument similar to a mandolin, while the other, a heavy-set fellow in black suit and dark glasses, is hammering away at a small electric keyboard with built in drum rhythm machine. In front of them, approving patrons toss plate after ceramic plate to the floor, where they shatter at the feet of U2's Bono Vox, who is demonstrating that a rock singer from Ireland can be quite a lively dancer.

Though this seems like some sort of international celebration, it's only another pre-show dinner for U2. The band which has been touring Britain non-stop since the release of "Boy", has garnered more than the usual amount of attention. Since early last year, the media have been touting U2 as the Next Big Thing. If all the publicity weren't enough, Island Records President Chris Blackwell proclaimed the group the label's most important signing since King Crimson.

In concert, the loquacious Bono tries to play down all the hype – he regularly tells audiences to "forget all that stuff you may have read and make up your own minds" – but privately he concurs with the press. "I don't mean to sound arrogant," he tells me after the dancing has died down, "but even at this stage, I do feel that we are meant to be one of the great groups. There's a certain spark, a certain chemistry, that was special about the Stones, The Who and the Beatles, and I think it's also special about U2."

A mighty boast, to be sure. But "Boy", scheduled for late-January U.S. release, does indicate that U2 is a band to be reckoned with. Their highly original sound can best be described as pop music with brains. It's accessible and melodic combining the dreamy, atmospheric qualities of a band like Television, with a hard rock edge not unlike The Who's. In particular, Edge's guitar playing and Bono's singing stand out; the lyrical guitar lines slice through every song, while the vocals are rugged, urgent and heartfelt.

The title "Boy" is appropriate and significant: not only are the band members young, but the bulk of their songs deal with the dreams and frustrations of childhood. "We're playing to audiences in Britain that range in age from 17 to 25," Bono explains. "There is massive unemployment, and there is real disillusionment. U2's music is about getting up and doing something about it. People like Bruce Springsteen carry hope. Like The Who – 'Won't Get Fooled Again'. I mean, there is a song of endurance, and that's the attitude of the great bands. We want our audience to think about their actions and where they are going, to realise the pressures that are on them, but at the same time not to give up."

U2 · BOY

— 4 —

Especially for cassette-buyers here are some of the lyrics to "Boy". The other songs on "Boy" which weren't printed on the sleeve, plus the lyrics to the songs on "October" will follow in future issues.

THE OCEAN

A picture in grey, Dorian Gray,
Just me by the sea.
And I felt like a star.

I thought the world could go far,
If they listened to what I said.

The Ocean, the Ocean
Washes my feet.
Splashes the soul of my shoes.

When I looked around,
The world couldn't be found.
Just me by the sea.

SHADOWS AND TALL TREES

Back to the cold restless streets at night
I talk to myself about tomorrow night.
Walls of white protest, a gravestone in name
Who is it now? it's always the same.

Who is it now? who calls me inside
Are the leaves on the trees just a living disguise?
I walk the sweet rain tragicomedy
I'll walk home again to the street melody.

But I know oh no
But I know oh no
I know

Shadows and tall trees
Shadows and tall trees
Shadows and tall trees
Shadows and tall trees

Life through a window, a discoloured pain,
Mrs Brown's washing is always the same.
I walk the sweet rain tragicomedy
I'll walk home again to the street melody.

(Out there)
Do you feel in me, anything redeeming,
Any worthwhile feeling
Is life like a tightrope? hanging on my ceiling.

But I know oh no
But I know oh no
I know

Shadows and Tall Trees.

PRODUCED BY STEVE LILLYWHITE
AVAILABLE ON RECORD AND ON 1 + 1 CASSETTE

© 1980 Lyrics Reproduced By Kind Permission Of Blue Mountain Music Ltd.

U2 · BOY

— 5 —

TWILIGHT

I look into his eyes, they're closed
But I see something.
A teacher told me why, I laugh
When old men cry.

My body grows and grows,
It frightens me, you know.
The old man tried to walk me home,
I thought he should have known.

Twilight
Twilight
Twilight
Twilight

Lost my way,
Night and day,
Can't find my way.

(In the shadow boy meets man
In the shadow boy meets man).

I'm running in the rain.
I'm caught in a late night play.
It's all and everything,
I'm soaking through the skin.

Twilight
Twilight
Twilight
Twilight

Darkened days,
Lost my way,
Night and day,
Can't find my way.

(In the shadow boy meets man
In the shadow boy meets man).

I WILL FOLLOW

I was on the outside, when you said,
You said you needed me.
I was looking at myself, I was blind,
I could not see.

A boy tries hard to be a man,
His mother takes him by his hand.
If he stops to think he starts to cry.
Oh why?

If you walkaway, walkaway
I walkaway, walkaway — I will follow.

I was on the inside.
When they pulled the four walls down.
You looked through the window, I was lost,
I am found.

If you walkaway, walkaway
I walkaway, walkaway — I will follow.

(Your eyes make a circle,
I see you when I go in there).

If you walkaway, walkaway
I walkaway, walkaway — I will follow.
I will follow

I will follow . . .

· I WILL FOLLOW ·

Bono : Singer
The Edge : Guitar Player
Adam Clayton : Bass Player
Larry : Drummer

U2

Producer : Steve Lillywhite
Manager : Paul McGuinness

Engineer : Paul Thomas
Assistant : Kevin Moloney

Sleeve Design/Layout : Bono, Rapid Exteriors
"Boy" Photographs : Hugo McGuinness
U2 Photographs : Phil Sheils

Tour Manager : Tim Nicholson
Crew : John Kennedy, Pod, Amigo O'Herlihy

Studio : Windmill Lane, Dublin
Mastered At The Sound Clinic By John Dent

Agent Dublin : Dave Kavanagh, Road Runner
Agent London : Ian Wilson, Wasted Talent

SIDE ONE : 1. I Will Follow 2. Twilight 3. An Cat Dubh 4. Into The Heart 5. Out Of Control
SIDE TWO : 1. Stories For Boys 2. The Ocean 3. A Day Without Me 4. Another Time, Another Place 5. The Electric Co. 6. Shadows And Tall Trees.

© 1980 Lyrics Reproduced By Kind Permission Of Blue Mountain Music Ltd.

— 6 —

U2's
FIRST AMERICAN WRITE-UP!
RS 19.2.81

U2: HERE COMES THE "NEXT BIG THING"
by James Henke

Here I am, an American writer, dining with an Irish band in a Greek restaurant in the heart of England. Strange? Well, so is the scene that's unfolding in front of me. A few feet away, two musicians are seated on a platform. One is playing bazouki, a string instrument similar to a mandolin, while the other, a heavy-set fellow in black suit and dark glasses, is hammering away at a small electric keyboard with built in drum rhythm machine. In front of them, approving patrons toss plate after ceramic plate to the floor, where they shatter at the feet of U2's Bono Vox, who is demonstrating that a rock singer from Ireland can be quite a lively dancer.

Though this seems like some sort of international celebration, it's only another pre-show dinner for U2. The band which has been touring Britain non-stop since the release of "Boy", has garnered more than the usual amount of attention. Since early last year, the media have been touting U2 as the Next Big Thing. If all the publicity weren't enough, Island Records President Chris Blackwell proclaimed the group the label's most important signing since King Crimson.

In concert, the loquacious Bono tries to play down all the hype – he regularly tells audiences to "forget all that stuff you may have read and make up your own minds" – but privately he concurs with the press. "I don't mean to sound arrogant," he tells me after the dancing has died down, "but even at this stage, I do feel that we are meant to be one of the great groups. There's a certain spark, a certain chemistry, that was special about the Stones, the Who and the Beatles, and I think it's also special about U2."

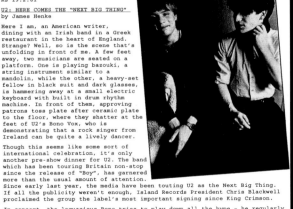

A mighty boast, to be sure. But "Boy", scheduled for late-January U.S. release, does indicate that U2 is a band to be reckoned with. Their highly original sound can best be described as pop music with brains. It's accessible and melodic combining the dreamy, atmospheric qualities of a band like Television, with a hard rock edge not unlike The Who's. In particular, Edge's guitar playing and Bono's singing stand out; the lyrical guitar lines slice through every song, while the vocals are rugged, urgent and heartfelt.

The title "Boy" is appropriate and significant: not only are the band members young, but the bulk of their songs deal with the dreams and frustrations of childhood. "We're playing to audiences in Britain that range in

U2 OCTOBER

— 7 —

U2 *ISSUE 2*

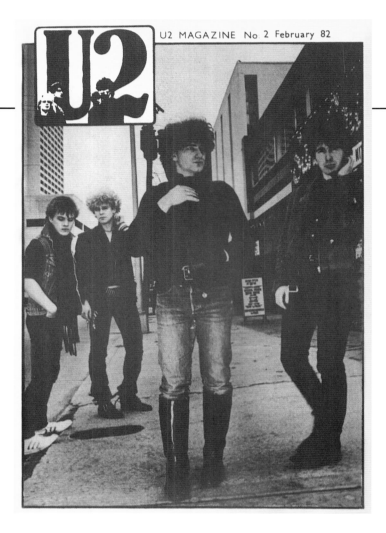

adrenalin starts to go crazy, your bones just seem to rattle and blood shoots up your veins. You think 'right, there is something about this band!'", says Bono as he tries to explain the reaction.

U2 are playing at a new peak. From the opening notes of "Gloria", they gave us all the classics old and new, plus a very special surprise – "Tomorrow" played live for the first time, complete with uillean pipes!

"We put our lives on the line and just kind of went for it … and when you see that kind of reaction you just feel … phew! It's very hard to talk about it really." Bono continues, "It's everything that we wanted when we were a garage band. We wanted that total thing, people just up."

U2's return to their home town of Dublin after a year touring and impressing the rest of the world was a tumultuous celebration.

This was the final date on the Irish tour that had also taken in Cork and Galway (the Belfast gig had unfortunately had to be postponed due to structural problems in the hall – but the show will be re-scheduled for the near future), and it was the first time that anyone had been allowed to play the RDS Main Hall as a stand up venue. The months of planning for approval paid off completely, and left no-one in any doubt that this was the finest Dublin would see this year.

The two support acts played to chants of "U2, U2," through their sets, and when U2 took the stage the massive hall was transformed to the intimacy of a small club – the atmosphere was electric, with a definite special magic in the air. "Your knees go weak, your

U2 at the R.D.S.

U2's return to their home town of Dublin after a year touring and impressing the rest of the world was a tumultuous celebration.

This was the final date on the Irish tour that had also taken in Cork and Galway (the Belfast gig had unfortunately had to be postponed due to structural problems in the hall – but the show will be re-scheduled for the near future), and it was the first time that anyone had been allowed to play the RDS Main Hall as a stand up venue. The months of planning for approval paid off completely, and left no-one in any doubt that this was the finest Dublin would see this year.

The two support acts played to chants of "U2, U2," through their sets, and when U2 took the stage the massive hall was transformed to the intimacy of a small club – the atmosphere was electric, with a definite special magic in the air. "Your knees go weak, your adrenalin starts to go crazy, your bones just seem to rattle and blood shoots up your veins. You think 'right, there is something about this band!'", says Bono as he tries to explain the reaction.

U2 are playing at a new peak. From the opening notes of "Gloria", they gave us all the classics old and new, plus a very special surprise – "Tomorrow" played live for the first time, complete with uillean pipes!

"We put our lives on the line and just kind of went for it … and when you see that kind of reaction you just feel … phew! It's very hard to talk about it really." Bono continues, "It's everything that we wanted when we were a garage band. We wanted that total thing, people just up."

U2 are unique. Their determination of purpose and clear-cut ideas mean they know exactly where they're heading. Bono: "U2 not about fashion. We don't want to be in fashion, because being in fashion is going out of fashion, you know?". "One thing I'm into is the type of people who are into us. They're prepared to give, they're a reaction-oriented audience."

Talking about some of the current trends in music, Bono continues emphatically, "If people like that sort of atmosphere in music, fine, but what I'd like to see is people burning the rulebooks … the rulebooks that say they have to like this type of music and nothing else. I think people should broaden their vision … there's some great music happening on ethnic fronts, like African music, and I'm particularly interested in traditional Irish music."

U2 OCTOBER DUBLIN R.D.S. Tuesday 26th January 1982.

"At the same time I'm sure there are some great pop songs, but I want more out of music than just that. I want music with that X factor, music with that heart and soul.

"I don't want to sound pretentious, but to me truth is like a two-edged sword, it cuts deep. I can tell when a singer is singing what's in his heart, or if he isn't. There's a big difference, and there's a lot of glossy pop songs that can maybe make us cry, but it's a bit like watching 'Lassie' or 'The Little House On The Prairie', you know, it's not <u>real</u> emotion, it's a kind of thin level of emotion.

"The truth is when that singer is saying something that comes from right down within him, and it affects you right down within you … and that's when you start talking about great music, as distinct from nice music.

U2

"Like the word 'nice' is a horrible word … music for lifts, music for supermarkets. I think that's fine if you're into shopping or going up and down, but I want more than that. Is that wrong? Is it wrong to want more out of music? I'm not suggesting U2 are Wagner; when it comes down to it we're just four people playing music the way we see it."

"In 'Rejoice' I said 'I can't change the world, but I can change a world in me'. Music can possibly direct you and change you as a person. I think the ultimate revolution is the one that goes on in a man. I'm not saying, 'join the revolution, be like us' … where you go is your decision."

"It's not a plan. We don't say 'let's be aggressive, let's really communicate and be passionate'. Sometimes to think about it is to destroy it. U2 is just natural, we're really just four people – within ourselves we have a very strong relationship, like a love between the band, which spreads into the crew, our sound engineer, to the management, even to the record company, and then spreads into the audience."

"I think people understand now that I'm not religious, they understand that I'm nearly anti-religion … when I talk of religion I'm talking about the force that's cut Ireland in two. I'm not religious at all, but I do believe in God very strongly, and I don't believe that we just exploded out of thin air, I can't believe it. I think it's a spiritual strength that's essential to the band. People have got to find their own way, I'm not into standing up and saying 'Hey, you should be into God!' My own life is exhilarating through an experience I feel, and I feel there's no point in talking about something which should be there in your life anyway. You don't have to preach about it."

"I've changed as U2 has gone through. When it started I was very drunk on being

Adam and Bono backstage at London Hammersmith Palais with "The Boss" – Bruce Springsteen.

'U.2.'
Adam Clayton Ph: 45... ...

When manager Paul McGuinness first met U2, Adam handed him the card on the left. At that time Adam was handling a lot of the management duties for U2, and doing very well at finding gigs for the group!

in a band, very confident, it was everything. I couldn't see the wood for the trees. You get bitter, you knock other bands … I had a lot of hate. That's changed my life, U2 has broadened my experience and allowed me to realise that wherever you go in the world people are still flesh and blood, and if they would only realise and stop hitting each other over the head."

<u>ON 'OCTOBER':</u>

"I'm much happier talking about 'October' now, because now it is clearer in my head. I listened to it last week for the first time in ages and I couldn't believe I was part of it. It's a <u>huge</u> record, I couldn't cope with it!

"I remember the pressure it was made under, I remember writing lyrics on the microphone, and at £50 an hour that's quite a pressure. Lillywhite was pacing up and down the studio … he coped really well. And the ironic thing about 'October' is that there's a sort of peace about the album, even though it was recorded under that pressure. A lot of people found 'October' hard to accept at first", Bono continues, "I mean, I used the word 'rejoice' precisely because I knew people have a mental block against it. It's a powerful word, it's lovely to say. It's implying more than 'get up and dance, baby'. I think 'October' goes into areas that most rock 'n roll bands ignore. When I listen to the album, something like 'Tomorrow', it actually <u>moves</u> me."

OCTOBER

ISLAND

Bono backstage with Paul and Ian Wilson.

U2 *ISSUE 3*

pound. That was my first instrument. It was an acoustic guitar and me and my elder brother Dick both played it, plonking away, all very rudimentary stuff, open chords and all that. The next stage was a note on the school board to the effect that 'Larry had wasted a lot of money on drums and was interested in finding other people to waste money on guitars' and stuff like that, so we all met in his kitchen one day. I think between us there was one kit of drums, one bass without amp ('I had a purple Marshall amp with a tatty little speaker that used to blow up every time I wound it up', protested Adam), one borrowed electric guitar

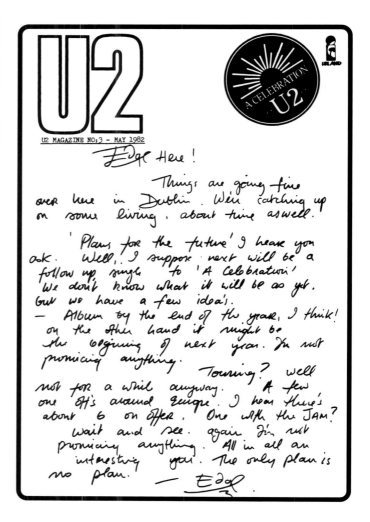

ON THE EDGE OF SUCCESS
by Tom Nolan

There aren't too many players who can honestly be said to have developed their own style on an instrument as cliche-ridden as the electric guitar, but undoubtedly one such musician is The Edge. In the five years since the band's inception, he has steadily evolved a unique approach that owes absolutely nothing to anyone, and indeed I can't think of anybody who sounds remotely like him.

So how did he manage to come up with his own sound in the first place? Obviously there were several factors, mainly connected with the way the band got together, as The Edge explains.

"I suppose the first link in the chain was a visit to the local jumble sale where I purchased a guitar for a

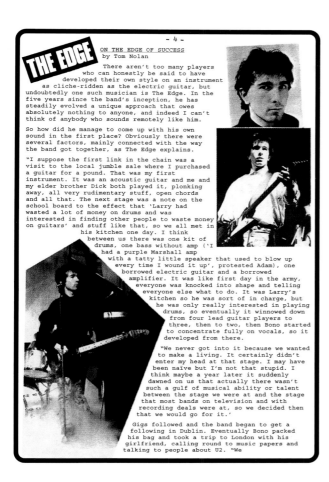

THE EDGE

ON THE EDGE OF SUCCESS
by Tom Nolan

- 4 -

There aren't too many players who can honestly be said to have developed their own style on an instrument as cliche-ridden as the electric guitar, but undoubtedly one such musician is The Edge. In the five years since the band's inception, he has steadily evolved a unique approach that owes absolutely nothing to anyone, and indeed I can't think of anybody who sounds remotely like him.

So how did he manage to come up with his own sound in the first place? Obviously there were several factors, mainly connected with the way the band got together, as The Edge explains.

"I suppose the first link in the chain was a visit to the local jumble sale where I purchased a guitar for a pound. That was my first instrument. It was an acoustic guitar and me and my elder brother Dick both played it, plonking away, all very rudimentary stuff, open chords and all that. The next stage was a note on the school board to the effect that 'Larry had wasted a lot of money on drums and was interested in finding other people to waste money on guitars' and stuff like that, so we all met in his kitchen one day. I think between us there was one kit of drums, one bass without amp ('I had a purple Marshall amp with a tatty little speaker that used to blow up every time I wound it up', protested Adam), one borrowed electric guitar and a borrowed amplifier. It was like first day in the army, everyone was knocked into shape and telling everyone else what to do. It was Larry's kitchen so he was sort of in charge, but he was only really interested in playing drums, so eventually it winnowed down from four lead guitar players to three, then to two, then Bono started to concentrate fully on vocals, so it developed from there.

"We never got into it because we wanted to make a living. It certainly didn't enter my head at that stage. I may have been naive but I'm not that stupid. I think maybe a year later it suddenly dawned on us that actually there wasn't such a gulf of musical ability or talent between the stage we were at and the stage that most bands on television and with recording deals were at, so we decided then that we would go for it.'

Gigs followed and the band began to get a following in Dublin. Eventually Bono packed his bag and took a trip to London with his girlfriend, calling round to music papers and talking to people about U2. "We

- 5 -

Edge does a US radio interview from backstage.

got a bit of interest going", recalled The Edge, "and during that six month stage we were talking to yourself."

This was a reference to the period in September '79 when I, as an EMI A&R man, went to Dublin to see them and decided there and then that this was the best new band around and must be signed immediately. Sadly I was alone in this opinion, and to my the band's intense disappointment the deal was unceremoniously booted out.

"That was a devastating period of our lives, as you can well imagine, but we rebounded quite well, and eventually we came and did a small London tour, and off the back of that and the subsequent Irish tour, we signed to Island Records about seven months later."

"Much earlier on we tried to do cover versions of things, but to be honest we were so bad at working out stuff that we just had to give it up and write our own songs, so by the time we came to realise there were other bands doing new things it was too late, because we already had our own style of writing. We just played together and things came out. We always try to do things differently, we never accept the normal, so it was mainly trial and error. I like a nice ringing sound on guitar, and most of my chords I find two strings and make them ring the same note, so it's almost like a 12-string sound. So for E I might play a B, E, E and B and make it ring. It works very well with the Gibson Explorer. It's funny because the bass end of the Explore was so awful that I used to stay away from the low strings, and a lot of the chords I played were very trebly, on the first four, or even three strings. I discovered that through using this one area of the fretboard I was developing a stylised way

CONT'D PAGE 8

A CELEBRATION · U2

---

and a borrowed amplifier. It was like first day in the army, everyone was knocked into shape and telling everyone else what to do. It was Larry's kitchen so he was sort of in charge, but he was only really interested in playing drums, so eventually it winnowed down from four lead guitar players to three, then to two, then Bono started to concentrate fully on vocals, so it developed from there.

"We never got into it because we wanted to make a living. It certainly didn't enter my head at that stage. I may have been naïve but I'm not that stupid. I think maybe a year later it suddenly dawned on us that actually there wasn't such a gulf of musical ability or talent between the stage we were at and the stage that most bands on television and with recording deals were at, so we decided then that we would go for it.'

Gigs followed and the band began to get a following in Dublin. Eventually Bono packed his bag and took a trip to London with his girlfriend, calling round to music papers and talking to people about U2. "We got a bit of interest going", recalled The Edge, "and during that six month stage we were talking to yourself."

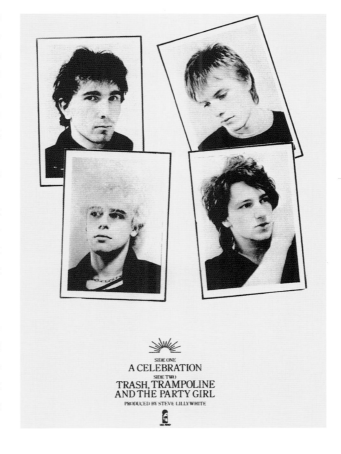

SIDE ONE
A CELEBRATION
SIDE TWO
TRASH, TRAMPOLINE
AND THE PARTY GIRL
PRODUCED BY STEVE LILLYWHITE

U2 *ISSUE 4*

U2 MAGAZINE No:4 August 82

A CELEBRATION IN BELGIUM

by Louise Adams, 10 Gig Mill Way, Norton,
Stourbridge, West Midlands DY8 3HN.

On 2nd July 1982, two coaches left London.
Destination Belgium. We travelled via Dover to Calais,
through France and over the border into Belgium. After
spending the night in Antwerp we travelled on to
Torhout, where the rock festival was held.

The opening act were Allez Allez, who have quite a
following in their native country. They were followed by
The Members, who received a warm reception. When
they left the stage the crowd became restless. A banner showing Bono's head in profile flapped regally in
the breeze. Final tests on equipment having been
made, the road crew left the stage to make way for
Bono, Larry, The Edge and Adam. U2 began with the
classic "Gloria" and were on stage for about an hour.
The singing sounded slightly strained and Bono
announced that "the singer is losing his voice". Who
cared? As he said, "who needs a voice when it comes
straight from the heart".

During one song, much to the delight of the crowd,
Bono climbed up the scaffolding on the side of the
stage and sang from a great height. The following
song was "I Fall Down", luckily he didn't. "It's for you"
announced Mr Hewson, and I believe it was. Encore
over with, U2 left the stage. They made a great impression on the devoted, and they also gained some new
fans. For me the rest of the show was an
anti-climax, although the Talking Heads were good.

Whilst leaving the concert ground we saw a red car.
I heard a tap on the window and saw Bono waving at
us. We were all wearing U2 t-shirts which had caught
his eye. For me this was the final personal touch I
admire so much in U2.

A group of weary travellers arrived in Dover eight
o'clock Sunday morning, bleary-eyed and clad in U2 t-
shirts, now rather crumpled. As the coach pulled out of
Dover, those who weren't asleep sang along to a U2
tape. We had listened to U2 in France, Belgium and
Britain almost non-stop since the trip began, I didn't
get tired of listening to them, and I don't think I ever will.

I would like to say hallo to the people from Dorset,
Manchester, Falkirk and Leicester and everyone else
on coaches one and two. I hope those who
exchanged addresses will write and hopefully become
friends. If anyone has any good photos I would like to
hear from them and obtain some copies.

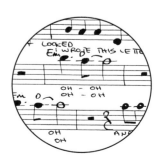

- 2 -

rock torhout

U2

A CELEBRATION IN BELGIUM

by Louise Adams, 10 Gig Mill Way, Norton, Stourbridge, West Midlands DY8 3HN.

On 2nd July 1982, two coaches left London. Destination Belgium. We travelled via Dover to Calais, through France and over the border into Belgium. After spending the night in Antwerp we travelled on to Torhout, where the rock festival was held.

The opening act were Allez Allez, who have quite a following in their native country. They were followed by The Members, who received a warm reception. When they left the stage the crowd became restless. A banner showing Bono's head in profile flapped regally in the breeze. Final tests on equipment having been made, the road crew left the stage to make way for Bono, Larry, The Edge and Adam. U2 began with the classic "Gloria" and were on stage for about an hour. The singing sounded slightly strained and Bono announced that "the singer is losing his voice". Who cared? As he said, "who needs a voice when it comes straight from the heart".

During one song, much to the delight of the crowd, Bono climbed up the scaffolding on the side of the stage and sang from a great height. The following song was "I Fall Down", luckily he didn't. "It's for you" announced Mr Hewson, and I believe it was. Encore over with, U2 left the stage. They made a great impression on the devoted, and they also gained some new fans. For me the rest of the show was an anti-climax, although the Talking Heads were good.

Whilst leaving the concert ground we saw a red car. I heard a tap on the window and saw Bono waving at us. We were all wearing U2 t-shirts which had caught his eye. For me this was the final personal touch I admire so much in U2.

A group of weary travellers arrived in Dover eight o'clock Sunday morning, bleary-eyed and clad in U2 t-shirts, now rather crumpled. As the coach pulled out of Dover, those who weren't asleep sang along to a U2 tape. We had listened to U2 in France, Belgium and Britain almost non-stop since the trip began, I didn't get tired of listening to them, and I don't think I ever will.

I would like to say hallo to the people from Dorset, Manchester, Falkirk and Leicester and everyone else on coaches one and two. I hope those who exchanged addresses will write and hopefully become friends. If anyone has any good photos I would like to hear from them and obtain some copies.

U2 U2 U2

A CELEBRATION U2

U2 in Chicago (Photo: Adrian Boot)   - 3 -

- 6 -

"Stranger in a Strange Land"

HEWSON/EVANS/MULLEN/CLAYTON

Copyright Blue Mountain Music Ltd
Reproduced by permission

U2 OCTOBER

- 7 -

"Scarlet"

HEWSON/EVANS/MULLEN/CLAYTON

Copyright Blue Mountain Music Ltd
Reproduced by permission

TOMORROW (U2)
Won't you come back tomorrow,
Won't you be back tomorrow,
can I sleep tonight?

Outside, somebody's outside,
somebody's knocking at the door,
there's a black car parked at
the side of the road,
don't go to the door, don't go to
the door.
I'm going out. I'm going outside
mother I'm going out there.

Won't you come back tomorrow,
Won't you come back tomorrow,
can I sleep tonight?

Who broke the window, who broke
down the door?
Who tore the curtain, and who was
it for?
Who heals the wounds, who heals the
scars?
Open the door, open the door.

Won't you be back tomorrow,
Won't you be back tomorrow,
can I sleep tonight?

'Cause I want you, I want you,
I want you to be back tomorrow,
Won't you be back tomorrow.
Open up, open up to the Lamb of God.
Open up, open up to the blind
to the love of He who made the blind
to see He's coming back, He's coming
back. Believe HIM. Jesus coming.

Reproduced by permission
Copyright Blue Mountain Music Ltd

U2 OCTOBER

15

HIGHLIGHTS OF U2, ISSUE 4

U2 *ISSUE 5*

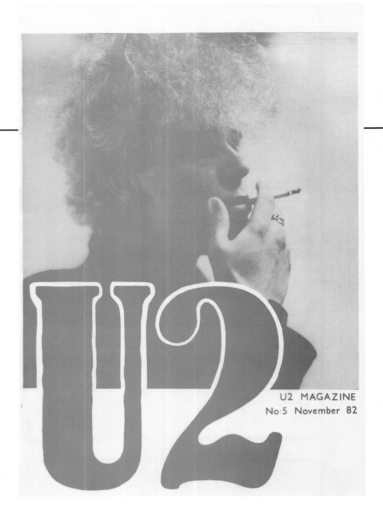

U2 MAGAZINE
No.5 November 82

U2's FIRST EUROPEAN TOUR

With U2 about to set out on a new tour of the U.K., Europe and Ireland, here are some recollections on their very first trip through Europe from Mike Gardner.

Contrary to the popular consensus of those who have seen U2 in concert or heard the masterfully executed "Boy" album, the band cannot run faster than a speeding bullet, stop express trains with their bare hands or leap tall buildings with a single bound. What they can do is far more impressive. The band take the conventions of straightforward pop, strip it bare, leave the essence of that accessibility in that music and then build, with atmosphere, raw emotion and a forceful passion, a sound that's as sturdy and powerful as it is fragile and moving.

The sound is epic without being lumbering, yet flexible enough to swell to mountainous emotional highs and swiftly but delicately shade the evocative quiet. The whole affair is conducted with an inventive infectious attack. To call them refreshing is an inadequate description for music that inspires the lift and optimism U2's work can release, whether in their erratic, chancy live experience or on the elegant "Boy".

It was after a five hour haul through the motorways of France, Belgium and Holland that photographer Virginia Turbett, Neil Storey and myself end up cruising the streets of the picture postcard Dutch town Appledoorne looking for the penultimate U2 venue on their first European jaunt. We make one circuit of the main streets and are then stuck at some traffic lights, trying to find a native who can direct us. A gaggle of males approach us and shadow gives way to the features of Larry, Adam, Bono, The Edge, manager Paul McGuinness and sundry crew. The usual pleasantries and greetings are interspersed with directions until the group saunter off towards the venue.

In the dressing room the band are warm and hospitable, more than eager to break the ice which they do with an abundance of enthusiasm and interest. Neil has brought the first finished copies of "Boy" with him for their inspection and there's the expected glee at holding the proof of the band's growth to date.

The hall is small and seedy and totally at odds with the ambiance of the neatly pressed town. But as the aching strains of The Edge's guitar pieces, the soft lull of Larry and Adam's rhythm pattern on "The Ocean", the large adjoining bar is left unpropped. "The Ocean" segues into the latent intent of the intro to "11 O'Clock Tick Tock" which explodes into the colour and passion that makes U2 in flight as potent and dramatic as an eagle swooping on its prey. The band play with tension as the bass pins down the flighty skinwork of drummer Larry with the shadowy stabs and prickles of The Edge's guitar simultaneously dancing and slicing through the throbbing power while the expressive and expansive Bono commands, focuses and embodies the energy.

U2's FIRST EUROPEAN TOUR

- 2 -

With U2 about to set out on a new tour of the U.K., Europe and Ireland, here are some recollections on their very first trip through Europe from Mike Gardner.

Contrary to the popular consensus of those who have seen U2 in concert or heard the masterfully executed "Boy" album, the band cannot run faster than a speeding bullet, stop express trains with their bare hands or leap tall buildings with a single bound. What they can do is far more impressive. The band take the conventions of straightforward pop, strip it bare, leave the essence of that accessibility in that music and then build, with atmosphere, raw emotion and a forceful passion, a sound that's as sturdy and powerful as it is fragile and moving.

THE EDGE

LARRY

BONO

The sound is epic without being lumbering, yet flexible enough to swell to mountainous emotional highs and swiftly but delicately shade the evocative quiet. The whole affair is conducted with an inventive infectious attack. To call them refreshing is an inadequate description for music that inspires the lift and optimism U2's work can release, whether in their erratic, chancy live experience or on the elegant "Boy".

ADAM CLAYTON

It was after a five hour haul through the motorways of France, Belgium and Holland that photographer Virginia Turbett, Neil Storey and myself end up cruising the streets of the picture postcard Dutch town Appledoorne looking for the penultimate U2 venue on their first European jaunt. We make one circuit of the main streets and are then stuck at some traffic lights, trying to find a native who can direct us. A gaggle of males approach us and shadow gives way to the features of Larry, Adam, Bono, The Edge, manager Paul McGuinness and sundry crew. The usual pleasantries and greetings are interspersed with directions until the group saunter off towards the venue.

In the dressing room the band are warm and hospitable, more than eager to break the ice which they do with an abundance of enthusiasm and interest. Neil has brought the first finished copies of "Boy" with him for their inspection and there's the expected glee at holding the proof of the band's growth to date.

The hall is small and seedy and totally at odds with the ambiance of the neatly pressed town. But as the aching strains of The Edge's guitar pieces, the soft lull of Larry and Adam's rhythm pattern on "The Ocean", the large adjoining bar is left unpropped. "The Ocean" segues into the latent intent of the intro to "11 O'Clock Tick Tock" which explodes into the colour and passion that makes U2 in flight as potent and dramatic as an eagle swooping on its prey. The band play with tension as the bass pins down the flighty skinwork of drummer Larry with the shadowy stabs and prickles of The Edge's guitar

- 3 -

simultaneously dancing and slicing through the throbbing power while the expressive and expansive Bono commands, focuses and embodies the energy. "I Will Follow", a passionate but impressionistic examination of the loss of security, thunders while the Dutch heads nod and bodies succumb to the insistent rhythm.

The fluid but latently evil "An Cat Dubh" has the loping bass and forthright rhythm igniting the spiky fretwork of The Edge while Bono calls on and articulates the hidden terror of the temptation and seduction the song speaks of before journeying to the moving "Into The Heart" which is committed without stifling the spark that makes it their most vital composition. During "Twilight" there is a re-enactment of that hoary old Hollywood scene where the starlet is thrust into the spotlight as the lead actress is ill and the hostile audience are broken down one by one by the natural charm of the newcomer until they rapturously accept her. The Appledoorne crowd need no such bait as one by one they physically start bending, moving and bopping to the music.

By the helter skelter effervescence of "Out Of Control" they are totally in the grip of the U2 magic. Their applause and appreciation is, at first, muted and restrained but they end up fighting to show the band that a few encores wouldn't exactly bomb.

The next day is changeable, varying from a dank grey drizzle to a warming sunshine that settles for drizzle the closer we get to Brussels, their last date before going back to Britain and Eire. There is only time for a quick lump of cheese and a drink and a few snapshots around the hotel with the ever-increasing U2 family and head for the gig five miles away. Nearly two hours and numerous wrong turns later we arrive, thoroughly exhausted, at the Klacik club, Bono's sniffles have taken on a more sinister tone and road manager Tim Nicholson is considerably concealing the fact that flu will knock him flat on his back within the next six hours.

The sound check is a weary affair, with the usual mixture of laboured graft and mischievous tedium. Everybody wanders aimlessly, searching the nooks and crannies of the club while the Bromley boys who came over for the gig sit and stare intently at the stage while the band play half-hearted fragments of their set. We are all more than pleased when it's over and we can go and hunt for a proper meal, since it has been some 10 hours since breakfast. We settle in a restaurant and on goes the tape recorder …

"The Dutch are a very interesting people. They are very aware of British music", claims Bono. "We played the Milky Way in Amsterdam which is seriously in the sixties. It hasn't changed. It's a time warp. Outside a girl collapsed in front of me and smashed her head on the pavement. Her boyfriend didn't seem to mind. She was smashed too. They were junkies just hanging around … a very sick sight.

"You can see the sordid side to Amsterdam. At first

- 4 -

sight it's beautiful, innocent, even a naive city. There's shop window prostitution and it's the European centre for the drugs market. It's like one of the songs on 'Boy' called 'An Cat Dubh' which describes the cat as a symbol of temptation. At first beautiful, the shape, you know, seductive. In the daylight it destroys a birdnest. Not for food, but for enjoyment and at the same time it comes up to you and strokes the side of your leg. Amsterdam is like that. It's beautiful, it's people are beautiful, but …"

"They're surprisingly well informed," interjects Adam. "By no means, at this stage, have we cracked England. Even for a band with our present status in England we've done surprisingly well. They know about us, they've heard our records, they've seen our pictures and they want to know more."

"I think they thought U2 were a post industrial funk band, very arty, very cultural but when they saw us as an aggressive performing act, when they saw the explosion of our personalities and our instruments on the stage they were taken aback," says Bono.

Part of what makes U2 so important is a determined belief in their destiny to become a noted and powerful force in contemporary music. "I believe that we combine the aspects of contemporary music that I find exciting," opines Bono. "Which is performance, aggressive live rock music, that is at the same time lyrical, because we mean what we say. We are talking. We are not just writing on topics, like say XTC, we come from the heart.

"Our overall impression is optimism, uplift, power, elation which very few acts, like The Who and Springsteen, possess. I believe we should be there because there's a lot of dross, a lot of unworthy music in our place. There are a lot of bands who should finish now."

U2 have an unswerving faith that they have the right to the Madison Square Gardens and saturation of the airwaves that success will bring eventually and while that sounds more than a little immodest, a little naive to others, the sentiments do strike a chord with those who have sampled the character and sturdiness of their chosen type of musical expression.

"Some have said that U2 music is for the head and the feet," re-calls Bono, "but I think it's music for the heart as well. It combines the three. Every night CONTD PAGE 9...

CONTD PAGE 9...

17

HIGHLIGHTS OF U2, ISSUE 5

U2 *ISSUE 6*

U2

WAR

U2 MAGAZINE No:6 February 83

WAR BREAKS OUT IN ENGLAND
by Louise Wates,
Sunbury-on-Thames, Middx.

December 82, and the long awaited U2 tour began. This is the tour that so many have waited for... the prelude to their coming album "War".

Manchester Apollo – Dec 2nd.
The day started for many, including myself, with the appearance of U2 at the back of the venue at about 4.45. The crowd of about twenty people clustered as Larry, Edge and Adam slipped through the doors leaving a defenceless though competent Bono at the mercy of the gabbling hordes.

After the arguments of who was going to have Bono's hat ended, he began to shake hands, sign record sleeves and generally make himself even more popular. Bono also showed his un-superstar nature by taking names with the intent of putting them on guest lists, answering questions and joking with fans. After about ten minutes, Bono began hustling the frost-bitten fans backstage leaving them behind the practising Larry, Edge and Adam with the words "It's the survival of the fittest now. "

Once in the warmth, the crowd began to thaw out finding that they could operate the finger used for clicking cameras. Several pictures later, we were again hustled away, this time to the front stalls where we privileged few listened to the soundchecks (plus bits of "Sunday Bloody Sunday", "Surrender" and "New Year's Day") whilst taking as many photos as we wished, leaning on the stage and chatting to U2 without being threatened by any irate roadies or security staff. All good things come to an end, though, and so we were dismissed so that we should queue with the other members of the audience, the real gig was about to begin.

"The Alarm" were supporting. They were not unreasonable but they were not what the audience wanted. What they did want didn't arrive until nearly nine o'clock. U2, cheered by a packed venue at last came on stage.

A heated hour and a half followed with many tracks from "Boy" and "October" and the readily welcomed "Sunday Bloody Sunday", "Surrender", and "New Year's Day" from the coming album "War" which The Edge informed me is to be released in February with the single released in early January. Also due a mention were "A Celebration" and the classic "11 O'Clock Tick Tock" played and greeted with the enthusiasm they produce.

Bono is not superhuman, but he is special. Whether he realises it or not, he has the audience eating out of his hand. When he says "sing" they sing. When he says "dance" they dance, when he says "up", the audience go up. Maybe it's because everyone seems to admire him for the powerful man that he is.

U2 WAR

- 2 -

"I Threw A Brick Through A Window" and "A Day Without Me" recorded live in Werchter, Belgium in July 1982.

In the January Hot Press Reader's Poll, U2 took No.1 Best Polling Act, No.1 Group, No.1 Live Band, No.1 Video with "A Celebration", No.2 Single with "A Celebration", No.2 Irish based Band, No.2 Instrumentalist for The Edge, No.3 Love of The Year, and No.5 Songwriter for Bono U2, and No.2 Male Singer for Bono.

SOME QUOTES ON "WAR"

Bono: "War" is about people, war between people, lovers, war between religions - Catholics and Protestants, war in Politics. War is about struggle, conflict and realisation. So there is a theme running through the songs but it is definitely not a concept album. We really wanted to make every song different, as far away from what people expect from us, I think there are only two songs that people will know as U2.

Bono: "War" is important to me, to the whole band, but make or break? I don't think so, more of a progressive build up. We have developed the sound, taking it a stage further. It is far more rhythmic with much more depth. "War" is our heaviest album yet.

Bono: A song called "Surrender" and another called "Sunday Bloody Sunday" were two I just hard to write after being in New York. There is so much happening over there, so much tension, I had to make a statement.

Bono: This band is hitting out against all the blippety blop aural wallpaper we have rammed down our throats on the radio and TV every day. I am personally bloody sick of every time I switch on the radio of being blasted with this contrived crap.

Bono: The idea on "War" was to possibly use different producers for each song or group of songs so the approach would vary throughout but in the end it didn't happen and we sorted it out with Steve. We understand each other and it works well for us. He has helped us grow and mature to understand recording techniques and translate our sound and ideas into reality.

- 3 -

HAPPY CHRISTMAS TOUR '82

WAR BREAKS OUT IN ENGLAND
by Louise Wates, Sunbury-- on-Thames, Middx.

December 82, and the long awaited U2 tour began. This is the tour that so many have waited for... the prelude to their coming album "War".

Manchester Apollo - Dec 2nd.

The day started for many, including myself, with the appearance of U2 at the back of the venue at about 4.45. The crowd of about twenty people clustered as Larry, Edge and Adam slipped through the doors leaving a defenceless though competent Bono at the mercy of the gabbling hordes.

After the arguments of who was going to have Bono's hat ended, he began to shake hands, sign record sleeves and generally make himself even more popular. Bono also showed his un-superstar nature by taking names with the intent of putting them on guest lists, answering questions and joking with fans. After about ten minutes, Bono began hustling the frost-bitten fans backstage leaving them behind the practising Larry, Edge and Adam with the words "It's the survival of the fittest now."

Once in the warmth, the crowd began to thaw out finding that they could operate the finger used for clicking cameras. Several pictures later, we were again hustled away, this time to the front stalls where we privileged few listened to the soundchecks (plus bits of "Sunday Bloody Sunday", "Surrender" and "New Year's Day") whilst taking as many photos as we wished, leaning on the stage and chatting to U2 without being threatened by any irate roadies or security staff. All good things come to an end, though, and so we were dismissed so that we should queue with the other members of the audience, the real gig was about to begin.

"The Alarm" were supporting. They were not unreasonable but they were not what the audience wanted. What they did want didn't arrive until nearly nine o'clock. U2, cheered by a packed venue at last came on stage.

A heated hour and a half followed with many tracks from "Boy" and "October" and the readily welcomed "Sunday Bloody Sunday", "Surrender", and "New Year's Day" from the coming album "War" which The Edge informed me is to be released in February with the single released in early January. Also due a mention were "A Celebration" and the classic "11 O'Clock Tick Tock" played and greeted with the enthusiasm they produce.

Bono is not superhuman, but he is special. Whether he realises it or not, he has the audience eating out of his hand. When he says "sing" they sing. When he says "dance" they dance, when he says "up", the audience go up. Maybe it's because everyone seems to admire him for the powerful man that he is.

- 9 -

U2 WAR

U2 *ISSUE 7*

U2 MAGAZINE No:7 May 83

U2 ON THE TUBE – 18TH MARCH 83

U2 Info was able to offer a limited number of complimentary tickets to members for the filming of The Tube. This was, unfortunately, restricted to people in the North-east only due to the very limited space in the studio, but I'm sure there'll be lots of other opportunities in the future. Here are some comments from those able to go …

As soon as we walked in we saw the U2 set and made a bee-line for the balcony above, which was an excellent view. We waited patiently for U2 to appear, but saw Big Country first and The Undertones, which I must say were really good – better than I expected.

Then at approx. 6.35 Jools and Paula Yates finally introduced U2. Cheers came from all directions. On walked Bono, at this moment the atmosphere suddenly turned into something different – a great feeling. Only one thing we noticed was Bono didn't look too happy when he walked on – I realise you can't be all smiles every minute of the day, but my heart went out to him at that moment. Pushing this aside they did a great and superb set. They first sang "Gloria" with such energy, then "Sunday Bloody Sunday", then came "New Year's Day", then a superb "I Will Follow". They came off the air and sang for us "Like A Song". That was it, over as quick as that, then I really did feel sad. We left the studio feeling pleased with ourselves that we travelled to Newcastle to see them, it was well worth it.
Linda Pearson, Middlesbrough.

I was one of the lucky ones who, thanks to you, was able to catch U2 on The Tube. The first group to come on were Big Country who sang two excellent songs with some brilliant guitar playing from Stuart Adamson. This got the audience nicely warmed up and ready for the next group, the very entertaining Undertones who treated us for half an hour before going on the air by telling jokes and playing some old favourites like "Get Over You".

By the end of their set, everyone was eagerly anticipating the arrival of U2 who surpassed every expectation I had of them. They began with "Gloria" and the reaction was amazing. Bono's voice was superb, reaching right to the heart, giving you no choice but to listen and enjoy.

By "New Year's Day" everyone had fallen under Bono's spell, singing along as though their lives depended on it. Next came the incredible "Sunday Bloody Sunday". "It's just a song!" cried Bono but we knew better. An invisible cloud of emotion generated by the band enveloped the captivated audience and when Bono sang, "Tonight, we can be as one", we knew what he meant.

Finally, as we all knew it had to, the end came and we were left numb, trying to understand what had just happened to us. U2 – that's what!
Alison, Ossett, W.Yorks.

U2 WAR

SUNDAY BLOODY SUNDAY

I can't believe the news today,
I can't close my eyes and make it go away.
How long, how long must we sing this song?
How long? Tonight we can be as one.
Broken bottles under children's feet,
Bodies strewn across a dead end street.
But I won't heed the battle call,
It puts my back up, puts my back up against the wall.

Sunday, bloody Sunday.
Sunday, bloody Sunday.

And the battle's just begun,
There's many lost, but tell me who has won?
The trenches dug within our hearts,
And mother's children, brothers, sisters torn apart.

Sunday, bloody Sunday.
Sunday, bloody Sunday.

How long, how long must we sing this song?
How long? Tonight we can be as one.
Tonight, tonight.

Sunday, bloody Sunday.
Sunday, bloody Sunday.

Wipe the tears from your eyes,
Wipe your tears away.
Wipe your bloodshot eyes.

Sunday, bloody Sunday.
Sunday, bloody Sunday.

And it's true we are immune,
When fact is fiction and TV is reality.
And today the millions cry,
We eat and drink while tomorrow they die.
the real battle just begun.
To claim the victory Jesus won,
On a Sunday, bloody Sunday.
Sunday, bloody Sunday.

NEW YEAR'S DAY

All is quiet on New Year's Day.
A world in white gets underway.
And I want to be with you,
Be with you night and day.
Nothing changes on New Year's Day.
I will be with you again.
I will be with you again.

Under a blood red sky
A crowd has gathered in black and white,
Arms entwined, the chosen few,
Newspapers say, it says it's true it's true.
And we can break through,
Though torn in two we can be one.
I will begin again, I will begin again.
Oh and maybe the time is right,
Oh maybe tonight.
I will be with you again.
I will be with you again.

And so we are told this is the golden age
And gold is the reason for the wars we wage,
Though I want to be with you,
To be with you night and day.
Nothing changes on New Year's Day.

SECONDS

It takes a second to say goodbye,
Say goodbye.
It takes a second to say goodbye,
Say goodbye, say bye bye where are you going to now?

fall, rise and ... fall, rise and ...
Lightning flashes across the sky
From east to west you do or die.
Like a thief in the night,
You see the world by candlelight.

fall, rise and ... fall, rise and ...
In an apartment on Times Square,
You can assemble; them anywhere.
Held to ransom, hell to pay.
A revolution every day.
U.S.S.R., D.D.R., London, New York, Peking.
It's the puppets, it's the puppets who pull the strings.

Say goodbye, say goodbye, Say goodbye, say goodbye,
It takes a second to say goodbye,
Push the button and pull the plug, say goodbye.

fall, rise and ... fall, rise and ...
They're doing the atomic bomb,
Do they know where the dance comes from?
Yes they're doing the atomic bomb,
They want you to sing along.
Say goodbye, say goodbye.

Excerpt from "Soldier Girls" courtesy of Contemporary Films

Especially for cassette collectors, here are some of the lyrics from "War". More next time ...

U2 WAR

LIKE A SONG

Like a song I have to sing,
I sing it for you.
Like the words I have to bring,
I bring them to you.
And in leather, lace or chains,
We stake our claim,
Revolution once again
But I won't,
I won't wear it on my sleeve.
I can see through this expression
And you know I don't believe.
I'm too old to lose, nothing to gain,
Exactly who are you?
Tonight, tomorrow's too late.

And we love to wear a badge, a uniform,
And we love to fly a flag,
But I won't let others live in hell,
As we divide against each other,
And we fight amongst ourselves.
Too set in our ways to try to rearrange,
Too right to be wrong, in this rebel song.
Let the bells ring out, is there nothing left?
Is honesty what you call it?

A generation without name, ripped and torn,
Nothing to lose, nothing to gain,
Nothing at all.
And if you can't help yourself,
We'll take a look around you,
When others need your time.
You say it's time to go it's your time.
Angry words won't stop the fight
Two wrongs won't make it right.
A new heart is what I need,
Oh God, make it bleed,
Is there nothing left?

SURRENDER

The city's alight
With lovers and lies
Bright blue eyes.
The city is bright,
Brighter than day tonight,
Surrender, Surrender,
Surrender, Surrender.

Sadie said she couldn't
Work out what it was all about
And so she let go.
Now Sadie's on the street
And the people she meets you know.
Shot tried to be a good girl
And a good wife.
Raise a good family.
Lead a good life.
It's not good enough
She got herself up on the 48th floor
Got to find out, find out
What she's living for.
Surrender, Surrender,
Surrender, Surrender.

The city's a fire,
A passionate flame
That knows me by name.
The city's desire
To take me for more and more.
It's in the street getting under my feet,
It's in the air it's everywhere I look for you,
It's in the things I do and say.
If I want to live, I've got to die to myself someday.

Papa sing my sing my song,
Papa sing my sing my song,
Papa sing my sing my song

DROWNING MAN

Take my hand
You know I'll be there
If you can I'll cross
The sky for your love,
For I have promised for
To be with you tonight
And for the time that will come.

Take my hand
You know I'll be there
If you can I'll cross
The sky for your love
And I understand
These winds and tides,
This change of times
Won't drag you away.
Hold on, hold on tightly,
Hold on and don't let go
Of my love.

The storms will pass
It won't be long now.
The storms will pass
But my love lasts forever.

And take my hand,
You know I'll be there,
If you can I'll cross the sky
for your love,
Give you what I hold dear,
Hold on, hold on tightly.
Hold on, hold on tightly.
Rise up, rise up with wings,
Like eagles you'll run, you'll run,
You'll run and not grow weary.

Take my hand, take my hand.
Hold on, hold on tightly.
Hold on, hold on tightly.
This love lasts forever,
This love lasts forever,
Take my hand,
Take my hand.

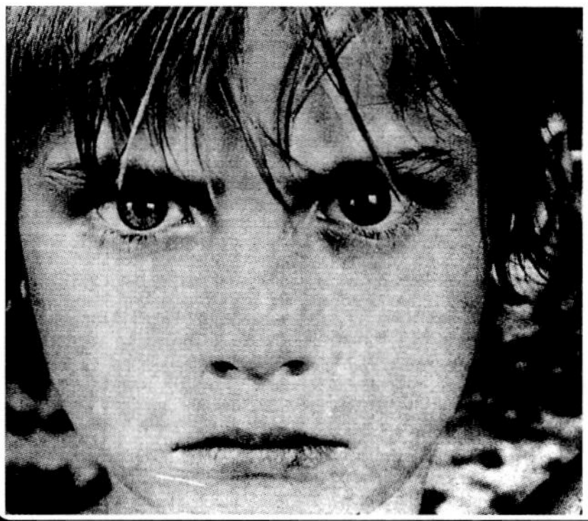

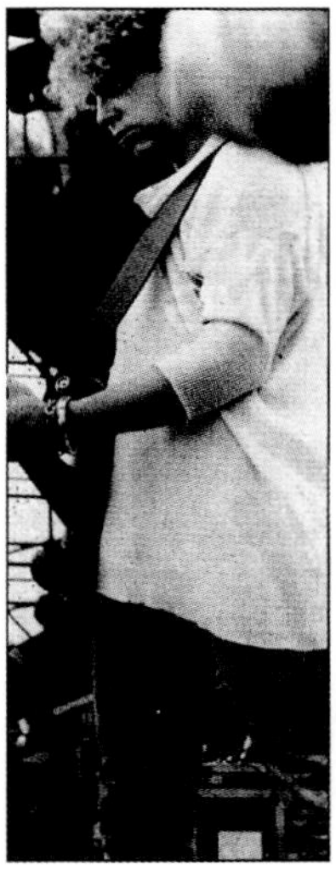

U2 has by now earned considerable crust, which they would split an even four ways if they didn't insist on pouring most of it back into their own recording (thereby retaining creative control) and touring. Their second American tour campaign supporting "October" was long, hard and costly. But they were determined to find their U.S. audience, and it seemed radio was not ready to help. So they broke one of their rules and took second billing to the J. Geils Band (at Peter Wolf's personal request) for the resultant exposure.

Even though they have had virtually no time off from their 1979 signing until Bono's honeymoon last August, the band refuses to complain. They have a mission, and they are decidedly unified in their determination. "When people ask us what our influences are", says Bono, "we always say, 'Each other'".

My first look at U2 came in the fall of 1980, just after "Boy"s release. Island Records' publicist Neil Storey shanghaied me from the arrivals gate at Heathrow Airport directly down to Southampton College, where we walked in on U2 a few minutes before a gig. All four band members were twenty-one or younger: Larry Mullen, who organised the band by posting a notice at Mt Temple Comprehensive school after being kicked out of the Artane Boys' (marching) Band for wearing long hair; Adam Clayton, who Bono says, "couldn't even dance" at the time he picked up the bass; The Edge, who had quickly gone from acoustic noodler to budding guitar hero through a seemingly innate gift; and Bono, born Paul Hewson, with the slapdash good looks and unselfconscious swagger to match his drive. "It had been a long time," recalls Dublin rock writer Bill Graham of an early U2 gig, "since I'd seen a singer who _went_ for an audience that way, all the time watching their eyes."

Their stage show was much too large in scope for that low-ceilinged, underpopulated function room at Southampton College. The Edge's clarion calls on the treble strings, Larry's martial ferocity and Bono's upthrust arm showed an expansive, hot-blooded streak that had been developed naturally in what Bono called "a garage band", as they went from being utter novices to playing in open market squares to the soused and skeptical local teenagers, to the kind of reputation that enabled them - before they even had a contract - to fill Ireland's largest concert hall. They stood against the pretensions of the new wave's idealogues, against the "gop" on U.S. radio, against the elitism of fashion bands like Visage.

They went a long way on Bono's tirelessness, his fervour with a mike in his hand. "When you think, 'Oh, screw it, I'm not gonna climb this mountain,'" says Adam, "he's the type of person who'll hit you in the ass and get you going. It doesn't make you a lot of friends, but it's a great ability to have."

Bono gave The Edge his nickname, but he's a bit cryptic about why. When he's asked, he grasps Edge's long, chiseled jaw and turns it in profile: "The Edge." Then, after a pause: "Let's just say he's on the border between something and nothing."

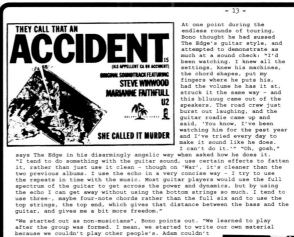

THEY CALL THAT AN ACCIDENT. (ITS APPELENT CA IN ACCIDENT)

ORIGINAL SOUNDTRACK FEATURING
STEVE WINWOOD
MARIANNE FAITHFULL
U2

SHE CALLED IT MURDER

At one point during the endless rounds of touring, Bono thought he had sussed The Edge's guitar style, and attempted to demonstrate as much at a sound check: "I'd been watching. I knew all the settings, knew his machines, the chord shapes, where he puts his, my fingers where he puts his, had the volume he has it at, struck it the same way - and this blluuug came out of the speakers. The road crew just burst out laughing, and the guitar roadie came up and said, 'You know, I've been watching him for the past year and I've tried every day to make it sound like he does. I can't do it.'" "Oh, gosh," says The Edge in his disarmingly angelic way when asked how he does it. "I tend to do something with the guitar sound, use certain effects to fatten it, rather than just use it clean - though on 'War', it's cleaner than the two previous albums. I use the echo in a very concise way - I try to use the repeats in time with the music. Most guitar players would use the full spectrum of the guitar to get across the power and dynamics, but by using the echo I can get away without using the bottom strings so much. I tend to use three-, maybe four-note chords rather than the full six and to use the top strings, the top end, which gives that distance between the bass and the guitar, and gives me a bit more freedom."

"We started out as non-musicians", Bono points out. "We learned to play after the group was formed. I mean, we started to write our own material because we couldn't play other people's. Adam couldn't slap in time when he joined, Edge could play sort of bad acoustic. Larry had his military drumming, and I started singing 'cause I couldn't play guitar."

Adam concurs. "In the past, when we went in the studio, we simply didn't know our craft well enough. On 'War' you can hear more of the arrangements coming from a bass-and-drum thing; the rhythm section's standing up. That means Edge doesn't have to play as much. On the first two albums, knowingly or not, he was covering up for a rhythm section that wasn't quite mature. We're a much tougher band now." During a playback of "War"s "Surrender", I catch Adam's eye after hearing a particularly canny bass run. He grins wickedly: "Little something I picked up from Tina Weymouth." Like his bandmates, Adam stoked his adolescent rock fantasies with the likes of Talking Heads, Patti Smith, and Television (The Edge clearly carries a few of Tom Verlaine's arrows in his quiver). But Adam's not unmindful of the Stones: "I was just listening to Bill Wyman last week, and he is all over the place with his bass playing, but the one thing he never tampers with is where he doesn't play, and that, I think, is the key to the Stones' sort of sloppy but rhythmic feel."

TWO HEARTS BEAT AS ONE

U2 *ISSUE 8*

U2 MAGAZINE No: 8 August 83

U2 AT THE CENTRUM – WORCESTER, MASS. 6.83
by Dave Mawson

There's always something refreshing about a band that plays rock 'n' roll the way it was meant to be played – stripped down to its bare essentials, a voice, a bass, a guitar and some drums. It s all the more satisfying when the fundamentals are executed by a band as invigorating and innovative as U2.

In just a little more than three years, these four young men have catapulted from the clubs of their native Ireland to the top of their profession. Last night, an ecstatic crowd of about 10,000 in the Centrum learned why.

Cramming 17 songs into 85 minutes at breakneck speed, U2 demonstrated why they are one of the freshest acts on the musical scene today. Their repertoire of relentless, crashing dance music and potent political rockers translates almost as well in an arena as it does on vinyl. The show had been billed as U2's first arena show, but after playing to a quarter-million people at the US Festival in California a few weeks ago, the band certainly wasn't new to the experience.

They opened with "Out Of Control", the perfect choice for the moment. It sent the crowd out of control. By the time lead singer Bono made it to the second verse of the next song, "Twilight", an eager fan had thrown one of the arena chairs on stage. Bono promptly joined in the spirit by doing a two-step on the prone seat. Three months ago, U2 had played to two sold out crowds at Boston's Orpheum Theatre. Last night, Bono decided early in the set to put any ill minds at ease about how the band would play in an arena the size of the Centrum. "Tonight we're going to turn this large complex into a living room", he declared.

Well, not quite. But the band came prepared for the task. Huge speakers lined both sides of the stage, and the volume level could have challenged any one of the

heavy metal monsters. Which is not to say the show was unnecessarily loud. The sound was crisp and clean, with The Edge's ringing guitar piercing through the hall.

U2 followed Bono's proclamation with a non-stop stream of some of the band's best tunes – "Two Hearts Beat As One", "Seconds", "Sunday Bloody Sunday", and one of the night's highlights, "The Electric Co."

Bono, one of the most frantic and inexhaustible performers you'll ever see, was in constant motion. When not planting a flagpole raised during "Surrender" in between two speakers, he was moving from one side of the stage to the other, leaving a crew of roadies scurrying in his wake. The Edge is a stunning guitar player. His soaring leads sometimes obscure the fact that he must play the part of two guitarists on most songs. And on "New Year's Day", he has the unenviable task of having to trade off on guitar and piano.

Because Bono and The Edge are such dynamic performers, and thus share most of the spotlight, it's almost too easy to forget drummer Larry Mullen Jr and bassist Adam Clayton. But they form a powerful duo and Clayton's intricate fills make this one-guitar band all the more palatable.

By the time U2 wrapped up the regular set with "Gloria", only 60 minutes had ticked off the clock. Despite such a fierce pace, they came back to perform "Party Girl", only to see Bono mobbed on stage by a group of about a dozen women, one of whom tried to handcuff herself to his leg.

"In any other city, there would have been a riot by now," he said good-naturedly. And he was right. But there wasn't. There were just four more songs and a lot of satisfied customers.

- 10 -

from Newcastle, Jimmy, Martin the Drunk!, and 'La, La, La, La' for a great time. Richard Smith, 81 Gants Hill Crescent, Gants Hill, Ilford, Essex IG2 6TS. Wants either the 1981 NME Dancin' Master tape w. "An Cat Dubh" live or "I Will Follow/Out of Control(Live)" single in exchange for either soundtracks of Last American Virgin ("I Will Follow") or "They Call That An Accident" (2 versions of October) or the 12" of "Sunday Bloody Sunday".

THE U2 "ANOTHER TIME, ANOTHER PLACE" QUIZ

Many thanks to Barry Cross from Oxford for putting this quiz together. Use each of the 23 clues below, and fit each answer on to the grid. The correct answers will only fit onto the 23 lines in the correct order, allowing for the one letter already provided by the vertical line of "Another Time, Another Place". If you have any ideas for a crossword or similar puzzle on U2, send it in and I'll try to use it in a future issue. Here are the clues:

1. The Studio, 2. Co-produced U2's debut, 3. A day without him, 4. Location for a Celebration, 5. U2.3 but not boy, 6. First Island release to be co-produced by U2, 7. Produced by Bill Whelan, 8. The black cat, 9. Working title for 'October' album, 10. Will Vincent Kilduff be back, 11. Inspiration for 'Shadows And Tall Trees', 12. The message from 'Scarlet', 13. US remix man, 14. She got herself up on the 48th floor, 15. The Edge AKA, 16. Kenny Fradley shines through, 17. Whatever happened to him, 18. Bono's Wah! Heat choice, 19. Paul McCartney also had one, 20. Trash, Trampoline and her, 21. Edge's brother is still one, 22. Did he only produce at 11 O'Clock, 23. The boy. Good luck! Answers next time.

TORHOUT ROCK 83 - U2 LIVE IN BELGIUM - 2nd July 1983
By Christina Glass, Stakeford, Northumberland.

What can I say? The best I've ever seen? It certainly was! The day of the festival was warm and sunny and the field crowded with French, Belgians and English, not forgetting Scots and Irish! We managed to get right to the front so we could lean on the barriers and look onto the stage. We caught all of the Eurythmics, whose set was surprisingly good, largely due to Annie Lennox's

U2 *ISSUE 9*

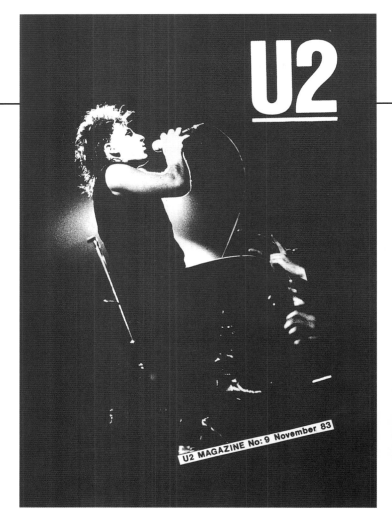

U2 MAGAZINE No: 9 November 83

U2 LIVE – PHOENIX PARK FESTIVAL
Sunday August 14th 1983
by Colm Kavanagh, Arklow, Co Wicklow, Eire

A day to remember? It certainly was!! Over 20,000 people from Ireland, Britain, the Continent and even America made their way to the Phoenix Park to celebrate the homecoming of U2.

The music started with Dublin duo Pat O'Donnell and Steve Belton. They were followed by the Northern Irish band Perfect Crime. Led by Gregory Grey they gave a good show before departing the stage. After an hour of reggae from Steel Pulse, the Scottish connection started when Big Country came on stage. They brought a bopping crowd to life with an excellent set including "Fields Of Fire", "In A Big Country", "The Storm", and their new single "Chance".

After a set from Eurythmics, the next band to appear were the excellent Simple Minds who left the crowd feeling drained. On a radio programme during the week Jim Kerr paid U2 a compliment. He said he had an advantage over Bono in that he did not have to follow him. Anyway, they gave an excellent performance, the highlights being "New Gold Dream" and "The American". When they left the stage, everyone pushed forward to get nearer to it. All of us up front were being crushed, but it was worth it!

U2 PEN-PALS/SWOPS AND TRADES SECTION

To contact other friends and fans of U2, send in your name and address and we will include it here. You can also include U2 items that you're offering to swap if you wish, like the early deleted singles, etc, but please keep the listing fairly brief.

Maria Ludvigsson, Linjestigen 8, 58266 Linkoping, Sweden.
Jacqueline Dixon, 13 Wood Close, Hatfield, Herts AL10 8TU.
Paula Treacy, 6 Castleknock, Ballincollig, Co. Cork, Eire.
David Leppard, 12 Tytheing Close, Newton St Cyres, Exeter, Devon EX5 5DB.
Ced Teague, 42 Buckingham Street, Redfern, 2016 N.S.W., Australia.
Claudia Katarajn, 28 Buckley Ave, N Sunshine 3020, Melbourne, Victoria, Australia.
Catherine Povey, 17 Weighton Road, Harrow Weald, Middx.
Paul Copeland, 50 Broome Grove, Wivenhoe, Essex C07 9QU. Would like any U2 live tapes.
Kevin Haney, 16 Throstle Ave, Wigston, Cumbria CA7 9QZ. Would like to hear from U2 fans in Dublin or New Zealand.
Duncan Fraser, 21C Park Road, Aberdeen, Scotland AB2 1NY.
Julie Jones, 89 Charles Street, Tonypandy, Rhondda, S.Wales CF40 2AW.
J. Spurgen, 20 Manby Road, Great Malvern, Worcester, Worcs. Wants tapes of Hammersmith 82, Rockpalast 83.
Terry King, 248 Cambridge Road, Woburn, MA 01801, U.S.A.
Steve Jack, 487 Heather Court, Collydean, Glenrothes, Fife, Scotland.
Siobhan Kennedy, 33 Seaford Road, Harwood, Bolton B12 4BX.
Joanne Payne, 4 Wingard Close, Uphill, Weston-Super-Mare, Avon. Looking for U2 video VHS.
Sandi Anne Skies, 452 3rd Street, Blakely, PA 18447, U.S.A.
Sharron Roberts, 25 Lea Crescent, Newbold, Rugby, Warks CV21 1EX.
Ellen Dahl, 309 North Grand Ave, Monrovia, California 91016, United States.
Vicki Stevens, 646 Wagon Wheel Lane, Marysville 43040, United States.
Maureen Marr, 75 Frampton Road, Walton, Liverpool 14 5RN.
Jancy Jacobs, 17 Curtis House, Morecambe Street, London SE 17 1EB.
Helen Youlten, 47 St James Court, St James Road, Croydon, Surrey CHO 2SF.
Allan Hamilton, 2 Edward Ave, Renfrew, Strathclyde, Scotland PA 8QN. Wants to swap tapes.
Leon van den Bergh, Kapellerlaan 43, 4702 JN Rosendaal, Holland. Has Dutch 7" "I Will Follow (live)/Gloria" to swap for 7" "A Celebration". Also wants to swap live tapes.
Cola Kavanagh, 182 Fernhill, Arklow, Co. Wicklow, Eire.
Louise Smith, 38 Winkfield Row, Horndean, Portsmouth PO8 9TL.

On the next page are the answers to the "Another Time Another Place" quiz from Barry Cross, who was also responsible for the sketch on the left.

"Guitar hero of the eighties!"

U2: "War" (Island) Third albums are always dangerous because at this stage bands have lost their novelty value with the fans and the critics, and are often beginning to run out of ideas. All credit, then, to Bono and his friends for coming up with a collection of songs that are fresh, gutsy and unashamedly emotional. U2 (below right) are all from Dublin, and with this album they have perfected their melodic, rousing song-writing technique. As Bono explains in the interview below, "It's really the first proper U2 album."
The songs mix Bono's high, powerful voice with a solid rhythm section held together by drummer Larry. They have the ability to switch mid-song between the gutsy and the gentle (listen to "Refugee"). This will prove to be one of the great albums of 1983.

Below is a new quiz, a U2 Wordsearch put together by Selma Malik. The idea is to find the U2 song titles listed and these can be vertical, horizontal or diagonal on, the grid, eg.

```
        N
H C U O T   E       E
            C       R
            O       I
            E       F
            H       T
```

The song titles to find which are all included in there somewhere are: "A Celebration", "A Day Without Me", "An Cat Dubh", "Drowning Man", "Endless Deep", "Fire", "Gloria", "I Fall Down", "I Will Follow", "Into The Heart", "Is That All", "Like A Song", "New Year's Day", "October", "Out of Control", "Red Light", "Rejoice", "Scarlet", "Seconds", "Shadows And Tall Trees", "Stories For Boys", "Sunday Bloody Sunday", "Surrender", "The Electric Co", "The Ocean", "The Refugee", "Tomorrow", "Touch", "Treasure", "Twilight", "Two Hearts Beat As One", "With A Shout".

Thanks Selma. Solution will be printed next time.

U2 WORDSEARCH

```
I Z G A R M T E S L A R E Y A D N U S Q
S W E N C A S E G D E S W Y E A R C U S
T T C H O E I F H D W R R O S R A E D Y
H Y M L A S L R N O E R U C G R S N U T
A Y A O L U A E O F A E T S L L O X U T
T A D R O O R E B L A H G E A C L O H I
A R A E D R F S K R G T T U E E H E F S
L S E D U N S L E I A P H S F S R A A E
L T E S A A O O L F L T A G A E L T O N
V O T E J Y N I E I K P I H I L R S J O
L R D S R O W E B P W S T O D L A E Y S
O I N R M T C I W O E I X O N M D A H A
R E I U O I L W T Y W E W S E T O E Z T
T S O W O W O L T H E N D O T E U G R A
N F J J C R N C A O O A U S I N T O Y E
O O E S R D E I T T Y U R E S X O H T B
C R R O H W X D N O D X T S H E F B B S
F B M W E A W A T G B N E M D T L U O T
O O S N C O D N C O M E A L E A R D Y R
T Y L A R E A O F U U A R S W O Y T N A
U S V D W E S N W T O R N O W N A A E E
O O V O C H N C E O U T U U N O Z C R H
X E M O Z T O N I F Y C E S O B D N I O
A O E I N T O T H E H E A R T F W A F W
T H C U O T P O C C I R T C E L E E H T
T W Y A D N U S Y D O O L B Y A D N U S
```

The MC came on stage and to quote him, "Are ya happy? D'ya wanna hear the best in live music? Last December was the last time Bono, The Edge, Adam and Larry played in Ireland. In six short months U2 have conquered the world." Too right!!

The band appeared on stage. The crowd roared its approval. Flags flew high in the sky. U2 kicked off with "Out of Control" which had the crowd going wild. "Twilight" was next. Bono then dedicated a song to Jim Reilly whose brother was shot in Belfast the previous week. Before playing "Sunday Bloody Sunday", Bono noticed an Irish flag in the crowd. He asked for it to be passed up to him, and he tied it to a white flag onstage. "This is not a rebel song," said Bono, giving it everything he had. "Surrender", "October", "New Year's Day", "Gloria", and many more classic tracks continued. Bono told us it was Edge's birthday (which it wasn't, it's Aug 8th) and the crowd sang "Happy Birthday" to him.

The band made their exit but it wasn't long before they re-appeared. The crowd went wild yet again to the beat of "11 O'Clock Tick Tock" which was followed by "Trash, Trampoline and the Party Girl". The band left the stage again, but the crowd weren't finished yet. We wanted more, and that's what we got. They played the old favourite "I Will Follow" which had the exhausted crowd bopping endlessly. The final song of the evening, or rather, night showed how much U2 are respected and loved by their fans. "40" was the song, and long after it had finished and the band had disappeared the crowd just stood there singing "How long to sing this song?" for ages and ages. We even sang it on the way out. U2 had just proven to the people why they are the best band around.

U2 *ISSUE 10*

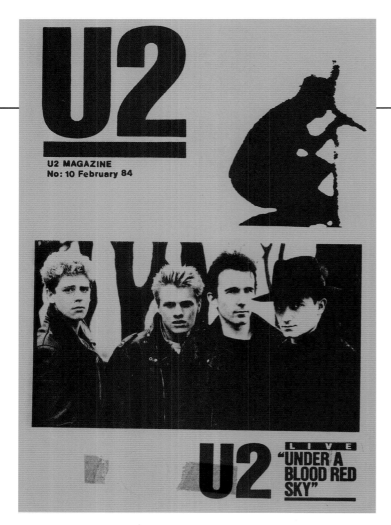

U2 MAGAZINE
No: 10 February 84

U2 "LIVE
UNDER A
BLOOD RED
SKY"

excellent set, including such favourites as "New Year's Day", "I Will Follow", "11 O'Clock Tick Tock" and of course "Sunday Bloody Sunday". The fact that the concert was taking place the night after the Harrod's bombing in London didn't go unnoticed by Bono – he felt that made the show all the more important.

The set came to a close with Mike Peters from The Alarm joining the band on stage for a powerful version of "Knocking On Heaven's Door". The encore was "40" with everyone joining in, and the chorus of 'How long, how long to sing this song' echoing out into the night.

U2 had made their point.

(There are some plans for an album and a video from this show apparently, but no details have been finalised yet.)

U2 ended a very hard-working year by headlining a show called "The Big One", a charity show for the Campaign for Nuclear Disarmament. The band don't often get the chance to do shows like this, and it did come in the middle of working on material for the new album, but they felt it was very important A lot of people had offered their services for the concert, so to fit everything in the sets were kept fairly short and included fine performances from Mari Wilson, Ian Dury, Hazel O'Connor, The Alarm, Style Council, Elvis Costello, and Costello and Paul Weller sang a duet of "My Ever Changing Moods".

After all this it was quite late when U2 came on as headliners, but there was no doubt in the minds of the audience as to who they had come to see. And U2 left no doubt in anyone's mind what sort of message they wanted to put across. They played an

"40"

– 10 –

I waited patiently for the Lord
He inclined and heard my cry
He brought me up out of the pit
Out of the miry clay

I will sing, sing a new song
I will sing, sing a new song
How long to sing this song
How long to sing this song
How long, how long, how long, how long
To sing this song

You set my feet upon a rock
And made my footsteps firm
Many will see
Many will see and hear

I will sing, sing a new song
I will sing, sing a new song
How long to sing this song
How long to sing this song
How long, how long, how long
How long to sing this song

LIVE
"UNDER A
BLOOD RED
SKY"

Music and lyrics by U2.
"40" © 1983 Blue Mountain Music Ltd
"Trash, Trampoline And The Party Girl"
© 1982 Blue Mountain Music Ltd.
Reproduced by permission.
Illustrated by Barry Cross 1983

U2

TRASH, TRAMPOLINE AND THE PARTY GIRL

I know a girl, a girl called party, party girl
I know she wants more than a party, party girl
And she won't tell me her name

I know a boy, a boy called trash, trash can
I know he does all that he can, when ban
And he won't tell me his name

I have a heart, a heart that's been a son
When I was three I thought the world revolved
Around as, I was wrong
And so I sing oh

And if you dance then dance with me
I know a girl, a girl called party, party girl
I know she wants more than a party, party girl
I know a boy, a boy called trampoline
You know what I mean
I think you know he wants
I think he knows what he wants

- 2 -

A theatrical show for peace produced by
Susannah York and Bill Bachle.

U2 ended a very hard-working year by headlining a show called "The Big One", a charity show for the Campaign for Nuclear Disarmament. The band don't often get the chance to do shows like this, and it did come in the middle of working on material for the new album, but they felt it was very important

A lot of people had offered their services for the concert, so to fit everything in the sets were kept fairly short and included fine performances from Mari Wilson, Ian Dury, Hazel O'Connor, The Alarm, Style Council, Elvis Costello, and Costello and Paul Weller sang a duet of "My Ever Changing Moods".

U2, COSTELLO, WELLER, DURY, O'CONNOR, WILSON
and many others appearing in 'The Big One'
a peace show on SUNDAY, DEC.18 7.00 pm.
£6,8 and up APOLLO
VICTORIA 01-834-6177/8/9

After all this it was quite late when U2 came on as headliners, but there was no doubt in the minds of the audience as to who they had come to see. And U2 left no doubt in anyone's mind what sort of message they wanted to put across. They played an excellent set, including such favourites as "New Year's Day", "I Will Follow", "11 O'Clock Tick Tock" and of course "Sunday Bloody Sunday". The fact that the concert was taking place the night after the Harrod's bombing in London didn't go unnoticed by Bono – he felt that made the show all the more important.

The set came to a close with Mike Peters from The Alarm joining the band on stage for a powerful version of "Knocking On Heaven's Door". The encore was "40" with everyone joining in, and the chorus of 'How long, how long to sing this song' echoing out into the night.

U2 had made their point.

(There are some plans for an album and a video from this show apparently, but no details have been finalised yet.)

The new album is likely to make quite a break with the past. After the War tour, Bono said, "Everyone feels a weight off their shoulders. We feel like we're in a new group now. I can't sleep at night with thoughts about the next record."

"It would be wrong for me to say, yes, we can change the world with a song. But every time I try writing that's where I'm at. I'm not stupid. I'm

---

1976, 7, 8, 9, 80, 81, 82, 83,

I WILL FOLLOW · AN CAT DUBH · OUT OF CONTROL · THE OCEAN · ANOTHER TIME, ANOTHER PLACE · SHADOWS AND TALL TREES · SECONDS · LIKE A SONG ... · THE REFUGEE · RED LIGHT · 40 · I FALL DOWN · REJOICE · TOMORROW · WITH A SHOUT · SCARLET · ENDLESS DEEP · TRASH TRAMPOLINE AND THE PARTY GIRL · BOY/GIRL · 11 O'CLOCK TICK TOCK · ANOTHER DAY · TWILIGHT .

U2 THANK YOU
HOME IS WHERE THE HEART

INTO THE HEART · STORIES FOR BOYS · A DAY WITHOUT ME · THE ELECTRIC CO · SUNDAY BLOODY SUNDAY · NEW YEARS DAY DROWNING MAN · TWO HEARTS BEAT AS ONE · SURRENDER · GLORIA · I THREW A BRICK THROUGH A WINDOW · FIRE · OCTOBER · STRANGER IN A STRANGE LAND · IS THAT ALL? · A CELEBRATION · J. SWALLOW · THINGS TO MAKE AND DO · TOUCH

1984 . . . . ?

U2 Live In Japan!
NEW YEARS HERO

文・小倉エージ

開演が訪れるとともに、わきあがる歓声。黒い垂れ幕があがると、場内は騒然となった。そして、メンバー4人が次々に登場するとともに、客席に立っていただれもが立ち上がって彼らを迎えた。11月26日、渋谷公会堂でのことだ。大阪を皮切りに始まったU2の、初の来日公演。幕開けを飾ったのはウト・オブ・コントロール。

- 8 -

- 9 -

U2 *ISSUE 11*

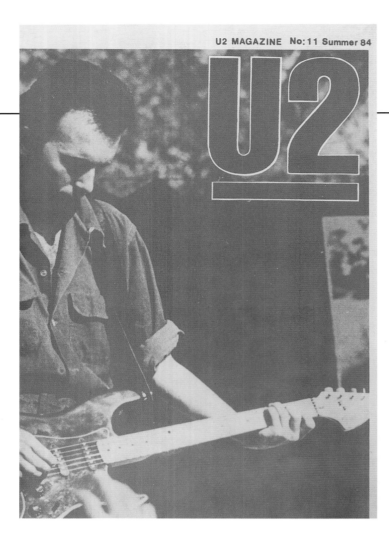

U2 MAGAZINE No:11 Summer 84

U2 MAGAZINE No.11 – SUMMER 1984

Hello!

Sorry for the delay on this issue, but I wanted to bring you the absolute latest news on how the new album is progressing. Everything is moving forward really smoothly and the band are getting on very well with Eno, who is producing. All the basic ideas are on tape, but they're continuing to experiment with different alternatives – one way to describe the sound may be that it combines the power of U2 with the ambient melodic phrasing favoured by Eno – but, well, just wait and see!

All the guys are very excited with the way the project is turning out. Bono says that they're surprising themselves with what's coming up, and that there is the same air of expectancy as when they were record-ing "Boy" – so it is a new beginning, really. And yes, Larry's come up with another killer drum sound.

The album release will be early autumn sometime, possibly September, and preceded by a single most likely. There'll be a U.K. tour to co-incide, so all U.K. members please be sure you've sent in your stamped addressed envelope marked tour dates as requested so we can send off the advance details as soon as they are available. The tour will continue on a world-wide basis, but the exact sequence and order of dates is still to be sorted out, so we'll keep you informed.

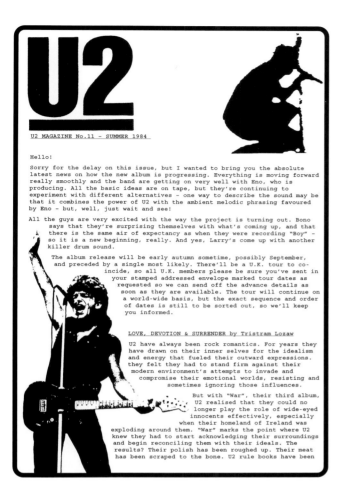

U2 MAGAZINE No.11 - SUMMER 1984

Hello!

Sorry for the delay on this issue, but I wanted to bring you the absolute latest news on how the new album is progressing. Everything is moving forward really smoothly and the band are getting on very well with Eno, who is producing. All the basic ideas are on tape, but they're continuing to experiment with different alternatives - one way to describe the sound may be that it combines the power of U2 with the ambient melodic phrasing favoured by Eno - but, well, just wait and see!

All the guys are very excited with the way the project is turning out. Bono says that they're surprising themselves with what's coming up, and that there is the same air of expectancy as when they were recording "Boy" - so it is a new beginning, really. And yes, Larry's come up with another killer drum sound.

The album release will be early autumn sometime, possibly September, and preceded by a single most likely. There'll be a U.K. tour to co-incide, so all U.K. members please be sure you've sent in your stamped addressed envelope marked tour dates as requested so we can send off the advance details as soon as they are available. The tour will continue on a world-wide basis, but the exact sequence and order of dates is still to be sorted out, so we'll keep you informed.

LOVE, DEVOTION & SURRENDER by Tristram Lozaw

U2 have always been rock romantics. For years they have drawn on their inner selves for the idealism and energy that fueled their outward expressions. they felt they had to stand firm against their modern environment's attempts to invade and compromise their emotional worlds, resisting and sometimes ignoring those influences.

But with "War", their third album, U2 realised that they could no longer play the role of wide-eyed innocents effectively, especially when their homeland of Ireland was exploding around them. "War" marks the point where U2 knew they had to start acknowledging their surroundings and begin reconciling them with their ideals. The results? Their polish has been roughed up. Their meat has been scraped to the bone. U2 rule books have been

LOVE, DEVOTION & SURRENDER

by Tristram Lozaw

U2 have always been rock romantics. For years they have drawn on their inner selves for the idealism and energy that fueled their outward expressions. they felt they had to stand firm against their modern environment's attempts to invade and compromise their emotional worlds, resisting and sometimes ignoring those influences.

But with "War", their third album, U2 realised that they could no longer play the role of wide-eyed innocents effectively, especially when their homeland of Ireland was exploding around them. "War" marks the point where U2 knew they had to start acknowledging their surroundings and begin reconciling them with their ideals. The results? Their polish has been roughed up. Their meat has been scraped to the bone. U2 rule books have been thrown out the window. And electricity flies off a vibrant album by a band that has been reborn.

This new outward approach has brought with it a flurry of activity and success. "New Year's Day" is U2's biggest single ever. "War", on which they enlisted the aid of talents as diverse as Steve Lillywhite, Kid Creole's Coconuts and Ken Fradley, is enjoying across the board airplay while it zips up the charts. In Paris, a video of "Two Hearts Beat As One" has just been completed, the same tune that master knob-twirler Francois Kervorkian is remixing for a 12" dance single. They played 36 dates in the U.K. and Europe in about as many days. There's talk in the European press that U2 is taking up where The Jam left off. And They're embarking on what promises to be a most rewarding tour of the U.S.

- 2 -

thrown out the window. And electricity flies off a vibrant album by a band that has been reborn.

This new outward approach has brought with it a flurry of activity and success. "New Year's Day" is U2's biggest single ever. "War", on which they enlisted the aid of talents as diverse as Steve Lillywhite, Kid Creole's Coconuts and Ken Fradley, is enjoying across the board airplay while it zips up the charts. In Paris, a video of "Two Hearts Beat As One" has just been completed, the same tune that master knob-twirler Francois Kervorkian is remixing for a 12" dance single. They played 36 dates in the U.K. and Europe in about as many days. There's talk in the European press that U2 is taking up where The Jam left off. And They're embarking on what promises to be a most rewarding tour of the U.S.

As people were lining up hours before U2 tickets would go on sale at the Orpheum box office (some had camped overnight), I was busy trying to track down U2's erstwhile vocalist, Bono. This task was made no easier when dates were continually being added to their tour of Europe. Nor by the fact that the band, understandably tired of being hounded by journalists, is now virtually off-limits to interviewers.

And though I'm sure that U2 and their families are equally as tired of being inundated by a growing legion of fans, my inquiries were met with nothing less than total courtesy by those whose lives I interrupted frequently - especially Bono's father. "U2 have, over the last few years, developed a party of people who maintain a vigilante-type watch on the band," commented Bono by phone from Dublin. "To me, to still be playing to the audience that bought our first record is an achievement, because even though the group has grown we haven't outgrown our audience, or vice versa. I've noticed that there are a lot more levels on which people are taken with the group now, and it's gone a little haywire." Backstage after their European shows, they'd meet an assortment of oddballs, professors, even people who were doing a thesis on the band and Edge's playing. "There's that extreme and then you have people that are into the band because they think Larry's fab or they like our denim jackets."

This difference of extremes in appeal is something that U2 has always wanted to achieve. But aren't they bothered by all the people tagging along now? "What meant more to me than the album going straight to number one were the faces on the front rows at our concerts - people who had been sleeping under hedges, in railway stations, people who had been travelling all over Europe to see us. But at the same time, to virtually be sharing hotel rooms with our audience really got in our hair.

TOP ALBUMS
1. U2, **WAR** Island
2. Michael Jackson, **THRILLER** Epic
3. R.E.M. **MURMUR** I.R.S
4. Talking Heads, **SPEAKING IN TOUNGES**
5. Big Country, **THE CROSSING**

U2 *ISSUE 12*

U2 MAGAZINE No: 12 Autumn 84

**ADAM CLAYTON IN CONVERSATION
WITH NEIL STOREY**

Windmill Lane, Dublin, Sunday 29th July

N: The album – how difficult has it been?

A: Well the album has been no more difficult than any other album to make – it's taken slightly longer this time. It's obviously not the right time for post-mortems at this point, as we haven't even finished yet, but certainly a lot of the reason why the album has taken slightly longer is the nature in which we did it. We started with a new producer for our fourth studio album, so it was a big change.

N: What were the reasons for choosing Eno as opposed to any of the other people that were mentioned at one point – the Jimmy Iovine's of this world and people like that?

A: I think they were all good ideas at the time, and we considered them but it came closer and closer to making a decision and none of them felt spot-on. I think the band basically has a very personal attitude to the way it works, and people around us who are close are important, and I think if we'd gone for somebody American it would have been very alien to our world and way of working. And there wasn't really anybody English who was available or right, that we felt 100% right about, until Brian came along.

N: Where did the original idea of using Brian come from?

A: I don't remember. It's one of those ideas that crops up – somebody says "What about using Brian Eno?" and people say "Yeah, that's interesting". I think it had been around for a while, I think we couldn't have done it if he had still been working with Talking Heads, and at the time when it had cropped up, he had been working with Talk-ing Heads, and it wouldn't have been right to have used him then. We wanted him to actually come to this project with something of a period to move away from Talking Heads and be prepared to start with a rock band again. And he was certainly interested and excited by that idea.

N: How surprised do you think he was by being approached by basically a rock 'n' roll band like yourselves?

A: I don't think he was surprised by us. I think some of the other people who approach him are the ones that surprise him – like Whitesnake, or whatever. He said he gets two or three requests a week, and most of them are fairly normal, but he said the odd time when he gets metal bands approaching him, he finds that very odd. Mind you, it's probably the next thing he'd do, knowing the way he thinks. (laughs)

- 5 -

WAR TOUR

This is the first in a new series of original maps covering U2's touring schedule from the earliest days through to the present. We start off with the U.K. War Tour 1983, and in future a different one will be included with each issue.

ABERDEEN, FEBRUARY 27

DUNDEE, FEBRUARY 26.

EDINBURGH, FEBRUARY 25

GLASGOW MARCH 24

NEWCASTLE, MARCH 1, 26.

U2, THE WAR TOUR

LANCASTER, MARCH 2.

LIVERPOOL, MARCH 3 + 25

LEEDS, MARCH 18

MANCHESTER MARCH 19

SHEFFIELD MARCH 17

STOKE, MARCH 4

DERBY MARCH 20

NOTTINGHAM, MARCH 28

BIRMINGHAM MARCH 10, 27

IPSWICH MARCH 15.

CARDIFF MARCH 11

BRISTOL MARCH 7

LONDON - HAMMERSMITH ODEON MARCH 14, 21 HAMMERSMITH PALAIS MARCH 22, 29.

EXETER MARCH 8.

POOLE MARCH 9

PORTSMOUTH MARCH 6.

BRIGHTON MARCH 13

(c) N Storey/ Ardvreck 1984

U2 *ISSUE 13*

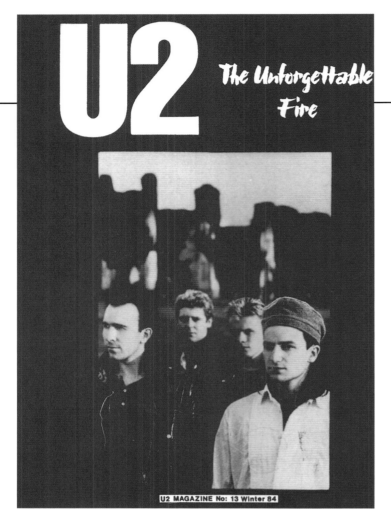

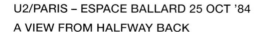

U2 MAGAZINE No: 13 Winter 84

U2/PARIS – ESPACE BALLARD 25 OCT '84
A VIEW FROM HALFWAY BACK

by Peter Marschall

Parts in the rain sidewalk cafés near deserted half fin-ished and forgotten glasses of wine left on sodden tables. Car lights glisten on the cobbles of the Champs Elysees. The Eiffel Tower, enshrouded in mist, surveys all like some giant meccano monstrosity, strangely compelling in its ugliness. Paris in the rain – U2 at Espace Ballard.

Espace Ballard is not your average rock 'n roll venue, oh no John; it's a vast tent (think big top and then some). Outside the smell of sausages and frites frying on outsize barbecues, inside 12,000 Parisians; banner-waving, cigarette lighter holding, noisy Parisians.

The lights darken, the eerie sound of "4th Of July" echoes through the canvas. As U2 quietly walk on stage the Espace Ballard erupts – Paris has waited patiently for U2 for a long time.

The familiar howl of Edge's guitar signals the start of "11 O'Clock Tick Tock". Bono stalking the stage, the audience already singing along, the song building and building until that guitar solo burns into the audience. A pause, then "I Will Follow", the flag-wavers to the front of the stage nearly falling over each other in their excitement. Songs one would expect to come late on in a set are played first – for them Christmas is liable to come twice this year.

The opening chords of "Wire" are greeted quietly – the noisy adrenalin rush of the audience ebbing until the song, building on its own intensity, claws its way through. On that showing "Wire" is likely to become one of the all-time great U2 live tunes. And then sud-denly all is quiet, Bono singing his tribute to Martin Luther King – "M.L.K.", the words, fuelled by massive, resonant keyboards courtesy Edge haunt each corner of this already rain-soaked building. The version of 'The Unforgettable Fire' that follows is stunning in its simplicity. Edge alternating between guitar and his, by now, growing bank of keyboards. Not as long as the recorded version, it lacks that final instrumental climax, moving too quickly on to "Surrender". The crowd, back on home territory, surge forward as the band play on through "Two Hearts", "Seconds" and on into "Sunday Bloody Sunday".

BAD

- 14 -

If you twist and turn away
If you tear yourself in two again
If I could, yes I would, if I could I would
Let it go
Surrender, dislocate

If I could throw this lifeless lifeline to the wind
Leave this heart of clay
See you walk, walk away
Into the night and through the rain
Into the half light and through the flame
If I could - through myself, set your spirit free
I'd lead your heart away, see you break, breakaway
Into the light and to the day
To let it go and so to find a way
To let it go and so find a way
I'm wide awake
I'm wide awake
Wide awake
I'm not sleeping, oh no no

If you should ask then maybe they tell you what I
Would say
True colours fly in blue and black
Blue silken sky and burning flag
Colours clash, collide in blood shot eyes
If I could you know I would, if I could I would
Let it go
This desperation
Dislocation, separation, condemnation, revelation
In temptation, isolation, desolation
Let it go, and so find a way
To let it go and so find a way
To let it go, oh no, and so to find a way
I'm wide awake
I'm wide awake
Wide awake
I'm not sleeping, oh no no

Sleep, sleep tonight and may your dreams be realised
If the thundercloud passes rain
So let it rain
Rain down on he

So let it be, so let it be
Sleep, sleep tonight and may your dreams be realised
If the thundercloud passes rain
So let it rain
Let it rain, rain on he

Music U2, Words Bono
© 1984 Blue Mountain Music Ltd.
Reproduced by permission.
Illustration and layout Barry Cross 1984.

U2

The Unforgettable Fire

And your heart beats so slow, through the rain and fallen snow
across the fields of mourning, to a light that's in the distance
Oh don't sorrow, no don't weep for tonight, at last
I am coming home
I am coming home

(A Sort of Homecoming)
© Blue Mountain Music Ltd

U2 MAGAZINE No: 14 Spring 85

THE PRODUCERS: STEVE LILLYWHITE

Interview by Geoff Parkyn –
West London mid-March

Geoff: So did you hit it off with U2 from the word go?

Steve: Yes. There weren't that many producers around who were doing the new sorts of music. It worked out well.

Geoff: You stayed over in Dublin to work on the album at Windmill Lane?

Steve: That was in the days when, I think everyone will agree, Windmill Lane wasn't the world class studio it is now. It was the best in Ireland, but to be honest that wasn't saying a lot. So for the sorts of tehcnical things we had I think it turned out quite well. The album was called 'Boy' and the mood of everybody on it was childish. All the silly noises on 'I Will Follow' in the middle section, me and Bono … I'll always remember this … Bono was breaking bottles in the back and I had a push-bike upside down on its saddle, turning the wheels and running a knife along the spokes. All silly things like that …

Geoff: So it was very spontaneous then?

Steve: Yes, it was, it was a vibe and it was great. Even in those days Bono didn't have all the lyrics written, even for the first album.

Geoff: Usually for a first album most of the songs have been played live for a while.

Steve: Yes. The first album was the easiest in that respect. It was the most rehearsed of all the albums I did with them. Even then it wasn't as rehearsed as virtually everyone else's first album. I can remember the record company not really thinking 'Boy' was that good, and it didn't do very much over here, but in America where the band were doing some touring – 'I Will Follow' started getting some radio play and all of a sudden it looked like a healthy base to start the band's career.

Geoff: Did you spend much time with them between recording 'Boy' and 'October'?

Steve: Yes, I went on tour with them.

Geoff: So you could see the different developments and changes?

Steve: They were growing as people, mentally they were becoming aware. The London scene's a thriving music scene – everything was happening compared to Dublin in those days. So for them everything was new and it was like being born in a lot of ways – getting lots of new ideas together. Then it was time to do the second album.

LYRICS 9

U2 The Unforgettable Fire

Ice, your only rivers run cold
These city lights, they shine as silver and gold
Duck from the night, your eyes as black as coal
Walk on by, walk on through
Walk till you run and don't look back
For here I am

Carnival, the wheels fly and the colours spin
Throughout the hall, red wine that punctures the skin
Face to face, in a dry and waterless place
Walk on by, walk on through
So sad to besiege your love so hang on
Stay this time
Stay tonight in a lie
I'm only asking but I, I think you know
Come on take me away
Come on take me away
Come on take me home
Home again

And if the mountains should crumble
Or disappear into the sea
Not a tear, no not I
Stay this time
Stay tonight in a lie
Ever after is loving time
And if you save your love
Save your tear
Don't push me too far
Don't push me too far
Tonight
Tonight

© 1984 Blue Mountain Music Ltd
Music U2, Words Bono
Reproduced by permission
Illustration and layout
Barry Cross 1984

12 LYRICS

P R O M E N A D E

Earth, sky, scenery, is she coming back again, men of straw, snooker hall
Words that build or destroy, dirt dry, bone, sand and stone
Barbed wire fence cut me down
I'd like to be around in a spiral staircase to the higher ground
And I like a firework, explode
Roman candle, lightning, lights up the sky
In cracked streets trample under foot
Sidestep, sidewalk
I see you stare into open space
Have I got closer now, behind the face
Oh tell me, Cherry dance with me
Turn me around tonight
Up through spiral staircase to the higher ground
Slide show, seaside town, coca cola, football, radio, radio, radio …

© 1984 Blue Mountain Music Ltd
Music U2, Words Bono
Reproduced by permission
Illustration Barry Cross 1984

Geoff: After touring constantly for a year or so …

Steve: Right. And no-one really thinking, "Hang on, we've got to write songs". They had about three weeks to rehearse, and they had about ten ideas for tracks. They didn't have any completed songs, put it that way – they were musical pieces. So we went in the studio and recorded these musical pieces, and then Bono was going in and singing his heart out without any lyrics, and whatever came out … He'd do say five vocal tapes and I'd sit through them and they'd all be completely different. I'd go through each of the vocal tapes and make a composite tape up, which had a rough idea of what I thought was a good melody – flicking between the faders. Bono would take that away and carry on writing the words, a better version of what he was singing. Then he'd go in a sing it again. Bono does have difficulty in sitting down and actually writing words out – he sings whatever comes out. It's a very painful process, for him – I'm sure he'd admit this – he puts himself through a lot of hardship to come out with what he feels are his best lyrics.

35

HIGHLIGHTS OF U2, ISSUE 14

U2 *ISSUE 15*

U2 MAGAZINE No: 15 Summer 85

NEWS

U2's appearance at the massive Live Aid show is the last official date for a while, and marks the end of a period of constant touring that began when the band set off for Australia last year. Plans for the immediate future are to have a rest and start writing some more songs.

Along the lines of the "Unforgettable Fire" 12" release, is a new release in the U.S., which is "U2 Wide Awake In America". It's described as "A special low-priced collection of live recordings and out takes from The Unforgettable Fire tour and album 1984-85" and comes with some superb photography by Matt Mahurin. Tracks are "Bad (Live)", "A Sort Of Homecoming (Live)" and the two studio tracks are "Three Sunrises" and "Love Comes Tumbling".

It has been done before apparently, but it's the first time I've heard of it – U2's highly inventive road crew have been putting together their own tour newsheet over the last few months. It is packed with stories and in-jokes about the concerts and personalities along the way. Put together with the help of some clever computer graphics, and most of the work being done on the tour bus, it's been coming out on a more-or-less weekly basis under the title "De Voibe"!

The "Live Aid" concert simultaneously at Wembley Stadium and the JFK Stadium in Philadelphia on July 13th represents a remarkable achievement, and of course U2 have been involved from the very beginning when Bono and Adam flew over for the day to help record the single "Do They Know It's Christmas". If you wish to contribute and help this worthy cause, the address for any donations is: "BAND AID TRUST", c/o Stoy Hayward, 8 Baker Street, London WIM 1DJ.

I apologise for the fact that we have not been able to bring you the interview with U2's sound man Joe O'Herlihy in this issue, but due to various technical problems with the tape, it became impossible. I can assure you it will be included in the Autumn/Fall issue.

LIVE AID

JULY 13th

U2 *ISSUE 16*

U2
U2 MAGAZINE No: 16
Autumn / Fall 85

BACKTRACK
U2 – London Lyceum Christmas 81

What can I say? That U2 were an experience that defies the written word? That the atmosphere was one of sheer jubilation? Or maybe just that if you missed them live, you missed one of the most joyous and inspiring events of the year.

Imagine the Lyceum transformed into a hall of celebration, where U2's followers could gather to pay tribute to the band they know should have been much, much bigger in 1981. We were overwhelmed by their music and lifted by their feeling, and the world outside seemed a million miles away as we were carried into a land of passion and beauty.

U2 are striving for, and almost reaching, perfection. The audience had expected something special and

what they got was an evening to treasure, an evening of such emotion that only those with no heart or soul could have failed to be moved. We danced, waved and smiled, and Bono smiled back. At times he looked surprisingly like Rod Stewart, especially in profile, but unlike Stewart, his humanity shines through. It was obvious that he just couldn't quite believe the reaction – he looked out with awe at the seething mass of people – but he responded magnificently, rising to the occasion with the ease of one who believes implicitly in what he is doing.

The band opened with 'Gloria', a hymn-like song performed with such intensity that I wondered if Bono's voice would be able to take the strain if he carried on with such force throughout the set. There was no problem, however, for although the vocals became huskier, the power and purity were still there, soaring above the haunting, sliding guitar which provided the ideal backing.

U2 played all the songs I love best. 'Another Time, Another Place', 'Out Of Control', 'I Will Follow', 'I Fall Down' and so many more, played warmth and feeling, and for one fan at the front it was all too much.

He clambered onto the stage to embrace Bono, who grabbed his hand, danced a little jig, then walked him off to the wings before a bouncer could eject him more forcibly. This sounds a bit of a non-event in print, but if you could have been there and seen the expression of pure delight on the faces of the crowd, you'd understand how important an unselfconscious act like that was to them. It confirmed their trust in him. I hope I've conveyed even a fraction of U2's strength and brilliance because it's hard to analyse and almost impossible to dscribe. "What can I say but thank you," murmered Bono, lost for words after a particularly rapturous response. I know exactly how he felt, because I felt the same way about them.

Karen Swayne, *Sounds*

PROPAGANDA

AUTUMN 1985 – WINTER 1999

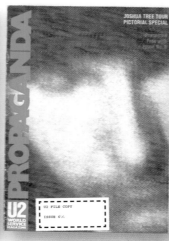

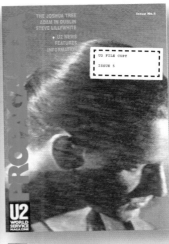

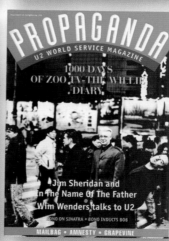

U2 THE BEST OF PROPAGANDA

THE MODERN DRUMMER

LAST YEAR, IN CELEBRATION OF WINNING THE READERS' POLL OF AMERICAN MAGAZINE 'MODERN DRUMMER', LARRY GAVE HIS FIRST MAJOR PRESS INTERVIEW IN YEARS. BEING SUCH A RARE EVENT, AND SUCH A GOOD INTERVIEW, IT IS REPEATED HERE.

Voted Number One in the Up & Coming category of MD's 1985 Readers Poll, Larry Mullen. Jr., is a different drummer A universal blend of past and future, East and West, primitive and classical, his sound is huge and heroic. Even before he began drumming with U2 at the age of 16, he was, in his own words, "unteachable". Logic and reason do not define his approach to drumming; spirit and instinct do. He treats each song as an experiment.

U2 baseman Adam Clayton refers to Larry's "dignity" as a drummer and adds. "He won't play anything that isn't natural to him". Assigned with a long shopping list of percussive paraphernalia to set up for experimentation in Larry's new home, drum roadie Tom Mullally describes Larry as "not demanding". But Mullally continues, "If he gets an idea, we work bloody hard to make sure it happens. He'll turn everything upside down".

Rebelling against the clutter in so much music, Larry allows the freshness and freedom of the open space to be important, and in the drummer's dangerous world of time and space, he knows when to hit and when not to hit. At 23 he's a young master. Unlike most musicians his age, he seems to have already lost his taste for "stardom", if he ever had it.

This interview explores the thoughts of a drummer who holds his ground. Whatever it took for Larry Mullen, Jr., to become himself, he made it. And he is truly one of the most gifted and innovative drummers in the world today.

LARRY: Let me say first of all that I don't do interviews, ever. I did them when the band first started and then I stopped because I didn't enjoy them. I've seen issues of *Modern Drummer.* I like what the magazine does, so I decided to do this. But I'm not a talker, I hope you can make sense of what I say. I saw a piece on Russ Kunkel about how musical he is and all that. I don't deserve that kind of praise in a technical sense; I don't consider myself great by any means. I wouldn't want the magazine to make me something I'm **not**. But what I do feel is that, if I'm going to do an interview, I want people

> Somebody says, "There's the drummer from U2." Another person answers, "So what?"

to know that you don't have to be a technical drummer. You can follow your own rules and be in a successful band.

I: I think you're underestimating yourself.

LARRY: Maybe. There's no harm in that. It means that I'll continue to grow hopefully.

I: Your music projects a global consciousness, but your roots are firmly in Ireland. What was it like to grow up there?

LARRY: There's no comparison with America or even Europe. It's a very isolated country – a totally different world. Things like abortion, contraception, and pornography don't exist. You have to fight – very hard – if you want to do anything different. To be in a band is really, really difficult. There's nowhere to play. But it's an interesting and beautiful place, too. I live there now; I wouldn't live anywhere else. It doesn't have the pressures of rock'n'roll. Somebody says, "There's the drummer from U2". Another person answers "So what?" In America or anywhere else, you come out of the hotel, and people want to take bits out of you. In Ireland, people have respect, and they leave you alone.

I: Did you spend much time by the ocean? Sounds of the ocean come across in some of your bass drum and cymbal work.

LARRY: Yes, I grew up in Dublin. You've always got the sea. From where I lived, it's about 500 yards down the road. Dublin has about a million people, but if you go just a mile outside the city, it's very peaceful, with green trees, and all the things you'd imagine are in Ireland.

I: Were you into native Irish music?

LARRY: Well obviously I listened to it. When I was growing up there wasn't one rock'n'roll station in Dublin. There was a station that

THE MODERN DRUMMER

played an occasional Beatles' song, but if you wanted to hear rock'n'roll, you had to tune in to a pirate radio station or a British radio station like Radio Luxembourg. I'd have my pocket radio under my bed, trying to tune into Radio Luxembourg so I could hear the charts. It wasn't until around the last five years that new bands would come to Ireland; before that, very few came. The Stones came about two years ago, which was the first time since '76 or '77. Now rock'n'roll is big in Ireland. It's just that very few can survive playing it or doing anything original.

I: How did you come to be a drummer?

LARRY: I started at about nine; I used to play piano. The teacher was a really nice lady, but one day she said "Larry, you're not going to make it". (laughs) She suggested that I try something else. I was delighted, because I had wanted to say the same thing to her a year before that.

I: But your parents were making you take lessons?

LARRY: Well, they thought it would be good for me to be exposed to music, and since I liked music, I went along with it. But I wasn't good at piano; I didn't practice much. So, as I walked away from my last piano lesson at the College of Music, I heard somebody playing drums. I turned around to my old lady and said "You hear that? **I** want to do that" She said "Okay. If you want to do that, you'll pay for it yourself". So at nine years of age I saved up a bit of money and I got nine pounds for my first term of drum instruction. I wasn't very good at learning or technique; I didn't practice much, because I was far more interested in doing my own thing. I wanted to play along with records like Bowie and the Stones. I didn't want to go through the rudiments – paradiddles and all that stuff, you know. I carried on with this teacher for about two years, and I just got bored. This is terrible, but he passed away, and (pauses) I mean I was only a kid: I said "Wow, Divine Intervention! I don't have to do

this anymore!" (laughs) So I joined a military style band: fife and drum – all that sort of stuff.

I: Why did you want to join that? It seems like more regimentation.

LARRY: It was more of a goof, because there were girls in this band, in the Color Guard.

I: I've seen some of those bands in competition. They can be quite sophisticated in their musicianship.

LARRY: Not this one. It was more "Let's have a good time and march in the St. Patrick's

Day parade in Dublin". They would try to make us read music as well, and I **could** read, but this other guy and I said, "This sounds too drab off the sheet." So we just threw the sheet music away and invented our **own** things. I was in that band for two years, including the early days of U2.

I: I've read that you got kicked out of a military band.

LARRY: That was another band, the Artane Boys' Band. The band I was just telling you about was a bit more loose - a little freer. The Artane band was too rigid for me. I was in for three days, and they told me to get my hair cut. And at the time, it was my pride and

joy – you know shoulder length golden locks. So I got it cut a few inches, and they told me to cut it more. So I told them to stick it, and I left! (laughs) I'd forgotten about that. I had a stage too, when a guy tried to teach me jazz drumming, but again, the same problem. This teacher was really into Steven Gadd: Steve Gadd was his idol. I think Steve Gadd is a great drummer, but this teacher would play Gadd's records and tell me to play that. I was rehearsing with U2 as well so I

gave it up. I just couldn't sit there and imitate someone else.

I: The story has it that you founded U2.

LARRY: Yes, and I was in charge for about three days! (laughs) We were all in the same school, and the prospect of leaving school and getting a job wasn't there. There were no jobs to get. It was like we were all going nowhere, so we decided to go nowhere together and form a band. Our school was an experimental, interdenominational school, quite liberal and open. We had to do our work, and if we were interested in sports or music, for instance, we were actually

"I didn't want to go through the rudiments – paradiddles and all that stuff, I just got bored."

given time. They gave us a room to practice in. There were very few schools in Ireland like that. Most were Christian Brothers schools where you studied, did your work, and that was **it**. We started the band as punk rock was bursting on the scene, and when we heard it, we said "Wow, this is amazing. This is energy!" Music was getting so boring. There seemed to be so much conveyor-belt rock where they'd just take the money and run, but punk rock had raw power. A lot of bands couldn't play, but they had something to say. They gave it inspiration.
I: Did you ever think that the isolation, and maybe even the adversity, you experienced in your formative years in Ireland was an advantage?
LARRY; Yes. I don't honestly think a band like U2 could have come from anywhere else. We had time to grow at our own pace, protected and away from the circus of the rock'n'roll culture. We can be ourselves, be with our families, and do all the things **human beings** are meant to do. Our music comes from being around real people in the real world. The title *The Unforgettable Fire* comes from a book we saw of paintings that were done by survivors of Hiroshima. And if you listen very closely to Bono's lyrics in "Bad" from that album, he touches on the huge heroin problem, especially in Dublin, and everything that surrounds it. We're very aware of those things. But go to London, and what some people are influenced by is the fantasy "scene" – the clothes, the dancing girls, how many drugs you can take. We just leave that behind. That's not what this band is about.
I: You talk to the public about clean living and spirituality, but you manage to walk a thin line: You're not wimps. You're still legitimate rock'n'rollers.
LARRY: All the sex and drugs in rock is so old, so boring, and so pretentious. I suppose some people think you have to go along with that old image to be a legitimate rock'n'roller, but why should we pretend? If you actually meet a lot of big name rock'n'roll bands as human beings, you find they're a lot straighter than you think.

It's a big game, and we don't play it. People can make up their own minds about U2. People who see us live know it's not "wimp rock".
I: How would you describe your drum style, Larry?
LARRY: Well, I never thought of it as a **style** until somebody said, "You know, you have a really unique style". And I said "Oh really, what's a unique style?" It's hard for me to articulate what I do. Other people have to tell me what **they** think. Once, there were two professional session drummers on Irish TV who took the drumbeats from "Pride" and explained what they were in great musical terms, and explained how this technique was used. (chuckles) I mean they **could** be right, but **I** never thought of it like that! I just do what I do. I've developed into something myself. Sometimes people ring me up, or write and say, "We think you're fab. Can you give us hints on how to drum?" The only thing I can think of is something I learned myself and that is, "Hit 'em hard!" Just put everything into it; don't hold anything back.
I: But you know when to hit 'em soft too. You're capable of subtlety in your drumming.
LARRY: Yes, we like to put light and shade into the music as well – not always hammering away. There are times to be lighter, but still it's strong. There are times to come down and go back up again. I don't hit the drums at the same intensity all the time.
I: Of course one of the standard critiques of rock drummers is that they know nothing about dynamics.
LARRY: It may be true of a lot of drummers, but certainly not of all of them. You can't generalise, especially now. There are so many new drummers with new ideas. It **could** be said, though, that in the past I was sometimes just heavy handed, but I think that, over the last few years, I've started to listen to music a **lot** more in terms of light and shade. It's a question of maturity – of actually listening to more music and seeing other drummers. I was never interested in other drummers until about two or three years ago.
I: "Drowning Man" on *War,*

"I was never interested in other drummers until about two or three years ago."

comes to mind as an example of light and shade. The bass drum resonates as if from the depths of the ocean, with a stirring sense of ebb and flow.
LARRY: That song just evolved spontaneously. I did it with a 24" marching-band bass drum that I put on a chair, and just hit with a mallet and with my hands. It was recorded in Windmill Lane, the studio in Dublin that we use. It's an **amazing** place, with its own character. You can get an **immaculate** drum sound in the hallway, which is solid stone walls with a really high ceiling. I set my kit out there, and they put mic's all the way down from the very, very top of the stairwell. I've recorded many songs out there.
I: You also use brushes on "Drowning Man"
LARRY: Yes, and on "Bad" too, among others. A while back, I started to use brushes on different songs, and it seemed then that it was catching on. Are you familiar with the band Echo & The Bunnymen? They did a complete album with just brushes; I really like it. The only thing is that so many drummers are using brushes now that I've sort of stayed away from it slightly.
I: There seems to be an Oriental streak in your playing, which I noticed first on "Drowning Man".
LARRY: Oh, did you get Oriental flavours in that? In *The Unforgettable Fire,* there are many Oriental touches, even in the design of the album cover, with the rich purply colour and the calligraphy. When we went to Japan, we avoided all the "touristy" trappings. Most bands stay in rock'n'roll hotels there, we stayed in traditional Japanese hotels and ate at traditional Japanese restaurants. Everywhere we went, we heard the traditional music, we were all influenced by it.
I: You must also be aware of the marching-band influence, evident especially on *War.*

THE MODERN DRUMMER

LARRY: Oh, yeah. I see it, although it's not something I cultivated. It was just there. It was very, very natural. Again it was a case of someone asking me if I were ever in a marching band, because they could hear it in my style, and I said "Oh really, can you?" I didn't realise it, because it wasn't a conscious decision on my part.

"Hit 'em hard!"

I: The sense of open space is prominent in your drumming. There are times when you allow the absolute maximum space between beats; you hold it to the last fraction of a second.
LARRY: Yes, I like gaps; I like to be able to **feel** the music – not to clutter the songs. Lots of new drummers tend to fill in all the gaps and leave no space. Technically, a lot of drummers leave me standing miles away, but they don't leave gaps. It may sound good for their bands, but it's just not for me. I've been really getting into R&B drummers. They're right down to earth – simple. All those jazz-head drummers are just so complex. It's like going to college. It's like "How intelligent you are? How many big words do you know?" It doesn't really matter ultimately.
I: There are some who would say that the technique – all those big words, if you will – gives you a greater vocabulary to convey the musical message.
LARRY: Well. To me it's like the difference between a novel and a poem. Sometimes, you can say everything in one line or even one word. I don't mean to knock anybody; there's room for everyone. But what happened to the whole punk thing – just getting up and doing what you feel? I'm into the **spirit**, not into the musicianship.

DRUMMING: MULLEN STYLE

Larry Mullen, Jr., has an interesting and driving approach to drumming. Anyone who has witnessed a U2 performance can attest to Larry's power and intensity.
The examples below demonstrate Larry's dynamic style from U2's most recent album, *The Unforgettable Fire* (Island Records, 90231-1). The examples are excerpts of the basic patterns he performs and embellishes on.

1. "A short Homecoming"

2. "In the name of Love"

Verse

Chorus

3. "The Unforgettable Fire"

4. "Promenade" Larry performs this song with brushes. ♩ = 138

5. "Bad". From the closing sections of the song with the snares off.

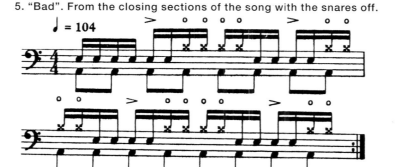

THE MAN WHO MISTOOK HIS WIFE FOR A HAT

I'm reading a great book called 'The man who mistook his wife for a hat' by Oliver Sacks. It's a book about neurology case histories, and as well as being a bit of a laugh it's a fascinating insight into the way the human brain works. The title comes from one case in particular.

This man's brain had been damaged and what it meant was that he could no longer transform visual images into reality. They were totally abstract and meant nothing to him intellectually. It was as if somebody who had been blind all their life suddenly could see, but they saw just 'things', they hadn't learned what was light and shade, and what was a human face, and so on. Some of the symptoms of this problem were that he could no longer recognise faces. He could see chins, he could see eyes, noses, ears, hair, but he could not assimilate that and decide on who the individual was. He could only recognise people from his hearing their voices. So, for instance, if somebody came up to him, he could describe them but he couldn't decide who they were. He was continually mixing things up, like he'd look at his feet and not be able to decide whether there were shoes on his feet or not – he could mistake his shoes for his feet, a fire hydrant he would mistake for a child. When he mistook his wife for a hat, he thought she was a coat stand, and he was actually trying to find his hat. He put his hand out and grabbed her head, thinking it was his hat.

His whole life was centred around music, he was a great musician. In order to do simple things like eat, or dress, he made songs about them, so he would hum, as he did things. As long as he stuck to a strict routine, and he knew exactly where his clothes were, he could get it together, but if he was interrupted he could no longer figure out what he was doing. He'd lost his ability to look at his trousers and see them as trousers, but in song form it made some sort of sense to him.

"He basically died, I think".

THE EDGE

SELF AID FOR IRELAND

It was the greatest night in the history of Irish Music. Bono sang 'C'mon Everybody'. Everybody did.

IS THERE ANYBODY HERE FROM DUBLIN?! ▽

Eire's Sunday Tribune of May the eighteenth got it about right with their front page colour photo of Bono in full-concert flight and the gigantic headline 'JOBS, CASH, AND ROCK'N'ROLL'. For the fourteen hour long Bob Geldof-inspired Self Aid Concert of the previous day saw more than 1,200 jobs pledged in the war against catastrophic levels of Irish unemployment. It also raised more than £500,000 in donations from generous Irish TV viewers who watched the marathon rock spectacular at home. It was the most impressive line-up of Irish rock'n'roll history ever mounted on the Emerald Isle. Virtual unknowns like Brush Shiels and De Danann brushed shoulders and shared stage with virtual legends like Bob Geldof and his Boomtown Rats, Van Morrison, Elvis Costello and of course U2.

Bono admitted to not identifying with the unemployed in every aspect of their depressing situations – "I've been in this band since I was sixteen and now I'm twenty six" – but he did what he does best. He lifted hearts. "This is a song about pride…. Don't let them take it away!" The majestic acoustic rendering of Pride followed a bizarre, but frantically enjoyable opening cover version of the Eddie Cochran standard C'mon Everybody. Sunday Bloody Sunday led into the perfect non-sermonising political statement, Dylan's Maggie's Farm. With Edge, Larry and Adam relishing the rare opportunity to plunder the catalogue of rock's great anthems, Bono updated the interpretations with chilling references to ever-present nuclear catastrophe. "Chernobyl's got me on the run" he intoned, in a brief trip through Lennon's Cold Turkey. Eerie tapes of political ranting and F-1 11's blared in the background. Bad closed the euphorically received set. A great Irish rock occasion, a feast of music for 30,000 fans in the Royal Dublin Showground and a million Irish TV viewers. But for 1,200 of Ireland's unemployed, Self Aid was even more. It was a job and a brighter future.

M W

△ C'MON EVERYBODY!!

ELVIS TRIES TO REMEMBER
▽ HOW TO SPELL DECLAN

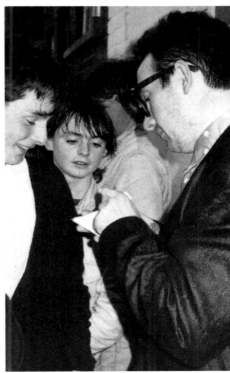

△ BOB GIVES IT SOME WELLY

◁ THE CALM BEFORE THE STORM

△ BONO: JACKET BY FIFI-TRIXIBELL

FIFI-TRIXIBELL MODELLING
▽ HER OWN VERSION

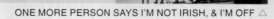
ONE MORE PERSON SAYS I'M NOT IRISH, & I'M OFF △

"AINT GONNA WORK ON △
MAGGIE'S FARM NO MORE"

GUTTER PRESS HACK REPORTERS ▽

LARRY MAKES A BID FOR
CENTRE STAGE ▽

LIFE OF BRIAN

Brian Eno, co-producer of U2's Unforgettable Fire, has recently been back in Ireland, working with the band on the initial stages of their new album. He is, however, also the creator of a touring exhibition of 'Works Constructed with Sound & Light'. Its most recent appearances have been in London, entitled "Place # 11", Grenoble, France, as "Place # 12" and appropriately enough, "Place # 13" in Dublin. The exhibition runs from June 4th at the Douglas Hyde Gallery, Trinity College.

LIFE OF **BRIAN**

For many a U2 fan, the news that Brian Eno was to produce their fourth studio album back in 1984, was greeted with blank expressions and a deafening silence. Brian who? Oh, Brian Eno. Yes, name rings a bell. Used to have something to do with Roxy Music didn't he? Or was it Talking Heads? Or David Bowie perhaps. But isn't he one of those avante-garde types, a 'critics-favourite' who never sells (m)any records? Intellectual sort. Yes, that's it, something to do with 'ambient music'. Music without words. Or drums. Music for Airports. Music for Films. Music for Compact-Disc Owners.

Serious

In fact, due to a combination of serious artistic obsession, serious care to avoid the press and serious disdain for public profile (which most pop-stars view as essential) Brian Eno, in the 12 years since leaving Roxy Music, has successfully become Mr. Anonymous Music Maker. He looks like your next-door neighbour. Come to think of it, perhaps he is. Through the late seventies and into the eighties the trail of his particular artistic quest has become a little clearer, making a couple of albums with David Bowie ('Low' and 'Heroes') recording 'My Life in the Bush of Ghosts' with David Byrne, producing a few albums for Talking Heads ('Remain in Light', 'More Songs about Buildings and Food' and 'Fear of Music') and most relevantly 'The Unforgettable Fire' for U2. He's already had a prolonged working visit to Dublin this year and is to be, at least partially, involved in producing the next vinyl epic from Larry, Adam, Edge and Bono.

Discreet Music

Meanwhile, throughout the last decade, he has continued to create individually, and in collaboration with similar musical minds, a growing library of what has been termed 'ambient music' – always experimental, occasionally off-the-wall, usually beautiful, and invariably soothing and meditative. Just occasionally the adjectives 'self-indulgent', 'repetitive' and 'tranquillising' have also been appropriate for this preoccupation with ambience or atmospheric sound. A description or review won't fit into words. He's been painting pictures with sound, big bold strokes like a sunset in non-drip gloss.

Eno is regarded as part of the rock fraternity but his is the strangest kind of 'rock music' you ever heard – one English magazine got it about right when they headlined a feature on Eno with the phrase 'Still Twisting Without the Shout'. Nobody shouts on records like 'Music for Airports' or 'Music for Films', nobody so much as more than whispers on 'Discreet Music' or the compact-disc only release 'Thursday Afternoon'.

Exhibitions

In his most recent artistic foray, the unique 'Sound and Light Constructions' currently travelling Europe, a British Library-like reverence and solemnity is required of the

> ## Once I'd met Bono I knew I had to work with him.

bemused punters as, with hushed tones, they view his surreal model landscapes creatively lit and re-lit to the appropriately discreet background of Eno-ambience. They're musical light-scapes I suppose. While a manic world roars by outside, Eno has created a womb-like existence of warmth and peace, a tranquil landscape where hearts get cautioned if they beat too loudly. Visitors sit and lounge and walk, soothed by Eno's aural-visual sculpting. Definitely No Shouting.

Entertaining journalists and assorted pop-luminaries at the opening of its London showing, Eno is glad to hear that PROPAGANDA is represented.

"The guys in U2 are always asking me what I do, apart from music....well here it is. I hope they come and see it!"

ENO ON U2

So how did a strict No-Shouter get involved with the band who wrote 'With a Shout'? One English music-paper described their artistic union as about as unlikely as the Pope contracting Aids. It transpires that U2 originally contacted Eno in 1982 and he turned them flat down. More than once. "But they just kept on nagging at me," says Eno "So much so that I listened to some of their old material which didn't particularly inspire me".

Eventually and reluctantly Eno agreed to meet the band. Problem solved. "Once I'd met Bono I knew I had to work with him. I thought there was something about him – something that made the idea of spending time in a studio with him very interesting. His attitude struck me as very intelligent and inspiring.

"He talked about how they work as a band, not in terms of playing and so forth, but in terms of contribution, what contributed to the identity of the band as a whole. I hadn't heard anyone talking about a band like that in a long time –

and so on that basis, out of curiosity, I agreed to work with them".

It was a meeting that did the trick for the band as well, as The Edge recalls: "It wasn't until we met the guy that we were finally committed to the idea of him producing because he is a very, very honest no-bullshit kind of person".

Energy and Atmosphere

For a musician whose production style is more of a wash, an ambience in fact, than the characteristic stamp and brand of a Steve Lillywhite who'd produced the first three U2 studio albums, the U2 of the past was not a problem.

"I wasn't previously acquainted with their work and had no such blindfold to work against. To tell you the truth I was unsure at the outset of what they wanted or expected from me.

"I emphasised that if I worked with them the record would not sound like anything else they'd done and perhaps would be a problem". Quite the opposite as it turned out. Bono puts it best! "There's always been two sides to U2, the energy and the atmosphere. With Steve Lillywhite it was always the energy that showed, but Brian Eno is helping bring out the atmosphere again".

In The Studio

The time in Slane Castle was a trip to be relished, a temporary move from his Woodbridge, Suffolk home – a house at the bottom of his parents' garden – to a romantic Irish port, a huge stately ballroom and the lighting of an unforgettable fire. He describes working with U2 as one of the most enjoyable experiences of his life.

"As people and artists they were refreshing and innovative – we both learned a lot. I was mystified at their reasons for asking me particularly. I wanted to discover just what it was they wanted from me and it transpired that their vision of how their new record should sound worked well in this context".

"They knew that I would encourage the new side to them instead of harping at the old. But producing is not my job really and I don't intend to make a habit of it".

Since his production work on 'The Unforgettable Fire' and 'Wide Awake in America' Brian Eno has released 'The Pearl' with American pianist Harold Budd, 'Hybrid' with Michael Brook and Daniel Lanois and 'Voices' with Roger Eno and Daniel Lanois. He also scored the theme music to 'Creation of the Universe' (USA:tv) and 'Before the Jungle Gods' (Australia:film). Meanwhile his video installations have visited Holland, Italy, Canada, England, Germany and Sweden. Their recent Dublin visit meant the members of U2 could find out just what else Brian Eno does do beside his music. 'More Dark than Shark' is a book of paintings and illustrations by Russell Mills depicting 10 years of Eno's songs (Faber and Faber £16.50) and 'More Blank than Frank' is a selected compilation of Brian's favourite songs released to coincide.

Brian Eno's middle name is 'Prolific',
MW

The Edge on working in the studio with Eno, and Daniel Lanois:

"Brian will say something like 'these speakers don't inspire me. They have a particularly hard sound and this is the second mix we've had trouble with. Let's make the decision now, and bring in some new speakers.

"Our attitude would have been 'Ah, I'm sure they're alright' kinda Irish, not following through an instinct. Brian and Danny have great follow through. I would choose a guitar to play a certain part, and Danny would say "Well, Edge, that guitar sound nice, but that guitar over there, I've noticed whenever you've played it, it inspires you. Why don't you use that one?".

U2
WORLD
SERVICE
MAGAZINE

PROP

HOPE ON THE

U2 HEADED A PARTY OF EIGHT BANDS, 36 MUSICIANS, 200 TOUR PERSONNEL AND 250 TONS OF EQUIPMENT ON A JOURNEY OF HOPE FROM THE WEST ON TO THE EAST.

"A Conspiracy of Hope". That was the title given to the series of concerts across America, in which U2 were involved. There were six shows in all, over a two week period starting in San Francisco on June 4th, and winding across the States to finish at the Giants Stadium in New Jersey, just over the river from New York City.

The artists on the bill varied from night to night, but the basis of the tour consisted of U2, Sting, Peter Gabriel, Lou Reed, The Neville Brothers, Jackson Browne and Joan Baez and Bryan Adams.

Everybody involved had come together to support Amnesty International, and help celebrate their 25th birthday. There were plenty of surprises along the way, but one surprise that no-one had bargained for was the vast fun-factor that would be involved. Despite the serious nature of the tour's aim, there was much more hilarity en route – largely due to the huge number of people on the tour.

There were about 200 in all, counting band members, road crews, managers, promoters, etc., etc. Everyone was travelling on the same aeroplane – a chartered 707 with no rules – so the potential for fun was vast.

Everyone met up in San Francisco for the first of the many press conferences, on June 3rd. A rough diary outline of events follows:
June 3rd – San Francisco Cow Palace. Soundchecks and Press conference. Finding things unnecessarily dull at the press conference, Bono attempted to break the formal atmosphere a little. "What songs will you be playing for

Amnesty?", asked a reporter, "Yummy, Yummy, Yummy, I've got love in my tummy" replies Bono. Nobody laughs, the U2 crew go into hysterics.
June 4th – San Francisco – show day. First night nerves all round, but everything ran exactly to plan. After the show everyone was pleased, relieved and ready for more.
June 5th – Travel day to Los Angeles. Press conference on arrival for artists, a fun-packed evening load-in awaits the road crew.
June 6th – Los Angeles, The (Fabulous) Forum. Being within spitting distance of Hollywood, the stars flocked to the hippest point in the known universe. A mound of mega-stars huddled backstage, with a slightly larger mound of press photographers taking pictures of them. On stage, surprise appearances came from Bob Geldof and Eurythmic Dave Stewart, Bob Dylan (gasp) and Tom Petty, with compering spots from Jamie Lee Curtis plus Madonna and Sean Penn, who narrowly avoided a full-scale slanging match with the audience. Meanwhile, backstage, Jack Nicholson arrived and the press squad completely ignored everybody else, even Sigue Sigue Sputnik. U2 bought the house down.
June 7th – Flight to Denver. Everyone's loosened up, with the various parties beginning to intermingle. Peter Gabriel arrived, video camera on shoulder, and there it stayed.
June 8th – Denver McNichols Arena. All the bands are in great form now. Joan Baez and Aaron Neville did a vocal rendition of Amazing Grace, which was quite something. It was the birthday of Amnesty's

Mary Daly, who received a bouquet during the finale, presented by Bono.
June 11th – Atlanta Omni. Issue 2 of Propaganda arrived which put everyone in a good mood – or was it the day off? Sting's jazz band mysteriously reappeared as The Police! During U2's rendition of 'Sun City' with Lou Reed guesting on vocals, Bono goes into "Vicious ....." Lou Reed gapes, and signals to Bono to carry on. Bono smirks, carries on and instantly forgets the words.
June 12th – Flight to Chicago. In flight behaviour reached an all-time low. Just as the plane lifted off, three masked individuals "flew" up the centre aisle, capes fluttering, carrying a huge tape recorder blaring the Superman theme. It'll end in tears.
June 13th – Chicago Rosemont. The second to last show – how time flies when you're having fun. A stunning show – Jack Healey's ranting and raving about Amnesty would be enough to make Atilla the Hun join up.

> **Bono:**
> "You'd have to be deaf, dumb and blind not to hit back at the injustice of the world we live in."

ROAD

Sting:
"It's one thing to reflect the mood of the time, but it's much harder to change the times."

June 14th – Complete anarchy descended on the flight to New York, as a massive pillow fight broke out, by way of a farewell. Hilarious, half a 707 buried in a white snow storm of pillow hurling frenzy. The air hostesses just joined in.

U2 slip off to an Anti Apartheid rally in New York City. It's all go at Giants' Stadium, in preparation for the TV broadcast tomorrow.

June 15th – The 'Conspiracy of Hope' ends live on TV with a million more guest artists and comperes joining in. These included Muhammed Ali, Third World, Joni Mitchell, Santana and the awesome Yoko Ono.

The usual finale, 'I Shall be Released' closes the show, during which several real 'prisoners of conscience' whom Amnesty have helped release, join the assembled gathering of musicians on stage. A very moving moment, and it reminded everyone yet again of what it was we came here to achieve.

Peter Gabriel:
"What I really want to be able to say about my own music is maybe that I contributed something to make a better world."

CONSPIRACY OF HOPE
Show schedule – Los Angeles

5:00	Dinner
6:00	**Doors Open**
6:00	Amnesty Logo rolldrops in – House music
6:50	Tape – Olatunji House lights to ½ (4.55")
6:55	Video Nelson Mandela (4'30") House lights to black
7:00	Bill Graham intro Nevilles
7:00	Neville Bros/Joan Baez
7:25	Lou Reed to holding area
7:30	Nevilles/Joan off
	Bill Thanks
	No music – House black
	Rolldrops/Stage lights
7:35	Bill intro Lou Reed – Lou on
8:00	Lou Reed off/Bill Thanks
	Rolldrops/Audio/Stage lights/House music
	Jackson Browne to holding area
8:05	Bill intro Jackson Browne – Jackson on
8:20	Jackson off/Bill Thanks/Stage lights
	Bill intro Amnesty Videos (Vintage)
8:30	Bob Dylan/Tom Petty to holding area
8:35	Bill intro Dylan/Petty
8:50	Dylan/Petty off/Bill Thanks
	Full House lights
	House music/Rolldrops/Intermission
9:15	Peter Gabriel to holding area
9:20	Bill intro Gabriel
9:50	Gabriel off/Bill Thanks
	House lights full
	House music
	Rolldrops
10:00	Bob Geldof/Dave Stewart to holding area
10:05	Geldof/Steward on
10:10	Geldof/Steward off/Bill Thanks
	Stage lights only/No music/No Rolldrops
10:15	Bryan Adams to holding area
10:20	Bill intro Bryan Adams
10:50	Bryan off/Bill Thanks
	Stage lights only
	Bill intro Jack Healy
	Amnesty Videos (Personality)
	House music
11:00	Sting to holding area
11:05	Sting On - No Intro
11:40	Sting off/Bill Thanks
	House lights
	House music/Rolldrops
11:55	U2 to holding area
12:00	Bill intro
	U2
	"Sun City"
	"I shall be released" (Finale)
	House to ¼ at (+ .30)
	House to ½ at (+ .60)
12...?	End
	Olatunji
	Rolldrops
	House lights

HOPE ON THE ROAD

After the tour Adam and The Edge spent a little time reflecting on the whole event:

How did you enjoy getting back into live shows after almost a year off the road?
Adam: It was very good. What was nice about it was that we had such a good reason to be out there.
Edge: Yes, what a great way to get back into live shows! We always knew it would be a great deal more fun than a usual tour because of all the other artists involved, and we'd be travelling in one plane, staying in the same hotels and there'd be plenty of getting to know the other guys on the tour – but I don't think anyone imagined it would be quite as much fun as it was. We were on tour with some brilliant people, like Lou Reed, The Nevilles, Peter Gabriel, and of course 'Sting' and latterly The Police, so with that collection of interesting characters it made touring totally fascinating.

Also because of the distances between the shows, it meant there had to be a day clear for the equipment to make it, which meant we weren't killing ourselves in terms of schedule either. We could see a lot of the other artists and people on the tour, and get it together at press conferences, radio and TV interviews, and so on.

The fact it was for such a great cause obviously multiplied the enjoyment by ten immediately. Plus the Amnesty people, like Jack Healey and Mary Daly to name but two, were just great people to be around for a couple of weeks.

What about the actual shows - was it a new experience, or more like 'back in the old routine?'
E: Both really. Some of it was like a U2 gig – the audience were great and very reminiscent of a U2 tour, very responsive and seemed to know exactly what was happening, why they were there and why we were there. Because we were only doing 40 minutes every night, though, it meant there was a lot less pressure on us to 'headline' or whatever. We had a lot of the good points of touring, and very few of the bad points. It really was a great way to tour.

How did it feel sharing a headline with The Police, after opening for them at Gateshead only three years ago?
E: It was funny – I don't think it really struck us, because we'd started off with Sting, who was on right before us, so when it switched to The Police it wasn't quite such a big thing any more because we'd become confident enough over the previous three shows. It was obviously a piece of history, though.

Did you get the impression this was a kind of farewell appearance for The Police?
E: I don't know. Maybe we won't see them together again, but I didn't get that feeling from them particularly.

Were there any shows you enjoyed particularly?
E: I'd have to say Chicago. I mean they were all great, but in Chicago we had SUCH a good audience, they were fantastic. Plus, it was the fifth show in, so everything was really happening at that stage.

Any of the other artists you enjoyed particularly?
A: I enjoyed them all for different reasons. I guess I enjoyed watching Peter Gabriel every night, but at the same time I also enjoyed Sting with his jazz band and

Lou Reed's band. I liked the Neville Brothers a lot.

E: I love the Nevilles. I loved Peter Gabriel – and Sting, in a way, too. There were high points in everybody's sets, but I particularly enjoyed those three.

Were there any great moments offstage?

E: There's so many… ! The fights were always good fun – the pillow fight was great and the Superman episode was funny.

A: I really enjoyed hanging out in people's dressing rooms before we'd go on. Great moments don't always need an explosion.

E: The jam sessions in Atlanta – now they were good. We were in this hotel for three nights, and in the bar was this 'cover' band. The first night everyone was a bit sheepish. I hit the sack about twelve, but later on various musicians began to hit the stage. Bono was up there, and Peter Gabriel, with Manou from his band. Joan Baez, and I think Larry and Adam. They went through a whole load of R&B classics that everyone knew, through various stages of the very late evening.

The next night was the same. I was there for that, and to see someone like Lou Reed get up and play 'Vicious' and some of his songs he hasn't played for so long was quite something. Everyone got up there and just went for it, in front of all these other musicians. It was a really good feeling.

How was the Giants' Stadium show?

E: That was our first Stadium show in the States and it wasn't too bad really – I felt quite good. The TV lights that MTV had put in meant it was totally different to the other nights. It was off-putting at the beginning, but I managed to ignore them and went for it – I had a great time on stage. I didn't feel intimidated by the size of the place either – OK it was big, but I didn't find it a problem.

Personally I felt that the overall event fell apart a bit in New York. The bill got a little out of hand and it diffused some of the potency of the

earlier shows around the States, because it was overladen with 'special guests'. It killed it a little I think.

A: We knew the event was going to be beefed up for Giants Stadium. I think had we known beforehand that the original package was going to be so successful, we wouldn't have opted to boost the bill for the last show. But I think that having made that decision – and that was the basis on which we agreed to play outdoors – it was swings and roundabouts really.

What about the MTV broadcast??

E: What I saw of it seemed fairly professional, but as I said, the bill was a bit 'iffy'. I didn't think it was all that fantastic.

Do you think there's any future in 'benefits' as such, now that everyone seems to be holding charity music events?

A: As long as the actual event is inspired – if the people have put work into it to make it appealing to the public, then it survives as a benefit. It's foolish to think that people only go to these events

because they are termed a 'benefit'!

The reason people go to benefits, is because they like what's going on. If people who wish to be involved in them are prepared to put in the time and the energy to do it properly, then there's no reason why they should have a limited life span. It's only when people become greedy and lazy that benefits don't function as what they're meant to be.

Did you see Geldof play in L.A.?

A: Yeah, he was good – but he only had one song to play!

HOPE ON THE ROAD

Tell me about the Anti Apartheid rally you went to in New York.

A: It was a large rally – there were marches coming in from the East and West. Meeting in Central Park. We didn't get in from Chicago till late so I didn't know how the day went, but apparently there were around 60,000 people there.

Various bands played – Little Steven did a set. Peter Gabriel got up and did 'Biko' and Black Uhuru were there too – I think just about every black band from New York must have been there! We all got up and did Sun City with Little Steven. It was more for moral support than anything – turn up and be counted.

Are you looking forward to getting back to the album after all the excitement?

A: It'll be good to get stuck in. There's a couple of extra songs needed, but so far, so good.

Do you think doing these live shows will lead to a better album?

E: It might – I hope it does. What would have been a help would have been to get out and play some of the new songs live, but it became obvious to everyone (lastly to me), that to do material no-one knew would have been a bad thing. We really had to go out there and do the 'greatest hits', but we did mess around with a few cover versions like 'Maggies Farm', 'Help' and in 'Bad' Bono would do his various meanderings. 'C'mon Everybody' we did once too.

'Maggies Farm' developed into something quite astounding – do you think we'll see that again?

E: Oh, I'm sure of it.

So, it'll be heads down for the rest of the year?

E: The basic plan is to go back, do some writing and demoing by ourselves, and then get stuck into the album proper in August.

No more surprise appearances for a while, then?

E: No, no more surprise appearances.

TOUR SNAPSHOTS

Here is a selection of moments from the Amnesty tour, lifted from our family album. The camera never lies, so here's the grim truth.

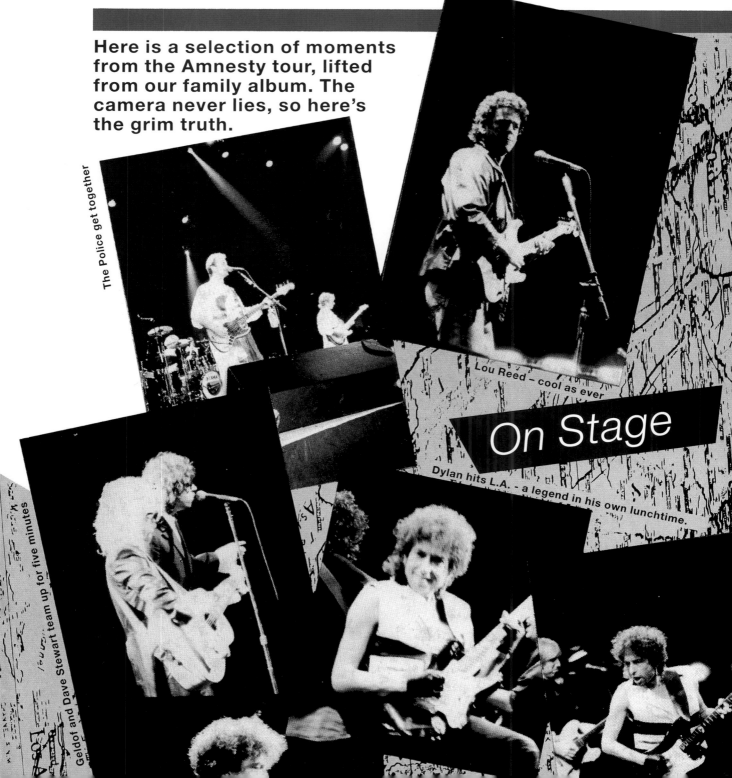

The Police get together

Lou Reed – cool as ever

On Stage

Dylan hits L.A. – a legend in his own lunchtime.

Geldof and Dave Stewart team up for five minutes

In-flight Entertainment

The legendary pillow fight – spot the singer in mid-fling

Peter Gabriel's careful documentation goes on ...

... and on ...

... and on ...

... and on ...

... and on!

Amnesty's Jack Healy

It's Thursday so this must be ...

In flight crew inactivity

Joan promoting dental health

Say cheese

U2 THE BEST OF PROPAGANDA

Star Liggers

A Thompson or two

Michael J Filmstar

Monsieur Howard Jones

Yes! It really is Mono and Badonna!
(.....and Sean too)

Kevin Killen reads the goss

Back door Propagandists

... and this is Harvey Goldsmith

...igh tension and drama at a press conference

Salivating Press Hounds

THE ENDURING CHILL
BONO AND THE TWO AMERICAS

BONO IS SITTING WITH A GLASS OF BEER IN HIS HAND. EASTENDERS IS BLARING FROM THE TV SCREEN HIGH ON A SHELF IN THIS CROWDED PUB DOWN BY THE RIVER IN OCTOBER-ALBUM-COVER COUNTRY. THE PEOPLE OF DUBLIN, ANOTHER DAY OVER, ARE OUT DRINKING AND TALKING AT FULL VOLUME ALL AROUND AND FINALLY U2'S MAIN MAN HAS FOUND TIME TO TALK TO PROPAGANDA. THE CONVERSATION IS CASUAL, AND WANDERS ONTO THE SUBJECT OF RECORDS AND BOOKS.

What kind of books have you been reading recently?
Bono: "I've been reading American stuff this year, a lot of black poets. Robert Hayden and people like that. I read this fantastic book that Maria from "Lone Justice" lent me, called "Now Let Us Praise Famous

Men". It's an amazing book which is an account of the Depression in the dustbowl of the United States in the 1930s. I worked hard to get a copy of that as it's very difficult to get hold of.

I've also been reading a lot by a writer called Flannery O'Connor.

How did you come across Flannery O'Connor? Not many people read her today.
Actually, Bruce Springsteen and I had a conversation about writers. A lot of his writing has that 'Grapes of Wrath' scenery ...I thought he'd have read somebody like (John) Steinbeck – which of course he had – but he said to me that a far more important influence was Flannery O'Connor. And he thought, considering the music we were making, that it might be something I should read. I don't think he knew what he was saying because I've never felt such sympathy with a writer in America before.

Do you feel a lot of sympathy for America?
Well I have a kind of love-hate relationship with America. I love the place, I love the people. One of the things I hate is that such a trusting people could have put their trust in a guy like Ronald Reagan. He may be a sincere man, but he is sincerely wrong in so many cases.

For instance in South America. There is no question in my mind that the people of America through their taxes are paying for the equipment that is used to torture people in El Salvador. In my trip to Salvador

THE ENDURING CHILL
BONO AND THE TWO AMERICAS

Have you ever encountered the kind of racist attitudes she describes in her books?

I've never come up against black and white racism of that kind although I've come up against Protestant and Catholic bigotry which is the same thing. The Irish can really relate to the black people. They say the Irish are the white blacks – I mean we like to think we have the same soul. We definitely share the same sort of spirit of 'up against all odds we'll do it'.

I spent some time on the Amnesty International tour with the Neville Brothers, a remarkable r'n'b band. Cyril Neville was on his way to vote when Martin Luther King was assassinated and he became a very angry man in the Black Power movement and at one stage he lost faith in voting and in trying to do anything through the proper channels. He just wanted to get back at the white man who had for long persecuted the black man. I learnt to understand a lot of the anger and resentment that the black community has, but I've never seen it in operation.

What's your favourite Flannery O'Connor story?

The Enduring Chill. It's a very sad and pathetic portrait of a guy, a very unromantic piece of writing and it's just so powerful the way it describes his death as an enduring chill, that begins slowly.

There are few happy endings in her stories, as there are few in life generally.

But there is great hope in her books in a way, there is some

"If you give someone a colour television, a house, a car, and two weeks vacation a year... they'll agree to anything and stop asking questions."

I met with mothers of children who had disappeared. They have never found where their children went or where their bodies were buried. They are presumed dead.

Actually, there's a song which may be on the new LP called 'Mothers of the Disappeared'. There's no question in my mind of the Reagan administration's involvement in backing the regime that is commiting these atrocities.

I doubt if the people of America are even aware of this. It's not my position to lecture them or tell them their place or to even open their eyes up to it in a very visual way but it is affecting me and it affects the words I write and the music we make.

"*I started to see the western world as a desert*"

You're a believer, yet you've gone on record to attack religion, and talked about the dangers of establishment religion. Flannery O'Connor seems to be doing the same thing because she caricatures religious figures, not for having a faith but for just having this institution around them.

Yeah. Sadly, religion like politics attracts both the worst and the best kinds of people, often the worst.

hope there. Like my favourite book of hers is Wise Blood. A guy called Hazel Motes sets up a Church without Christ and then his mate sets up this other rival church of God without Christ. I live in Ireland and Ireland is full of sects and weird religious cults.

Do you know, the two subjects that you just can't talk about in Ireland are religion and politics and they're probably all that I do talk about!

THE ENDURING CHILL
BONO AND THE TWO AMERICAS

Flannery O'Connor wrote that … 'The sharper the light of faith, the more glaring are apt to be the distortions the writer sees in life around him'.

An old but very wise man once said to me that you should never fight darkness with light, you should just make the light brighter. A lot of people are anti-this or anti-that, or against this or against-that but I find myself attracted to people who are for things rather than against things.

It's far easier to destroy than to build and words are capable of either.

Let's not get too heavy, though, because Flannery O'Connor is also a hilariously funny writer and Hazel Motes in Wise Blood is one of her funniest characters.

How is the new record going?

When people ask us if the album is going well I usually say yes, but if I do I'm probably lying!

Actually it is going better than most of our records have gone. It's funny, we're all far more positive and optimistic about it at this stage than usual. But as much as the music is going well I have to say that it has been a difficult year for U2 and that light and shade is on the record. I hope the ultimate effects will be uplifting ones but we really have waded through the shit on this record.

One thing that really annoys me about the music business is

movement came some very powerful people like John Lennon, and poets like Jim Morrison.

A song that says so much to me even now is John Lennon's 'Gimme Some Truth'. 'No short haired yellow-bellied son-of-tricky-dicky's going to mother-hubbard short-soap me for a pocketful of hope'. 'All I want is the truth, gimme the truth'.

A lot of people want to get up off their ass and get out and do some good but they don't really know what to do.

What you've got to do to get through to the heart of things and say 'Look Mister, the money you're taking home at the end of the week, in your paypacket , is paying for instruments of torture in South America for instance'. Or 'Look Mister, your defence budget could be used to feed the hungry'. I just read a statistic that says that for ten minutes of the world's defence budget we could cure the number one killer disease in the world which is malaria. Ten minutes. That gets through.

You went to Africa last year didn't you?

Look – there's a lot of people who'd love to take a month off and help out in Ethiopia. You hear these cries from different parts of the world, most people hear these cries but they're not in a position to attend to that and check it out and see if there's anything they can do. The only thing I can do is write songs.

What have you found most encouraging recently?

One thing this year has made me feel better. One thing has more than anything made me feel good as a performer, as a songwriter and as a member of U2. I got a letter from a U2 fan club and they told me about these clubs they were setting up, maybe once a month. They listen to U2 music and watched our videos – not just ours but also Peter Gabriel, The Waterboys and younger groups like Cactus World News and R.E.M.

I saw this hand out about it – they had a fee. It was sort of five dollars to join the club, and I thought 'what a rip-off, charging to listen to U2 music'. But then I turned it over and discovered they were using the five dollars to support families in the third world, and they spent their evening, as well as listening to music and watching videos, writing postcards for Amnesty International.

"I'm not really aware of what's in the charts at the moment"

Are you concerned not to lose touch now that the band has reached such a level of success?

I suppose in going to Africa and Central America I was injecting myself with a severe dose of reality, but I don't think being a pop star is any more cocooned than living in a semi-detached house with suburban lawns. I think that's just as detached from the real world. They're as bad and as good as each other. I came from that background.

the suffering artist cliché where you get a lot of these middle-class kids sticking needles in their arms so they can perform, so they can know what it's like man. Anyone with their eyes or ears open in this world can see suffering.

There's two kinds of people, there's those that are asleep and those that are awake. I've used my music to wake me up and if it wakes other people up on the way that's OK because we get used to the sound of a bomb going off in Belfast and to the roll call of bad news on television, we get used to the fact that a third of the population on earth are starving. We get used to all these things and we eventually fall asleep in the comfort of our freedom.

There's a guy called Francis Schaeffer and he says that we're entering into a new era of fascism. It won't be like the fascism of Mussolini or Hitler, it'll be fascism with a smile and a warm handshake. It'll be based on personal peace and prosperity. In other words if you give someone a colour television, a house, a car, and two weeks vacation a year...they'll agree to anything and stop asking questions.

So there's a need for raised voices – like the American radical students of the sixties?

I've been very inspired by the 60s protest movements in America. Drugs may have diluted that movement, but their music played an important part in the ending of the Vietnam war and out of that

I live in London and I see the troubles in the North of Ireland every night on the news but a few weeks ago I went to Belfast and walked the streets for myself. It frightened me and I realised how much I was numb to it, I was asleep to it....

It always gets back to this! You see all this going on out there and you think 'Well, what the hell can I do about it?' For a lot of people there's not a lot you can do about it and all I believe is that everyone in their own way has a position they have to take and if that's as a mother with snotty nosed kids or a guy in a factory just doing the best they can or being a schoolteacher or a farmer, you just find your ground, your place and you just do the best you can to shine a light on the shit that's out there. That's all.

My position is that I write songs, I'm in a band and I just hope that when it's all over for U2 that in some way we made the light a bit brighter. Maybe just tore off a corner of the darkness. That's all I can do and everyone can do it in their own way.

The biggest compliment anyone can pay U2 as performers is that they get out and do something themselves.

They get out and they chip away themselves at those boulders that are in the path of progress, if you like, and they just smash them up with their own hands and they can do that whatever way they want and if that's writing postcards for Amnesty International....that was a thrill. I just thought 'Well, that's it'. I love for instance hearing bands come up to us after gigs and saying 'We formed a band after your concert.

That's the best thing that can ever come about for me, that somebody gets out and does it for themselves in whatever way. I really love that phrase 'a conspiracy of hope' and I really hope it could be applied to U2 and its organisation. It applies to the way we do our work, our merchandising, our magazine.... (I hope!), it's just whatever you do if you can just do it with a bit

> *"The biggest compliment anyone can pay U2... is that they get out and do something themselves"*

of dignity. I don't think U2 have walked on anybody or kicked anyone in the balls. I don't think we have ... we may have kicked each other in the balls a few times – but that's another story.

How did your experience in Ethiopia affect you?
I find the time I spent in Africa a little difficult to deal with. I worked on the edge of the desert and I remember looking out at what was a very proud people, a very upright people.

that kind of thing.
    Before that I grew up on reel-to-reel tapes of The Jimi Hendrix Experience, The Who, the classic rock'n'roll bands and back into the Beatles and Elvis. I missed pop music. It passed me by.
    But I also missed roots music. I even disliked roots music. Around the time of October I began to get interested in traditional Irish music and those roots. Since meeting people like Charlie Whisker, a painter who I paint

THE ENDURING CHILL
BONO AND THE TWO AMERICAS

I started to think not about what they hadn't got, but what they had.

What I couldn't cope with was when I came home and I saw the waste of the land in the west, and I saw little spoilt children and I saw people fat, not physically fat but mentally...that's what I couldn't cope with, I started thinking it was us that lived in a desert, because although people are rich here, physically, they're very poor spiritually and in Africa the opposite is true.

So what kind of music do you like to listen to when you're not working.

I have Peter Case's record and like it, that's a great song 'Three Days Straight'.

My record collection started in 1976 with the punk groups and the first post-punk groups like Patti Smith and Television,

with and a blues man, I've got interested in a lot of blues records... Silver and Gold was the first I wrote in that style. But since then I've been listening to a lot of black music, John Lee Hooker, Muddy Waters, a lot of gospel music, James Cleveland, The Rev. Theophilus Someone... I can't remember his name!

B.B. King was here recently and he asked me to produce him. I don't know if we can work it out but I think he's got a remarkable voice. I think the reason that I disliked blues music and gospel music is that I saw it all done very badly by these twelve bar blues bands which used to play in the Strip down Baggot Street and it was just really dog-eared and boring. And then you've got this really naff and soppy soap-opera gospel music that you get nowadays.

> *"I'd like to be a soul singer – that's my aim."*

I'd like to be a soul singer- that's my aim. Of white music I've been listening to Van Morrison a lot because I think he's one of the finest white soul-singers and Janis Joplin, God bless her. Her version of Ball and Chain really puts me on my back. Y'know – when she breaks down in the middle of the live version and starts ripping into people. I can understand that as a performer. I'm not really very aware of what's in the charts at the moment. I would like to be a little bit more aware. Sometimes when I'm driving I turn on the radio but driving through inner city Dublin you might as well be driving down Manhattan for all the silk-soul that dominates the radio. I like black music but I find the silk-soul aspect of it a bit hard to handle. I prefer the more raucous and raw black music.

THE JOS

The four members of U2 talk about the

UA TREE

new album and the current tour.

How does it feel to have finally finished the record?

BONO "Finishing the album is like having been in a black hole, or a room with blinds closed and then you go out into the lights and everything dazzles you, it's so brilliant. That's what it's like because essentially a studio is just a big black hole in the ground.

When you start making a record you'll go into the studio for, say, ten hours, and you'll get eight hours work done, but towards the end of the project you'll be spending twenty hours in the studio and getting two hours work done. At the end of the recording we called everyone round for a party, a pool tournament to celebrate the end of the album, but we ended up not being able to go to our own party because we were working right up to the last minute, and that was our third night in a row!

So that's what it's like – it's like being down a black hole and coming out to the light everything looks clear again."

But you're pleased with the record, obviously?

"Yeah, I'm as pleased with the record as I can ever be pleased with a record – y'know I'm very rarely happy with our own work. I suppose more than any other record, probably since our first, it's a very complete record....it's a collection of different points of view.

The significant thing about the record for me is that I had to 'come clean' as a word-writer. Instead of trying to capture the elusive message of the music, which is what I'd normally try to do with my words, I wanted to speak out specifically, but without a placard, and without my John Lennon handbook!"

71

THE JOSHUA TREE

What were the chief inspirations for this record?

"America – the continent as opposed to the country. It has had quite an effect on me, and on my own life.

I love being there, I love America, I love the feeling of the wide open spaces, I love the deserts, I love the mountain ranges, I even love the cities. So having fallen in love with America over the years that we've been there on tour, I then had to 'deal with' America and the way it was affecting me, because America's having such an effect on the world at the moment. On this record I had to deal with it on a political level for the first time, if in a subtle way.

I don't think it's my position to ever use the stage as a soapbox, so I've tried on this record to get across some of our feelings, hopefully in a more subtle and intelligent way, using symbols.

THE BLUES

"And then also, you see, I had discovered The Blues in the meantime and discovered American Music. In doing the Silver and Gold session with Keith Richard, he was playing blues music for me, but not only blues music, he played country music, 50s American pop music – all those influences. Then there was my own background in Patti Smith and Bob Dylan, I mean there's always been that American input. So musically as well – all that was coming through.

What do you hope people will get from this record?

"I've no idea. I've no idea what people will get from the record.
I have to say there's a side of me that can't quite work out why anyone would buy a U2 LP. I think I might buy one… It's the same as I feel about a U2 concert. I mean I've never been to a U2 concert. I've been at one, but I've never been to one!

Do you still feel U2's live work is important?

"Oh yes. I don't like making records. I really don't like making records. I like writing songs, I like writing words but I don't enjoy making records. I do enjoy being on the road. There's a sort of travelling person in us all, the sort of gypsy, we are gypsies of a kind. I like moving about from place to place, but you can get lost along the way, y'know. I got lost along the way on the last tour definitely, on the Unforgettable Fire tour, I really did lose it a little bit. I'm attracted to that on-the-road feeling of fraternity, I suppose. Our entourage, if you want to call it that, is a kind of ball of chaos, but in a nice way. And as anyone who knows me will tell you, I feel at home in chaos, so the chaos of touring life suits me. In a way it's easy, maybe too easy for me, to stand there and be packed into a suitcase and taken away. I get up in the mornings in a hotel room, and I don't have to clean up, I don't have to do anything formal. Things like that tend to fall about my ears a bit unless there's good people looking after us.

What would you say is the common thread that runs through all U2's work?

"Us I suppose. U2 is the common thread. There's still the same commitment to each other, to four people. Four guys in the band. I was disappointed with Live Aid, with the Live Aid book, because of the fact that they didn't recognise that there was four people in U2. That bugged me. I mean, I don't think it bugged the others that much, they just found it funny, but it got to me, because we're four people.

So you feel the four of you are still a strong unit?

"The four of us feel pretty good together, but I must say that on tour, as much as the overall feeling is one of a

" I don't think it's my position to ever use the stage as a soapbox."

family or street-gang, I actually do spend a lot of time on my own within that structure.

What I like about being on a bus or being on a plane is that I can read, for instance, or have a game of cards with someone, but generally I get into a kind of trance on my own, because it takes so much energy for me to go up on stage at night.

Often, because I'm not a trained singer, I just can't sing for two hours and then talk the next day. I have to just sit there – I do and people will come up and talk to me and I nod and make signals, but generally, through the day I'm really out of order.

As well as the positive feelings, there seems to be a lot of darkness on "The Joshua Tree"....

"Well...1986 was a real paradox of a year. In 1985 we had achieved some sort of peak in our music life. The Unforgettable Fire, which was kind of a radical LP, had done very well for us. Our tours round the world had all sold out and it almost got silly with the demand for tickets. Then there were things like Live Aid; there was a reason to feel very good not only about U2, but about rock & roll music in general. Coming home from all that back down to earth in Dublin, in 1986, didn't prove to be as easy as I'd thought it might be.

The year was difficult for other reasons, with a few personal tragedies, so I felt 1986 was something of a desert for me.

I thought the photographs in the tour programme from the ghost town were really powerful...

I'm glad you found that. I found that too. I'm surprised nobody else is saying that. The shots I think are really special.

It's Bodie, one of the oldest ghost towns in America. It's an interesting place to visit. It's a gold rush town left as a monument to the mining community and to the out-west lifestyle. Literally there's plates on the table,

the whole thing. It's almost eerie, the feeling about it. The thing is though, if you drive through some of the European cities now, late at night, city centres that were once thriving, vibrant places now are shut down and closed. A lot of people just don't have money to go out any more, so some of our own cities are like ghost towns, and I liked the parallel with the western ghost town.

Tell me about the desert shoot – how did you find that Joshua tree?

"I still don't know where that Joshua tree is, we just spotted it by the roadside. Anton Corbijn, our photographer, was the first to see it, so he called "stop the bus" and went racing across the desert.

The thing is though, Anton is Dutch and speaks with an accent, so he has quite a curious way of pronouncing "Joshua Tree", he kind of says "Yoshua Tree", and this became quite a funny thing – we were all talking about Yoshua Trees", so there was a bit of sense of humour involved in calling the album The Joshua Tree, as well as for the more serious reasons. When we took the photographs, we thought it was a very powerful visual graphic image. We then drove off, and I don't know if we'll ever find that Joshua tree again. I don't know if anyone will ever find that Joshua tree again – I hope that if people do find the Joshua tree they won't cut it down and take it home and stick it to the wall – or bring it to a gig!!! ("Hey Baaano! I got yer tree!")

Anton really is a very funny man, but his photographs are very serious, which is, in a way, quite like us, because people think that we're very serious people because we take our music seriously. It's just that when it comes to being on stage, Monty Python we're not. Off-stage it's a different story. Anton makes us laugh so much, for a guy who portrays us in such a serious light, we spend most of the time calling for an ambulance!"

"1986 was a real paradox of a year"

"It captures something that Bono has live."

THE JOSHUA TREE

ADAM

"In the desert four people stand out really strongly."

"I think the feelings of last year are contained in the record, in as much as that I think people seem to have become a lot more politically aware over the past couple of years. People seem to realise that to not vote is the worst possible thing you can do, you've got to get involved in what's going on.

That's what started to develop with Live Aid. I think people became aware that their opinion was important and I think the record challenges people's opinions – well, not challenging their opinions as such, but forces them to have opinions. If that's the ultimate effect of the record I think it's worthwhile.

NAIVETY

"It's a record that admits a few truths about ourselves. It says, "yeah, we know the way things are but we're not going to let it get us down.

I think a certain amount of the naivety that was present in our earlier work is more in perspective. I think it's still there, I think it's essentially U2, but I think the maturing process is taking place. But at the same time that maturity has given us a self-confidence in what we are, which is a noisy rock & roll band, and there's no way that's gonna change!

BARREN

"With each record we've always looked for some sort of location to inspire the tone of what we were doing and I think the desert is so many things to us. The desert was immensely inspirational to us as a mental image for this record.

Most people would take the desert on face value and think it's some kind of barren place, but I think in the right frame of mind it's also a very positive image, because you can actually do something with a blank canvas, which is effectively what the desert is.

In the desert four people stand out really strongly, and I think the record reflects four different personalities. At the same time, I found from our experience of doing the shoots and being in the desert, that it isn't really a lonely or frightening place, it's actually very peaceful and tranquil. There's something about it that is comforting.

The most extraordinary thing was that the desert was actually freezing. It was a bit

> ## "It's a record that admits a few truths about ourselves."

of a shock, because we'd psyched ourselves up into finally doing something where there'd be sunshine, and there was lots of buying of different lotions before we left, to make sure our noses didn't go red, and in fact our noses did go red – but from the cold.

JOSHUA TREE PARK

"I don't think the '60s connotations of the Joshua tree are too relevant as regards what we're doing. I think it's a bit of a sidetrack, but at the same time an interesting sidetrack. To the best of my knowledge Joshua Tree Park in California was where the centre of mind-expanding drug culture developed – I think a lot of people took acid and turned into Joshua trees as far as I can work out.

COOPED UP

"Normally we haven't had that much time to hang out on street corners between tours. Since we've been off the road, we've had to get back to normal and learn how to live on our own and wash shirts and stuff. Having done all that for a while, with only the odd little bursts of live activity, plus being cooped up in a studio for the best part of six months I think we're actually dying for things to return to normality. Being on the road is very simple – you know what you're doing the next day and you know the reasons why you're doing it. There's not really any time to get bored.

HOPES

"I hope we learn a lot on this tour. I hope we learn the weaknesses and the strengths of what we've done, to enable us to stretch ourselves even more the next time round. I wouldn't want for us to get bored by it. I hope the power of the music continues to build. It is there to get you through the next couple of years and it becomes your strength and your weakness. I'll be happy as long as at the end of the next two years we're saying, 'yeah, it was good, but I think we can do another one that's better'".

What would you say would be an overall view of "The Joshua Tree"

LARRY "There isn't really an overall view of this album. Whereas with Unforgettable Fire there was a real continuity between all the songs, this is slightly different. It's an album of songs, each song saying a different thing, touching areas that we haven't touched before. There's a lot more emotion, especially in the singing, that there hasn't been on any of the other records. It captures something that Bono has live, which we haven't done before.

When you're making a record either the instruments serve the song, or the song serves the instruments. I mean sometimes, everyone's playing a certain part and it's all very correct and musical, but this isn't like that. It's more like we're serving the song, we're playing to the song, and we're also playing to the vocal. It's a different approach and one we've not really taken before, it's much more fluid.

When I come off the road I'm a different person. On the road you become slightly tense, and it's difficult to conduct relationships. The relationship within the band becomes different – not strained at all, but just different. Relationships with everyone become different. It's a working relationship.

EDGE "The chief influences for 'The Joshua Tree' really have been tours and time spent discovering that clichés about America weren't true. America is constantly surprising you and you discover that there's so many different sides to it which you initially didn't imagine were there.

Yet at the same time it seems to be a land where* clichés very easily spring up. It's so extreme. For a film-maker or a musician it's a land full of things that are larger than life.

The music of America we really weren't particularly interested in, or we really

didn't know much about it when we first formed the band. Really in going to the States and seeing the culture first hand we began to get closer to the music of America.

RE-ASSESSING

"In just a social context, people like T-Bone Burnett, Robbie Robertson, the sort of artists that we've met, have made us reassess our opinion of American artists and American music, because there is this European, well certainly English, attitude to American rock & roll that it is in some way inferior – that American rock is just jaded and lifeless, whereas in fact like the country itself, the clichés about the music don't hold true under close inspection.

I think since really falling in love with the country – this crazy place full of contradictions and paradoxes – we've started falling in love with the music of the place. A lot of stuff that we didn't have much time for when we first formed the group. We've been discovering anything from B.B.King, Robert Johnson, Hank Williams, Patsie Klein, Johnny Cash, Merle Haggard – all these artists who are a million miles from where we were coming from. I'm not suggesting that we love everything that they do, but there's certainly something that they're dealing with which is opening up for us now and has really only started becoming important for us recently.

WATERSHED

"So that's definitely one huge watershed of inspiration for the record. I think we've also discovered some of the same sort of music in Ireland through artists like Christie Moore and the Dubliners. It's very interesting to see how Ireland is so rich in music like that, call it 'folk' music, or whatever. Woodie Guthrie called it music to live to, as opposed to music to die to.

The fact is that Irish folk music was a kind of seminal influence for a lot of early American folk. The Irish seem to provide a lot of the

THE JOSHUA TREE

instrumentation, like fiddles, acoustic guitars and the way the music is presented is very similar. The ballad format of bringing in characters and the stories, that's all very much an Irish tradition.

THE SONG

"The other great influence is a heightened awareness of the concept of 'the song' as a sort of art form all of its own. The song can at the same time be challenging and limiting, but limiting in a positive sense, in that there is a discipline in the art of song writing. If you submit yourself to it you can do a lot within the final result. If you've done it well, it can be a timeless thing crossing all boundaries, universal in its appeal and hopefully have a life that will be longer than any of the people who wrote it.

That was also a bit of a revelation for us, to be thinking about songs in that way. Whereas before if songs came along it was really just luck, we never really considered the song as an essential part of our records.

Up to now our records have been a collection of things that were songs, and also things that were very definitely not songs – experimental musical pieces, lyrically experimental as well as musically experimental. I think on this record we've really attempted to strip down the music so it really has that kind of trim, disciplined outlined. I think we've managed to – every track on the record has an identity of its own, but the record holds together as one. That's because they are songs rather than parts of one whole concept.

THEMES

"I think the open endedness of previous records was because the lyrics were open ended. They were obviously written with one idea in mind

"I think it will just be a much more dangerous stage presence."

but they could equally be interpreted in another way. I think this record is pinned down a little more. So that the lyrics have a more obvious single main theme. Within that main theme there are a number of ways the lyrics can be interpreted, but that one idea is expressed a little more concisely and forcibly than before.

But still there is a good deal of a positive ambiguity. I do like some songs that are totally open book, but I do appreciate a bit of mystery where you can make up your own mind about the fine print.

THE DESERT SONGS

"The desert idea was one which we'd had for a while which seemed right. The Joshua tree was an image which came to us really during the shoot, and just seemed like the right image to tie all our ideas together, in focus. We could have called the record "The desert songs", but the Joshua tree has other images related to it and is a little more subtle in its connection with the desert. It's something we decided on instinct almost…. It has a spiritual aspect, which this record has and also a great deal of mystery. It's appropriate on many levels.

It's like hope pushed to the limit, and love pushed to the limit. There's a certain aridness to the album, but at the same time there is hope, there is life there, but still it's not a very pleasant landscape. It's still pretty bedraggled and parched.

The Joshua tree is standing there in the middle of this barrenness, there's so many great images there. In fact the sleeve photograph is taken in death valley and you can see this dry riverbed down below, this dry riverbed in the desert, which is another fantastic image.

THE LIVE SHOW

"I think it will be quite radically different to the Unforgettable Fire tour. I think it'll be probably closer to Live Aid and the Amnesty

shows where there was an emphasis more on a dangerous feeling on stage, where we didn't really know quite what was going to happen. There was a certain energy that we were able to feed off. A feeling that literally anything could happen at any moment, and I for one really enjoyed that energy.

DANGER

"As a band we've always been very cautious about destroying the carefully prepared show that we'd been working on for a number of weeks or months on tour. Obviously within it there was space for improvisation, but there was a certain level that we always worked to. We'd improve the show to a very high standard and not tamper with it too much. Maybe we're feeling now like we'd like to be a little less precious about it. Even if it means that we do some bad shows, we'd like to at least try and throw the whole thing into a state of flux, where every show was going to be different. Some nights I think it'll pay dividends and it'll be magic, some nights maybe not, but the instinct there is to try to push things as far as we can, and improvise a lot during the shows.

It succeeded in the Amnesty shows, but I'm not sure how it'll fare when we've got two hours instead of 35 minutes. I'm looking forward to that. I think that it will just be a much more dangerous stage presence. It'll certainly keep us on our toes anyway.

WHERE THE STREETS HAVE NO NAME

I want to run
I want to hide
I want to tear down the walls
That hold me inside
I want to reach out and touch the flame
Where the streets have no name

I want to feel sunlight on my face
See that dust cloud disappear without a trace
I want to take shelter from the poison rain
Where the streets have no name

Where the streets have no name
Where the streets have no name
Still building then burning down love
Burning down love
And when I go there
I go there with you
It's all I can do

The city's a flood
And our love turns to rust
We're beaten and blown by the wind
Trampled in dust
I'll show you a place
High on a desert plain
Where the streets have no name

Where the streets have no name
Where the streets have no name
Still building then burning down love
Burning down love
And when I go there
I go there with you
It's all I can do

Our love turns to rust
We're beaten and blown by the wind
Blown by the wind
When I go there
I go there with you
It's all I can do

BONO "Where the streets have no name", that's more like the U2 of old than any of the other songs on the LP. Because it's a sketch – I was just trying to sketch a location, maybe a spiritual location, maybe a romantic location, I was trying to sketch a feeling. I often feel very claustrophobic in a city, a feeling of wanting to break out of that city, and a feeling of wanting to go somewhere where the values of the city and the values of our society don't hold you down.

An interesting story that somebody told me once, is that in Belfast, by what street somebody lives on you can tell not only their religion, but tell how much money they're making – literally by which side of the road they live on, because the further you go up the hill the more expensive the houses become. You can almost tell what the people are earning by the name of the street they live on and what side of that street they live on. That said something to me, and so I started writing about a place where the streets have no name ....'

THE BODIE SHOOT

PICTURES FROM A GHOST TOWN

FAME, FORTUNE & FRANK SINATRA

SIX MONTHS INTO THE JOSHUA TREE TOUR, THE EDGE HAS BREAKFAST IN A HOTEL ROOM IN MUNICH AND REFLECTS ON THE TOUR SO FAR. THE HIGHPOINTS, THE HIGHER POINTS, AND WHAT TO DO NEXT...

So tell me about seeing Frank Sinatra first of all....

"Ah, Frank Sinatra that was fantastic... what a vibe!

"Can you imagine coming into Las Vegas, 'Never Never Land', and actually going to a Frank Sinatra show? I mean the setting was perfect, probably if we'd seen him in McGonagles in Dublin it wouldn't have been quite so magic but in the Golden Nugget in Las Vegas at one in the morning after the Hagler/Leonard fight, it was amazing. His voice was in great shape. He seemed also to be giving us a rough autobiography in the songs giving you a glimpse of what he was about as a person. Each song showing a different side of him – and he is incredibly chauvinistic and incredibly old fashioned in that sense, but at the same time it was honest.

"Before Frank went on, they introduced us (U2) to the audience, which was a real buzz – got us to stand up and said who we were and they applauded us. It was hysterical, I mean Gregory Peck was there, and all manner of folks, and they made a real song and dance about it. That was funny."

"After Sinatra's set we went back and had a few words with him. He was great – it's hard to make an assessment of somebody in five minutes, but he was talking music which was good. Y'know after all these years he was talking about the Tommy Dorsey Orchestra and working with Buddy Rich and we were talking about his band and how good we thought they were.

"Frank's obviously been very influenced by The Blue Nile, but you can forgive him that!"

What did you make of Las Vegas as a whole?

"One got the feeling that the whole of Las Vegas was desperately wanting to be taken seriously, as a proper city and a proper place to live and bring up your kids, and all that stuff, as opposed to its image which is a kind of giant Butlins. They were just delighted that a band of U2's credibility would go and play there. Though actually we were there precisely for the reason they were pretending didn't exist. To see all the gambling, to see all the strangeness of the American people coming with their savings for the year to Las Vegas generally to lose it all."

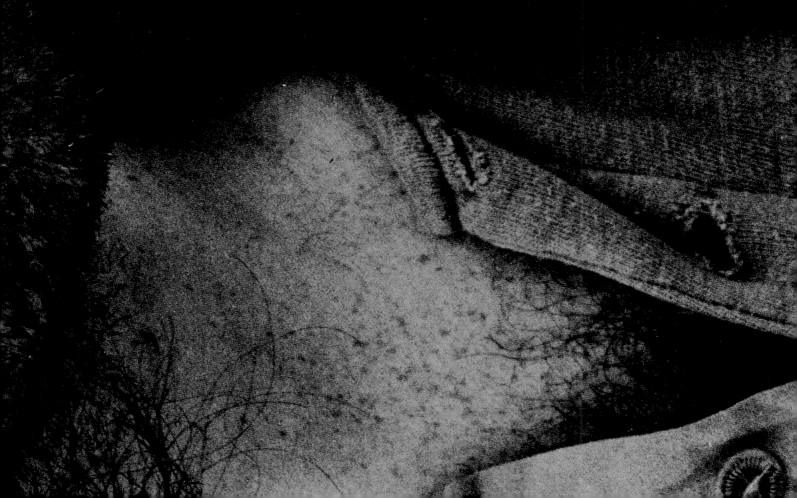

FAME, FORTUNE & FRANK SINATRA

"We found that fascinating and that's why we went there. The 'Still Haven't Found What I'm Looking For' video was perfect in that location. It was a real laugh doing that.

"There was a lot of people around and we got followed around by this huge gang of people. It wasn't a problem though, because movies mean so much in America that people will do anything if there's a film crew around. You can get a permit to shoot almost anywhere."

Like an L.A. rooftop, for instance?

"We did get a permit to shoot on the rooftop in L.A. for the 'Streets' video. The trouble was when the radio stations started announcing it as a free concert the Chief of Police got a bit freaked, especially as he heard the announcements in his car on his way to work.

"The Beatles comparison wasn't really intentional. We wanted to do something in a side of Los Angeles that no-one really ever sees, which is the downtown area. Everyone always sees Sunset Strip, and the film side and all that, but downtown L.A. is a fascinating place although very dangerous and very tough. We felt that that song for us has that feeling of escape from an urban situation. The roof top in downtown L.A. was certainly very colourful, and we felt it was a good place to do the shoot, and set up the song well.

"There's a certain equality there, it's a funny thing, you get to the bottom and you find on your toes.

"Playing outdoors was a huge worry, because I've never been an outdoor show that I really thought was great. Once we got started though we were fine, in fact we're so pleased with the way the outdoor shows went that we decided to add more outdoor shows to the American tour.

"Now, I don't know whether we're being fooled, because there is an argument that the first fifty rows are going to think it's great, but beyond that you have your problem. But my impression has been that, out of the good outdoor shows, which has been a high percentage, that the atmosphere stretches well beyond those first fifty rows. Whether it gets to the very back I don't know, but I think it gets close to containing the whole audience.

"The one thing that seems to affect it is whether we have darkness or not. If you have darkness the atmosphere is much more intense than if you're dealing with daylight.

"This business of video screens is interesting. A lot of the outdoor shows I've seen recently have had video screens, and I think that although they can be good for the people at the very, very back, I think it's a real distraction.

"One got the feeling that the whole of Las Vegas was desperately wanting to be taken seriously."

"Success on this level has never been the main motivation for this group."

to be dealt with on my part, that I do really have to be aggressive, or it would not really happen.

"I mean, U2 is about the contrasts within the group within the music, about the contradiction. Bono can be very relaxed, I can be very uptight and aggressive, but the reverse is true. Bono can get really freaked out, so the rest of us rally round and get it together. Both sorts of shows are very different, but work out in their own ways. Like Bono climbing onto the roof of the stage in Madrid! That was a bit of nostalgia. It was very funny – though I don't know if Bono realised how high it was."

With the Joshua Tree, U2 has suddenly become a media event – are you happy with the way you are perceived in the press?

"You kind of have to take your hands off that and say, well, what the press do is what they want to do. You could lose a lot of sleep over what Time magazine were writing about you, or whatever, but at some point you have to say well, whatever they're going to do, they're going to do, so let them.

"Early on if we were misquoted, or if someone made something up about us we'd get very pissed off but now you just

whites, blacks, Hispanics, Puerto Ricans, Mexicans, everyone's on a level, no-one's better off than anyone else and you get a suspension of the racial tensions.

"We spend quite a bit of time in this area of L.A., and we did some photographs on the roof of a building called the Million Dollar Hotel. It was originally an incredibly expensive hotel when downtown L.A. was an expensive and salubrious part of town, but now it's falling apart and is let out as really cheap accommodation. Apparently a lot of mental patients and people from state institutions, when they are released back into the big bad world are put into this hotel. But there's a real community feeling. We talked to a couple of guys in the lobby of this place, some white, some Chicano, and you sensed that they all knew they were in the same predicament which gave them a sense of community, which I found heartening that people in that position stuck together".

"You never know what to expect in Europe."

So, how did you find playing in Europe after America?

"Well, America was such fun that I felt Europe might be an anticlimax, but it wasn't. You never really know what to expect in Europe, which is good from our point of view. In America pretty much wherever you are your audiences tend to be similar. The things that they like, the jokes that they get, favourite songs, and so on, there's not much variation. In Europe there's an awful lot of variation. For instance the language barrier means that in some countries audiences seem to understand almost everything – lyrics, Bono's comments from stage, whatever. In a lot of countries they understand little of that, which generally means throwing a lot of emphasis beck on to the music. That's challenging and keeps you

"Great sound is important. Just to have four guys on stage I think is important. It's not like an enormous array of musicians, there's only four of us, you hear the sound, and it's very straightforward, it's very simple. When you get into screens and extra musicians and backing tapes it becomes a more complex thing. A U2 show is very easy to relate to, because there's nothing to it. That guy sings into that mike, it comes out there and that's it."

"We're constantly fighting to produce the best music we can"

Bono's really loosened up this time round, but you seem to be even more intense – you've even trashed a couple of guitars.

"Bono can be relaxed now, but I don't think I should be. If I got relaxed on stage the whole thing would probably fall apart! There's so much stuff that has

have to accept that that's what newspapers and journalists are about.

"Newspapers aren't about telling people what's actually going on, they're about selling papers, they're as commercially minded as any other. They have to be, and sometimes you're the victim of that.

"They make up stories, embroider stories, misquote you. It was quite funny the tour bus story, by the time the press finished with it it sounded like U2 were having a pitched battle with the Belgian mafia!"

Are you beginning to get America out of your system?
"Ah, we're only just scratching the surface. We're still very interested in America, but for the next record I'd like to produce a rock and roll record. A no bullshit record, with guitar, bass and drums and good songs."

ever experience again what we're experiencing now. So in one sense this is it, as far as touring goes, as far as being in a band goes, the whole buzz of it. I'm in it right now, and next time it won't mean the same at all.

"It's kind of interesting to think that this is as good as it gets. I'm not really worried about it, it's just an observation".

"You see success on this level has never been the main motivation for this group – we've never had any qualms about going after it, we almost assumed it – but the things that we're really fighting for are musical things."

Things are very different now to how they were on previous tours – how have you had to adapt personally?

"Well, to be honest I don't really find it that different. I find it a bit more exhilarating, being out in front of 70,000 as opposed to 7,000, it's a bit of a buzz. That's different, but as far as our day-to-day life and how we get on with each other goes, it's pretty much as it used to be. The internal thing is still very close. We let a lot of that stuff just wash over us without letting it affect us."

What would you put that down to?

"Attitude really. I mean 'the big time'...this sounds funny but I suppose we always assumed it would happen. But what we're constantly fighting for is to produce the best music we can produce, the best lyrics, the best shows, and the actual achievement of the band doesn't affect that. It doesn't really surprise us or phase us that much. But we're still determined to do what we can to ensure that in this position we do the best we can do."

FAME, FORTUNE & FRANK SINATRA

Do you think you're capable of that! This was supposed to be a rock and roll record to some extent, but you ended up with a much bigger production.

"Well, there's rock and roll, and rock and roll. I think the spirit of rock and roll is what I'm talking about. The modern state of rock and roll is pathetic. It's just the pits. What I'm talking about is like what rock and roll meant when it first happened. A feeling of 'what the hell is going on?'"

A bit like punk was ....?

"I think that punk was born out of disillusionment, but with rock and roll people had never thought they could feel like this before. It suddenly took everybody aback, and it was new. To get that now is kind of hard, but that's what we'd aim for."

**U2 used to be "The biggest cult band in the world" – Bono said U2 were "always on the way but never arriving".
Clearly you have arrived now – does it worry you that this might be your peak?**

"It has occurred to me but it doesn't really bother me. One thing that did occur to me the other day was that this is a peak of one kind, in that it's the first tour that we've done on this level, and I don't think we can

THE SIGHTS OF

Joshua Tree

THE TOUR WOULDN'T HAVE BEEN COMPLETE WITHOUT A VISIT TO CALIFORNIA'S "JOSHUA TREE NATIONAL PARK" NEXT TO WHICH IS A TINY TOWN CALLED "JOSHUA TREE, CALIFORNIA". HERE'S A BRIEF GUIDED TOUR

ABSOLUTE McGUINNESS

Paul McGuinness is sitting in his management caravan deep in the heart of back-stage territory behind the huge walls of the Los Angeles Coliseum. It seems that only bearers of passes coated in platinum make it this far. U2 are about to play their second successive show to 75,000 devoted Californians. He is not phased by the statistics, by the money, or by the hurricane of attention at the centre of which stands the group he manages. Against all the odds in a crowded schedule he finds time to talk to PROPAGANDA

TEN YEARS ON, DID YOU EVER THINK IT WOULD COME TO THIS?
"Yes, I did. Actually I'd no idea what it would be but I knew it would be this big. I knew it the first time I saw them. I could have been wrong but I only needed to be right once. I saw this band and decided to risk everything on them."

BUT YOU ALSO DECIDED EARLY THAT U2 WOULDN'T BE THE GREATEST BAND EVER WITHOUT A VERY CLEAR STRATEGY. THEY WOULD NOT MAKE IT BY ACCIDENT.
"No, it could never have been accidental and the idea that it might have happened that way is ludicrous. We had a plan and had to work at it: even though the plan changes all the time we have always felt we knew what we were doing."
FOR EXAMPLE YEARS SPENT SLOGGING AROUND AMERICA TRYING TO BUILD AN AUDIENCE WHILE SO MANY OTHERS WERE INTENT ONLY ON GAINING A HIT SINGLE.
"Yes, I always felt that our interests and the record company's were quite different. The record company is a source of finance for a baby band but by

attempting to have hit singles you become a hostage to your next record. The touring base that we built up was really a means of defending ourselves from that. It would not be possible too for the record company to say, 'This band has no support, we'd better drop them and not spend any more money on them.'
"Clearly we did have support, large support, and that's very impressive."

BUT IT TAKES A LOT LONGER TO 'MAKE IT'
"True, it's a lot longer, but it's basically a conservative approach because we were not prepared to risk what we had on the chances of having a hit single next time out and the time after that. Bands that must have hit singles every time are always in jeopardy and we wouldn't allow it to go that way."

U2 HAVE ALWAYS HAD A 'SOFTLY, SOFTLY' APPROACH. THEY HAVE NEVER COME ACROSS, IN THE MARKETING AREA, AS BRASH.
"We've always controlled our own graphics and packaging and timing and for a long time we thought that every group did

87

ABSOLUTE McGUINNESS, ISSUE 7

ABSOLUTE McGUINNESS

that. We thought it was so clearly the right way to do it that we were quite surprised when we would meet other artists who would say, 'We really didn't like the sleeve on our album ....' We'd say, 'You didn't like the album sleeve? Well why didn't you change it? It's your responsibility.'

"There were other artists who somehow regard a video as something that happens to them, something that comes up and bites them – a video is every bit as much part of the band's work as the sound recordings and the performances."

THE BAND HAVE GROWN UP AND MATURED IN THEIR TEN YEARS TOGETHER BUT HOW ELSE DO YOU THINK THEY HAVE CHANGED?
"They have become much better players. Right from the beginning I always understood very clearly that you didn't have to be a very good player to be in this band. I thought it was one of their greatest strengths that it was not about how fast you could play or what a virtuoso you were on such and such an instrument. That has changed and because they have now become very good musicians and so the band is a much more flexible unit – they can now play anything which used not to be true. The reason U2 started writing songs is because they couldn't play anyone else's."

DO YOU THINK YOU'D BE IMPRESSED BY U2 UF YOU WEREN'T THEIR MANAGER AND HAD NEVER COME ACROSS THEM UNTIL THE JOSHUA TREE TOUR?
"Sure. I do actually think that. At this stage I'm a connoisseur and the shows that I like are the ones like last night's (L.A. Coliseum, November 17, 1987), one of the best shows of the whole tour. I can't remember an outdoor show that was as good as that one."

WHAT MARKS U2 OUT FROM THE REST?
"In very basic terms it's what everyone always loved about rock'n'roll, certainly what I always loved about it when I was a kid – the idea of four guys up on a stage making

this enormous noise in that way. In that way U2 has retained its original simplicity as a group. I don't like to go to, for instance, a Rolling Stones concert, and see a lot of backing musicians buried at the side of the stage and gangs of backing singers. I want to know the names of the four or five people in the group and I want to know that they've been there for ever. One of the interesting things about watching a band like the Beatles or the early Rolling Stones was all the peripheral data that you could obtain by reading the newspapers – they were interesting as media figures as well as performers."

WHEN YOU SAW THE BEATLES OR STONES DID YOU EVER THINK 'I'D LOVE TO HAVE A BAND LIKE THIS'?
"Sure. I was always interested to know that Brian Epstein was behind the Beatles and Andrew Oldham was behind the Rolling Stones. In my teens I would probably have known the names of all the managers of the groups as well as all the groups."

DO YOU EVER WAKE UP IN THE MORNING AND THINK 'I DID IT, WE MADE IT, WE'RE THERE!'?
"No, not at all. Without complaining about it which would be really stupid, it is as hard as it ever was or much harder to do the work, for the band as well as myself…it's that old cliché about staying at the top. We're not going to surrender to anyone else.

It is a very competitive business and the charts are a very graphic image of how

competitive popular music is. There is no such thing as rock'n'roll made for private reasons – you make a rock'n'roll record for a minimum of $50,000 these days and if you're using those resources you'd better have a good enough reason. To use that money and waste it is dreadful."

LAST NIGHT THE BAND MEMBERS WERE TALKING TO ELVIS'S DAUGHTER LISA MARIE AFTER THE SHOW, ANOTHER TIME BOB DYLAN TURNED UP TO DO A SONG WITH THEM ON STAGE – WHEN THAT HAPPENS DO YOU GET A LITTLE SHOCK?
"Yeah. It's one of the great pleasures of what we do that sooner or later – in fact very quickly – you meet all the other people who are doing it,

The best thing about the Joshua Tree is that they can do ten times better than that.

because often their experiences are very similar. Someone was explaining to me this week that the reason that so many actors and stars live in Hollywood is because you can actually talk to other stars rather than talk to people who say 'What's it like being a star?' I don't think I would like to live like that and I don't think the band would, but it's certainly a very reasonable view. Very early on we got to know the Talking Heads and The Police and The Pretenders and The Clash – we'd bump into them at airports or hotels – and it's not like a meeting of normal strangers because there's an enormous amount of previous information already there, you'd have heard all their records and read all the press, and so a normal

guarded introduction between two strangers isn't appropriate – you start talking about things you have in common.

"If they're nice people it's all a pleasure, but I'm not starstruck at all. I'm certainly not starstruck with U2, although I'm sometimes stunned when they bring something off like the Joshua Tree for example."

AFTER THE EXPERIMENTAL NATURE OF THE UNFORGETTABLE FIRE?
"I thought that was a wonderful record but the Joshua Tree was an extraordinary achievement. The best thing about the Joshua Tree – marvellous and magnificent as it is – is that they can do ten times better than that.

They can make much better records than that. The group is just beginning, and it's more fun that I thought it could possibly be."

ORIGINALLY IT WAS JUST THE FIVE OF YOU. HOW HAS YOUR ROLE CHANGED IN TEN YEARS?
"The whole thing has become a very complex organisation with hundreds of people in our employment on the night of a big show. If you include our staging crew then we have a tour party for this American tour of about 180 people '...and the buck stops with me'. I am responsible to the band for that organisation. It's a big responsibility but it's a delight as well because over the years we have been able to attract people into that organisation who are now just the best in the world. I was always very inclined to delegate – not to people who just happened to be there but to people who could do it. We now have some extraordinary people working for us, whose own achievements over the years have been just as significant as the band's."

One of the interesting things about watching a band like the Beatles or the early Rolling Stones was ...they were interesting as media figures as well as performers.

ABSOLUTE McGUINNESS

YOU MUST HAVE SEEN HUNDREDS AND HUNDREDS OF U2 SHOWS, DO YOU EVER SNEAK OFF AND GET A DRINK INSTEAD?

"Oh yes I do, absolutely and I'd be a terrible liar if I didn't admit it. There are parts of the show where I'll go off and sit down and make some phone-calls for example – it's quite peaceful backstage during the show, funnily enough, and that's the time of day when I can speak to the people in the organisation who have been wanting to speak to me all day. I like to watch the show and I would never put myself in a position where I couldn't. But you can't watch it with equal concentration hundreds of times a year.

"Last night for example I watched the whole show, it was just so great that I couldn't take my eyes off it."

IN 1987, FOR WHAT IT'S WORTH, U2 HAVE BEEN 'THE BIGGEST BAND IN THE WORLD' WHERE DO U2 GO NEXT?

"I don't think we know and until now we have always known that we were moving onward and upward. Now I think we will start to play around with it a bit more – like with the film for example.

"There is a strong feeling that we should not do long tours in future but concentrate on short tours, not particularly tied in to the release of an album. We've always had this model campaign which involved producing an album, promoting it, doing press and videos and then touring the world on it with the live show – but that cycle now takes two or three years if you include time to recover afterwards. We may change that quite radically in the future and start going home more often – familiarities are a factor.

"Versus that are the financial difficulties which are quite considerable – once you start up an overhead like this tour those 180 mouths still have to be fed every day whether we are playing or not. Days off are expensive. At the same time the morale and the stamina of the band is a finite quantity and if you played every night for seven nights a week it would disappear, no-one would watch the tour and all the fun would go out of it."

BONO ONCE SAID THAT ONE OF THE THINGS MOST LIKELY TO THREATEN THE BAND AS THEY BECAME INCREASINGLY SUCCESSFUL WAS THE WEALTH THEY WOULD INEVITABLY ACCRUE? IS THAT A CONSTANT THREAT?

"It would be very embarrassing to be good at everything else and bad at business and certainly we try to make our operations profitable. We were able to stop worrying about money a few years ago which was nice and didn't do any harm as far as I can see. It just meant that you could have a car which didn't break down all the time and that if we wanted to go to London to see a concert we could go without counting the cost."

WHAT WAS THE MOST DIFFICULT PERIOD IN THE HISTORY OF U2 SO FAR?

"I think without any doubt the October tour and leading into the War tour. I think it was 'a character-forming period' which was pretty well covered by Eamonn Dunphy in the book."

I can express myself very forcefully when I need to, so can Bono.

THERE ARE CONFLICTING REPORTS ABOUT THE RESPONSE OF U2 TO 'UNFORGETTABLE FIRE' THE BOOK THEY COMMISSIONED FROM EAMONN DUNPHY. IT RECEIVED THE BAND'S 'ENDORSAL' BUT NOT, APPARENTLY, UNQUALIFIED SATISFACTION.

"In many ways we intensely regret having done the book because Eamonn took us absolutely at our word and I suppose that we didn't think he would dig as deeply as he would and find out the things that he did. He's a very skilled reporter and he found out enormous amounts of information. There is stuff in the book that I certainly didn't know and in the end it is so clearly his work and not ours that I'm proud of it –
when you compare it to Bruce Springsteen books which are absolutely authorised there is no comparison. I think U2 fans are smart enough to see that.

"It is a pity that Eamonn Dunphy reneged on his promise to let us correct errors, I suppose he was pressurised by his publisher.

"The coverage of people's personal lives and family lives is something I think that none of us anticipated – the idea that people I meet in future will know all this stuff about me aged eight or Adam aged four.... I could do without it sometimes."

HOW DO YOU 'MANAGE' SOMEONE LIKE BONO?
"Well it's nothing to do with control, my job is to provide the environment in which they can do their work."

DURING THE WAR TOUR EVEN THE OTHER BAND MEMBERS WERE ON RECORD AS BEING WORRIED ABOUT BONO'S ANTICS DURING CONCERTS, CLAMBERING INTO THE STAGE ROOF FOR EXAMPLE."
"I can express myself very forcefully when I need to, and so can Bono. There were times when he was doing very dangerous things that not only put him in danger, which I cared about, but also other people in the audience – it was a bad period. He would regularly agree never to do it again but at some frustrating point during the show he would go out there again and

start climbing up the rigging – it was infuriating and very worrying for his friends. I'm his friend as well as his manager."

SO WHAT HAPPENS WHEN YOU HAVE BUST-UPS IN U2?
"We tend to have them in a very, very careful way. One of the things about living with the same five people over ten years is that it teaches you to have disagreements very carefully – nobody wants to start discussions by saying 'Well, this is my point of view and anyone who wants to disagree with me can fuck off'. That would paralyse our operation, so they never start like that. With any luck you should be able to arrive at a position where everyone's feelings are clear and then the decision must be taken bearing in mind all those opinions.

"One of the first things I learned years ago was that if I lost my temper with anyone the best thing to do was apologise – the quicker you apologise for bad behaviour, and there's plenty of that, the better."

WHAT ABOUT THE JOYS OF WORKING WITH U2?
"Well they are the best and we have known each other for so long – we've been in each others' houses and bedrooms and pockets for ten years now. I can't think of any other group of people that I could imagine being exposed to for so long and so intensely that I would still be on speaking terms with."

ARE YOU STILL PALS?
"Yes, very much and also we have the secret knowledge of what really happened.

Outsiders have an imagination based on some information of what happened over the years but at the end of the day the only people who have the real knowledge of what really happened are the four members of the band and, shortly afterwards, me. Even though history gets re-written as you go along, as much by us as by anyone else, the memory of those days is always at the back of our minds."

DO ALL THESE BUSINESS DEALINGS, INEVITABLE WITH ANY MAJOR BAND, THREATEN TO DIVORCE YOU FROM THE SPIRIT OF U2?
"No, no, no, I see enough of them – the nice thing about this kind of tour is that the power has shifted. In the early days I would often have to run off the tour to New York or Los Angeles to try and get somebody to do something they weren't willing to do or to get them to do it better. Now people come to us and that makes the tour the centre of power for business decisions like that. I love all that stuff, it's what I enjoy – making deals and negotiation and defending our position. We're very thorough."

YOU'RE BRANCHING OUT INTO MANAGEMENT OF OTHER ARTISTS ALSO?
"Not really, it's just that I'm giving the Pretenders, well it's Chrissie (Hynde) in fact, some help at the moment, and I'm not sure whether it's true to call it full management but it may turn into that in the future. We've known them for years and she clearly needed some help this year because she got rid of her previous

manager. I'm very happy to do that and to be a friend as well – what it turns into in the long run remains to be seen."

HAVE YOU GOT A LIFE OUTSIDE U2?
"Not this year! I have a family and two small children and I am looking forward to seeing them."

WHAT ABOUT YOUR FAVOURITE BANDS?
"Elvis Presley, The Beatles and The Stones and The Who are favourites. They are the real legends for me, the people who made the biggest changes.

"I never liked Zeppelin, funnily enough, and it was U2 who turned me onto them which is rather strange considering our ages."

WHAT ARE YOUR FAVOURITE U2 SONGS?
" 'Bad' I think has always been my favourite song. 'One Tree Hill' I think is stunning as well, though it hasn't been performed much on this tour because it's very difficult.

"I always liked 'An Cat Dubh' - one of the first, if you like, of U2's tempo experiments, and that had a great mood. I like 'Tomorrow' and '11 o'clock Tick Tock' – I wouldn't mind having that back in the set.

"It's a problem having so many to choose from these days but it's also a tremendous luxury. When we first started playing we only had ten songs and we used to play some of them twice which was really a bit embarrassing."

ARE YOU STILL A U2 FAN?
"Enormously. I love them."

One of the things about living with the same five people over ten years is that it teaches you to have disagreements very carefully.

LIVIN' IN

★ ★ ★ ★ ★ ★ ★ ★ ★ ★ ★ ★ ★ ★

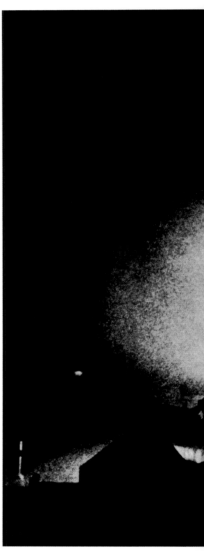

It's been six months now since U2 moved en masse to Los Angeles. This time it isn't the usual on-tour-hotels-and-living-out-of-suitcases situation. The band rented two houses for themselves and one for the handful of crew who are with them – this has been long-term encampment. So what's everyone doing out there? Well, quite simply it's just a matter of mixing and producing the entire soundtrack for their forthcoming concert/documentary film "U2: Rattle & Hum," putting together a complete live album, recording a half dozen or so new studio tracks, filming the final documentary sequences for the movie and keeping an eye on the editing of the movie itself. Not to mention approving artwork for the new album/cassette/CD/singles, the movie publicity and even a "Rattle & Hum" book. By comparison, being on tour looks like a holiday. Despite the pressure though, Adam took the time to make a phone call to PROPAGANDA to say how it's all going.

"Ah, it's going fine" he says, making light of what everyone knows is a killing work schedule. "I think if we tried to look at the big picture we'd get very confused. We're just taking each day as it comes and hoping that by the time we get to the deadline that all the parts will fit together. It's very difficult to monitor all the separate areas whether it's live mixes for the movie, live mixes for the album, studio work, and so on. We

AMERICA

★ ★

just press on hoping we're working on the right bits of the jigsaw."

How is Phil Joanou (U2 film director) getting on with all the editing work?
"Phil's very relaxed actually. It was good for him to have a bit of time away from it, when we came back to do the Dublin filming last month. When he was in Dublin he was under a lot of pressure, but now we've got back here he seems far more relaxed and can see a bit straighter.

"The movie isn't something that we're attending to every day at this stage. We'll see a rough cut then later another and another."

How are you approaching work for the soundtrack?
"Jimmy (Lovine) is co-ordinating all the film soundtrack plus doing the studio work on the new tracks. The Edge is working with Jimmy because he knows what the live tracks will be and the various technical problems of mixing the live material for the movie reproduction."

Having always recorded in Dublin, working in L.A. must be a very different experience. Is it easier working without the distractions of being at home?
"Yes, it does seem to be happening a little quicker. It's easier to try out different ideas here. You just say to Jimmy, right we'd like to try some backing singers on this, can you get some people down this evening – and they arrive and they know what they're doing. It's the same if you want to try percussion or keyboards or anything. You can find instruments and you can find players and that does make the whole thing more rewarding to see ideas coming together much faster."

'Los Angeles is so diverse – there are two sides to it there's the glamour side and then there's the homelessness'

In what ways is it harder for you, being away from home?

"I don't think it's really any harder, although the pace does become a little slower once the backing tracks are done. In the studio you're working with people who don't have the perspective of the people we work with in Dublin. Pat McCarthy at Windmill Lane for example would know instinctively when a track is finished, he knows what the vibe is. But here, because the guys are used to working in a different way they don't quite know when a track is done. It's not a big problem, it's just a different approach."

How are the rest of the band coping with living in Los Angeles?

"Larry's getting on fine with L.A. – that's because he's in

Dublin at the moment! The Edge is great. Edge has got great stamina for just going in every day and getting on with it. He doesn't get overwhelmed by the process at all. He enjoys studios and trying out the different ideas.

"Bono always gets a buzz out

of being away and being in a place like this. Los Angeles is so diverse – there are two sides to it, there's the glamour side and then there's the homelessness and the poverty here which we've seen before in the Downtown area where we shot the

"You can see on MTV and stuff like that, that we're still very much in the public eye, but I think there's a natural cycle when people know that you're working and that there's something about to be released, that public attention does come back onto you. It's happening quite naturally, but we're avoiding it as much as possible. There's a lot of invitations coming in where people would like us to attend events or whatever – but it's really a case or let's get the work out of the way first."

Can you give away anything about the new album?
"Nothing final yet by any means, but it's looking like maybe two sides live and two studio, as we've got a lot of songs together. We'll see."

"Like I said, it seems to be happening quickly. I always hate saying that because you can so easily get tripped up, bud it does feel like it's happening OK.

"The deadlines are all getting slightly close, so we've stopped looking at the numbers on the calendar. We're just going to keep working flat out until we get the phone call that says it's got to be ready tomorrow....!

Streets video. Those things are still going on – nothing changes.

"There's always a lot to go looking for and lots of interesting people to meet, but there isn't a feeling of belonging – you do feel like an alien. You realise that you think differently to everyone else. You do notice a difference to being at home."

And how about yourself – how do you get on with L.A.?
"Remember there was a character in a kid's comic called 'Piper Peter' or something, who could play a tune on his magical pipe and the billboards would come alive – well that's the feeling of L.A. It feels like everyone's a part of something, but they don't really know what. Everyone is a star and it's really very difficult to find normal low-key things to do without everything being a big production number. Even finding an ordinary bar to drink in is difficult.

"Having said that, we don't really have much time for socialising. There are times like late at night when you can go out to a bar or night club, but you have to accept that it's not going to be like going out in Dublin where you can just go somewhere and talk. It is a glamour town and that's the way it works."

Is U2 getting much attention there at the moment?

'A STRING

Earlier in the year the Hendricks Gallery in Dublin put on an exhibition of paintings, drawings and photographs by four Dublin artists. The artists were Charlie Whisker, who entitled his exhibit "This Then is That", Derek Rowen (alias "Guggi") with "The First Friday", Gavin Friday with "Ididn'tcomeuptheliffeyinabubble" and Bono, giving the first and only public exhibition of his photographs of Ethiopia. There were twenty five photographs in all, which Bono called "A String of Pearls". Almost all the pictures are the profoundly beautiful faces of Ethiopian people with whom he was working, when he and his wife Ali made the trip to Wello, a northern province of Ethiopia in September 1985. Their visit was organised and kept a secret by World Vision, and proceeds from the sale of the limited edition prints and book will go to Concern/World Vision Ireland.

OF PEARLS'

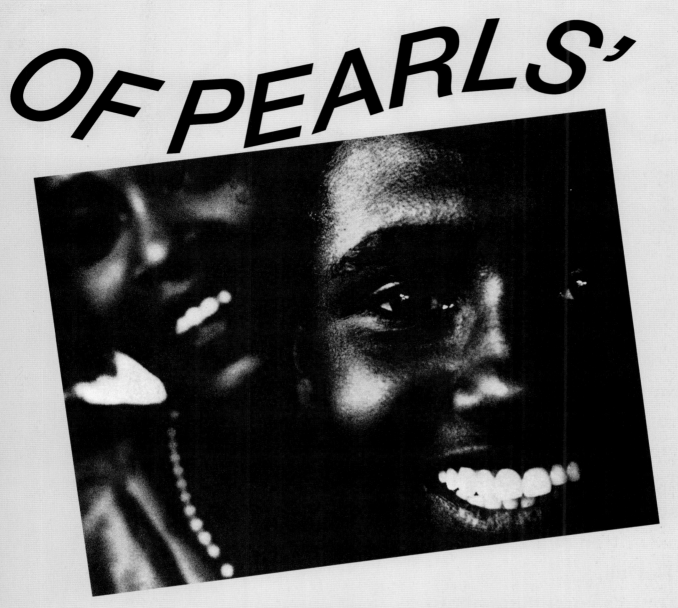

"Ajibar was high up in the mountains in Wello. At night the winds were so cold they could cut you.

The feeding centre was a tin-can town of wood, wire and corrugated iron. For a second it could have been Belsen – but here the barbed wire was to keep people out, not in.

At first as we walked through the camp, we kept our eyes down and were so overpowered by the suffering we saw around us that I couldn't even take my camera out of its case.

Weeks later a different but more lasting impression set in of the beauty and strength of spirit of the Ethiopian people. It was then I started taking photographs, not to deny the waste of human life that was and still is Ethiopia but to make the people and therefore the tragedy real by bringing their sense of dignity back into the picture.

In the end we received more from the Ethiopian people than we could ever give."

Bono 1987

SOUND

Soundchecks have always been important for U2. Not simply to get things sounding right, but also as a time to just play and run through ideas. Soundchecks have produced countless new U2 songs and sounds – even a song like "Pride" which was written at a soundcheck in Hawaii.

There's something about working on ideas within the context of a tour that is different to a rehearsal room or recording studio. The Edge in particular uses soundchecks to find new sounds and techniques. You'll often see him working on stage almost till doors open.

CHECKS

BONO

off the record

BONO is sitting in the boardroom at U2's Windmill Lane headquarters in Dublin. It is late afternoon in early winter and he has just finished a "business meeting" with Edge and Paul McGuiness, the kind of meetings of which there are more and more but in which he is getting "less and less involved".

1988 has nearly run out. Rattle and Hum the double album is in the shops and in the record books, the fastest – selling album of all time, beating Michael Jackson's Bad which itself had beaten The Joshua Tree. Nobody was cheering it into the record books though, says Bono, the aim is to be the best not merely the biggest. Rattle and Hum the Book – of the Film of the Record – is also in the shops and also in the best-seller lists. It is the first U2-associated book that the band have expressed unreserved pleasure with. Rattle and Hum the Film has opened to rave reviews and long queues of fans eager to see the band without the disadvantage of sitting through a warm-up act. They exit the cinema after the showing only to queue up again for the next performance.

Bono, like the rest of the band, has been to the charity premieres of the film – in aid of Amnesty International – in Dublin, in London, in Los Angeles and in Madrid. After a year living in America 'doing post-production' on the film with director Phil Joanou and getting the album together with producer Jimmy Iovine the band are finally back in Ireland. Back home. This time for a proper break. Despite preliminary discussions about

going out on the road in New Zealand, Australia and Japan in the spring, they have decided to leave it until the autumn. They want to be ready not just willing when the campaign resumes.

"As boring as it might sound," explains Bono, "I'm just into reading and writing at the moment." He's been reading Tenessee Williams and Eugene O'Neill, Charles Bukowski and John Fantay. He's done some travelling too, along the way discovering the music of Guy Clarke, Lee Clayton, Johnny Cash – with whom he spend a day and began to write a song – and John Prime. But no discovery was more exciting than an old bluesman in Memphis.

"In Memphis recently Adam and I went out into the cotton fields and found this off limits juke-joint one Sunday afternoon where they serve moonshine and play the blues."

"We found one of the old bluesmen there who didn't leave to go to Chicago like Muddy Waters, BB King and the others. He was playing in this shed, this kind of dwelling right on the edge of the cotton field. It was an extraordinary music."

He also cites appreciating recent work by Sonic Youth, REM and The Subterraneans.

"But I feel very cut off from

the present because I'm locked in the past and also, in a weird way, the future. I've been listening to a lot of psychedelic music, the warping of sounds, the more avant-garde music of John Cage and Philip Glass."

Meanwhile for the benefit of PROPAGANDA, which he describes as "obviously the best fan magazine in the world", Bono has suspended his recent 'no interviews at the moment' policy and found time to talk about the present, the past and the future and U2's role in the big picture.

His words are often halting, uncertain and far more considered than usual. "I'm not as verbal about the music anymore. I feel it's all still inside me and that's why I'm writing and writing. And if I'm writing then I can't really talk."

But if he is far less verbal in conversation than before, he is far more articulate in his songwriting, which is where we start.

Judging by the new material on Rattle and Hum and the continuing trend to put new songs on B-sides of the single releases, you have been doing a lot of songwriting since last year?
Yes, in one way it's a way of withdrawing from the megadom, the helter-skelter, the hurdy-gurdy of it all... it's trying to simplify it and just

bring it down to three and a half minutes, to a song.

Songwriting is the one area that I – that we – have complete control of. Nobody intrudes into that place where you write a song, where you write words.... So I find that has become a kind of safe-haven. I've had to simplify it all, just get it down to the song. It's that one thing that you have completely to yourself.

What are you doing now that you're home again?
Well writing songs yes, but also trying to catch up on a lot of people that I lost touch with. I have a lot of people around here that are really close friends like Guggi who is a painter or Gavin Friday who has his own album coming out.... That kind of thing.

Apart from the hullabaloo of the premieres have you been to see the film privately?
The first time I went to see it was a private screening in Los Angeles about a month and a half before it was released. That's when I saw the film with my eyes open, most of the rest of the time I see it with my eyes closed. I look but I don't see it.

But in Los Angeles recently me and Adam went again, with cap and glasses on we just went into the back of a cinema that was showing it.

Was it like being at your first ever U2 gig, being in the audience when you were on the stage?
It was an odd experience because I've never been to a U2 concert. I think it's the closest I'll ever get to a U2 concert. It was great because there were two beautiful black girls sitting in front of us who had no idea that we were sitting behind them. And every time Adam came on they just screamed and jumped on each other with excitement. It was hysterical. I was jumping on him.

In Spain at the Madrid premiere they just about tore the cinema down, it was unbelievable. I love that about the Spanish, I love it. They out-riot the Irish any day, that was wonderful. But the way

I've seen it best has been with just ten people in a small cinema, before it came out and I really enjoyed it.

Would you change anything or is it gone now?
It's gone now. I think we were pretty uncompromising in the making of the movie. A lot of people would have liked it to have gone various other different ways. It could have been like The Monkees with the outtakes – there's some ridiculous outtakes. It could have been an in-depth psychoanalysis of the band.

It could have been those things and people could have got to know us more as people but we felt very strongly that this was about us as musicians first and foremost.

A British film critic said that from the band's few comments in the film he longed to know more about your views as individuals.
We thought we were better at playing music than we were at talking. It was like we could have three minutes of rap or three minutes of Bullet the Blue Sky and we just thought we were better at Bullet the Blue Sky.

Also we are feeling a little over-exposed in a way and we were kind of withdrawing a bit and hiding behind our music more. That is after all what's most important to us. We didn't want to focus too much on our personalities. We also felt that it was cool that Larry came through more because he's normally trapped behind the drum kit so it seemed to make sense that he came upfront.

It also took the focus off you, the film affirmed that this is a band.
That's correct, that was first and foremost in our thinking behind it. I felt that my say is when I sing, I write the words. So let Larry do some talking for a change, let Edge do some talking.

Joanou turned out to be quite an inspired choice to direct, there's even been talk of another collaboration, perhaps you doing music for his next film.

We haven't talked much about another project but I really enjoyed working with him. He certainly has seen the dark side as well as the light side of U2. We're pretty paranoid people. When you start filming us we're a bit like the Indians who feel like you're raking our soul. We're always asking "Who's the white man with the camera?" We wanted to scalp him half the time.

We're right to be a bit suspicious but he won us over because he wanted to make a film about the music. Because we feel that's what is extraordinary about U2. And I think he has made a remarkable film, I don't know how he did it.

You once described Blood Red Sky as the end of U2 part one. Is Rattle and Hum the end of U2 part two?
Yeah. We might have a full stop to come. It's just about there. Maybe we'll release a single or something that will finish it.

You talked recently about the Prince approach to recording, to put more and more records out. You're also writing constantly. Do you want to get U2 albums pouring out?
I do. I want to make another record and another. I also want to play. I have a feeling we'll play this year, definitely Australia, New Zealand and Japan but perhaps back through England and Scotland as well. I don't think there will be an LP out by then but I think we might put some songs out by then.

We're in a kind of reckless period. I mean we're not carefully planning things. We're being a lot more careless about the design of U2. We want to be able to be more spontaneous. There's no grand plan. The idea is just to make records and put them out, and play the places we want to play.

Back in the early days you talked about being the biggest band in the world. What do you do once you've become that?
Being the biggest band in the world is not as important as being the best. The best

'There's no grand plan. The idea is just to make records and put them out'

'I think real U2 fans have a very clear idea of what we're about. Probably clearer than we do'

being the most vital, the most reflective of what's going on.... That's all part of being the best.

Tunnel of Love, for example, is miles better than Born in the USA but only sold about one tenth as many copies. In a way Rattle and Hum could have been that too, after The Joshua Tree, but unfortunately everybody likes it.
Yes, true, we made it hard for people to love, you couldn't put out a more mixed up record. I mean we really worked hard at that. We worked hard at messing it up for the masses and they still went out and bought it. It is an amazing feeling that the audience is kind of as hip as you are.

When Desire went to number one in England it seemed all wrong. For a song like this to be on Top of the Pops, to be on pop radio stations, it seemed like interference from another channel.
I don't know how that happened but it did the trick. Yes we really wound up the compression on that.

Have you got America out of the way yet?
The only problem is looking for a place that isn't America. You've just for to turn on the television here and it's like living in America. Same as when you go to England... we're all kind of living in America.

Will another culture influence the groups so greatly, will there ever be an African U2 period?
Well it's fair to say that the blues is not just an American art-form. It's African, re-interpreted. Three chords are Irish, Scottish. But Africa and South America and these places ... I can feel a widening of our vision musically speaking. We just got caught up in this blues and gospel it just seems so alive, and you just feel your way.

A couple of years back you were with T-Bone Burnett and he played you some of his songs and then asked you to play some of yours. And you realised that yours didn't work like that. Now you could do that, you could play him yours.
Yeah and I do. We really enjoy that. In fact only last week I was in a bar in Nashville with Cowboy Jack Clement and Adam. There was a guy up on stage with greased back hair, about fifty or maybe a forty year old man who has been through a lot more than most. He is up there playing songs, a famous country songwriter, playing to a bar of fifteen people and his song was 'If I were in your shoes I'd walk out on me'.

Anyway, Cowboy Jack got up and he played some songs. And myself and Adam got up and we played some songs to this fifteen, twenty people who had no idea that we were in a band. We played Love Rescue Me. I got down from the platform and this old Indian was standing at the bar. He called me over and he said "D'you write that tune?"

I said "Yeah."

He said "Good song .... But you can't play it."

I loved it, it was great. He loved the songs but thought we couldn't play them, that we really messed them up and he was just hoping it wasn't any writer that he respected. The audience liked them too even though we couldn't play them.

Have you been writing recently?
Well I've written a whole pile of stuff, a whole pile of prose poems: 'Elvis is alive, We're dead', that's one of them. I've written a song for Nina Simone called 'Love is Blindness but I Don't Want to See'. I wrote a gospel tune for the Neville Brothers called 'One Love'. If somebody's music inspires me I write them a song.

You've talked of stages of writing.
To see like a songwriter is the easiest. Everyone can be in a situation and you see behind the surface of things, or see a person's motive for saying something. Hearing like a writer is a lot harder, you've got to really listen. Thinking like a writer is the next step and then you are. I find that I'm more interested in writing now than in just writing

songs. I have a lot of unfinished work. I'm not saying where I am in that. I think I know where I am in that but I think there are these stages of development in a writer.

Would you consider sending your prose to a publisher under a pseudonym?
Yeah. Definitely. That'd be the test and I don't doubt that I'll do that at some stage. I'm sure that'll be the last I'll hear of it as well.

Do you like PROPAGANDA?
I really like it. I think it's one of the best laid out magazines apart from anything else. It also makes me laugh. I never seem to know what's going in and so I'm as anxious as anyone to read what Edge etc. thinks of me. It's obviously the best magazine of its kind in the world. I have never seen a better one. And as soon as I do you're sacked! I really do think it's the best. I'm actually really proud of PROPAGANDA.

There are hundreds of U2 fanzines around the world. You see some sometimes. Do you have any favourites?
My favourite at the moment is ADAM. Because they don't like any other member of the band other than his lordship. I'm a big fan of that magazine.

Do you like U2 fans?
Yeah. I married one. I'm best friends with another. Also those fans who have the most to say send letters and we get to read the more interesting letters. I usually get the ones that people have put a lot of time into. I think real U2 fans have a very clear idea of what we're about. Probably clearer than we do.

What I love about a lot of the U2 fanzines is that they enjoy the imperfections of the band too, they love the weak side of U2 as well as the strong side. They enjoy our failings, they enjoy the mistakes we make as much as our successes. When you hit the nail on the head it's wonderful but when you hit your finger it maybe says more about you.

Many people want to set up a myth about U2.
But I don't think U2 fans are a part of that. I think the media would like to paint a picture of U2 and they have a rather cartoonish image of what U2 are. They have that because they haven't really listened to our music, they haven't really seen what U2 are about. They have this cartoon picture of us. Their image of U2 is based on the singles or a few broad strokes like a TV appearance whereas our audience are on a completely different level. The media occasionally get it right but mostly get it wrong with U2. The fans have a clear picture of what we are because they are immersed in the music.

I think it's just a minority of fans that go overboard. I think the real U2 audiences out there know us for what we are.

For example the 'spokes-man of a generation' stuff about me is not from U2 fans, it's from the media.

A lot of the fans who came to Dublin are just into Dublin, or Ireland or the band or all three. It's a trek. There are stupid people in the world and – I hate to say this – but there are some stupid U2 fans. Some stupid U2 fans think that we have all the answers and that maybe we can save their world. But the majority of U2 fans are much smarter than that.

Joe O'Herlihy was telling me earlier that ten years ago last October he played his first date with you. Can you remember 1978?
We're a lucky band to have found Joe O'Herlihy. Actually 1978 was a really exciting time for U2. We had just discovered F sharp minor. So we had the fourth chord and we'd only had three up to then.

It was in '78 that we started actually being able to play in McGonagles in town and just started to discover what U2 were. '77, '78 and '79 are a bit blurred for me. I could be talking about any one of those three years.

Any hankerings to play McGonagles again?
No, I must say I prefer playing Wembley Arena, I really do, that is no joke. The music never seemed to fit into those places, they always seemed too small. The music seemed too big for McGonagles. We wanted to blow the roof off. I always felt like that. We needed to find a bigger place to play even if there weren't any people there …. just to fit the music in.

When I think of '78 I think more of Lipton Village, the whole street gang, of not going to bed at night, of lying on my back on O'Connell Street on my birthday, of a policeman waking me up, of an all-girl punk group called The Boy Scouts of the Virgin Prunes, of U2, of putting on street performances, of the butt end of punk....

Are you ever surprised to be sitting here ten years on?
I'm very glad that we're not still playing McGonagles. Although I like going there, I much prefer not playing there.

Some of the songs you are writing now could almost be written for small clubs.
Well that's true and it's why we enjoyed playing the Dominion Theatre in London for the Jamaica relief thing in October. It was interesting because the songs fit into the place.

One reviewer said recently that now you're at the top you want to be a garage band again.
It'd be a pretty psychedelic garage I can tell you. The biggest shock I got at the Smile Jamaica thing was the people singing the refrain to Love Rescue Me. It was an extraordinary thing and it did feel that the song had been around for years … not weeks. Smart lot aren't they?

In the middle years you talked a lot about breaking down the barriers between the audience and performer. Does that become more difficult the bigger you get?
We actually stopped trying to do that. I stopped trying to do that physically, stopped trying to leave the stage and go into the audience and actually instead we tried to do it in the songs. That's the best way of breaking down that barrier.

Is it ever a pain being at

the top, being a businessman, having to go to meetings, talk about money, discuss merchandise?
Actually I go to less meetings now than I used to. I'm feeling very cut off at the moment from U2 the Organisation, and I find myself seeking refuge in the songs. I think the only way I can feel like that is that I know we have the best possible people in the world working for us.

Everybody in this building makes it possible for us to let go and let them.

The Band didn't do many interviews this time around and you did hardly anything.
I wouldn't agree to do an interview unless I really wanted to do it. I just felt this time around that I didn't have much to say ... as you have found out. I find now that I'm not quite as good at articulating in conversation what I have to say but I'm better at articulating it in songs. And I find that I'm talking to less people but writing more songs.

Do you ever read the press about U2?
I read some but not all.

When it's about you do you ever recognise yourself in it?
For a period there I didn't know I was the person they were talking about. I honestly had no idea who they were talking about. It really foxed me, it vexed me. I thought, 'Who is this guy I don't think I like him ... it's not me.'

It's not just the interviews, they are more or less me, but it's the portrayals generally by the press. Whoever that guy was he definitely needed a holiday. It seemed very one-dimensional, a very hollow version of the group that came across. In one interview I'd be deadly serious, in another I'd be completely mischievous. I just realised that people get a clearer glimpse of who you are through the music than through any interview you may do.

Edge says how you've matured as a songwriter. Is it a new approach to songwriting or have you more to say?
I haven't mastered the art of songwriting but I find at the moment that I just enjoy writing words. I've learnt a lot from Bob Dylan and from T-Bone Burnett but I've learnt the most from Edge, Larry and Adam. I write all the time. It's so simple this songwriting, it can't be taken away from you. It's just you, a piece of paper, a pen or just sitting with a guitar or a piano. It seems like sanity amidst all the madness of being with a big group. I'm more rather than less interested in that than anything else.

Love Rescue Me was written with Bob Dylan. How did that come about?
What happened with Love Rescue Me doesn't often happen but when it does it feels really worthwhile. I just woke up with that song in my head. I said to myself, Right I'll go and have a cup of coffee' and I couldn't. I couldn't even go and have a cup of coffee or have breakfast because it was so strong. I was wishing it wasn't there almost but I thought, well, I'll just start writing it down:
    'Love Rescue Me
    From the night's insanity'
    That was the first line and I don't think it even made it to the song.
    Love Rescue Me
    Come forward and speak to me
    Raise me up don't let me fall
    No man is my enemy
    My own hands imprison me
    Love Rescue Me
    I wrote that verse straight off, melody, everything, and thought Well ... what's that about? I'll get back to that.' I was going out to see Dylan that day and I just played it to him and we started working on it and the picture emerged.

People talk of the muse. Are there times when you just need to capture it immediately while it's here?
Well some songs seem to write themselves, whereas others you really have to work at. That was written in minutes. Desire also was written pretty quickly. I really enjoy it when they come real

quick. There was a lot of verses that were left out of Love Rescue Me. We wrote a whole pile of verses .... The only logic that each verse shares is the refrain Love Rescue Me. I like the randomness of it, the wandering way it goes.

It might be the theme of the whole album.
Yes, there might not be any other logic to it, that's correct.

You wrote a song with T-Bone a couple of years back. Having a Wonderful Time Wish You Were Her.
I really like that song but I didn't write much of it. T-Bone was very generous in giving me 50% of the song. I really love it. I've written others with T-Bone like Purple Heart on his last album, I think we've started another one. He's working on his next LP – the one to answer every question ever asked. It's called 'I Can Explain Everything.

T-Bone's heart is as tall as he is.

You've stayed in Ireland when so many others have left, particularly successful artists. How come?
We can afford to. We can afford the high price of a pint. Actually I've a funny feeling that it's the little things that I hate about Ireland that I secretly love. I probably like the hard times that they give us here. It makes a change. It definitely works against you rather than for you that you're in U2. People are incredibly cynical about success. It's stupid but it comes from years of associating success with oppression.

People who had money here in Ireland years ago were people who were not Irish people but English people or Scandinavian people, going back 700 years. When the country began we were not an aggressive race of people. In the Dark Ages we were more into study, the monastic life, this was a safe haven for monasteries all over while Europe was in the Dark Ages. For that reason people came to Ireland and took advantage of that. Now I don't think people can quite believe that we are independent .... If

'Why are we in this band? To make music. Let's keep on making music, that's the only way we can survive being in a big band'

'For years we had to do so many things just to stay solvent'

you're successful here you must have screwed somebody over because that has been the history of success.

Does it feel good when you come back to Ireland after being away from home for so long?
I love it here. I don't know what it would be like if I couldn't leave here. I don't know how I'd feel. The fact is I can leave any day, any week, I want. But if I wanted a divorce here and I couldn't get one or if I had to pay half my wages out every week in high taxes, then I don't know how I'd feel.

Do you go driving around the country when you're at home?
I love the West of Ireland. I do it all the time, just drive in the car. I'll probably do it this week. I like being rained on, I like the wildness of the Irish climate.

Do you get bothered by people?
No, people in the West of Ireland couldn't care less who you are. If I was a star footballer in the Mayo team then I'd be a big celebrity but rock'n'roll means nothing to them. These are fishermen and farmers.

What about Dublin, do you still love it?
I don't see as much of the city as I used to. When I was 17 and a hustler for U2, when I went round the city with my U2 tapes knocking on doors, handing them out and when I used to work in the centre, then I loved the city of Dublin. I used to go down and pretend I was a student at Trinity and get the subsidised lunches and all that. I really got into Dublin then. Now I don't feel as free just to roam the city. If I do it now it's usually after 2 am.

Do you ever play Boy or October or War?
I'm trying to think of the last time. I think Boy and War are the more popular albums of that earlier period but I think my favourite in a way is October. It's Adam's favourite too. I really like I Fall Down and October and Tomorrow. I

like Gloria too although I don't like the way I sing Gloria. I don't like Rejoice, I've gone off that, I find it hard to listen to. I find it hard to listen to our records – I really do.

With such a large repertoire of songs many of them can't be performed live, perhaps ever again. Do you ever miss the chance to play Stories for Boys or Into the Heart or I fall Down?
Into the Heart/An Cat Dubh, there's something I really enjoyed playing live, perhaps there could be a possibility of us playing that live again. I can't imagine us playing Stories for Boys again, it wouldn't seem right. We played Out of Control on the last tour.

Does it seem like almost another band?
We keep breaking up the band and forming it again, you know that. But sometimes it does feel like another band, it really does.

So what will you do next?
I feel that we're going to make some really great rock'n'roll records, some great ... what is it nowadays... CD's just doesn't feel the same... we're going to print some really cool information! Definitely where we're at now is to simplify. Why are we in this band? To make music. Let's keep on making music, that's the only way we can survive being in a big band.

Will you mind if in a couple of years time you release an album which only sells a couple of million?
No. Absolutely not. I expect to go down in terms of sales. We worked hard at it on Rattle and Hum but it didn't work! The great thing about being in a band this big ... Have I said this before?

You haven't said it yet.
Oh – that's the reason I'm not doing interviews at the moment –we just don't need to do anything and we can just do anything we want to. There's just a great sense of waywardness in the group at the moment. We feel we'll do what we want to do and when we want to do it.
I think this is a great atmosphere to release records in. We don't have to do a tour that lasts a year and nearly kills us anymore – just so that we don't lose a fortune. For years we had to do so many things just to stay solvent.
We have always made the music that we wanted to but the schedule, the timescale, was dictated by whether we could afford to. That's the excitement of being in U2 at the moment.
'Where to now Captain?
I don't know Captain what do you think?'
It's anywhere. We just point the Starship Enterprise in the right direction and our audience had proved to be an elastic kind of audience. They're into the where-to-next kind of approach. They're one step ahead of us in some ways. Rather than to have to lead the audience around by the nose we get the sense that they're right behind you every step of the way.
We thought if we stripped away the U2 sound completely, if we immersed ourselves in gospel music, country, soul... we're bound to shake off at least 50% of U2 fans: they can't cope with this. But they really could. We might have the most elastic audience when you think of what we've gone through in the last five years. As long as the songs are good they'll go with us all the way. When we start writing shit songs then I'll know that it's over.

AT THE MOVIES

★★★★★★★★★★★★★★★★★★★

Having finally finished the Rattle and Hum film and album the band went straight into movie premiere madness. Rattle and Hum premiered in five cities – Dublin, London, Madrid. New York and Los Angeles.

Bono, Edge, Larry and Adam attended all of them. Some of the premieres – particularly Madrid as Bono recalls in the interview in this issue – ended up being just like U2 gigs, except that there was no backstage and the band were sitting in the middle of the audience. The result was complete mayhem of course but a good time was had by all.

The world premiere for the film was, of course, Dublin, Ireland and the band turned up complete with instrumentation – as you can see – just in case of an emergency. In boring London a couple of days later the police refused permission for an impromptu performance and the fans had to make do with the film.

RATTLE AND LIVE

THE E D
ON H

The Edge is in Dublin in the Spring. He is getting rid of his old record player and trying out a new one ("My old stuff is like 8 years old and it's all bits and pieces, the original amp, some beaten up speakers…"), visiting obscure record shops to feed his interest in cajun and Zydeco and preparing to undertake some research into how to play guitar as he never really found out .

"I'm trying to figure out what I'm going to do," he explains. "We have more time off now than we've had since the beginning of the eighties. This time is time to do the things that we've never been able to do in the past. For me at the moment just to be able to go home and listen to music is incredible."

Although it is holiday time, the first real break since the band started with the film now gone to become a video, the Rattle and Hum single releases arriving periodically and the b-sides recorded, there is still work to be done. Mixed in with the leisure are early preparations for the next long player, meetings with potential single-release video directors and "simultaneously baby-sitting over the phone a remix that's going on in LA of Love Comes To Town."

But it is also a time for reflection, relaxation, some definite travelling – Edge is preparing to accompany Paul McGuiness to Moscow for the launch of the Greenpeace album on which the band are featured – some reading and lots of catching up.

In fact it is his new record player that Edge cites as his excuse for forgetting his appointment with PROPAGANDA. Well, he is on holiday.

ALTHOUGH YOU'VE BEEN OFF THE ROAD FOR OVER A YEAR AND THE FILM's BEEN COMPLETED AND RELEASED FOR OVER 6 MONTHS, U2 CLEARLY DON'T JUST SHUT DOWN BETWEEN RECORDS, WHAT'S AN ORDINARY DAY LIKE?

There's no such thing as an ordinary day. Every day is different. There's quite a lot of small things going on – small by comparison with touring the world – like we're planning our next video, looking at the work of directors and talking to them, and simultaneously baby-sitting over the phone a remix that's going on in LA of Love Comes To Town. It's with the same producer Louis Silas, Jr. who did the Desire re-mix and he's also done one of God Part II.

We will usually get together as a band at least a couple of times a week to plan what we're going to do – like now on the video and also on the re-mix to decide on edits.

The b-sides are pretty much under control. We decided at the beginning of the year that we'd try and get all the b-sides out of the way because as always at the end of the album that was the last thing on our mind. So invariably that means going back into the studio which we did in late January.

We decided that we'd work on some covers because we've never actually done that before – recorded a pile of cover versions. We spent about five days in the studio and it was great fun just playing some of the old songs that we'd always wanted to play. Maria McKee came down and she sang with us. It was one of those really low-pressure sessions and I think we got some good stuff as a result.

We did everything and anything really: a version of

the old classic Unchained Melody, a version of Dancing Barefoot by Patti Smith, a version of that old soul song Everlasting Love – I don't even know who wrote it – and that's going to blow a few heads. We did about eight but some of them are too off the wall. A couple of real old soul classics with Maria may or may not see the light of day depending on how they seem when we've worked on them. Dancing Barefoot certainly will come out on the single and Unchained Melody and Everlasting Love will be on the second single. God Part II – the re-mix – will probably not be a single release but come as part of a package with one of the next two released, a give-away track. As the song in its conception is based around a real solid drum machine beat we felt it would really lend itself to being treated in a dub-dance way. It's a great re-mix and we've cut up and put in some political speeches by Martin Luther King – just tiny little sentences with no real flow, snippets. We also had a little of JFK – almost inaudible – and a bit of John Lennon since the song is God Part II and we felt it would be only correct to have him represented.

On the Desire re-mix we used some TV news – whatever was on that night – and on When Love Comes To Town we're going to use some gospel radio snippets.

BUT BEING OFF THE ROAD AND DESPITE THE WORK THAT NEEDS TO BE DONE YOU MUST STILL GET A LOT MORE TIME TO RELAX AND TAKE LIFE EASIER. WHAT RECORDS HAVE YOU BEEN LISTENING TO?

There's a great record shop in Dublin called Cladding Records which has got all the records that I could never find

in this country. So I spent a couple of hours down there about a week ago and I'm going to have to go back because I only got through the cajuz/zydeco section – I got a lot of the old JD Miller sessions and a lot of old Queen Ida and Clifton Chenier, who is one of the main innovators of zydeco/accordion music. I'm fascinated with the clichés before they became set. This is the era when rock'n'roll was being invented. It's not like someone woke up one morning and here it was, so you see all sorts of strains of what eventually became rock'n'roll through this music. You find the 12-bar which obviously came from blues, but you find it used in a much more upbeat excited way. A lot of these songs were produced and written as singles and in the Louisiana area they were extremely successful and they've got a real 'up' sensibility which I like: the beat of the songs is almost a shuffle-thing. We're only recently becoming hip to the shuffle and it's a whole world: there's snare on 2 and 4 or kick drum on 1 and 3. It's a whole different thing, a whole different world rhythmically. I'm still mesmerised by the whole kind of groove this music sets up. It's the most exciting thing to hear.

WHAT ABOUT READING, I NOTICE IN THE OFFICE THAT ADAM HAS BEEN SENT A COPY OF AN ANDY WARHOL BIOGRAPHY BY A FAN AND THAT BONO HAS BEEN SENT A COPY OF THE KORAN.
(Laughter). I haven't been doing much reading lately although I just bought Salman Rushdie's book, it sounds heavy.
Fans tend for some reason to send me copies of this book The Prophet by Khali Gibrain. I've got about 14 copies and I don't know why but it seems

to be their favourite for me. The last thing I read was by Truman Capote – I have a big collection of his short stories – also I have a lot of Flannery O'Connor, some Raymond Carver, again short stories … there's something good about America. I don't relate to English culture, the British use of the English language. I tend to prefer the use of language that the American authors use. I like Irish writers for the same reasons. With Irish writers they tend to borrow a lot from the spoken word, quite subtle, and colourful and the vocabulary is smaller but it communicates in a stronger way. The words are not as important as where they are placed and their sound. I suppose it's more musical.

ANY FILMS?
I try to go to the cinema whenever I can. I saw Wim Wenders' Wings of Desire last night for the first time and I think I'll have to go and see it again. Maybe I was half asleep. I think I was too close to the screen because I had to keep looking up at the screen from the subtitles. I loved the story. We actually screened a couple of films recently in doing research for our video, the Fellini movie Le

Strada and some of the old Godard movies because we're working on a particular train of thought. It reinforced my belief that black and white is a superior medium cinematically – much better than colour which is just flatter. Nobody thinks of colour in a cinematic way, only in a realistic way.

THAT'S WHY IT WAS SO STRIKING WHEN RATTLE AND HUM WENT TO COLOUR TWO THIRDS OF THE WAY THROUGH. THE VIEWER HAD FORGOTTEN COLOUR EXISTED UNTIL THEN.
Well the main budget was the colour shoot and we were a bit uneasy about the fact that we were presenting Paramount with a movie that was about 60% black and white. Studios are very concerned about 'getting the budget on the screen.'
But we just kept on having to lose colour and add black and white. That was the way it worked out and I think it was the right decision. I don't feel we were wrong but we wondered how people in the studio would react to this when so much money had gone into the colour and we were going back to the black and white.

> "My old stuff is like 8 years old and it's all bits and pieces, the original amp, some beaten up speakers …"

MAYBE YOU COULD INTRODUCE A NEW BLACK-AND-WHITICISING PROCESS FOR COLOUR FILMS.

That would be great!!

DO YOU GET TO DO TRAVELLING IN TIME OFF?

I've been wanting to go to Russia for a couple of years now. It seems like when we were in Los Angeles there were more Russians there than I'd ever met in my life before. For some reason – Perestroika probably – there are more Russians currently in America than have ever gone over in the previous fifty years. From a musician's and artist's point of view it's a great time because Russia is opening up. Brian Eno has just been over there to produce a Russian group called Zvucki Mu.

AREN'T MOST OF THESE ACTS HEAVY METAL OR GLAM-ROCK BANDS?

That was my impression and for years I was very disappointed when I heard any Eastern Block bands because they were always either jazz-fusion or heavy metal. But Zvucki Mu are the Talking Heads of Russia – their whole emphasis is unusual. I have a translation of their lyrics and they are very ironic, quite thinly veiled criticism of the government. It's not really hard to figure out what they're talking about, they're quite satirical.

ARE THERE U2 BOOTLEG RECORDS AVAILABLE IN RUSSIA

We're very big on the underground scene in Russia. Unfortunately what happens is that one album goes in and then 10,000 cassettes are made of it and the quality is terrible. This song on the Greenpeace record, Pride (in The Name of Love) is the first official release of a U2 song in Russia.

But there's a lot of places I'd like to get to that I haven't managed to so far ... I'm fascinated with Cuba and would like to go there sometime. As it happens there is a direct flight from Shannon Airport to Havana in Cuba. I intend getting on it one weekend.

I also wanted to spend some time in New Orleans and particularly to check out the jazz and blues festival. New Orleans has fascinated me for years.

IN CONTRAST TO 'TOUR MADNESS' NOW THAT YOU'RE HOME YOU MUST HAVE TO DO THE WASHING UP?

Absolutely. I suppose that's refreshing in some ways but what I really want to do in this time is get my studio going in my basement and I've also decided that I'm going to do some of my own research on my guitar playing – on the technique of playing. I've always really survived on the work that we were doing at that time.

THE EDGE IS GOING TO LEARN TO PLAY GUITAR?

I'm going to start working on aspects of my playing to see what happens.

AFTER DOING THE SOUNDTRACK FOR HEROINE YOU SAID YOU WOULDN'T DO ANOTHER FILM SOUNDTRACK. DO YOU FEEL THE SAME WAY?

Unless it was something that I just couldn't refuse I wouldn't want to do anything like that right now. Soundtracks are great ... if that's all you're doing at the time. But for me right now U2 is what I'm interested in doing and especially our next record. It won't be for quite some time but that's what I'm really thinking of right now.

I RECENTLY PUT TOGETHER A

COMPILATION OF B-SIDES AND MORE UNUSUAL U2 MATERIAL WHICH IS TO U2 WHAT THE AMBIENT SERIES IS TO BRIAN ENO'S WORK. SONGS LIKE SCARLET, OCTOBER, BASS TRAP, LOVE COMES TUMBLING, FORTY, WALK TO THE WATER... A MEDITATIVE, REFLECTIVE SIDE OF THE BAND THAT IS OFTEN IGNORED. IT ISN'T SOMETHING THAT CAME WITH BRIAN ENO DOING UNFORGETTABLE FIRE, IT'S BEEN THERE SINCE AN CAT DUBH.

Yeah. One of the reasons we were interested in Brian Eno – and I'd been a fan of his for years – was that part of what we were interested in musically was to create a kind of landscape that could bring you into a different kind of mood. Eno has really taken that on and the whole New Age thing is terrible because suddenly he has been pigeon-holed with all that music: it has lumped some of the most pretentious garbage in with some records I really care about and like. It's awful. As an idea, as a direction New Age is a cul de sac and yet within it are some things which are really exciting and really worthwhile.

I think that at the moment we ourselves would not do a record like that. It's a side of the band that will come out in albums and is fine as a facet of the group but to do an album exclusively of that sort of thing would be as bad as doing one exclusively of the opposite of it. It would instantly be described as a New Age album and I think would be totally misunderstood right now.

BUT THIS SIDE OF THE BAND, THE AMBIENT U2, A LOT OF WHICH SEEMS TO BE YOUR INFLUENCE, IS LARGELY IGNORED BY THE CRITICS.

Well, it's funny because on the War Record the song that I was most into was Drowning Man which I still think is one of my top five U2 songs ever. And it was totally ignored. I don't know if it's because those songs take a little more time to unravel and get to know or whether it's just something that I particularly

THE EDGE

liked and not many others do.

WOULD YOU LIKE TO PLAY THAT LIVE AGAIN?

We thought about it but it never really worked live, we tried a few times. The subtlety of the thing was too volatile to be consistent – some nights it would be great other nights it would just be awful.

WHAT OTHER SONGS ARE IN YOUR U2 TOP FIVE?

On the new record All I Want is You, God Part II and Desire – I'm very proud of them. On previous records I think Running To Stand Still was a great piece of work. Also With or Without You because at that moment it was something no-one had heard of before although it's since become a kind of format or style and even for us we now accept it as kind of established. But when we first released it, it was like 'Will anyone play this?'

DO YOU EVER PLAY BOY, OCTOBER OR WAR?

Very, very occasionally. I'm very aware that we have come a long way since the first few albums . That's not to say that I don't like them or that I'm

discounting them but I think we have changed a lot as a band since those early days. Off the early records my 'hits' are definitely I Will Follow – that recording was one of the classic singles of that period. I don't know why it wasn't a hit because it has everything going for it. It's really something. I looked at the multi-track sheets the other day and whereas at this stage in order to get some more flexibility into the mixes we've gone to 48 tracks, I looked at the old track sheet and we only used half of a 24 track. The drums are on 6 tracks, one guitar track, two vocal tracks, bass track. That recording is really minimal, really simple and was done in a day, and mixed another half day. It was really uncomplicated and had a lot of energy ... a real instant thing.

WHAT ABOUT OCTOBER?

On October I like Tomorrow and Stranger in a Strange Land ... they're probably my two favourites. The only one that has survived in our stage set is October the piano song ... we gave up doing Gloria a year or so ago.

WAR?

On War I love Forty ... it is a great song. I have fond memories of being thrown out of the studio because we had to finish the song at the end of the session. It was literally a case of great inspiration at the eleventh hour.
We had this song which was about a five minute song and made up of various sections and we just edited the verses out of it and put all the bridges and choruses together and it became Forty. The verses have a different drumbeat: it was an attempt at a song with different rhythms in it. We just chopped up the offending section and stuck it together and then I just remember going in and doing some backing vocals and I think the melody came from another song. We had the verse melody but the chorus melody came from something else... it all went into the pot and came out like that. It was literally in a couple of hours that it was all put together.

I SUPPOSE YOU'D NEVER GET KICKED OUT OF STUDIOS THESE DAYS?

Well that's not true. We had to leave the studio quickly in LA recently!

ARE RECORDS LIKE OCTOBER AND WAR UNDERRATED CRITICALLY AND OVERLOOKED PUBLICALLY? BOY WOWED THE CRITICS, OCTOBER AND WAR ANNOYED THEM FOR DIFFERENT REASONS, AND UNFORGETTABLE FIRE WOOED THEM AGAIN. OCTOBER FOR EXAMPLE OFTEN SEEMS FORGOTTEN IN THE U2 CATALOGUE.

Yes. As a record a lot of people say 'My favourite album is October' but it sold less in America than any of the others – although in the UK it has outsold Boy. But people find it and they either love it or they don't. It's a side of U2 that we haven't really shown on any other record. It's kind of us with our backs so against the wall that we have to just take chances and release things that we're not fully sure about and work with lyrics that have been lost and so on.
There's a lot of anguish in that record, let's put it that way. At this stage I can laugh at it but at that stage it was not funny, getting that record together was do or die. It was literally a case of finishing the record and releasing it or else we folded financially.
And at that time Island Records were fantastic but they must have been saying to themselves: 'We put X amount of money into this band and the first album did OK – critically it did good but sales only OK – and they haven't had a hit ...' If we had defaulted on our schedules or cancelled the tour or whatever ... it would have been very difficult to come back.

DO YOU GET BORED NOW THAT YOU'RE OUT OF THE EYE OF THE HURRICANE OF TOUR, FILM AND RECORD? IS THERE A CULTURE SHOCK WHEN EVERYTHING STOPS? DOES IT TAKE DISCIPLINE TO GET UP IN THE

MORNING AND GET ON WITH THE NEXT PROJECT? IN OTHER WORDS HAVE YOU STILL GOT THE HUNGER?

Absolutely. And we're still thinking ahead. Instantly we finish one thing – almost before we finish it – we go on to the next thing. The two things on my mind right now are the tour of Australia, New Zealand and Japan in the autumn and the next record which we'll probably start to record in early 1990 although we'll have done quite a lot of work before we go on the road. So that's what my time is spent on.
But not having a short term purpose tends to open you up to other projects which are really not worth following up. I think getting bored would be a really good thing to do. The problem is there's a tendency for anyone who's really been busy for a long time – when you suddenly find you're not busy – to start finding things, a kind of workaholism.
There's so many things we're offered and when you're not doing anything they all sound interesting. But I don't want to do anything at the moment. This is an important time for us.

WHEN YOU GET TO AUSTRALIA AND NEW ZEALAND IN THE AUTUMN

IT WILL BE FIVE YEARS SINCE YOUR ONLY PREVIOUS TOUR THERE. DO YOU FEEL LIKE YOU OWE THEM ONE?
Well we owe it to ourselves to go to Australia because we know it's going to be great. The reason that we didn't go last time was because we knew it wouldn't have been great for us or the audience. So the time is right, I feel delighted that we can finally get down there. We loved every moment of our time down there on the Unforgettable Fire tour.

IF BLOOD RED SKY WAS END OF U2 PART 1, IS RATTLE AND HUM END OF U2 PART 2. IS IT A WATERSHED?
I'd like to think it was the end of U2's exploration of America but I honestly don't think it is. There's more there for us. I think there might be another record at least before we get into other things.

NOW THAT YOU'VE BEEN TO THE TOP ONE THING TO DO WOULD BE TO GO DOWN. BONO SAYS YOU TRIED TO LOSE A FEW FANS WITH RATTLE AND HUM BUT THEY STILL BOUGHT IN MILLIONS.
The record was a definite attempt at side-stepping. With Desire we felt that if we could establish the rock and roll single again or have a rock and roll single that was not going to please the DJs but be a real spanner in their playlists then that was a good thing for a big band to do. So few big bands take any risks – Prince seems to be the exception.
But we do and nobody seems to notice or care and to an extent, although we did it for ourselves, that surprised me … the fact that no-one else really noticed.

PRESUMABLY YOU'LL GO ON WITH THAT BECAUSE PART OF YOUR RESPONSIBILITY YOU'VE SAID IS TO TRY AND CHANGE THE MUSICAL ATMOSPHERE?
Well that's the only fun thing that a big band can do … mess around. The challenge is to mess around, let's throw another spanner in the works. The thing about being established is that people get very boring because the challenge is no longer achieving success – you have that – so what else turns you on? You have to invent challenges in a sense.

WHAT'S THE NEXT CHALLENGE?
Well the next record. I like Rattle and Hum and I like The Joshua Tree a lot – those two records in particular are my favourites – but I can see us doing much better work even than those two records. We still haven't done what we set out to achieve when we first formed the group. As we went along we saw further ahead what we could manage to do and we still haven't done all that.

THE TROUBLE WITH SUCCESS IS THAT YOU BECOME EMBRACED BY THE ESTABLISHMENT WHETHER IT'S THE MUSIC INDUSTRY IN AMERICA OR RADIO ONE IN THE UK.
Take Angel of Harlem for example. There was a lot of resistance to that record because it wasn't one thing or another. Was it a soul song or was it a rock and roll song or was it a pop song? What was it? In America the radio stations want something easy to define – if it's a rock song we'll play it on the album stations, if it's a pop song then we'll play it on the pop stations – if you give them a hybrid they all get very upset. It doesn't fit, it won't go anywhere. I enjoy that sensation – of puzzling people – and to he honest I think Angel of Harlem is probably the closest thing to a pop song that we'll ever do – I mean that in the positive sense of the word 'pop'.

DO YOU EVER THINK 'WHAT IF LARRY AND I HAD STAYED ON DOING SESSIONS WITH THE DRIFTING COWBOYS IN 1977?'
Well we weren't being offered a job at that stage and I don't think we were under any illusions. We were definitely journeymen or apprentices and these guys were like 40 years old and had been touring the country probably all their lives. We were just along for the ride. But the guy did say one thing to us, he said, 'There's no money in rock'n'roll but if you get together a collection of country cover versions in your band I can set you up with as many shows as you can play'. He said we could play 7 nights a week on the bookings they turned down.

TEMPTING?
No, to be honest. Country music right then was not something I was terribly interested in. At that moment I could think of nothing more interesting than Patti Smith and Television. I'm sure I'll run into that guy one of these days – he sold me my first electric guitar as well.

"The only fun thing that a big band can do is mess around. Let's throw a spanner in the works."

ANTON CORBIJN

ANTON CORBIJN is in more U2 photographs than anyone else except the band members themselves. You can't see him, of course, because he's behind the camera. He's the lensman that U2 return to time and again to capture them for press and posterity.

As well as many of the photos you see in magazines and newspapers, Anton, a Dutchman of 34 years standing, has shot U2 for four of the band's album covers: War; The Unforgettable Fire; The Joshua Tree *and* Rattle and Hum. *He has also been responsible for the bulk of material in tour programmes from* War *onwards.*

He takes pictures in black and white – at least he did until now. With the publication this spring of his first book, a high-quality and highly expensive collection of his music portraitures from 15 years of professional lensmanship, he ends his black and white era. He has gone colour. The book, which includes John Cale, Elvis Costello, Johnny Rotten, Ry Cooder, The Slits, David Bowie, and U2, is called Famouz *and opens with a photo of Anton himself, which he asked Bono to take. A neat reversal of roles. For this issue of* Propoganda *we asked Anton if he would choose his personal favourites from his U2 portfolio of thousands of photos from over a dozen photo sessions – some lasting three or four days. They appear over the next few pages along with his comments on why he likes them.*

Anton bought his first camera when he was 18 and went to an open-air concert to take his first snaps – black and white naturally. He was surprised to find them good enough for publication in a local Dutch music magazine. Photography had other merits for Anton too: "I was very shy as a teenager and until I had a camera I didn't even go to concerts on my own. But when I had a camera I felt like I could go to the front of the stage because I had this little excuse in my hand ... that's half the reason I got into photography." Over the years his love of music, which got him interested in photography, has developed into an obsession with photography itself. After attending photographic college in The Hague, he worked with another local photographer for just under a year before setting up on his own. Within three years he had exhausted all the bands he wanted to take pictures of in his home country and in 1979 decided

to move to England. He wanted pictures from the country that was giving the world everything from Joy Division – his favourite band at the time – to Elvis Costello. It was about this time that he took one of his most famous photographs by persuading the camera-shy Joy Division to let him work with them. One of the resultant photos captured the moment eerily: "I had this idea. They'd be in a tunnel with Ian Curtis looking the other way. One photo turned out to be the now-famous shot of Ian Curtis turning around to the camera as the rest of the band walk away ... when he died, half a year later, it looked like a prophecy." Appearing like a leisurely step up the ladder of success in retrospect, by that autumn Anton had persuaded the *NME* to let him cover his first concert for them – Bill Haley and The Comets at The Venue in London. "I was quite persistent, in fact I was in great demand pretty quickly." Following a much-praised photo-session with Joe

Jackson, within six months Anton was the main man at the music paper and shot about 20 of their cover stories in the next year, from David Bowie and Mick Jagger to Captain Beefheart and the Undertones.

"I used to have the people very low down in the frame, with the effect that you can jump in and join them. It could be because Holland's landscapes are very low." But most importantly for our story, through the *NME* he bumped into a young Irish band called U2.

"I had been asked by a Dutch magazine to take photos of U2 but declined because I thought they were a heavy metal band. I thought, no, I'm not going to do U2."

When the *NME* made the same request in the spring of '82 – with the extra incentive of a trip to New Orleans thrown in – he happily compromised. He also liked the band on meeting, even though their first gig was "a bit too rock 'n' roll" for him. U2 liked Anton too – and his camera work. Later that year they invited him to Sweden to do "the snow shot" on the inside sleeve of the *War* album. After that they just kept on inviting him.

Anton doubts if anyone has taken more pictures of the band, and is equally confident that he has taken more pictures of them than anyone else – if you see what we mean. "But," he adds, "I don't like being known as 'the U2 photographer' because I work with a lot of other people continuously."

Compared to many groups he works with, Anton says U2 are "very good but very demanding" – especially Bono. "He always wants to create new things but neither does he want to let old things go. But it's always pleasant to work with them, never unpleasant. They like to look good, like anyone else, but for public images they don't like

to be jokey either. We take quite a lot of photos where they are laughing but they don't get published – except occasionally, like the one I put in *The Unforgettable Fire* book and in the first tour programme taken in Sweden." Despite the impression from the published pictures of the band, Anton says that the photo-taking itself is not a particularly serious business, but because his work is serious and the band's music is serious, a serious end-result is not surprising. "But we do have a good time," he assures. "There is a lot of laughing going on despite the seriousness."

The creative ideas for the sessions are also a mixture of photographer and band. For example, the *Rattle and Hum* sleeve was the band's idea which Anton "merely executed for them", but *The Joshua Tree* sleeve was his. Although the individual members of the band are different (Adam: "Very interested in the results."; Larry: "Easily bored but easy to take."; Edge: "Always looks the same – that's why we've got him jumping on the recent single sleeve."; Bono: "Quite hard to photograph because he has so many different faces but is therefore my favourite."), Anton always strives to present the band as a group. "For me their approach is that of a group, even though people tend to make Bono more prominent because he is the singer. There is a great band feeling with U2 which I really like and the best pictures portray the band as this force standing there.

"Many other people approach me and ask me to do with them what I do with U2 – especially what we got around *The Joshua Tree* period – you can't of course. They are U2."

The book is an important milestone for Anton and he doesn't want it seen as just another collection of pop stars. "It's a photography book and they're all musicians – it's not a rock book."

With the publication of *Famouz* he begins a new era, still working in photography much of the time, but increasingly experimenting in colour and doing more and

more work with STATE, the video company he has begun with two partners. Apart from his well-known direction for bands like Echo and the Bunnymen (*Seven Seas*, *Bring on the Dancing Horses*) and Depeche Mode (*Museo Depeche Mode*), he has recently been working with less well-known European bands including The Rainbirds.

"I think because I'm foreign I listen to sounds more than words, so my videos are sometimes a bit surreal." Just as Anton has achieved a unique look in rock photography, so with video he is always experimenting – using Super-8s, for example, as he did with Depeche Mode. "I really believe in Super-8, not in the hand-held shaky way it's usually done but for its tone, for the way it makes people more realistic. You can't use glamour. I never liked glamour, it doesn't suit me."

Anton comments on his own U2 portfolio favourites.

LARRY – Sweden 1982.
"This is the day after the "New Year's Day" video-shooting. It's the first picture of him where I realized his great photo potential. He was not enough used to me by then to tell me to get on with it, but he was probably very bored when we took this shot."

U2 – CALIFORNIA 1986.
"One of the best groupshots I ever took, period. Their looks, the heat, the rounding-globe effect, the bloody tree – it has everything and more. I am very happy and proud of this photo and it brings back great memories as well. There is a great shot of The Band by Elliot Landy taken in the '60s where they are all standing in a line in a field, which I always have loved, and this shot has the same sort of feeling."

ADAM – Sweden 1985.
"We seem for some reason to end up in Sweden quite a lot and usually in the coldest months of the year unfortunately. This might have something to do with the snow I guess. Anyway, this is Adam during the Unforgettable Fire *video and it was my first work for four months (I had been ill) and with this shot I realised all was not lost (for me that is). Adam is hard to photograph, but always great company and it's very rewarding to get a good photo of him."*

EDGE – Los Angeles 1987. *"Can't really say why I picked this shot of Edge – I have quite a lot of good photos of him, but somehow I never printed this one and it strikes me looking at it that Edge is probably the only one I could imagine living on a rooftop and thinking nothing bizarre of it."*

U2 – San Francisco 1988. *"With this photo I wanted to create the feeling of a great liveband off stage – the rawness of it and the night-feeling most of the live concerts have, of course. It was done to coincide with the Rattle & Hum album and we spent two days in SF – great town for photos. By minimalizing content (I actually use this 'method' often) you get usually a stronger sense of content. You can tell that this photo was taken in the US for instance."*

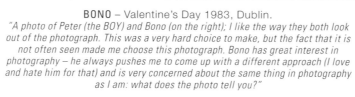

BONO – Valentine's Day 1983, Dublin.
"A photo of Peter (the BOY) and Bono (on the right); I like the way they both look
out of the photograph. This was a very hard choice to make, but the fact that it is
not often seen made me choose this photograph. Bono has great interest in
photography – he always pushes me to come up with a different approach (I love
and hate him for that) and is very concerned about the same thing in photography
as I am: what does the photo tell you?"

THE EARLY DAYS

This autumn sees the publication of a new book recording the very earliest Dublin days of U2. Bill Graham, a senior writer with the Irish rock magazine Hot Press, is the author of U2, The Early Days – Another Time Another Place (Mandarin £3.99 (UK.), $9.95 (Aus), $12.95 (NZ). Graham was captivated by the fledgeling group in their very earliest incarnations in the late '70s and it was he who introduced them to Paul McGuinness, their manager ever since. The book is humbly described as "A biographical sketch in words and pictures". Bill Graham has been in consultation with the band as the book has progressed and here we reproduce an early section from his story.

Dublin, 26 February 1980. U2 are playing the National Stadium to an admiring throng of friends and fans. Bono proudly introduces "Another Day", their second single for CBS Ireland, predicting, "It won't be out on the CBS label for long. I can tell you that story."

He isn't glibly boasting. Bono knows, you see. He knows that among the 1,200 at the Stadium is an aristocratically mannered Englishman, Bill Stewart, head of A&R at Island, and he's about to sign U2. It didn't matter much that Island would eventually pass on "Another Day" and open U2's account with the Martin Hannett-produced "11 O'Clock Tick Tock". Bono's speaking the symbolic truth. U2 have cracked it. They've finally won a serious long-term recording contract – that Holy Grail that had eluded most of their Irish contemporaries.

Theirs has also been a most precocious success. Except for Adam Clayton, U2's members are still in their teens. Two years ago, Larry Mullen and the Edge were still students at Mount Temple, while Bono was finishing an extra school year to get the Irish-language qualification that would allow him to enter

university. In these two intervening years, U2 have passed all their local tests. They've established the basics of a unique style, founded on Bono's theatrical presentation and the Edge's ringing guitar. They've also found an ambitious and equally astute manager in Paul McGuinness and a more sizeable, committed audience than any of their Dublin contemporaries – victories won against local apathy and even some enmity.

So U2 can celebrate on this Tuesday night. And not just because of Bill Stewart's presence inviting them to Island. Young, unsigned Irish bands aren't meant to play the National Stadium. It's for securely popular acts – traditional music institutions like the Chieftains or the Bothy Band, or country artists like Emmylou Harris or Merle Haggard if they're passing through town. Yet here are U2, proclaiming their party, welcoming their 1,200 to the Stadium, showing they count in Dublin. Two months away from his twentieth birthday, Bono takes a step back from the microphone and then speaks, mingling his pride with late teenage, adolescent awe: "We're here in the Stadium. Big lights, big record-player – the whole beans."

So, tonight, U2 can conduct their own city's symphony. Before "Shadows and Tall Trees" – the tall trees, those slim amber streetlamps that lay their spectral lights and shadows on the night-life hopes of Dublin youth – Bono will comment, "Dim the lights, we feel embarrassed," and then try out a tin whistle for a few callow, squirting phrases. On "A Day Without Me", later to be their second Island single, he injects a couplet about his girlfriend and future wife, Alison Stewart: "If Alison's dreaming, what's at stake?" His vocals aren't yet polished. On "Stories For Boys" he's almost a Bowie soundalike, as if the laughing gnome had lodged in his throat. But mostly, there's a straining breathlessness, as if he's gulping at experiences that can be neither swallowed nor digested.

At the Stadium, U2 are still self-consciously and intentionally juvenile. But not juvenile delinquents. This is a band who have diverged from punk's bad-boy and bad-girl models. Bono prefers to play the Fool – incidentally the title of an early and unrecorded U2 song – a role he claims is borrowed from studying Shakespeare at school. Bono's Fool plays up to and with adolescent confusion, scurrying around the stage on

U2
THE EARLY DAYS

"Boy/Girl" like a hyperactive and over-impressionable manikin on his first date. For U2 are a strange paradox: they're actually confessing to and using uncoolness, vulnerability and insecurity as artistic devices when nearly all their contemporaries slap on a mask.

A paradox that had already confused many, it would continue to do so through so much of U2's career. They had reversed the terms. Other bands – and not only in Ireland – would cultivate images of poise and control and then be outmanoeuvred by the music business. Yet U2, and especially Bono, who never feared to play the gauche Fool, would retain control where it counted and rarely be outplayed.

Yet coupled with their feeling of triumph that night, their sense of achievement in convincing both Island's Bill Stewart and the other 1,200 in the Stadium, there was a deep sigh of relief. For U2's first two years involved an audacious gamble in their determination to design their career as they desired. The U2 paradox of being oddly normal had made them controversial creatures, a band who had both divided their own home scene in Dublin and generated no small degree of incomprehension in the British record companies that had first hoped and then hesitated to sign them. Instinctively and incurably romantic and utopian, U2 had gone against the grain of those punk attitudes that, by 1980, were hardening into marginalization and antisocial cynicism. Or – that paradox again – as Bono confessed, introducing another unrecorded song and most consciously echoing John Lennon, "The Dream Is Over". Yet if, like the hippie dream Lennon had lamented, the punk fantasy was now over, U2's own romance was only just beginning. They had bypassed their Dublin competitors. Through the '80s, they would gradually overhaul and then outpace all but a handful of their UK counterparts. It is highly arguable that their early isolated Irish experiences both hardened U2 and gave them the hunger for the task. By their genes, by their early

essential bloodings, ye shall know a band. U2 were born into a scene that was a blank slate, and they had the bravado and instinctive insight to scrawl their own signature on the board. They found their own fulfilment by recognizing that they weren't tied by rigid expectations of what rock should or shouldn't be. Beginning in a backwater, U2 would redefine Ireland's often incoherent aspirations.

Outside Ireland, U2 would initially be viewed as another post-punk provincial prodigy regularly associated with Simple Minds and Echo and the Bunnymen to the latter's oft-quoted dismay. And from the same vantage point, the pre-punk Dublin of '76 would have seemed little different from any lacklustre provincial British city, where lethargic hippie survivors shuffled round a limited pub circuit, its musos the remnants of yet another scene that the London A&R men would have forgotten but for the fact that they had hardly bothered to notice it in the first place.

Yet, in many respects, Dublin had more in common with Continental European cities, closer in its lack of amenities and its patchwork rock tradition to Antwerp or Helsinki than Aberdeen or Cardiff. Like those Continental cities, the summit of pop ambition was victory at the annual Eurovision Song Contest. The light-entertainment values that had been routed in Britain since the mid '60s still held sway over rock. Typically, until a network of pirate radio stations emerged in '77, there wasn't even a national pop radio channel.

After all, I introduced them to their manager and spent a month's campaign of persuasion, often over bottles of cheap red Burgundy in a Dublin night-club called Pierre's, laying siege to an initially sceptical Paul McGuinness.

But actually I can't remember that first date. I can recall how, when and why I first met them – another matter entirely – but my first three or four dates with U2 are now a blur, a jumble of impressions from all those shows.

Later Bono would talk of U2 using "the primary colours". of rock in their classic four-man line-up, and the basic elements were there from the start. Whereas in the spring of '78 every other young Dublin guitarist was still trying to emulate the pneumatic-drill rhythm style of punk, the Edge even then preferred bursts of quicksilver chiming melody. And Bono already had an insatiable compulsion to communicate. Totally unable to freeze into any studied pose, he could be jabberingly eager, always likely to overrun a verse or chorus and destroy the other's cues and timing with some spontaneous vocal or stage stunt. Through Bono, U2 rejected rock's manneredness. Never afraid to look flustered or foolish – in many ways, the worst crime in the book of rules – Bono was reversing rock's ideas of sophistication. Later he would conceive of himself as "an offering to the audience" and he already had the ability to rivet their attention. Of course, with that magnetism there were many mistakes. But Bono learned to use them; he rarely repeated the same error.

Very soon, I started to bore everyone, my colleagues at Hot Press and other Dublin musicians, with my praise for the band. In time, people in Dublin would tell me I discovered U2. Untrue, since there are many more with a right to that claim: Steve Averill, Jackie Hayden, Dave McCullough, Chris Westwood, Rob Partridge, Annie Roseberry and Bill Stewart, to name only the most prominent. Or Chas De Whalley, Charlie Eyre and Tom Nolan, and the A&R scouts who tried and failed to sign U2 to respectively CBS, A&M, and EMI. The real truth is one every successful band knows – U2 were always rather skilled at discovering people to discover them!

They needed that persistence and persuasiveness in a scene with limited opportunities. Early U2 can't be understood without a detailed examination of their Irish background. For even the punk rebellion would have its own peculiarly ambiguous meanings specific to Ireland alone.

ADAM

TALKS

It's summer and everybody in U2 is off on holiday. When they return preparations will begin in earnest for the autumn tour of Australia, New Zealand, the Far East and a clutch of European dates. Unlike Larry, Edge and Bono, Adam has decided to stay at home in Dublin for the break, having been away to both the US and Australia in the months since Rattle and Hum was released.

It was November '88 when the band were last in the public eye and Adam rehearses his diary as something like this: "Most of November was taken up attending premieres and meeting people; then there was the album release and all that boring stuff like photo sessions and meeting people; in January and February we really got into B-sides with the intention of coming up with some new songs but in fact we recorded some cover versions; I don't know what happened to the rest of the year. There's always something going on but we haven't been touring, have we? ... er, Smile Jamaica ... was that January? ... no, that was October ... oh, videos like "All I Want Is You" – that was another month ... it seems like we've been in the studio or rehearsing every day since ..."

When U2 are off the road, or not making an album, they cannot close down completely. If it's not business as usual, it is business as unusual. Sitting in the boardroom of the band's Windmill Lane offices Adam tries – unsuccessfully – to describe a 'normal day': "You start the day by opening the mail and then you gradually get into making phone calls; then around two in the afternoon you start rehearsing ... er ..." His voice trails away. Well, good try, but the problem is that U2 is not exactly a 9–5 job and there are few 'normal' days. There are constant factors, though: "The phone rings every five minutes – 'Do you want to do this ... Do you want to do that?' The requests range

from 'Can you meet me for lunch?' to 'Can you open my supermarket?' and it's incredibly confusing because we're not heads of state, we're businessmen, we're musicians. None of us wants all that crap but it's there the minute you open your door. Although you just want to be left alone ... to play your guitar in your bedroom the way you used to ... suddenly there's all these people demanding bits of you and in the end I just say 'No' to pretty much everything." Unfortunately, he laughs, "Even saying no to everything takes up most of your time ... it's a ridiculous situation to find yourself in."

Which is why the opportunity U2's position now gives them to make music at their leisure and continue their exploration of other kinds of music is so important. At the turn of the year, as Edge described in PROPAGANDA 10, the band recorded perhaps 10 different cover versions for possible use as B-sides, some of which – like "Everlasting Love" and "Unchained Melody" – have already seen the light of day, others of which may never. "Some just didn't work," explained Adam. "It wasn't right for us to do some of them. Like the old Creedence number "Fortunate Son" – it was a great idea as it refers to the draft-dodgers in Vietnam, the Senators' sons avoiding the draft. When we looked at it, it was in the middle of the Senator Dan Quayle controversy but that soon passed and it didn't work when we'd finished it. "Another song was that Bruce Cockburn song, 'If I Had a Rocket Launcher', which again is great when Bruce Cockburn does it but it just doesn't happen for us." Relaxed and eagerly anticipating his holiday, he says the direction of the next album is completely unpredictable ("Bono will change his mind from one end of the day to the next so it's best to wait until you hear a positive noise on what's happening") but says that "God Part II" hints, for him, at the direction they're heading towards. "It's a fresh sound, not that clichéd rock 'n' roll sound."

He cites his favourite U2 songs as "Love Comes Tumbling" ("a great melancholy tune and very simple") and his favourite memories as filming "Under a Blood Red Sky" ("pretty hectic, it felt like the end of the world") and "Getting back from America after the October tour when we couldn't pay the crew." He claims to have vivid memories of touring round Europe in the back of a VW van in the early '80s but says that he does not miss it.

And with the conveniences of home and familiar surroundings, Adam has also been keeping his ear to the ground and catching up on listening to music – of all kinds. He's been listening to the new Neneh Cherry record, to Van Morrison's "Avalon Sunset" – "But I'm always listening to him so it doesn't really count" – to The Pixies and The Triffids, to traditional Irish sessions music and to African music. "I don't like anyone new at the moment unless they're rap. NWA is something I've just come across – a tape given to me by Chris Blackwell, which is the heaviest black New York rap, and if there was censorship there'd be bleeps all the way through but it's got a good attitude."

SO HOW DOES THE BASS PLAYER IN U2 COPE WITH THE DEMANDS OF OPENING NEW SHOPPING CENTRES? HOW DO YOU TAKE TIME OFF?

I get to enjoy a lot of music. I was down at a session in Galway a couple of weeks ago with Sharon Shannon, who is the accordion player in The Waterboys, Philip King, a traditional singer here, and some others, and we were just down in this hotel for three days of music and late nights. People just got on with the music in this small room and that is my idea of fun. A couple of weekends ago I went to the Glastonbury Festival, which was good fun, and did a number with The Flowers, which was great – very, very good.

HOW DID THAT COME ABOUT?

The Flowers were playing there and just said, "Look, come over with a bunch of people," and we did. The first night I slept on the floor of one of The Flowers' rooms, and the second night it was so much hassle to leave the field that I just slept in the field. A couple of days into Glastonbury they said, "Do you want to do a number?" I couldn't really refuse. There wasn't a lot of new talent around, although I enjoyed established acts like Elvis Costello and The Waterboys. It was very relaxed. And I really enjoyed playing the song with The Flowers.

HOW DID YOU ENJOY THE DOMINION GIG?

Loved it. That was fun – that was rock and roll. A great, great night.

WHAT ABOUT TRAVELING – YOU SEEM TO DO A BIT?

I went to Australia earlier in the year to see a friend. I also shot off to the US for 10 days with Bono to drive from LA to New Orleans after the premieres last year. That was great fun, except what we didn't realize was that the radio knew where we were going – typical American stuff. We were arriving in these towns wondering how the hell did they know that we were around. We'd check into a hotel on the edge of town and decide to go into town for a quiet drink and there'd be all these people who'd know we were there. After three or four days of travelling and the same thing happening someone finally admitted that the radio stations were linking up and transmitting the information because you bump into people and you tell them what you're doing and they were transmitting across the country what we were doing.

SO YOU WERE INCOGNITO BUT YOU WEREN'T IN FACT?

You can't be incognito with Bono.

CAN YOU BE INCOGNITO ON YOUR OWN?

No problem (laughs).

HOW DO YOU GET AROUND AT HOME IN DUBLIN WITHOUT INTERRUPTION?

Well, you have to be careful, to pick the right time. For example, you don't want to go shopping after school's out in the afternoon. It's like rush hour – you avoid it if you can.

WHAT ABOUT AUSTRALIA?

There I stayed with a friend of mine who is building himself a house at the moment but suspended building while I was there. Digging the foundations he suddenly hit the rock and he had to get a rock-breaker. The rock-breaker cost the same amount of money that it was for studio time, which really blew my mind – I think studio time is about £150 an hour and this rock-breaker is also £150 an hour. It took four days to dig through this rock.

YOU'VE BEEN TO AUSTRALIA A FEW TIMES?

Yes, I like it, I like the people. It's a long long way from Europe and America so you get a very, very different feeling and it's a very, very old land. That spirit of survival and pioneering is still very much here. In America the land has been conquered by the white man, but in Australia it's not really like that. Man exists on the land … you can go to places and you could be the first person walking there since the Creation or whatever. Also if you build there you literally have to build yourself – there's no such thing as plumbed water, everyone collects rainwater … just things like that. I like the spirit of the people, which is very much about preservation.

ARE YOU LOOKING FORWARD TO TOURING AUSTRALIA?

Yes it was fairly crazy in '84, but this time around I suppose it will be the same because we're not really playing that many more shows.

ON TOUR IS ONE PLACE VERY MUCH LIKE ANOTHER BECAUSE THERE'S NO TIME TO TAKE THEM IN?

Each place is like a hotel room to a stage to a limo to a hotel room to a stage. We build in time-off sometimes but you can't get in and out of a hotel without bodyguards, which is stupid … being in Australia will be nice.

DOES TOURING GET YOU DOWN AFTER A WHILE?

I sort of like touring. I think that the piss-off about it is that you do put a great deal of effort into trying to produce a great show and play good songs and at the end of the day it appears to be so unimportant in terms of the way people perceive it.

SO YOU CAN DO THE GREATEST SHOW YOU'VE EVER DONE AND SOMETIMES PEOPLE DON'T APPRECIATE IT AS MUCH AS SEEING YOU OR TOUCHING YOU?

Yes, it's very much a personal appearance.

DID THE LAST TOUR EXHAUST YOU?

Yeah, it was a bitch.

IS BEING IN U2 A DIFFERENT LEVEL OF INTENSITY WHEN YOU'RE OFF THE ROAD?

It never goes away. People always want something. It's a bit like being a parent – certainly since the '80s. I'm looking forward to the tour but I always know it's a case of grin and bear it.

DO YOU EVER FEEL SLIGHTLY FRIGHTENED BY GOING OUT IN FRONT OF 25,000 PEOPLE?

I don't mind those big places.

I'd much rather have fled the country and lived in the middle of the bush or something like that.

YOU'VE MENTIONED THAT YOU'RE ATTACHED TO PLAYING SMALL CLUBS?
I've love to play in small clubs, and practically it is possible … just plug in like we did at the film premieres. It helps if you play places that are off the regular trail. But for the moment it may be that we don't really want to.

ARE THE DALTONS STILL AROUND … HAVE YOU SEEN BETTY LATELY?
Yes, she's still around, she's doing well.

IS SHE GOING TO AUSTRALIA?
I don't know. She'd have awful problems with the heat there. She doesn't like travelling too far north of Atlanta – then it's kind of Philistine territory – and she doesn't like going too far south either. She's a homebird really. I don't think Australians will see her because it's a long trip and it'd really take the stuffing out of her.

WHAT ABOUT WHEN YOU'RE OFF THE ROAD – IF LARRY IS DOING MOTHER, FOR EXAMPLE, WHAT DO YOU GET UP TO?
I never particularly like to claim responsibility. I'm just willing to do other things. It just seems that U2 takes up an awful lot of energy. I do go off and play sometimes but it's difficult.

IF THERE WAS A LOCAL IRISH TRADITIONAL BAND WHO ASKED YOU TO GO OFF AND PLAY WITH THEM THREE NIGHTS A WEEK, WOULD THAT APPEAL?
Yeah, that would.

WHAT DON'T YOU LIKE ABOUT YOUR JOB IN U2?
I don't like meetings. You have to be a sort of businessman at this stage and sign cheques and all that sort of stuff and I hate that side of it. Have the meetings round the pub!

IF IT HADN'T COME TOGETHER IN 1978 WHAT DO YOU IMAGINE YOU'D BE DOING NOW?
I don't really know, it's so impossible to say. I'm sure I'd have probably dropped out somewhere, I wouldn't

particularly have liked to have been a part of any system or society – having a job and each year improving your circumstances or whatever. I'd much rather have fled the country and lived in the middle of the bush or something like that.

SO U2 RESCUED YOU FROM THOSE EARLY DAYS WHERE YOU ARE PICTURED IN AFGHAN COATS?
No, I gave it up, I sold my Afghan coat for a bass guitar. Who knows? I may have gone into a more arty thing – I could just as easily have turned right at Greenland, if you like, and gone into a real artsy-fartsy thing.

ROCK 'N' ROLL IS MAXIMIZE, MAXIMIZE?
That's what seems to happen. The challenge is how big can it get? I'd love to go in and do a record in two weeks and put it out like The Cowboy Junkies have just done with *Trinity Sessions* after one day. But you have to be brave and I don't know if U2 could do it because it would be just so confusing for the public. They wouldn't know what the hell was going on. It would be great in a way – but in another way, *Rattle and Hum* was meant to be that – in terms of the simplicity of it – and it's irritating that people don't seem to have realized that. They've judged it as a proper studio album, which it wasn't. If you view it as a bonus you can't beat it.

DID THE '80s BELONG TO U2?
Maybe, but what about Prince, Madonna … it must be Madonna that typifies the '80s. But for bands it may be true of us.

DID THE THOUGHT EVER OCCUR TO YOU AT THE BEGINNING OF THE '80s THAT THIS WOULD BE THE CASE?
A lot of it was punk and nobody could really see much beyond that. With the first club tours of England it was great but when we got to America and started to spend long periods of time there it became much more a case of getting our heads down

and working out that we could go all the way. For me it crystallized gradually but I always thought there was no point doing it unless we could go the whole way – but I didn't know what that was. Also being Irish made us different. What's happened in the Irish music scene since we started out is great. There is an infrastructure and there are Irish bands producing records all the time. It just wasn't so when we started out and it's very satisfying – much more so than maybe a lot of the other stuff people feel we ought to be pleased about. The fact that there's a real industry and people don't have to go away to England – that's exciting.

WHAT AMBITIONS DO YOU HAVE IN THE GROUP AT THIS STAGE?
To grow old gracefully is the only option left. It's important that we don't get into the old rock star syndrome.

DO YOU HAVE ANY REGRETS FROM THE SUCCESS OF U2 TO DATE – LIKE EAMONN DUNPHY'S BOOK, FOR EXAMPLE?
Not really because whoever writes your book, you're not going to agree completely because it's not your story. Everybody knew we didn't write the book, everybody knew they were buying Eamonn Dunphy's version of it.

IS THIS WHY THE BAND HAVEN'T GIVEN PERMISSION FOR SOUNDTRACKS TO ADVERTS OR ACCEPTED SPONSORSHIP UNLIKE MANY OTHER GROUPS?
We just ignore most requests

because fortunately we don't need the money, which means we can stick with the principle. Having been successful you don't have to prostitute yourself like that. This commercialization is the changing face of the music business and it will become harder and harder for new talent to break through.

VAN MORRISON IS ONE WHO HAS GRADUATED GRACEFULLY – HE'S JUST A MUSICIAN
His interview in the *NME* recently was interesting because he was saying at one period he was getting so much hype and expectations from the papers that he suddenly lost contact with the music, and there were all

these bigger responsibilities being placed on him that he didn't want and that really got in the way of his creativity. That was when he dropped out for a while – that's an interesting point.
I think the same thing is happening these days: I find it quite shocking the level of commercialization that happens to music. Every advert is music, the glossy magazines, the clothes that people wear on *Top of the Pops* – it's all directed at youth culture and an exploitation of it. I think that *Smash Hits* and *Number One*

> To grow old gracefully is the only option left. It's important that we don't get into the old rock star syndrome.

are as much a part of it as record companies. It's a blatant exploitation.

You have more time for the best fanzines – you bumped into the *Prattle and Fun* editorial team recently?

I met them outside here. I really like *Prattle and Fun*. It's a bit of a laugh. It's not the 'irreverence' that's amusing but that they obviously seem to understand the people in the band, which I like. I like it when people understand where you're at, and they do, and they're giving back something, which is nice.

GENERALLY FANZINES CAN TEND TO BE SLIGHTLY DEVOTIONAL

Yes, they can be horrible in that sense. I read them if they have insights and if they're fun, which is what *Prattle and Fun* is – A.D.A.M. too. The more sycophantic ones I don't really bother with. They don't interest me, but I'm sure some people enjoy them. But as for the music press themselves, in many ways they have destroyed the

I just want to be able to walk into a pub, have somebody buy me a drink and sit down and have a chat

mystique and power of music and made it into something that seems to go quite naturally into this tabloid format – *MM* and *NME* are grooming acts who will then go in the glossies and then into the popular press. And what they have managed to destroy is any rootsy cult bands after the first couple of features they have done.

I read less and less of the press about the band, unless we've just released a record. What I call music and musicians I see getting so separate from the entertainment business now. The entertainment business is videos and TV, and all that glitz and glamour, but musicians are about something else – about communications, about feelings, emotions ... not about entertainment only.

WAS IT A DISAPPOINTMENT THAT THE FILM DIDN'T ATTRACT THAT GREAT AUDIENCES AFTER THE INITIAL RUSH?

Again that's a funny thing because we deliberately tried to put the brake on the hyping of that film. Once you get into the world of movies you can spend weeks just promoting a

film, going to interviews, TV shows and premieres for its release to give it a big build up. But we said that we're not doing public appearances, we're going to the premieres and that's it – any other hype you can sort out yourselves. This is because it was a musical film and people could go and see it for the music and that was it – we didn't care whether it grossed £30 million or whatever the figures were – and we got out of that reasonably intact. We just wanted to make a great film that we could be proud of in 10 or 20 years' time and that's what we did, and we made a record as well. But we weren't going to hype it up as the greatest rock 'n' roll film ever.

SO WHAT'S YOUR PERSONAL AMBITION NOW?

I just want to be able to walk into a pub, have somebody buy me a drink and sit down and have a chat – because that's the hardest thing in the world to achieve. It's really that simple.

ADAM TALKS

Bringing it all back home

For the U2 Love Comes To Town Tour Programme, the band commissioned Niall Stokes, editor of Irish rock magazine Hot Press, to sum up something of their musical journey over the decade that brought them to BB King and Love Town. As the vast majority of Propaganda readers are in the US and UK, which the Love Town Tour couldn't visit, here we reproduce the article that set the scene for the tour.

Ten years ago, as the first U2 three-track 12-inch single hit the shops in Dublin, only the most visionary pundit could have foreseen the emergence of the theme which inspires the band's 1989 tour. Back then, the world of rock 'n' roll was divided ostensibly on a strict them-and-us basis, with the emerging breed of young musicians rolling in on the high tide of the new-wave boom, conspicuously kicking out the jams and rejecting the legacy of the previous 20-odd years of music, since Elvis Presley's genius was first captured on tape by Sam Philips in Sun Studios, all the way down in Memphis, in the southern states of the US of A, in 1956.

On the surface U2 might have seemed to fit that prescription. Exuding the kind of freshness, vitality and originality towards which many of their contemporaries could only aspire, they were singular in their style and approach and determined to do it their own way, learning their craft and their instruments on the run, and casting scarcely a reflective glance over the weight of rock 'n' roll tradition, or the roots music from which the beast had been spawned, as they went.

In the closing years of the '70s, among the majority of young musicians, gospel, soul, country and blues were seen as the musics of another time, another place, another culture. For white urban rock 'n' rollers the imperative seemed clear: to create a noise that expressed the frustration, the anger and the alienation they felt, not just in relation to establishment values in general, but about the music business and what it had become in particular. Punk and the 'new wave' that followed was seen as a fresh start, rock 'n' roll reinventing itself by rediscovering the garage band ethic – but in that headlong, speed-accelerated rush to capture the spirit of the hour, perspectives were too often distorted, with the vast and inter-related traditions of popular music, roots music and rock 'n' roll being neglected, forgotten and ignored. It was just one of the reasons why, in the long run, punk became a cul-de-sac for so many, and the majority of even the most promising and prominent bands of the time were destined ultimately to self-destruct.

To those who knew them, even at the time of the release of their exhilarating first single, U2 distinguished themselves from their contemporaries in their sense of open-mindedness and curiosity. Rather than presuming that they knew it all, they wanted to learn. Rather than relying on hearsay and prejudice, they wanted to really know. It took some time – but it should have come as no great surprise when that curiosity manifested itself in a desire to dig back into the music's past, to seek out, understand and encompass the variety of strands that make rock 'n' roll the vibrant and powerful form which it has undeniably become.

The fascination was first articulated when Bono reflected publicly on the role acoustic instruments might have in meeting the challenge which music would inevitably face in a technologically transformed world. "I was watching *Blade Runner,* which seemed to be set some place where Los Angeles meets Tokyo towards the turn of the century," he told *Hot Press* in 1983, "but somehow the Vangelis soundtrack didn't click, somehow I could image an ethnic soundtrack being more suitable. I remember thinking about the fact that people wouldn't want pure electronic music in the '90s – who wants electronic music in an electronic age? There's a humanity that's needed and the music of the '90s, I believe, will encompass ethnic sounds, cajun, reggae, Irish, blues or hybrids that would be a merger between the available technology and ethnic sounds."

Once the issue had been identified, however, the band's appetite for induction became almost insatiable. In Robbie Robertson's timeless phrase, U2 had caught the fever. And, inevitably, the search for the essence took them to the States, where blues, folk, gospel, country and soul influences mingle and intertwine in the most magnificently rich musical tapestry on planet earth.

From *The Unforgettable Fire* through *The Joshua Tree* to *Rattle And Hum*, the band's grasp of the roots was becoming firmer, their capacity to incorporate and transform them through their music more sure. It was a measure of just how far U2 had travelled on their journey to the heart of rock 'n' roll that *Rattle And Hum* could itself bring the various strands of rhythm 'n' blues, gospel, folk, country and rock 'n' roll together with such complete command. There is, of course, a degree of irony in an Irish band travelling to America to discover these roots. African sounds have had a significant influence on the pulse of American music, and flavours have crept up from the Caribbean too. But among the major sources of all those strands that would ultimately be reunited in rock 'n' roll is European folk music and within that configuration the strongest influence was undoubtedly Gaelic, including Welsh, Scottish and – predominantly – Irish elements.

During the 19th century, as the continent of North America was being opened up, thousands poured out of famine-stricken Ireland, a deprived and oppressed people seeking a new promised land where the crushed dream of freedom, independence and dignity might finally be more fully realized. They took with them little in the way of possessions – but in their hearts they carried a torch for one of the greatest motherlodes of musical magic in the known world, in the songs, ballads, and ceili and dance music of the home country.

In what was to become the melting pot of the United States, that music was absorbed, integrated and re-made, its melodic strength being paralleled in country and western, its highstepping in cajun and its sorrow in the blues. And thus, in a sense, U2 have travelled deep into the heart of America, only to find themselves musically closer to home than they'd ever previously been. The question is often asked: Can a white man sing the blues? In a sense, for U2 fans, *Rattle And Hum* settled that debate once and for all, underlining as it does just how short a step it is from the transportation ballad, written and sung by the Edge, "Van Dieman's Land" (a song of particular relevance to Australian audiences, themselves based in a land where dispossessed Irish were also destined to find themselves), to a country-blues-like "Love Rescue Me", and on to the triumphant electric blues-power of "When Loves Comes To Town."

Sometimes you have to look backwards to move forward. Every now and then we all need to check where we're coming from to know where

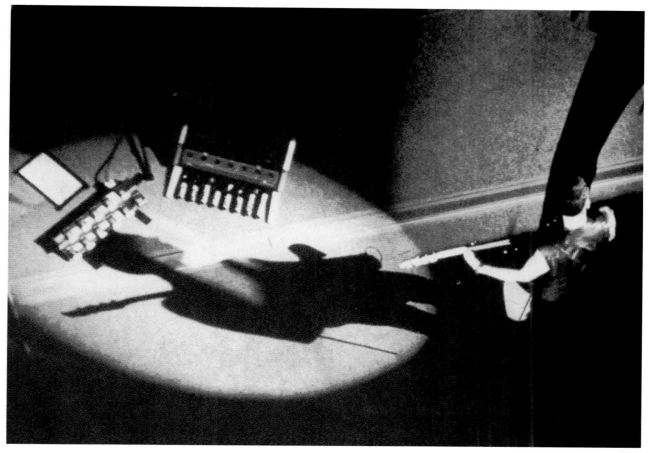

we're aiming to go. U2's search for musical roots, however, has gone beyond any mere national or geographic considerations. It's become a quest to preserve what was once defined as the true spirit of rock 'n' roll.

"Music's become too scientific," Edge told *Hot Press* on the launch of *Rattle And Hum*. "It's lost that spark and energy that it had in the '50s and '60s. When I listen to most modern records I hear a producer, I don't hear musicians interacting, and that quality – that missing quality – is something we were trying to get back to in our own music." And so U2 travelled down the Mississippi to the cradle of rock 'n' roll, in Studios in Memphis, to record some of *Rattle And Hum's* most potent music.

"You go into the Sun room and it's a modest studio," Adam says. "It's got the old acoustic tiles on the wall, and the pictures of Elvis and Roy Orbison and Jerry Lee and Carl Perkins – it's just history. You don't take a lot of technology into a studio like that – just the smallest amount of equipment you can do with. And you try to get back to the feeling of making rock 'n' roll without having huge banks of Marshalls or whatever.

Just strip it back and play the simplest thing you can."

It's history but it's also humanity. It's four guys and some cohorts in a studio making raw, powerful, spontaneous music to the best of their ability – and refusing to tart it up afterwards in the way that so many rock 'n' roll records have been in the '80s. It's music made for the hell of it – the spirit, the emotion, the message taking precedence over the pseudo-sophistications of the medium.

And what cohorts! Bob Dylan on "Love Rescue Me", the Memphis Horns on the magnificent "Angel Of Harlem" – and on "When Love Comes To Town" the greatest blues guitarist of them all, BB King. "We thought: we have this thing U2. Now let's put it aside, almost, and let's get lost in this music," Bono explained to *Hot Press* ...

"We were in there as apprentices – it was quite obvious. You only have to see the movie to see the look on my face of sheer embarrassment talking to BB King, sitting next to this great blues man".

But the master paid his own compliment to the apprentice, commenting on the power of the song's "heavy" lyrics and expressing his astonishment that they could have

been written by so young a songwriter: *"I used to make love under a red sunset, I was making promises I was soon to forget. She was pale to the lace on her wedding gown, But I left her standing before love came to town."*

He had a point.

Can a white man sing the blues? As BB King would doubtless be the first to acknowledge, no one race, creed or colour has a patent on the trials, tribulations, heartbreak and pain that run like a powerful seam through the human condition. No one, black, white, brown, yellow or red has a monopoly on the experience of being marginalized, dispossessed, alienated and oppressed.

The Irish in Ireland, the Aborigines in Australia, the Red Indians in America, the Blacks in South Africa, the Palestinians in the occupied territories, the Mothers of the Disappeared in Argentina – at one time or another we all have felt that same feeling of powerlessness in the face of a dominant culture and we have turned, if not always then at least often, to music to express our sorrow, our anger, our defiance ... and our pride. We are all in this together.

THE LOVE TOWN TOUR

" *I think we'll all look back on LoveTown with affection,*" said Bono when it was over. "*I think it'll seem like an eccentric kind of a tour, which we did just because we wanted to. It didn't make much sense, it was a lot of fun and it's absolutely nothing to do with where we're headed next ...*"

U2's lighting director, Peter Williams, spent the LoveTown Tour not only cueing his spotoperators and conducting the stage-lights but also making notes for *Propaganda*. Here we carry his own unique spy-on-the-wall review of the tour, from BB King's 64th birthday party in Sydney Harbour to New Year's Eve and 700 million listeners.

*I*t had been five years since U2 played in Australia, so there was a lot of catching up to do. Consequently the band spent over two months there, performing 23 concerts, to kick off the LoveTown tour.
Full production rehearsals began at the beginning of September in Sydney's Homebush Sports Centre. This followed many weeks of band rehearsals back at home in Dublin, working through U2's large repertoire, making decisions as to what songs to try in the live show this time out; which new ones will work best, which old ones should stay and which should go. The first three shows were in Perth, Western Australia. They were the first full U2 shows anywhere for nearly two years, so understandably there was a good deal of anticipation all round. The song to open the tour was "Hawkmoon 269" – something of a lateral choice for an opener, particularly when performed in almost total darkness, but it was clear this was going to be something new, not merely an extension of the *Joshua Tree* Tour.
It was also clear that the Australian audiences were more than ready to see U2. Tickets for all the concerts sold out almost instantly, and the crowd response was extremely enthusiastic to say the very least. After Perth came Sydney, Brisbane, Melbourne, more Sydney, Adelaide and then a little more Sydney to do three concerts which had been postponed, due to some "very psychedelic germs which decided to hold their annual general meeting in my throat," as Bono put it.
Being in each Australian city for so long allowed the band to settle in a

good deal more than on a usual touring schedule. There was time for the place to become very familiar. There was plenty of time off too, which allowed everybody to take advantage of the Australian summer, a very pleasant change from U2's previous habit of finding the coldest places on earth to play and make videos.

The last three Sydney concerts were filmed by Australian film director Richard Lowenstein. Richard and his team have a somewhat free-form approach to film-making (the 'scrapbook' style of his work can be seen in the *Desire* and *Angel of Harlem* videos), which the band felt would be a good way to document the LoveTown Tour.

It wasn't going to be *Rattle & Hum II*, rather a much more informal look at the tour, its environment and the city of Sydney (with its own version of LoveTown – the red light area of King's Cross). The resulting half-hour film was shown on European television over Christmas.

While in Sydney B.B. King celebrated his 64th birthday. If that wasn't an excuse for a party, then what was? Spending a little time with B.B., who is so young in spirit, it becomes impossible to comprehend that he's as old as the average grandparent. This is one way cool grown-up, and here was a party to prove it. U2 rented a boat with just enough room for a live band and some dancing space, then, with all of the tour personnel aboard, set out into Sydney harbour for a day afloat in the Australian spring sunshine. With plenty to eat and drink (and even a cake in the shape of his guitar, Lucille) it was inevitable that B.B. would end up playing some birthday blues. This he did, accompanied by Bono and anyone who happened to be within arms' reach at the time. The party boat sailed on until after dark, with a firework display to accompany it back to shore.

133

PROPAGANDA

U2 WORLD SERVICE MAGAZINE

B O N O
SONGWRITING BY ACCIDENT

As preparations for the recording of a new U2 record gather momentum, Bono takes time out to talk to *Propaganda* about the Irish in the World Cup, Edge as "a maniac" on their "abstract" latest recordings, songwriting by accident and the importance of Air-India sick bags in the creation of new material. Oh, and a new number presently called "Sick Puppy".

"When the Love Town Tour ran out at the beginning of the year," recalls Bono, "We all ran out as well." And little has been seen or heard of the members of U2 since then. So what have they been up to, where have they been, what are they doing and when will we see them next? These were some of the questions that *Propaganda* readers have been eager to get answers to as the months have passed since the Love Town Tour. Despite the fact that the band have not been doing any interviews and have rarely been in the public eye, Bono happily broke the silence – "as it's our magazine" – for an hour or two to fill fans in on some of those answers.
For a start, there was the small matter of Ireland's national football team featuring successfully in the World Cup in Italy. Not content with Larry having written the Irish team song for Italia 90, everyone in the band flew to Italy to watch the players compete. It was an unforgettable experience for Bono: "Where we were sitting at the match with Italy, the atmosphere was very Italian. There was a giant Italian mascot dressed as a sort of bullfighter with a world cup on his head and two cymbals, one on each arm, which on every Italian offensive were bashed together … I think Larry wanted to put his head between the cymbals."
For a few memorable weeks Jack Charlton, the Irish team manager, was "bigger than the Pope" and the country ground to a virtual standstill. In fact Italy is one of the band's favourite countries to visit – they've been three times this year, staying in Rome and Turin. But the year has also been a lot about staying at home, and for Bono, being a family man with Ali and young Jordan. Not that being in the family way was a novel experience for him. "In one sense I've been a family man ever since I joined this band," he quips. "But being at home for a while would, you imagine, soften you out and lay you back but it doesn't really do that to me. "At home ol' Captain Paranoia won't let us sit too easy. The advantage is that there are very few distractions and it becomes a time for evaluation of what

you do. But I do a lot of my writing when we're on the road, on the back of Air-India sick bags and on tablecloths in restaurants, or when I come in at six o'clock in the morning and maybe I shouldn't have been out so late." Coming home is a useful time to decipher the ideas written on tablecloths and to slip tapes of band soundchecks into the home cassette player to try and get some kind of objective view of how the band are doing musically. "Home is like the lab," he continues. "When we're at home, we usually focus on what has happened to us when we're away." And even when they're at home – that is off the touring road – there is still a lot of

I do a lot of my writing when we're on the road, on the back of Air-India sick bags and on tablecloths in restaurants, or when I come in at six o'clock in the morning and maybe I shouldn't have been out so late.

being away. In fact, he says, racking his memory to remember the diary for 1990 to date, "The day after the last concert in Amsterdam I went out on a boat and sailed away."
He "sailed" to America, family in tow, "to tie up some loose ends." This included a memorable few weeks' stay in New Orleans, where the Neville Brothers, born and bred in the city, were their guides. But it was not all leisure time – there was work to be done. Bono ended up writing songs with The Nevilles, notably "Jah Love", which appears on their recent *Brother's Keeper* release. Another song he wrote with them is entitled "Kingdom Come".
Hiring a Cherokee van, Bono, Ali and Jordan set off across America for a few weeks: "The van was really a device to keep us all together and we just drove and drove and drove …" The writing continued unabated. In Los Angeles, for example, Bono continued work on a screenplay called *The Million Dollar Hotel* with Canadian playwright Nicholas Klein. He calls it a black comedy, "a Peyton place on acid". In San Francisco

he was scribbling bits and pieces for a play that is set there, also a prose-poem, "which may or may not be a song", entitled "Ballad of New Orleans". "These are kind of the loose ends left over by *The Joshua Tree* and *Rattle and Hum*, just different projects which may never see the light of day," says Bono. But he is certain, in their own way, even these diverse projects will contribute to the overall U2 mix in the same way that Larry's continuing interest in country music or Adam's passion for the sounds of urban black America will contribute.
"That's what *Clockwork Orange* was about. That's the reason I'm having a go at this play and this poetry – it's to experiment and bring back the results of the experiment to U2. Adam, Larry and Edge bring back their findings to U2 and the band becomes a melting pot for the four of us. That's the exciting thing about a band."
By April the Cherokee trip was over and the Family Bono had returned to Dublin again to continue writing and musical experimentation with the other members of the band. Everyone's minds were focused on the next long-playing record – what would it be and how would it arrive? I wondered how the band goes about getting a new record together. For U2 it usually takes two forms.
"One is what we've been doing for the last few months and what we will be doing for the next few months – we come together and just improvise, just play, just see what happens. It's songwriting by accident as opposed to by numbers," explains Bono. "You wait for that special moment and you build the music around that moment and then out of the mood of the music come the words.
"As a lyricist that can be difficult for me. Sometimes the words just come straight from the music but sometimes they don't and I've got to try and listen in to the music, to what it's saying and then try to put words to it."
That's one approach. The other process is a more formal way of songwriting, where one of the band will have an idea that they've written on

We're not a band who just get up on stage and play the songs – the songs are either an all-out experience or they are nothing. There is no in-between U2 songs – you either perform it completely and utterly or you stop performing it.

guitar or piano and they bring it to Bono to write words for it. Or Bono has a musical idea and takes it to them to see where they can take it. "Edge would be experimenting in the studio with an atmosphere or a mood or a drumbeat and he would develop it more on his own and it would actually look more like a song – you will have a rough idea of what this piece is and the next step is to hone it down as opposed to completely develop it."

He cites "Where The Streets Have No Name" and "Unforgettable Fire" as examples of songs that developed this way. This time around, in preparation for the new album, the band have been at the first stage this past summer: "It's the earlier, more experimental approach at present. We feel that with *The Joshua Tree* and *Rattle and Hum* we got to grips with a certain kind of songwriting and though we enjoy that, still the most exciting way to songwrite is in improvisation, in experimenting when you create something new."

Inevitably there is a lot of wastage in this process. Bono explained that they are probably working with about 50 different ideas for new songs at the moment, ranging from sound-ideas to almost complete numbers: "It's fifty musical ideas but that's everything from a sampled piece from *Clockwork Orange* to a ballad."

Sometime this autumn that number will be whittled down to about 30 different pieces from which the songs on the next record will be born. "It's the first time we've ever had that many make it through ... but this is still quite early on. Not all the ideas will necessarily require a lot of honing down in the

recording studio. We might decide to leave a piece unhoned down like we did with "Bad" on *The Unforgettable Fire* – you leave it as it arrives. Or you might rewrite and rewrite."

Those decisions will be made before Christmas, after which they will look back at all the material to date and "actually start working out formally what the record is."

When we're at home, we usually focus on what has happened to us when we're away.

After spending a few weeks in Berlin demo-ing, in the New Year they'll stand back and see where they think the record should go.

"Although it sounds a bit trippy to say it, oftentimes the record takes on a life of its own. We've all got ideas about where we'd like the record to go but rather than decide and then go out and make it, we're just following each person's vision and then we'll see."

Inevitably, of the score of songs that fail to make it on to the LP, many will be recorded and put on B-sides, continuing a valuable tradition of releasing additional U2 material to their audience. But it's the album that we await with eager anticipation. "We want to make a record that pushes out the boundaries a bit, not just for ourselves but in terms of what people are used to hearing on the radio or on records. We want to start abusing the technology that's available – this has always been an important side of U2."

So, the all-important question, what does Bono think, at this early stage, the album is shaping up like? What clues to its direction?

"I don't know how abstract the record will end up but it has started quite abstract – a lot of very, very aggressive guitar playing. Edge is like a maniac at the moment. It's not going to be a laid-back record, I can tell you that."

This sounds as though there is some continuity with the sounds created for the unreleased *Clockwork Orange* soundtrack.

"*Clockwork Orange* was a great springboard for our record because it was a question of us realizing that the only limits you have as an artist are your imagination. You are only limited by your ability to imagine a sound structure – you are not limited by your ability to play something anymore. In the early days, when we didn't play very well, we would have been limited by our ability to play but we're actually playing very well at the moment – there is no limit. That is both exciting and frightening – there are so many options, so many different ways you can go."

He is confident that the band are

starting out fresh for the '90s, refreshed by their experience of the last few years in looking through rock's back-catalogue.

"We're beginning again for the '90s. The sky's the limit and we want to be forward-looking. We've looked back and learnt so much in this period – from working with the blues and gospel and jazz, and working with people like Bob Dylan, B.B. King and Roy Orbison. We've been sponging, soaking up any decent information we could get. There's a generation dying out that might not be here in twenty years' time and the whole point of *Rattle and Hum* was to say, 'Look we're fans of these people'." Bono believes the band needed to "study under" people such as B.B. King and Bob Dylan because they provide a link with the past that will soon be lost. But while *Rattle and Hum* paid homage to the story of rock and roll music, it was only a stopping-off point for U2. And in parts it also pointed to their future direction. "The idea was to learn the information and to bring it back and synthesize it into a new direction for U2."

In Bono's view, the song from that recording which most clearly points to the next U2 is "God Part II". As usual, while the 'pieces' do not have fixed titles as yet, many of them have 'working titles' – some of them with a peculiar resonance, as Bono reveals. "Provisional titles" he calls them, insisting that they wouldn't make sense to anyone but the band, but when pressed he lets slip a couple as teasers. "Well, we've got a really great soul song, in the tradition of Sly and The Family Stone, called 'Sick Puppy' ... I'm not sure if that'll be the title when we make the record. Another one is a full-frontal attack from the Edge called 'Ultra-violet'."

The trick now is to take the music of U2 into the future and this is why they are not rushing the business of writing and recording. It is the band's success to date that means they can afford to spend this time getting things right before making the record. "It's a great position for people to have put us in. I think the U2 audience wants us to make a great record and to be surprised by it. They don't want us to put out another record just because we have to and we won't put it out unless its a great record." He is certain that the band have not yet reached their creative peak: "We're a few records

---

Sometimes the words just come straight from the music but sometimes they don't and I've got to try and listen in to the music, to what it's saying and then try to put words to it.

N O

away from that."

If things run to schedule it is likely that the album will be in the shops by this time next year but after that it gets hazy again. The world tour, which successful bands like U2 normally embark on with the release of a new record, is not necessarily inevitable. Bono says that the band have to ask themselves some hard questions about prolonged live touring. Breaking a mammoth tour into shorter, bite-sized trips with regular returns home is not as straightforward as it appears on paper.

"We're weighing all that up at the moment. I used to think that we could come and go but it's not proving to be that easy because, for instance, if we did a two-month tour we'd only be getting good on the last week, but if you do a six-month tour maybe the last month is not as good."

The Love Town Tour taught the band a lot of lessons about how not to tour, not least the awkward experience of the singer losing his voice and the consequent cancelled shows.

"In Australia and New Zealand particularly I discovered what we really like and what we really don't like about playing live. We thought it would be great to go indoors and to play seven nights in a city, and to almost take over a city for a week: it would become a home away from home and everyone could see us up close, unlike these big outdoor-type events. But we actually realized that out of those seven dates that we played, maybe only four of

them would be at the level we would like. We started to realize that concerts have to be special and there is a momentum to coming into a city for a few days ... and then going out again." While Australia and New Zealand proved an enjoyable experience, he thinks other territories, under that sort of concert schedule, might have put more strain on the band. "We're not a band who just get up on stage and play the songs – the songs are either an all-out experience or they are nothing. There is no in-between U2 songs – you either perform it completely and utterly or you should stop performing it."

In fact in Australia he stopped singing "Bad" for the simple reason that he

> **Ideally I'd love to just go out and play an hour of new songs and have three great acts on the bill ... I'd have Elvis to open, then Jimi Hendrix and the Beach Boys before we go on. Followed by Bob Dylan. In fact I suppose we'd have to be the opening act!**

couldn't maintain the necessary intensity night after night: "It was taking away from the song to do that." While some fans were disappointed not to hear "Sunday Bloody Sunday", Bono believes that it would be wrong to play a song "without being able to put heart and soul into it".

"The question remains whether we are going to play any song night after night? I don't know – can we play "Pride" every night? If you notice the song is taking a turn for the worse, you've got to stop playing it for a while."

It is a problem heightened every time a new record is released, with handfuls of new songs demanding a live airing. Bono has toyed with the idea of simply going out on the road and performing only new material, maybe for just an hour at a time.

"I love the idea that in the past you'd hear the Stones or the Who or Jimi Hendrix or the Beatles – all these people on the same bill – and they'd all play twenty minutes. That sounds ideal to me, not just because it's easier on my voice but because I think rock 'n' roll should not be much longer than that." A bit like the Amnesty tour? "Yeah, I loved that. It's all about the intensity of the songs. Ideally I'd love to just go out and play an hour of new songs and have three great acts on the bill." Who else? "Let's see. I'd have Elvis to open, then Jimi Hendrix and the Beach Boys before we go on. Followed by Bob Dylan. In fact I suppose we'd have to be the opening act!"

I don't know how abstract the record will end up but it has started quite abstract – a lot of very, very aggressive guitar playing. Edge is like a maniac at the moment. It's not going to be a laid-back record.

Although it sounds a bit trippy to say, oftentimes the record takes on a life of its own. We've all got ideas about where we'd like the record to go but rather than decide and then go out and make it, we're just following each person's vision and then we'll see.

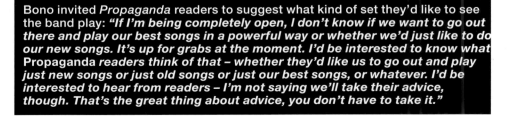

Bono invited *Propaganda* readers to suggest what kind of set they'd like to see the band play: *"If I'm being completely open, I don't know if we want to go out there and play our best songs in a powerful way or whether we'd just like to do our new songs. It's up for grabs at the moment. I'd be interested to know what* Propaganda *readers think of that – whether they'd like us to go out and play just new songs or just old songs or just our best songs, or whatever. I'd be interested to hear from readers – I'm not saying we'll take their advice, though. That's the great thing about advice, you don't have to take it."*

Word from the U2 office is that "an awful lot of lyrics" are being sent in for the attention of the band at the moment. Unfortunately for prospective songwriters who believe they might have a valuable contribution to make to the next U2 record, it is a policy of the band to leave such material unexamined. They've already written far too many songs to fit on the next record as it is.

Although there has been no formal word from the U2 camp on the recent cover version of "Where the Streets Have No Name", Adam Clayton was heard to mutter words to the effect that, "U2 are honoured that such a great group as the Pet Shop Boys felt they wanted to cover one of our songs". It is not known what expression Mr Clayton was wearing at the time.

The No Truth in This Rumour Corner. Stories that U2 will be releasing another full-length video of songs shot during the making of the *Rattle and Hum* film but not included in the final movie are without firm foundation. "It's not out of the question that we will ever do something of this kind," commented Paul McGuinness, "but there are no plans to release a video from the *Rattle and Hum* era in the foreseeable future. We don't feel under obligation to release everything we do to the public and we don't view fans of the band as librarians who want access to everything we ever do.
"The next record is the new U2 record and our 'back-pages', such as this footage, will remain private to the band, perhaps for ever."
He also pointed out that calls for a release of a compilation album of B-sides will have to remain unheeded as well. "It would be a complete distraction at this stage. I like the idea of doing something like this, say, for *Propaganda* readers at some point but I also like the fact that releasing those B-sides could devalue the original single releases themselves. But one day perhaps:'

A new U2 record is well under way as we report elsewhere in this issue of *Propaganda* – expect a single in September and the album a few weeks later – but the last person to ask what it's like is the band's manager Paul McGuinness. "If I'm in the studio I will listen to what the band are doing but I am a very poor judge of material that is only half-way finished," he admits. "The band all know that, so they don't bother playing it to me because it's a waste of time. It's embarrassing to say that but it's true." Mr McGuinness is a better judge nearer the end of the recording process: "I'm much better when it comes to nearly being finished – that's when they start to let me hear the material properly."

Early hints on the next U2 concerts suggest that spring 1992 looks promising with "somewhere-in-Europe" hosting the opening leg. Tentative plans are afoot for *Propaganda* subscribers to be offered preferential treatment for concert tickets. More information as it becomes available.
Don't write, we'll keep you informed. If you know other U2 fans who want to be guaranteed tickets, tell them what magazine they need to subscribe to. It begins with the letter 'P'.

THE BERLIN SESSIONS

It won't be called *Born in Berlin* but it was. When U2's new album hits the shops this autumn, the city of Berlin will have played a key role in its making. In the city's Hansa Studios, for many years in the shadow of the Berlin Wall and just a short walk from the centre of East Berlin, Edge, Larry, Bono and Adam set to work on writing and recording their new songs. The band spent two lengthy visits last autumn at 'Hansa by the Wall' – as the studio used to be called – working 16-hour days with Daniel Lanois in its famous Studio Two. They arrived on one of the last flights in to the old West Germany, hanging out with tens of thousands of others as the city celebrated Liberation Day and reunification. Although the Wall has now come down, the band stayed in what used to be East Berlin, renting a house that had formerly been East German Government property. It had been home, at various times, to Eastern Bloc politicians, including former Soviet premier Leonid Brezhnev. Its big, sparse rooms, home to

sound crew and band, felt like they were bugged even if they weren't – and if they weren't then they ought to have been. U2 got down to the serious business of making the new record after a few days' filming the video for Cole Porter's "Night and Day", their contribution to the Red Hot and Blue project. This was mostly shot in sub-zero temperatures on the balcony of the Berlin home of director Wim Wenders. "When they arrived for their recording, they worked very hard," recalled Matthias Hartt, Studio Manager at Hansa, which opened in 1972. "Studio Two has a unique sound. It is just right for them because it is such a big, live room."

For the last few years bands from the West have been thin on the ground at Hansa and West German groups have been the mainstay. Back in the mid '70s David Bowie recorded the classic albums *Low* (1976) and *Heroes* (1977) there. Later, some of rock's most creative talents made the trek to Hansa, including Iggy Pop, David Byrne, Nick Cave and The Birthday Party.

Matthias Hartt says he loved what he heard of the new U2 recordings. "They have a special way to record. They always like to go a step further, they always try to develop. It's going to be a great record."

145

"THE FLY,

IT'S THE SOU

MEN CHOP

THE JOS

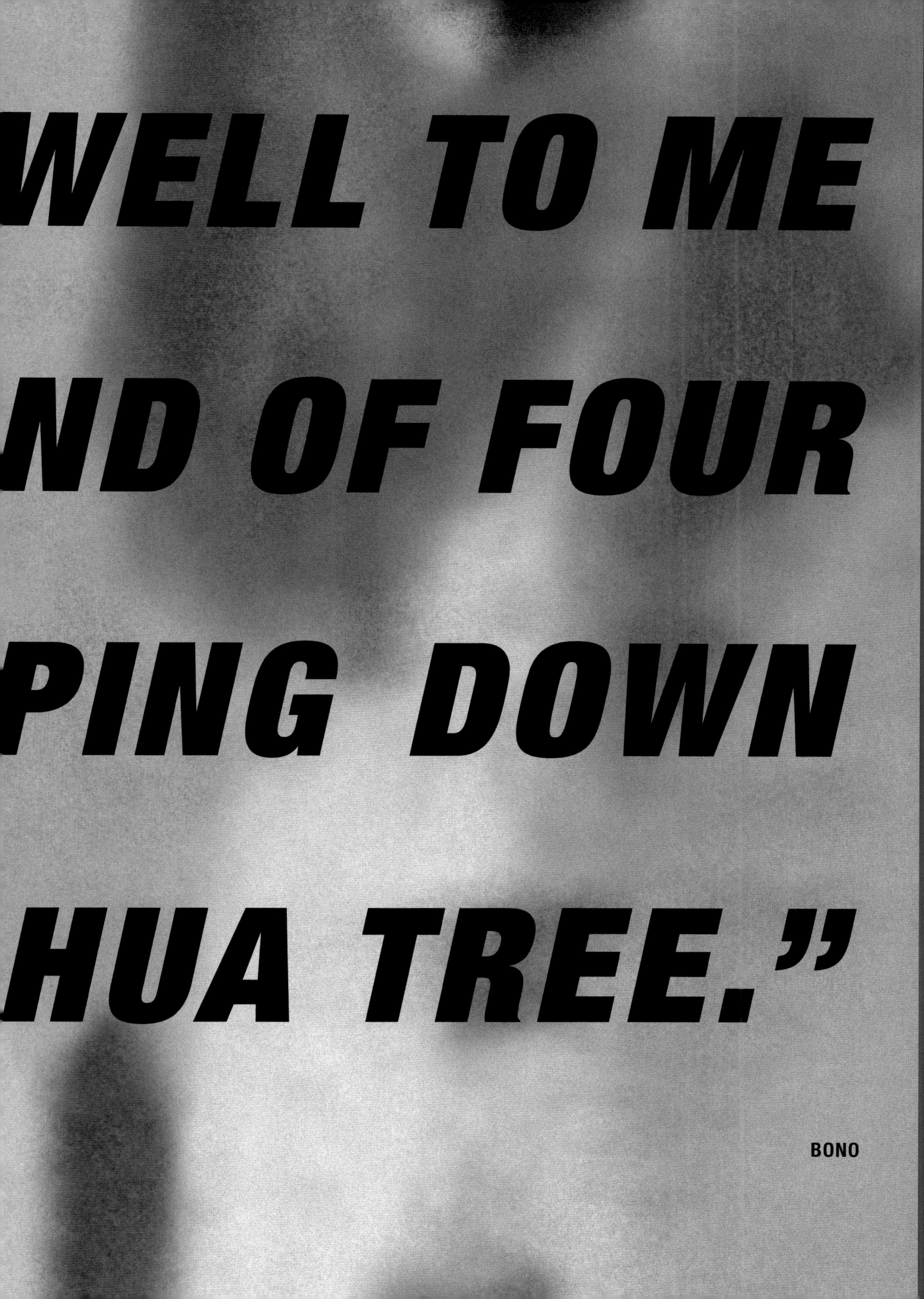

WELL TO ME

ND OF FOUR

PING DOWN

HUA TREE."

BONO

"All I know is that it feels like what I want right now. It's raw and rough and straightforward and down to the essence of things. Quite unpolished, in some ways, and I like that."
Edge

ACHTUNG BABY is the first U2 album of the 1990s. Their last public appearance was the climax of the Love Town Tour, when they saw in the new decade with an audience estimated to be in excess of 500 million tuned to a live broadcast of their concert at the Point Depot in Dublin.

There's a lot of songs on the record that I'll be proud to hear on the radio. Although *The Joshua Tree* had a lot of successful singles on it, that is not necessarily what we are about. We're not particularly into hit singles. Mind you, I need to do the roof of my house in the West so if we get a few hits away I won't be complaining."
Edge

U2 are the first band to be invited to sell their records in South Africa since a recent clarification of the United Nations policy on the cultural boycott of the country. This follows a mould-breaking agreement in which proceeds from *Achtung Baby* sales in South Africa – and other U2 albums – will raise funds for the benefit of anti-apartheid musicians' organizations. U2 have never performed in South Africa or allowed their records to be sold there. Their view was most clearly expressed in the song "Silver and Gold", one of the high points of the *Rattle and Hum* film. But in May this year the United Nations policy on the cultural boycott of South Africa was clarified at an International Symposium in Los Angeles to take into account recent moves towards dismantling apartheid. The Los Angeles Statement appeals to artists from abroad to assist in fundraising for non-racial organizations in the country, and to help in the training of South African artists. After consultations between U2's management, the Irish Anti-Apartheid Movement and the African National Congress, *Achtung Baby* and earlier releases will now be sold in South Africa to benefit the South African Musicians' Alliance and the Musicians' Alliance for People's Power, set up by Hugh Masekela. "The band feels very honoured to be able to contribute in any small way to the enormous task ahead of achieving democracy in South Africa," said Paul McGuinness, U2's manager.

"We've travelled a lot during the making of *Achtung Baby*, often with someone following us with a Super-8 – footage that may turn up in video clips. When you are in the studio for a long period of time you get very close to what you are recording and begin to lose perspective on it. The travelling has helped us to blast ourselves with the outside world. You can get lost in yourself in the studio – you need to open yourselves out."
Edge

Six days after its British release, "The Fly" entered the British Top 40 chart at Number One, displacing Brian Adams, who had been in the top spot for a record-breaking 16 weeks. The band heard the news in Morocco, where they were making a video for the second single from the album, "She Moves in Mysterious Ways". "The Fly" sold over 70,000 copies in the UK alone in the first week of release.

BERLIN'S HANSA STUDIOS, FOR YEARS IN THE SHADOW OF THE BERLIN WALL, WAS WHERE *ACHTUNG BABY* WAS BORN. U2 SPENT TWO LONG PERIODS STAYING IN GERMANY AND RECORDING AT 'HANSA BY THE WALL' IN LATE 1990 AND EARLY 1991. INCIDENTALLY, THE BAND STAYED IN A HOUSE THAT WAS ONCE THE PROPERTY OF THE EAST GERMAN GOVERNMENT AND HAD EVEN HOUSED FORMER SOVIET PREMIER LEONID BREZHNEV.

"IF YOU MANAGE TO GET THE FOUR OF THEM IN ONE ROOM WITH INSTRUMENTS IN THEIR HANDS, YOU'RE GOING TO GET RESULTS. THAT HAS A LOT TO DO WITH MY JOB – JUST GETTING THEM IN THE ROOM AND PLAYING." DANIEL LANOIS, PRODUCER.

Achtung Baby was honed in a studio that the band set up in Elsinor, a refurbished old house on the south Dublin coastline near Dalkey. Bono described the atmosphere in *Propaganda 14*: "It's a very over-the-top house we're in here, hence the over-the-top atmosphere of some of the songs at the moment. We've got plastic chandeliers, flock wallpaper, fake fires ... perfect for this record."

To coincide with the launch of "Achtung Baby", Island Records in London purchas
– one courtesy of Brian Eno no less – and placed them in suitably visible places arour
London. Later one will find itself being auctioned for charity while the others ar
could ever have imagined – they are being commandeered by U2s director Pete

It's official – "Achtung Baby" is a sexy record. So sexy in fact that the band
therapist Dr Ruth, to record a voiceover for American Commercials, which she wa
joke too – U2 taking the rise out of themselves – hence the suitably Germanic
televisions and radio stations throughout America. So if you thought it was just
U2 records, you were wrong. It's just the four of them having a laugh.

d and imported 6 trabant cars from Germany, hastily had them spray-painted
he UK. These included record-shop windows and a huge billboard in central
kely to find themselves travelling more miles than their original manufacturers
Villiams for use on the upcoming world tour. Watch this space.

reamt up the bizarre notion of inviting the world's most famous sex
appy to do. Island Records marketing department in the US saw the
ones of the good doctor announcing the release of "Achtung Baby" on
nother huge marketing machine churning out bland promotional ideas for

In between giving a talk to the European Parliament and putting in an installation in a cave in Lanzarote, Brian Eno, musical artist, full-time creative person and (Zoo) television consultant, found time to talk to Propaganda *about collaborating with U2 on records and on tour:*

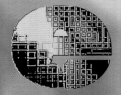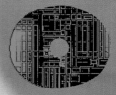

"What I like about being Brian Eno is that I am able to do such different things"

Brian Eno is standing outside the Civic Centre in Lakeland, Florida, next to a large satellite dish that bears the emblem 'Zoo TV'. In some ways he is responsible for the dish, or at least as responsible as anyone else. Bono has described Zoo TV as the idea of this former member of Roxy Music. "In collaboration, yes," comes the cautious reply from the man who made *Music for Airports.* "I mean the idea to make a stage set with a lot of different video sources was mine to make a chaos of information, and also the idea to have a lot of un-coordinated material happening together ..."

His very English voice, with just a hint of Suffolk in it, trails off and then begins again. "The idea of getting away from video being a way of helping people to see the band more easily ... this is video as a way of obscuring them, losing them sometimes in just a network of material."

Mr Eno, the man who made *My Life in The Bush of Ghosts* with David Byrne, is in Lakeland for two nights only. He is here as a kind of television consultant, a Zoo Television consultant, advising band and production team as to what is and isn't working visually during the rehearsals for the new tour. He kindly finds time to talk to *Propaganda,* but first has to fend off some rather more philosophical enquiries from Barry Devlin on behalf of Dreamchaser Films.

For example, when he has said that the video is obscuring said band, he is asked whether it is, therefore, "a metaphor for the kind of album it is ... or just a good idea?"

"I think it does connect a lot to some of the material on the album; 'Zoo Station' and 'The Fly' particularly. A lot of the material seems to be about people grasping at currents of information that are flying about and quite often in the songs you got a sound that is very non-typical of rock music.

"It is very crude and dirty, the sound of big machines. To me it is the sound of data flying about. I like the idea of making the concert the place where you intercept some of that. Which is what this is for of course." "This", as is clear from the direction of his right hand, is the satellite dish. He describes the new show as "a kind of sponge" soaking in local and satellite TV channels, phone-conversations, pre-prepared video material and live concert TV. Eno's original idea was to have all the monitors on wheels so that the entire architecture of the set was constantly moving. No doubt to the quiet relief of the crew, this proved impractical. He has also contributed himself a number of the filmed sequences for the Zoo TV showreels that turn up on the vidi-walls during the concert.

The man whose diary tells him that he will shortly be going to the Winter Gardens in New York to put in a sound installation called Tropical Rain Forest, clearly would not have been interested had Zoo TV merely turned into some kind of avant-garde version of video-reinforcement.

"Just the idea of seeing big people with microphones as opposed to little people with microphones is a very boring way to use video." On the other hand, after seeing a rehearsal, he was actually wondering if a little of the old reinforcement might not go amiss. "I thought we'd gone too far in the other direction and I imagined people after about four numbers thinking, 'Where are the band – this could be anyone we're looking at.'" But in the main he loves the messiness of the proceedings, the unruliness of the marriage of band and technology. In fact he says that "the idea of untidiness" was important all along from the birth of *Achtung Baby* in Berlin and Dublin, and as Zoo TV emerged swiftly on its heels. "This wasn't the kind of music where you set up a neat little stage with a nice screen at the back – it is really the opposite of computer music this. It

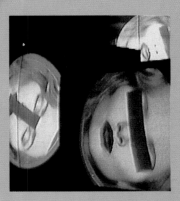

couldn't be more tactile than it is." Eno, as he has done for several years for U2, popped in and out of the recording studio as the new record was being made to observe, to interfere – and then, just as suddenly, to leave again while those remaining, namely the band and Daniel Lanois, reflected on whether he might just have something there.

One advantage for him over the others because of this was that he achieved a distance from the record as it was being created: "It was much easier to discern the whole identity of the album because I wasn't really listening to details. I'd come in and say, 'Yeah, this record has a particular feeling in this direction' and this industrial thing was one that I identified very early and very much encouraged. I thought that was a great new direction for it."

He was excited by the "industrial" elements, even taking to trying to unvarnish material he felt was over-done: "The intention was always to produce something less controlled into the whole thing, something that would be on the fringe of musical sound and just ordinary sound that you hear on the street." Eno knows the recording studio better than most people know their living room. It was in 1975 with the release of *Another Green World*, an album of song and instrumental miniatures, that he turned the recording studio into an essential tool in the compositional process itself. Discreet Music, in the same year, set a "self-regulating" musical system in motion and let it run its course with surprisingly appealing results.

Ten years later he released "Thursday Afternoon", a soundtrack to his video of the same name, and the first compact-disc-only recording. He became fascinated by the medium's potential as a way of painting – he studied to be a painter at art-school in the '60s – and has staged more than fifty installations of his work.

On the face of it, turning up for a week during the making of *Achtung Baby* and then leaving for a month or two, which he did at least five times, would appear likely to cause maximum irritation and distraction. He has a theory as to why, in contrast, it worked well. "A very

fascinating thing happens to people when they're listening to music for a long time, which is that they can hear it, even when it's not playing. So if you know a piece of music terribly well and the mix changes and the bass guitar goes very, very quiet, you still hear the

bass. You're so accustomed to it being there that you compensate and remake it in your mind."

He illustrates by citing the little-known fact that when you hear a piece of music down the phone-line, you also think you hear the bass line even though "it's not physically possible because the frequencies are too low". He returns to the studio situation: "I'd go in and say, 'The song has gone, whatever it is you liked about this song is not there anymore.' Sometimes, for example, the song would have disappeared under layers of overdubs. 'One' was like that, 'End of World' got like that at one point. 'Light My Way' also at one point. When people get excited about an idea it's usually to do with a particular combination of elements that exist then. They are excited so they work on it and they keep adding to it, and because they are familiar they are still hearing those original elements. But if you come along as an outsider you hear this huge crust over the top of the song and you don't hear those elements anymore."

I think the new show does connect a lot to the album, Zoo Station and The Fly particularly. A lot of the material seems to be about people grasping at currents of information that are flying about and quite often in the songs you got a sound that is very non-typical of rock music.

His job, he believes, was to strip things down a little and remind Daniel and the band members of what it was they liked about a song in the first place. He has worked with Daniel Lanois for many years, first introducing him to U2 in 1986 when he engineered *The Unforgettable Fire,* which Eno produced. He believes they are a good combination, now that, three albums later, the roles have changed: "Lanois creates long-term environments where magic may occur, whereas, what I'm good at is coming in and looking at the whole picture and saying, 'There's an implication here that you could take a lot further, are you interested in that?'" He also likes to concentrate on songs that "don't fit", songs that everyone may like but no one knows quite what to do about to make them work: "In a way I'm not so interested looking at the songs that are obvious great hits – I think they are solved problems. What thrills me is to see something that everyone knows has got something but they don't quite know what it is. To fiddle around with that for a while is

quite a lot of fun." His own favourites on *Achtung Baby* he cites as "So Cruel" and "The Fly": "It's lovely to have a song with such undertones of evil coming out."

Eno first became well-known as the androgynous synthesizer player in Roxy Music in the early '70s, later developing into one of rock's most sought after producers. Originally he didn't want to work with U2 at all. It was partly because he had had enough of rock music and partly because he didn't feel he wanted to wreck U2's career. "I was aware that if I did get involved in working with rock music my interest would be in making it less rocky and more diffuse, less directed towards the normal feelings of rock music." But the band persisted and he finally agreed to make *The Unforgettable Fire* with them. The marriage was creative healthy, the record winning critical praise for its departure from the direction of its predecessor, *War*, and they reunited for *The Joshua Tree*, again a success, this time winning a Grammy Award. Five years and another record later and he is on the road with them, advising on one of his strangest "installations", Zoo TV.

Over those years he believes U2 have changed significantly and also not changed at all. "They are much more ironic now and I don't mean by that that they are therefore not sincere because I think irony and sincerity aren't exclusive. But when I first met them they were entirely in the sincere mode and they were in the middle of thing but now they are capable of being in the middle of it but also standing outside it and realizing that they are playing with form and they can twist forms around."

He says they are not more "style-conscious" but are more "conscious of styles". "They are conscious that what they are doing is collaging together different emotional landscapes together." Ironically, while an

If you know a piece of music terribly well and the mix changes and the bass guitar goes very very quiet, you still hear the bass. You're so accustomed to it being there that you compensate and remake it in your mind.

unashamed fan of their music, he believes it is a non-musical element which is a key ingredient in their success; what he calls the lack of politics between the members. "In nearly all the bands that I've had experience of, there's been a huge under-the-surface diplomatic scene going on the whole time – this person can't work with that person unless this other one's present because he can talk to him through him and this person has to do overdubs because otherwise he gets in a real bad mood – that kind of thing takes up so much of the energy of ordinary bands."

They really are a group, the only real group I've ever met. They realize that intuitively and there is a great loyalty, perhaps because they realize that none of them would have been a musician without the others.

He says the biggest thing about U2 is the trust and loyalty amongst the members that they don't have to waste time and energy proving themselves to each other. "That means that all the attention is focused on the job which is, 'How do we make great music?' It doesn't mean that everyone agrees the whole time but it means that their attention is focused on what they are doing. What they are doing is not a vehicle for any of them to gain dominance politically over any others and it really is with a lot of bands."

Eno believes that *Achtung Baby* is a brave album, when it would have been all too easy to make a *Joshua Tree* Part Two, courage which stems from respect for their audience. "They don't have to be an innovative band, in fact it probably doesn't pay them to, they'd be better off financially just settling in to a rut."

He believes the U2 audience are respected in neither being given the same music again and "treated like dummies" nor in being given "any old experiments to look at ..." He is all too aware that successful artists can often go all "experimental", releasing any work in the name of art. This is intriguing coming from Eno, the great experimenter, who has made an art out of reinventing music by playing with its edges, who would like to see an official release of the notorious Berlin sessions bootlegs ("because they're great") and who persuaded them to put out Elvis Presley and America on *The Unforgettable Fire, a* work in progress if ever there was one.

"There was a thought to write words for it and do it again," he recalls, "but there was such a weird magic about that, that it would never have got back to that. It would never have happened again."

But then he did produce *The Joshua Tree* too, and that was hardly inaccessible. "I remember saying early on that this would be a really commercial record and at that time no one really believed that. I always had a lot of confidence in that one." He believes that *Rattle and Hum* "cleared the decks" for *Achtung Baby* to be as radical as it has turned out, which also bodes well for U2 being one of the very few bands not just over one decade, the eighties, but over two. "I think they've done it, they've certainly spanned this part of the decade."

It's in the chemistry and he senses that the chemistry is still very much there. "They really are a group, the only real group I've ever met. They realize that intuitively and there is a great loyalty, perhaps because they realize that none of them would have been a musician without the others." Then he adds, quizzically, "I can't imagine what kind of bands they would have ended up in."

157

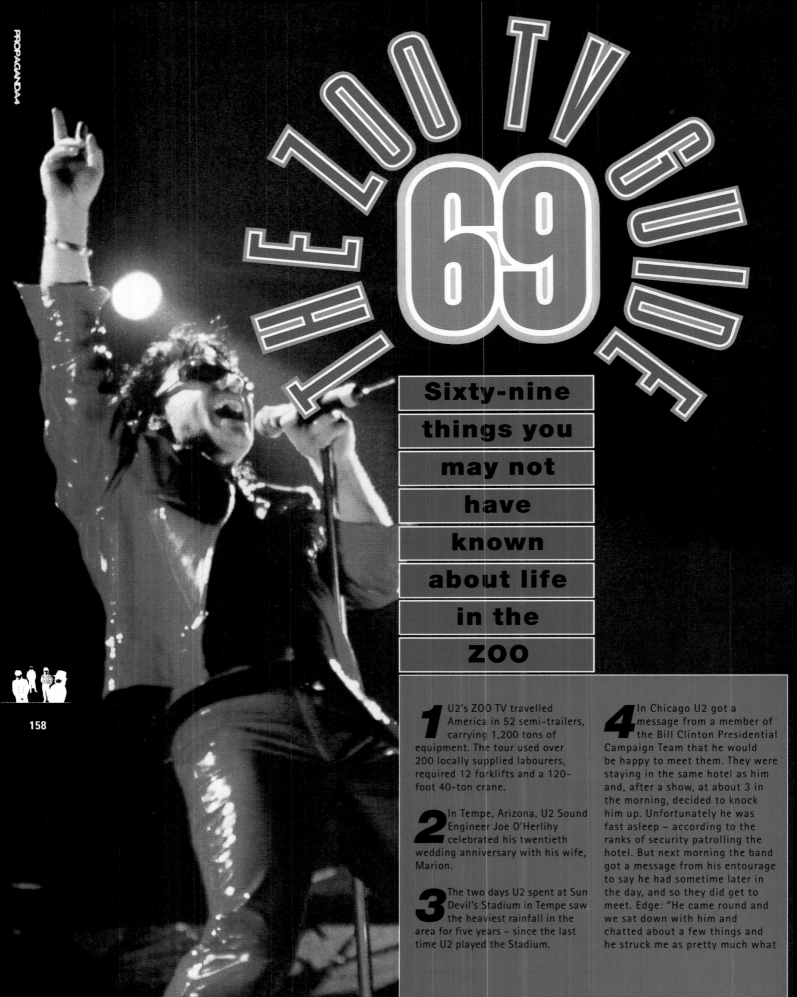

THE ZOO TV GUIDE
69

Sixty-nine things you may not have known about life in the ZOO

1 U2's ZOO TV travelled America in 52 semi-trailers, carrying 1,200 tons of equipment. The tour used over 200 locally supplied labourers, required 12 forklifts and a 120-foot 40-ton crane.

2 In Tempe, Arizona, U2 Sound Engineer Joe O'Herlihy celebrated his twentieth wedding anniversary with his wife, Marion.

3 The two days U2 spent at Sun Devil's Stadium in Tempe saw the heaviest rainfall in the area for five years – since the last time U2 played the Stadium.

4 In Chicago U2 got a message from a member of the Bill Clinton Presidential Campaign Team that he would be happy to meet them. They were staying in the same hotel as him and, after a show, at about 3 in the morning, decided to knock him up. Unfortunately he was fast asleep – according to the ranks of security patrolling the hotel. But next morning the band got a message from his entourage to say he had sometime later in the day, and so they did get to meet. Edge: "He came round and we sat down with him and chatted about a few things and he struck me as pretty much what

PROPAGANDA.5

69

THE ZOO TV GUIDE

159

he appears to be." But after he was elected President the band had to decline an invitation to play at his Washington Inauguration. Edge: "It's very dodgy to become too closely associated with politicians. We've had approaches over the years from a few politicians. We can support issues but not the candidate."

5 Two of the Trabants from the Zoo TV Tour later found fame of their own when they were featured on national TV in England on BBC1's *Tomorrow's World* in a special programme about Entertainment Technology.

6 At the four nights in Mexico City a new phenomenon was apparently created when, instead of merely holding up their lighters to express appreciation, the 22,000 fans began clicking them on and off to the rhythm of the songs. Not exactly the Mexican Wave but an excited lighting director said this phenomenon is one to be encouraged.

7 The sound system on the ZOO TV tour utilized over 1 million watts of power and had a total weight of 60,000 pounds – about 30 tons. There were two separate monitor mix positions, each with two consoles providing 160 channel input capacity. There were 26 on-stage mixes and 60 separate monitor speakers. The P.A. system comprised 176 speaker enclosures of various types utilising 312 18-inch woofers, 592 10-inch mid-range speakers and 604 high-frequency drivers. Front of house had three 40-channel consoles with a total input capability of 120 channels. It is a Clair Brothers sound system.

8 This is an example of a set-list from the ZOO TV tour by U2.

9 ZOO TV 's travelling army included over 180 members travelling in 12 buses as well as a 40-passenger chartered jet.

10 For the Freddie Mercury Tribute concert in April, U2 satellited across a live version of Until The End of the World. They were performing in Tacoma at the time of the concert – but in the interval the tribute concert was broadcast live to U2's Tacoma fans from England.

11 Edge, about those trabbies? "It's a surreal thing, they might as well be goldfish."

12 Four generators were used to power the ZOO TV show, using in excess of 3 miles of cable. These generators could provide enough power to run two city blocks of homes.

13 Malcolm Gerrie, producer of the ZOO TV special aired at the end of 1992 in 37 countries, said: "Zoo Television is a television programme about television, made by television, for television ... debunking television." The suitably preposterous press blurb from Channel Four in England ran as follows: "More anarchic than the Great Rock 'n' Roll Swindle, more intimate than In Bed With Madonna, more tongue-in-cheek than The Rocky Horror Picture Show, ZOO TV Featuring U2 promises to be the 'mother of all entertainment specials'. Pop and TV merge in a glorious orgy of over-indulgence as the mega-rock stars take control of the hype and media machine that made them and push it to breaking point." Right ...

14 Pee Wee Herman and Arnold Schwarzenegger both turned up in the Zoo.

8

SET 3
DRUG OF THE NATION
BEES/GEORGE
ZOO STATION
THE FLY
REAL THING
MYSTERIOUS WAYS
ONE
END OF THE WORLD
NEW YEARS DAY
LARRY
ARMS AROUND THE WORLD
ANGEL OF HARLEM
LOVETOWN
SATELLITE OF LOVE
ACCOUSTIC CRUEL
SUNDAY BLOODY SUNDAY
BULLET THE BLUE SKY
RUNNING TO STANDSTILL
STREETS
PRIDE
STILL HAVE'NT FOUND

DESIRE
LIGHT MY WAY
WITH OR WITHOUT YOU

LOVE IS BLINDNESS

20

15 Bono: "I don't know what ZOO TV is, so I guess it must be art."

16 The Edge's mum and dad came to the ZOO TV shows in Los Angeles and Vancouver.

17 At most rock shows the press photographers count themselves lucky if they get access to the security pit in front of the stage. During the ZOO TV tour, photographers were sometimes invited into a 'scizzor-lift' – a mobile platform – which lifted them up the side of the stage where The Fly would then perform right into their unbelieving lenses. The precise meaning of the moment was made clear to the audience by a large electronic sign flashing the words 'PHOTO OPPORTUNITY'.

18 The second show at Dodger's Stadium, Los Angeles, was on Halloween. TV Spook-Vamp 'Elvira' joined the show live by satellite to sing Happy Birthday to Larry.

19 U2 played the first rock show at Atlanta's spanking new Georgia Dome. Sadly the house technicians had not quite worked out the finer points of how to turn off all the lights in the building so some tights remained on for the first fifteen minutes of the show. A visit to the roof by U2 stage manager, Rocco Reedy, and his trusty hammer solved the problem.

20 Mandy Shaki, 17, and Jennifer Lind, 17, are U2 fans in Vancouver who came along to both stadium shows in the city. Mandy has been getting her *Propaganda* for six years. Her highlight of 1992 was in April at the indoor Vancouver show: "The ZOO TV concept is music, TV, information ... it's everything in excess."

21 Early on in the tour Larry and one of U2's security team acquired a pair of Harley Davidson Motorcycles. While everyone else drove or flew between shows, Larry often rode the trip on his Harley.

22 "Against a backdrop of flickering TV screens, Day-Glo Trabants and a bank of technology on Edge's side of the stage that looks like NASA Mission Control, Bono prowls the boards in a gold lame suit that harks back to vintage Elvis." (Sean O'Hagan in *The Face*).

23 The Fly made it to the cover of the British edition of *Vogue* magazine, along with supermodel Christy Turlington. Bono was the first male to grace the cover of the top fashion mag since Terence Stamp nearly three decades before.

24 The very first song – performed on the Outside Broadcast leg of the ZOO TV tour was 'Sunday Bloody Sunday' in Hershey, Pennsylvania. It was an experimental opening for the show and one that was not repeated.

25 The video release, 'Achtung Baby', the videos, the cameos and a whole lot of interference claims to offer the viewer "the truth, the whole truth and nothing like the truth". Apparently what you see is what you get and what you see is 1.31 inches of videotape per second. As well as a whole lot of interference the video also contains some songs including,
'Even Better Than The Real Thing' directed by Kevin Godley
'Mysterious Ways' directed by Stephane Sednaoui
'One' directed by Anton Corbijn
'The Fly' directed by Ritchie Smyth and Jon Klein
'Even Better than the Real Thing' directed by Ritchie Smyth
'One' directed by Mark Pellington
'Even Better Than The Real Thing' directed by Armando Gallo and Kampah
'One directed by Phil Joanou
'Until The End of the World' directed by Ritchie Smyth
and a whole lot of interference generally directed by Maurice Linnane.

26 Building the ZOO TV show took a minimum of 200 men and women over 40 hours to set up and required 12 mobile office trailers.

PROPAGANDA 7

27 At the Brit Awards in February, the annual ceremony of the British record industry in London, the Chairman insisted on having the category of 'Best Live Act 1992' in order to honour U2 for the Zoo TV tour. The band returned the compliment by flying across to receive it.

28 ZOO TV video crew member Richard Davis has got two grandchildren.

29 The fourth show in Mexico City was the last show for Ellen Darst who has worked with U2 for twelve years as Paul McGuinness's Management Associate in the US. Ellen moves on to work with Elecktra Records and will be much missed by all.

30 Press For Action: If you were a member of the press visiting the ZOO TV show you would be provided with the following helpful information by Dave Lemmink, Chief Engineer, Zoo TV. ZOO TV will provide the following for alt US and Canadian tour dates:
15 Composite NTSC baseband video feeds. Press Box connector is BNC female.
15 line-level mono audio feeds. Press Box connector is XLR male.
ZOO TV does NOT provide AC power so please come prepared with battery powered equipment. Please check your equipment before leaving your studio and bring alt necessary interconnect cables, our engineers are extremely busy prior to the show. Also note that many of the newer one-piece BetaCam ENG units will not accept an external video input. We cannot provide any taped video material without prior arrangements with U2 production management."

31 The surnames of the truck drivers on the ZOO TV tour were Herbert, Rich, Sallee, Jones, Stevens, Liss, Abbate, Harrison, McGeough, Lawson, Bjorklund, Bain, Kueblar, Plumley, Froneck, Hadley, Mederos, Lorenzana, Dodson, Puckett, Davis, Hereford, Marshall and Dipaola.

32 The singer came undone during one show. Edge recalls: "Bono split his pants one night mid-way through the set and he ended up asking a girl in the audience to gaffa tape him back together to finish the show. That was funny."
Another night: "We got mugged by two girls that jumped up on stage – they were like six foot three model types and full of energy. They basically jumped on Bono and myself on the b-stage like big Alsatian puppies completely out of control."

33 Peter 'Willie' Williams received the industry award of 'Lighting Designer of the Year' for the design of the ZOO TV show.

34 Members of the 'Emergency Broadcast Network' (who made, amongst other things, the now infamous video clip of George Bush singing 'We Will Rock You') brought their Satellite Dish Projector to Yankees Stadium in New York. They brought their Large dish into the stadium and set it up on the roof of the mixer tower, all without the aid of any tickets or working passes. When asked how they achieved such a feat, EBN's Gardener Post replied, "We're just so used to functioning without official credentials. Last year we did the whole Lollapalooza tour without passes of any sort..."

35 When U2 tickets went on sale in Los Angeles, Pacific Bell telephone company reported an incomprehensible 54 million phone call attempts in four hours, as redial buttons were pressed again and again...

161

THE ZOO TV GUIDE
69

36 EuroPop techno veterans Kraftwerk joined U2 for one show in Manchester, UK, as a protest gig against the Sellafield Nuclear Plant in the north of England.

37 A ZOO TV interview. *Propaganda -* Ready?
Singer – Ask me a question on sport.
Propaganda – Is the ZOO concept everything you thought it was going to be?
Guitarist – ZOO is not a concept, it is a way of life.
Propaganda – Has the ZOO ever gone completely out of control?
Guitarist – That's the whole idea. When it goes badly wrong it is at its best.
Propaganda – Has it ever gone badly right?
Singer – Yes. Willie, come on you get involved in this too.
Production Designer – For me the failure of the Los Angeles shows was that they went so well.
Singer – That's true.
Propaganda – Too smooth, a bit predictable?
Production Designer – 'Smooth' is not really a word which springs to mind for a U2 ZOO show. The LA shows were perhaps a little smooth though, which is a bit of a disappointment.
Singer – Actually, I really enjoyed the LA shows because it was one of those rare opportunities when I could think about singing and the music as opposed to just staying on my feet...
Production Designer – ... and not physically accosting any member of the band.
Propaganda – Paul McGuinness says he thinks your voice has improved still further on this tour.
Singer – Really ? That's very nice of him to say that: I've been having a lot of luck with my voice and I feel like I'm really enjoying singing on stage for the first time, as opposed to just shouting at people for a living, which is what the early eighties felt like.

I'm really enjoying being on stage and I Like the fact that we've got a script. It is not a jukebox that people just press a button and come out with a different song. ZOO TV is more than that, there is a beginning, middle and end to the show – we have got an opportunity to mess with it but only to a certain degree and then it falls apart in the wrong sort of way as opposed to when we get it working and it falls apart in the right sort of way.
Propaganda – One script, or several ?
Singer – There are a few different scripts but they have the same beginning, middle and end.
Propaganda – One American newspaper described the show as the one by which all other must be measured?
Singer – In the midst of this seventies revival happening here I think maybe the critics Like the show because it is at Least facing the future. It is the one concert you can go to these days and not hear Black Sabbath rifts.
Guitarist – More's the pity. But we're working on that.
Propaganda – Is there also a sense that this is a way forward with open-air stadium shows where before their prospects looked a bit bleak.
Guitarist – Stadium concerts are strange things and you have to accept that as a basic but once you have accepted that they are inherently weird, you say to yourself, well what are we going to do with it, where can we take it that will make it work.
Singer – Some people want to go back to the sixties when the music was fresh and new. Now, they say, you've got 50,000 or 80,000 people in a stadium looking down on the stage from on high but back then you just had 250,000 people in a field and nobody could see a thing.
Production Designer – Much cooler.
Singer – Yes. Much cooler. What is it Like at the back of the show, Willie?
Production Designer – I think

PROPAGANDA 9

we have shown many groups that they have no future in stadiums because we have found new and exciting ways of spending inconceivably large amounts of money. As an economic measure – from a management point of view – playing to a quarter of a million people on a postage stamp is far more attractive than going in and giving people the treat of their lives. Although I am stuck behind the lighting desk during shows I have it on good authority that the further away from the stage you get the better it gets because it is more visually

comprehensive – you can take it all in.
Singer – It's more of a trip, the drug fiends will go to the back.
Propaganda – This tour is even longer than the Joshua Tree tour. Are you at the point where you think, "I can't go out and sing these songs again." Do songs come up in the set and you think, "Oh, I could skip this one"?
Singer – There is not one song in this set I think that about. There used to be in other sets.
Guitarist – What was your most hated song from previous sets?
Singer – The hardest one for

me was "In God's Country". It was very hard to sing, it was in a range that was a little bit too high for me.
Guitarist – "Two Hearts Beat As One" was the one I used to hate the most from a playing point of view.
Production Designer – Those are my two favourite U2 songs of all time. (General laughter.)
Propaganda – What songs do you miss the most this time around?
Guitarist – Exit. We don't have enough of those hit singles in our set.
Propaganda – Are you disappointed you haven't had a

string of number ones this time around as you did with "The Joshua Tree" or did you expect that?
Singer – The only song that we thought might go to number one was "One".
Guitarist – We should have called it "Fourteen" because that's where it went in the charts. (More general laughter.)
Singer – Four.
Guitarist – Sorry, was it four?
Singer – We were a bit disappointed about that but then generally singles have choruses and that was the bit we missed in "One". There's

two kinds of U2 fans – there's the ones that want us to get to Number One because they just like the idea of us winning out there. Then there's the others who actually get disappointed when we get to number one because their little brother gets into it.

Production Designer – But at least "One" had five videos which is something that most songs don't get.

Propaganda – Do chauffeurs and police patrols make more sense in the world of ZOO TV?

Singer – You feel less guilty riding around in these ridiculous limos.

Guitarist – I think we mistakenly saw the trappings as important in '87 but I don't think we see them as significant at all now. We laugh at it now – that's the difference.

Propaganda – Hence the ZOO Lifestyle, from the stage into real life.

Guitarist – I took a taxi just last week and it was fine. (General laughter.)

Propaganda – When did you last wash your socks?

Guitarist – I don't know, you'd have to ask Finton.

Singer – He wouldn't touch the damn things.

Production Designer – The limos of course are now a performance art piece, like arriving today for a Sunday afternoon picnic in a San Francisco suburb in a stretch limo with a chauffeur.

Propaganda – You have now created a context whereby you make sense.

Singer/Guitarist/Production Designer – (Laughing.)

Guitarist – ZOO TV is ordinary life but just more realistic.

Production Designer – Exactly.

Propaganda (to Production Designer) – What was that you said to that guy from the lighting magazine who interviewed you?

Production Designer – I was being interviewed by a guy who last saw the indoor Joshua Tree tour who was thrilled to death with the minimalism and the German expressionism. He came back and saw this show after

heralding me as the bastion of minimalism and said to me, "So Willie, your watchword always used to be 'less is more' – what happened to that?"
So I said, "Well, less is more but I discovered that 'More' is even more."

All – (Laughing heads off.)

Propaganda – That sums up ZOO TV doesn't it.

Singer – Yes. Maximum minimalism, yes.

Propaganda – You are making contradiction an art really aren't you?

Singer – If it's not a contradiction it's not art.

Propaganda – How come "Sunday Bloody Sunday" ended up back in the set? Didn't you vow never to play that again?

Guitarist – We lied.

Singer – ZOO TV allows you to go back on things you have said and basically we gave Willie too much power.

Propaganda – There is a rumour that you couldn't remember how to play it and you had to send someone out to buy the CD. Is that true?

Guitarist – Yes. But that is not unusual.

Propaganda – Are there quite a few U2 songs that U2 don't know how to play?

Guitarist – Any that I haven't played in the last three weeks. That's part of the problem with being a guitar player who has never read music or even thought about how to notate what I play. It's all down to muscular memory. Once I have devised the parts and the ideas then I quite quickly forget how I arrived at them and I have to rely on memory to be able to play them again.

Propaganda – Has there been some historical revisionism of the "Rattle and Hum" era recently?

Singer – We're all for historical revisionism. We are the Gang of 4, the "politburo" after all.

Guitarist – History is relative.

Propaganda – In one or two interviews there's a feeling conveyed that maybe you lost your direction with "Rattle and Hum" slightly and it got a bit out of hand.

Guitarist – My line is that the only mistake we made is that when we first planned an album and a movie, we were thinking of a small record, something we would put together quickly and release – that it wouldn't be an epic, grand statement, but a step to one side, a collection of a few new songs and some live songs. The mistake was when we figured out that we had to go to a major studio to finance a film because without any of us ever noticing suddenly the whole project became even more mega, even more huge than the album that we had just had out, "The Joshua Tree".

It was sleight of hand, suddenly it just changed, and we didn't realize until it was out what was happening. It was when they started airbrushing my stubble out for the album sleeve that I realized there was something up.

Propaganda – From the perspective of fans it remains a favourite.

Singer – I think it is a really good record. The only thing that went wrong with it was the marketing around it, which went really over the top particularly in America and understandably got up people's noses. It was too much. But musically it was never where we were going, it was always a little detour. But there are some fine songs on there, I'm still into them anyway.

Propaganda – There was a guy who jumped on the stage the other night, around about "Bullet the Blue Sky" or "Running To Stand Still", who looked as if he took you by surprise?

Singer – He did surprise me. That is a pretty far gone point of the set – I wouldn't mess with me. But he got dragged into the performance, I was in a trance and I saw him but I hadn't come out of character so I knocked him over – gently, I was in control enough for that – and dragged him to the end of the b-stage and he went along with it. And I lay him down and thumped him in the chest.

Propaganda – Properly.

Singer - No, acting, and he went along with it really well, like he realised that he was part of the performance. But then he started to get palpitations and having difficulty breathing, a kind of after-shock, and I did have a split second where I had a fright when I thought, "Oh, no, is this where life starts imitating art!" You forget what it must be like when somebody else gets up onstage – it could scare you.

Propaganda – What's the story with the punchbag?

Production Designer – It's to save furniture and television bulbs.

Propaganda – You get pretty psyched up during the show.

Singer – I haven't worked it out at all yet – all I know is that certain songs can bully you, can get on your back and you can't shake them off during the performance. Some songs you actually can't leave, you can't get out of character – so sometimes the only way I can relax is to just hit something (laughs). It's an extraordinary thing that happens to you out there on stage, seconds are hours basically. And if something goes wrong, it is going wrong for a long time.

Propaganda – So when that song wouldn't start the other night...

Singer – Yeah, it's hours. It's like you're holding on to a lightning rod but if something goes wrong, sometimes the energy backfires. So I have a punchbag back there in the dressing room – rather than throwing the television out of the window.

38 Shows in Milan, Italy, were postponed by a day, due to a vital truck breaking down somewhere in the Pyrenees Mountains.

39 At the (very small) ASU activities centre in Tempe, Arizona, Bono kicked a cup of water from the stage, which remained full as it sailed over the crowd and landed directly on the lighting console. The console instantly ceased to function.

40 A mini-TV station was set up under the stage in each city where ZOO TV played, using live satellite broadcasts during the show. Bono used a channel changer to choose stations from the satellite feed. The video director, Carol Dodds, used a custom system developed for the tour by Philips Interactive Media called Cdi. It was the first time this kind of media has been used in a live show. She had 12 laser disc players, monitors containing the live television feeds and 5 camera systems which she mixed on site during each show it was a flexible system which could be changed nightly. There were four mega video screens, four Philips Video-Walls and 36 video monitors. The discs contained footage created by Kevin Godley, Brian Eno, Mark Pellington, Peter Williams, Carol Dodds and Emergency Broadcast Networks (EBN). There were also 18 projectors in use and a video crew of 18 people assisting Ms Dodds.

41 The estate of Keith Haring gave U2 permission to reproduce Haring's famous "Radiant Baby" logo on one of the Trabants. Thank you.

42 The ZOO TV Tour started in Lakeland, Florida (by Walt Disney World), rehearsed in Hershey, Pennsylvania (a theme park) and finished the U.S. Leg at Annaheim, California (by Disneyland). Is this significant?

43 At what other rock show do the audience get pizza thrown in for free? On several stops on the ZOO TV Tour, Bono took advantage of a conveniently placed telephone to call the local dial-a-pizza during the show. Sometimes for the entire audience. That was if he wasn't calling for a chat on a live sex-line, doing some Home Shopping or trying to get through for a chin wag with the President of the United States of America.

44 The stage set included 11 Trabant cars, two of which were suspended over the stage; all had lights inside and out. The Trabant was the People's Car of East Germany, and each one in the show was owned and used by East German families prior to the fall of the Eastern bloc. The cars are made of compressed cardboard, originally weighed 400lbs each and cost around $300. They were structurally modified and now weigh over 2000lbs each. They are decorated with artwork designed by Catherine Owens, Rene Castro and Peter Williams.

45 Heavy Duty is the name of one of the gallant gentlemen who drove the tour buses as the ZOO trundled across America. Normally the comprehensively tattooed Heavy drives a 39 Chevrolet at his 20-acre home in Tennessee where he has a 115-year-old house which he has been restoring. He has also toured with Paul McCartney, Paul Simon and The Grateful Dead. He says, "I enjoyed U2 the most. I've been a fan of theirs since day one, since I was buying imports of their records before they were released in the States." His favourite U2

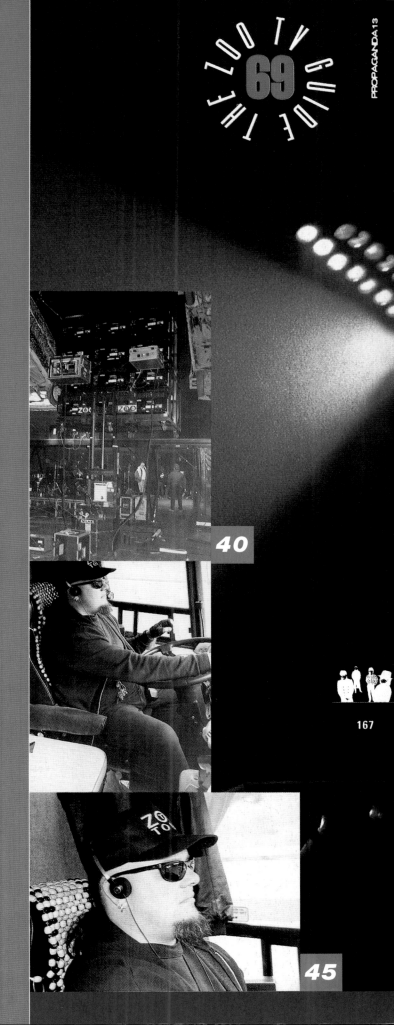

40

167

45

ZOO

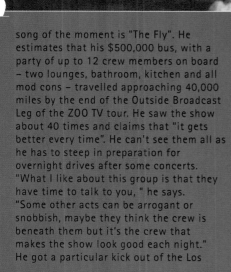

song of the moment is "The Fly". He estimates that his $500,000 bus, with a party of up to 12 crew members on board – two lounges, bathroom, kitchen and all mod cons – travelled approaching 40,000 miles by the end of the Outside Broadcast Leg of the ZOO TV tour. He saw the show about 40 times and claims that "it gets better every time". He can't see them all as he has to steep in preparation for overnight drives after some concerts. "What I like about this group is that they have time to talk to you, " he says. "Some other acts can be arrogant or snobbish, maybe they think the crew is beneath them but it's the crew that makes the show look good each night." He got a particular kick out of the Los

Angeles show, where the company included Jack Nicholson, Sean Connery, Met Gibson, Billy Idol, Sean Penn, Winona Ryder and Julia Roberts: "Hell, almost everybody in Hollywood was there, there were more stars than there were at the Oscars."

46 ZOO TV opened wide its heavily ironic arms to the media, which is a tiring business for the media's appetite is never sated. Edge: "I feel more and more like a politician on a campaign, constantly at the mercy of the media, doing interviews, being filmed. ZOO TV is life imitating art imitating politics."

47 Benny and Bjorn from ABBA joined U2 on stage in Stockholm for a rendition of "Dancing Queen" beneath the revolving mirrorball Trabant. The show was being broadcast live from The Globe in Stockholm to just one house, the home of competition winner John Harris of Nottinghamshire in England.

48 There was a fifteen-strong team of catering staff feeding the animals on the ZOO tour.

49 Robert Hilburn the Pop Music Critic of the Los Angeles Times wrote after two LA

shows on the ZOO TV tour that the
"Irish quartet demonstrated once again why it is the only contemporary band with the ambition and talent to once have been considered on the same level as the Beatles." He said that the "elaborate video-monitor system delivers such a startling sense of intimacy and immediacy to the proceedings that it may become the standard for stadium concerts in the '90s."

50 Greenpeace were present at all the ZOO TV shows. Kerry Mahoney and Kate Adams from Greenpeace travelled to each venue and worked with local members setting up tables for fund raising and information.

51 Three Grove-man lifts are used during the show.

52 Golf carts are used in some US stadiums to transport people around them because they are so vast. A golf cart from the Yankees Stadium show was found, later that night, abandoned in central Manhattan.

53 U2's Outside Broadcast video system includes a vast array of broadcast television production and projection equipment which filled two 48-foot semi-trailers and was run by a crew of 18 people. The production carried an entire video broadcast facility with the capacity for uplink/downlink and on-site editing. Some of the features of the system are:
23 inputs including:
4 Ikegami HL-55A CCD cameras with component CCUs
1 POV camera
10 Pioneer 8000 laserdisk playback decks
4 3/4" and Betacam SP playback decks
2 'BonoCams' (handheld video cameras)
1 Satellite dish and receiver
1 Philips CD-I player
47 simultaneous outputs including:
4 15" x 20" rear projection screens using 18 GE Talaria 5055HB light valve projectors
4 Philips 4 x 3 "Vidiwall" video walls
36 27" Barco monitors
1 Press feed
1 Auxiliary video feed (for stadiums with JumboTrons, Diamond Vision etc)
1 Satellite uplink feed
The system is run by four Personal Computers with customized hardware and software built specifically for the ZOO TV tour. A crew of three engineers control the system electronics from beneath the stage. The director and assistant director call the show from their perch on the second level of the mix platform in the front of house. They can view all the screens and also monitor all the system inputs from a remote switching console located in this position. Video projectionists control the video projectors from positions as high as 60 feet behind the large video screens flanking and hanging above the stage. The entire video system is worth over 3.5m US dollars. Typical system set-up time is approximately 10 hours and it is packed in racks and cases that fit under the performance stage. (And all this information comes to you from Dave Lemmink, Chief Engineer, ZOO TV.)

54 One fine day at rehearsals the entire scaffolding crew decided to shave their heads. It seemed like a good idea at the time.

THE ZOO TV GUIDE

55 Before the show every night on the Outside Broadcast leg of the ZOO TV Tour, U2 fans could enter the Video Confessional – a lavishly converted portaloo – and record a confession to camera. If it made the grade during playback, while the show was running, it was aired to the entire audience right before the encore of the concert.

56 ZOO TV is not a concept but a way of life, claimed The Edge. A way of life requires a form of hard currency – this was it.

57 You saw it here first. No sooner had the ZOO TV station ceased transmission for the winter, than British television programmes started unashamedly jumping on the bandwagon with Jonathan Ross' Saturday Night Zoo and the emergence of the ZOO TV phenomenon. *The Face* magazine, documenting the emergence of the genre in the UK, felt moved to emphasise that "ZOO TV isn't anything to do with U2". Hmmm.

U2 THE BEST OF PROPAGANDA

58 Important implement in order to keep the ZOO station clean.

59 Edge talking whilst in the Catering Marquee before the show in San Francisco: "I think ZOO TV can go further. I don't mean bigger – but it can be pushed further along the lines it is developing already. We make discoveries every now and again – like Emergency Broadcast Network, a group of video artists on the East Coast, who did the George Bush, 'We Will Rock You' sequence. I think we can take it further – it's not as zoo as it can be. There are still some wild, unorthodox, unpredictable, furry animals to go in this zoo.

We've a very a-la-carte attitude to technology, we find our own use for it. We're not interested in helping technology develop for the betterment of humankind so much as we are in using what is out there for our own selfish, fascist ends. Mostly what we do is abuse it by doing things with it that it wasn't designed to do – that's part of the fun. It's about trial and error, not necessarily knowing what you want but recognizing it when it hits you over the head.

A lot of our discoveries are made by accident. And even with the show we tried a lot of things that didn't work ... things that looked good on paper but were disastrous when we came to doing them. We've just kept the good things. It's all completely subjective, it's what you end up liking and what you end up thinking is great.

What I am enjoying about this tour is that people are even more mystified than ever before, not having a clue where we are coming from but still enjoying it. At times we allow the production to dominate and at times we don't. It's just a setting, a context for the material. And like any background you get bored with it after a while so you have to change it.

Once the visuals are in place I don't look at them, I'm thinking about performing the song. The visuals are there to support the performance and once they are in place I just concentrate on the performance, I don't really worry about the visuals.

ZOO TV is about ideas, more than about stage sets, the hardware is not what is important so much as the software.

55

SWITCHING SYSTEM

ZOO TV TOUR

HUSH

56

58

60 "U2's ZOO TV tour has grown into a thing of rich proportions; groovy, elevated, sad, but mostly just high on its own sense of the royal daftness of rock 'n' roll." Stuart Bailie in *NME*.

61 Without doubt the most overpriced hotel of the tour was in San Sebastian, Spain. The hotel charged management associate Sheila Roche $1200.00 for one long-distance phone call. Is this a record?

62 When finally having settled the astronomical bill for the whole touring party at the San Sebastian hotel, tour accountant Bob Koch was heard asking the hotel manager, "So which part of the hotel do we own now?"

63 Bono only broke two television monitors throughout the entire tour.

64 Rigger Warren Jones from New Zealand, took a day trip from El Paso, Texas, over the border into Mexico. Unfortunately upon his return he discovered that he had accidentally taken his three-year-old son's passport with him instead of his own. Four hours later U.S. immigration officials let him rejoin the tour.

171

65 In Vienna, Austria, Axl Rose joined Bono and The Edge on stage for a rendition of "Knocking On Heaven's Door"

66 Counting off the shows. Graffiti in the lighting console ... what a long strange, trip it's been.

THE ZOO TV GUIDE

67 Without U2's fans there would be... well... empty stadiums. But down at the front it can get a bit crushed.

68 Edge: "After this is over, I'll be glad to get home again. I might just go and read in a library for a while."

69 *Propaganda* World Exclusive – Photographic evidence of where the whole thing came from.

66

67

69

173

Satellite of Love

When Bill Carter flew to Italy from Sarajevo in June to interview U2 for Bosnian TV, he had no idea what he was getting himself into.

In the end he was responsible, night after night, for bringing ordinary people – from a country that has become a war-zone – live by satellite into the presence of thousands of U2 Zooropa concert fans.

This is Bill's own story.

We were driving at 140 km per hour down what is known as sniper's alley. Moments before the 'safe' zone, the bullets started to rip into the hood of the car. With a little evasive driving everyone in the car escaped injury. The passengers were Darko and Vlado with myself at the helm. It was after ten o'clock which in Sarajevo is a dangerous time to travel because it's after police hour, but we had a good reason to be out that late. We had just finished doing a live satellite link-up to the U2 concert in Bologna.

> Moments before the 'safe' zone, the bullets started to rip into the hood of the car. With a little evasive driving everyone in the car escaped injury.

The link-ups had started only the night before and I had the rest of the European schedule to organise for. The whole idea started way back in Verona, Italy, July 3rd at a U2 concert. I had been in Sarajevo since late March working on humanitarian food convoys and shooting a documentary during the month of May. After being in Sarajevo for that long, I had watched politicians of the world be completely apathetic and the United Nations run a mockery of an operation in Bosnia that included soldiers running goods on the black market and an inept political and military policy. I found myself becoming more involved with the way people save their minds in this absolutely insane situation.

Thus I started to think of ways to address the mental humanitarian issue. For twenty months this has been a besieged city that no one is allowed to leave. There is no electricity to most of the city, no constant water supply, and very little food. If they have to go through another winter

in these conditions a great deal of people will die from the sheer conditions of the cold. They have already cut down most of the city trees to have fuel for last winter. The conditions are inhumane. Add to that the constant barrage of shells and sniper's that kill people everyday.

Yet aside from all the politics and history involved in the war, the people are very cultured and sophisticated who are accustomed to rock 'n' roll, cafes and normal life. So I thought if anyone is going to reach out to give this kind of mental humanitarian help in the name of human rights it would be U2. Their history of music and their country's history makes the connection

> After a week and a half of faxes and phone calls to Dublin and London, I got a reply saying that Bono was interested in doing an interview for Sarajevo TV. I was off to Verona.

very real. So after a week and half of faxes and phone calls to Dublin and London, I got a reply saying that Bono was very interested in doing an interview for Sarajevo T.V. Since no one from the T.V. could actually leave Sarajevo I was to be their liaison. I was off to Verona with the blessing of Sarajevo T.V.

I got to Verona via boat from Croatia, and a car ride with my friends Jason Aplon and Ivana Sirovic, who were instrumental in making this all happen. I got to the venue and just before the concert I was told the interview would happen immediately before the show. The interview, more a conversation than an interview, was a little over ten minutes and very intense, with the conversation leaning itself to the human cycle of killing, with Bosnia being the focus of the conversation. A country in Europe that is facing a genocide only fifty years after the last one is an unacceptable event. It became obvious from the conversation that Bono had spent considerable time thinking about the war next door (only 45 minutes by jet) and had a strong feel for what was happening. In addition to the interview he offered me a tape of the whole Verona concert to show on Sarajevo T.V. The people of Sarajevo need this form of help more than any other, and it was extremely forthcoming.

After the show Bono and Edge wanted to know what they could do. What can U2 do? Up to this point I was still very much

their base. So that was set up through Dublin and we were on our way. At this point U2 pumped up the volume by saying they wanted to do the link-up every concert and to start as soon as possible: that was in two days in Marseilles, France. I was working very much by myself at this point and in a very real war situation. The Serbian attacks during this time were heavy with shells falling constantly, and I couldn't imagine getting ready in two days. It was all happening so fast and it was unclear what would be the format of the actual link.

Nevertheless, the first contact had been arranged to be by 'phone in

← mentally in Sarajevo and very tired. But when the biggest band in the world asked you what they can do ... I was a little stumped. What is needed is for Europe and the world to wake up to the problem and do something on a direct, political and, if necessary, military level. Bono and Edge both said it was time for something radical. Something to seriously jar people out of their numbness to what's happening in this continent. Don't let all the arguments and excuses of history and religion confuse the true issue. There is history and religion in every country and in every war: that doesn't justify the simple fact that people are dying and being starved for reasons they, as modem Europeans, don't understand. And it's not excusable that we sit and watch it happen.

As the conversation and evening came to an end, all of us had no good ideas as to what to do. But the band was very keen on going to and playing in the only existing disco in Sarajevo. Everyone was into it, but going to Sarajevo under any circumstance is dodgy and needs to be thought out. So the last words spoken that night in Verona were "Let's think of something and do it". With that, I and my friends returned to Croatia and were thinking a million miles a minute·

By the time we arrived back in Split, Croatia, Regine Moylett, the band's publicity manager, had already called and stressed that the band wanted to come and wanted to know had I thought of anything constructive and useful that the band could do. Indeed we had. Coming to Sarajevo was out, considering over the weekend that three thousand shells had fallen. This is where the satellite connection came to mind.

Jason and I thought that by using ZOO T.V.'s powerful medium I could be in Sarajevo and try a satellite link-up to the concert. At first the idea from all sides was for this to be in the Sarajevo disco, but for

various reasons that was impossible. I was focused on the Budapest and Wembley stadium concerts because of the politics of the two places. Both places would have a great deal of people from former Yugoslavia and by having people from Sarajevo speak to them they could see what was really happening. It was July 10th by the time I got back to Sarajevo and Budapest was on July 23rd and I had no idea of how this would work technically. Add to that the fact that there is very little way to communicate with the outside world once inside Sarajevo. To say the least I felt unsure how this was going to be pulled off.

After two days in Sarajevo and numerous inquiries into the technical aspects I found myself in the studio of EBU, European Broadcast Union. They are a rental up-link satellite house that almost all news agencies in Sarajevo use. All that needs to happen is that they give you an account and you pay your bills to Geneva,

How does one hang up the phone with fifty thousand people and U2 ... and walk into a war?

Marseilles. I had to run across the field to the very exposed Holiday Inn, dodging sniper fire, and arrange a satellite 'phone with Reuters, the news agency. They welcomed the idea and one hour after, Bono called from the venue live to Sarajevo via satellite phone. A very bizarre feeling to speak to Bono and to fifty thousand people over a phone. Surreal is the only word that comes to mind. How does one hang up the phone with fifty thousand people and U2 and walk into a war?

After I hung up, the concert in Marseilles went on while I ran back across the field to safety. The next link was in Bologna, Italy with Vlado and Darko,

which is where we begin this story. Darko and Vlado are Serbs living in a town, Sarajevo, that is extremely mixed, and are fighting for their lives against the Serbian Nationalist forces. Darko told the fifty thousand people that his parents live three kilometres from where we were standing and he hasn't seen them in over a year and has no way to contact them. We were standing in a dark hallway of the TN station. There is no electricity in Sarajevo and we were using battery lights.

The content of all the remaining link-ups, twelve in all, were live video feeds with someone from Sarajevo and myself speaking to the concert. Bono and I were strictly the facilitator for letting the person from Sarajevo speak. The link-ups had a double purpose: one was to use U2's voice to speak to Europe during this Zooropa tour and speak to them about a problem that is threatening the very base of human rights in Europe. Two was to give the people of Bosnia a voice to the outside world. The link itself was the importance for the people of Sarajevo. U2 represents to them the world they knew 18 months ago: there has been no connection since to the outside world, especially a live connection. The news that you see on T.V. edits people's lives and stories into 30 second sterile pieces. T.V. has allowed us to become numb to death, to life, and to the very world we live in. We've become buffered from the realities

of life. This connection into a rock 'n' roll concert represents where a live connection shouldn't be. But the contradiction itself is shocking enough to jar people out of their fantasies and into reality.

In Sarajevo the reaction from the people was tremendous. I went on the Bosnian radio and T.V. and did interviews on the local radio and newspapers. The people understood what was happening and they trusted it because I had been there long enough and they understood the genuineness of it. I have friends there, some that have died and some that are still

> In Sarajevo the reaction from the people was tremendous. I went on the Bosnian radio and TV and did interviews in local radio and newspapers. The people understood what was happening and they trusted it because I had been there long enough and they understood the genuineness of it.

alive but facing winter. Many people would tell me the spiritual uplift they felt due to the connection. You can turn off your T.V. but you can't turn off a concert. All the link-ups were very direct and they did not blame anyone for their predicament. They just wanted people to know that they are in fact normal and to let Europe know that this will become their problem if not

stopped. Fascism is not an idea that dies out but instead is fuelled like wild fire. To stop the war means the people running the war machine will have to face the piper: their own people and the rest of the world. As individuals they cannot do that. It would mean political suicide and the human ego won't let them quit.

The stress in doing these link-ups was tremendous. These were real people telling their real stories. That's a very hard thing to do. Add to that the absolute cynicism and rudeness we received from EBU and various other foreign media. Most of the foreign media were very receptive because they knew that I had been there for a while and this was not a U2 "thing" but instead a joint idea in giving the people here a medium to speak. Twice U2 management and myself got families together via the satellite link-up. At the Stockholm, Sweden concert Enes, a twenty--three year old fireman was with me in Sarajevo, and U2 had invited his wife and her family, who are from Sarajevo but living in Stockholm, to the concert. It was a phenomenal connection. They hadn't seen each other for seventeen months. He couldn't see her, but she could see him on the forty-foot screen which you could imagine was a shock.

There was another family link that happened, and the effect on the people in Sarajevo was tremendous. They were indebted and one mother told me that now she could die since she had spoken to her son.

Once we got to Wembley, after a month of concerts, I was thoroughly exhausted. I had seen a four-year-old have her head blown off by a sniper; a family down the road had committed suicide because they couldn't face another winter; expectations of intervention had come and gone and I was feeling pretty hopeless. In Wembley three women, a Serb, a Croat, and a Muslim, who had been friends for twenty-five years spoke to the crowd. They stressed that they wanted to live together. The reaction in the English press was astounding. They attacked U2 for exploitation and using a war situation in their concerts as being ridiculous. This wounded all those involved especially the people in Sarajevo. The journalists who wrote those articles never took the proper time to investigate how the project started. I invite all those journalists to come to Sarajevo with me and talk to the people there and see how it affected them. And the idea of having this in a rock 'n' roll show was that it was forcing people to see the reality exactly where they didn't think it would be.

All in all the whole experience was phenomenal. It all happened so fast. U2 was so quick to do something. It took my wildest idea of how to mentally help these people back in June to a much higher level by letting Bosnians speak to hundreds of thousands of people in a human way. A way any normal person couldn't deny. The concerns and reasons from everyone were so genuine and that's why it worked. By the end of it I was emotionally exhausted and the band invited me along for the Irish part of the

The whole experience was phenomenal – letting Bosnians speak to hundreds of thousands of people in a human way.

tour to relax, which was a bit surreal considering where I had come from after five months.

Anything we do as individuals is worth the effort. The people of Bosnia realise it is too difficult for all people to think of all the suffering going on in the world, but we must, to keep our humaneness, think of this situation where people are truly the victims of an unprecedented slaughter. People argue sometimes: it's too complicated, there are wars everywhere, or it's the cycle of life. To endorse the above arguments means history will continue to shape us whereas we should shape history. The sovereign people of Bosnia are victims of classic aggression of one country against another, western politicians' short-sighted policies, and the paralysed world caught in a constant state of confusion. The reality is that Europe and eventually the world will pay slowly for the passive role we have played in this war.

I felt the pressure of representing Bosnia and Sarajevo, trying to get their point across in a short three-four minute window of time. For U2, it's always a risk to seriously depress fifty thousand people who have paid twenty pounds to have a good time. It's always a risk doing a satellite link from anywhere, but especially from a place where a bomb could land on the roof at any second. But like the band said back in Verona, "It's time to do something radical." There are thousands of people who went to the U2 concerts that I hope now realise the people of Sarajevo are normal people who are being massacred by a fascism that destroyed this continent fifty years ago.

There are groups in Bosnia doing amazing charity work and they do need monetary help to continue. The most grass roots and genuine groups are:

The Serious Road Trip
Cradle Bowman House
7-12 Greenland Street
London NW 1 ON
England
Charity No. 1021945
Telephone: (44) – 71 – 916 9333
Fax: (44) – 71 – 916 9335

The Factory
35a Barrow Street
Dublin 2
Eire
Charity No. APP10807
Tel: (353) – 1 – 668 0721
Fax: (353) – 1 – 668 0715

Any donation would surely help the humanitarian efforts in Sarajevo, whose people survive 100% on humanitarian aid.

Bill Carter, 27, is a film-maker in San Francisco, California. He has recently completed a documentary on Sarajevo. ❤

Lights, Camera,

The German film director Wim Wenders and U2 are old collaborators. Wim shot a video for their contribution to the AIDS benefit album *Red Hot and Blue*, while they have contributed songs to his two recent films, *Until The End of the World* and *Faraway, So Close!* Last year Wim took a break from editing his film and U2 took a break from recording *Zooropa* to talk on the phone about films, the Zoo TV tour, the new Europe and media fatigue.

Wim Wenders (in Munich): *I'm sitting in an office. Alone, because I've sent everyone out. I thought it would be more cool if it was just us.*

Bono (in Dublin): We're here with just a few pizzas.

You're better off than me, I've only got some hazelnuts and nothing to break them with but my hands.

Bono: After working so hard on your film, I'd have thought you'd do that with your head. How long have you been working on it?

It's been non-stop for six months and we've got about three weeks left to wind it all up.

Bono: Worse than us!

I know! But I'm not sure: I've never been on tour like you. That must be worse than making films.

Bono: There is even worse, making a film about a tour.

You're warning me? It's nice not to ask anyway.

Bono: That's natural. We want to spare you.

How long are you going on tour for?

Edge: Until the end of August. And if it doesn't go too badly we'll go to Australia and Japan at the end of the year. For Europe, we don't need more than four months. What's making things more difficult in fact is that we've decided to record an album before we hit the road. In six weeks. It usually take us six months. That doesn't mean a lot, a stack of important tracks recorded in six days. But the way we work in the studio isn't the quickest.

So you're in the studio at the moment. Is that where I'm calling you?

Bono: Yep.

And you've given yourselves six weeks?

Bono: And we're slogging at it six days out of seven. We're taking just a day to get back to the real world. Only we're not sure that the real world is the best place to live, and everyone's really pleased to be back in the studio on Monday morning.

I know the feeling. I'm trying to rest on Sundays too.

Bono: How long have you been working on *Until the End of The World*?

Six years, in total. But the shooting only took six and a half months.

Bono: Hey, I met Simon Carmody in Dublin last night. He's a singer and a writer. Without knowing that we were going to call each other today he talked to me about your film; he loved it but thought it was too short. I immediately thought I must tell Wim that. I believe you've taken it back to its original length?

Yes, we've finished the trilogy: six hours of performance including two half-hour intervals.

Bono: Wow!

Achtung Baby

The film is definitely better now. And your song crops up in several countries: in a ghetto blaster in the States, in a garage in France. It's more like my original idea but since it had to be cut, heaps of songs suffered.

Edge: The restrictions on length and format imposed by business can be a real curse.

It's the same for a record isn't it?

Edge: A big yes. In fact, we're at a very interesting stage in this project with a different emphasis. We've come to think much more in terms of the whole thing. Not only the music and the words, but the visual as well. To the point where we are wondering whether to bring out the album without the usual first single taken from it, and replacing it with a video. You'd buy the album or the video of the single.

I see. Like for the show, have you got a lot of TVs on stage?

Bono: The TV thing for us is a way of making friends with your enemy. That's how we approach the Zoo TV Tour; we take over everything we're frightened of. Before we felt hemmed in by our status as the monsters of rock who perform in those ridiculous places called stadiums. That science-fiction vision of a mass of concrete and steel with chips and T-shirt stands. For a long time we behaved as though all that didn't exist and concentrated on the music. Now we've decided to integrate all those things that shocked us into the show, and we feel freeer. Hey! Adam's just arrived.

Adam: Hey Wim, how goes it?

Adam, it's a pleasure to hear you.

Adam: I really liked your new film. It looks perfect and I hope we'll be able to add our touch. You should get the tapes tomorrow.

No, I've got them.

Adam: Already?

Yes, just about an hour ago. I've listened to them once. Do you want me to talk about them now?

Adam: Not necessarily.

When I heard Johnny Cash on the first bit I was flabbergasted. What is it?

Bono: It's Brian Eno. I wasn't sure if the Johnny Cash would fit. Production fought to send it to you. The song we're most sure about is the one we've called "Faraway, So Close!", like the film.

I've listened to it once or twice. Wonderful. There are three versions on the tapes, one instrumental, a second called "Control Room", much more tender and sweet, while the third is more rock with an omnipresent guitar.

Bono: That's it. We've sent you the instrumental version because I thought that the words, even if they share some of the themes of the film, were too specific.

What you consider too specific is in fact very close to the film, the last couples about the fallen angel is superb.

Bono: It's a song about an impossible relationship and someone looking at what's happening. In those kind of situations, observing and the desire to intervene can poison everything.

Yes, it destroys everything. I really like the way that ties in with one of the film's big themes.

Bono: Good. There's another piece, "The Piano Song", with a humming accompaniment. It might fit in with the opening too if you're not too keen on "Faraway, So Close!".

I've listened to that too. The piano is super. Who's playing?

Edge: Me, I must apologise. All my mistakes give the impression of being professional, as if they were deliberate. In fact, we made it with them without trying to improve it.

OK, we'll talk about it again when I've really had time to absorb them ... One of the subjects of Until The End of The World is the image epidemic. I wonder whether the Zoo TV Tour and all the on-stage TVs weren't making a reference to that?

Bono: We are coming to a really interesting time in music where it seems as though classic guitar-based rock is short of ideas. For five years we've heard that rock is dead. We've never really thought of ourselves as a rock group but one feels that there are so many uncertainties that in fact anything is possible. One of the main interests in music is combining everything which has become part of the everyday background like TV programmes or cinema. Anything could happen in a kind of transformation where video games sell more than records, and where audio-visual formats are taking precedence over music. Most showbiz people are shit-scared. We find it stimulating. With the Zoo TV Tour we are getting near this point of transformation, and this over-load of images you refer to is precisely the language of Zoo TV. Richard Kearney, an Irish philosopher, deals with the death of images in his book (*The Awakening of the Imagination*). A theme which you got close to in *Until The End of The World*. The idea that images are manipulated to the point where our perception of reality has taken a knock.

Yes, there is an annihilation of perception. It doesn't mean anything more these days.

Bono: So much that when people see a woman's back on a beach they immediately think of shampoo or jeans. This association of ideas has polluted our way of looking at an image with unprejudiced eyes. Purists prefer to bury their head in the sand and ignore what's happening in the name of a claimed freshness. We're going the opposite way, we're forging into the future with open arms, curious about what is going to happen and confident. I'd like to know what you think since you, more than us, you're an image maker.

I'm listening to you. I feel that our professions are getting more and more alike, you're getting closer to images and me to sound. I used to say that my profession consisted of making images and that was true of my first films. I used to shoot, then I mixed and cut, then I remixed and cut and after two months work the final mix of the film was done in three days. These days it's different. I cut my images in two weeks and slave over the sound for six months. I am becoming more of a sound man than an image man. But that doesn't answer your question.

Bono: Don't worry. It's no big deal.

But to come back to it, one has the impression that images these days are always selling something and it is difficult to think about them while freeing them from their commercial function.

Bono: We suffered a bit from that in the 80's because U2 became a caricature, partly our fault I must admit. But we didn't have the slightest idea of the danger that could lead to. That's why we decided to change strategy for our tour and our next album, so that the greatest possible confusion reigns, making it synonymous with originality and erasing the caricatures which have been made around the group.

Yes, I know, as soon as you do what you know about perfectly you fall into the trap.

Bono: Exactly.

You don't start repeating yourself and that's the worst for anyone seeking to stay alert.

Bono: That's exactly what we felt in the studio. We don't worry about borrowing things from other groups. On the other hand, as soon as we noticed that we are back to the U2 sound, we stop everything.

I think that the style and form are less important than the spirit which guides you.

Bono: It's also at the point that when people say to us that we can't do this or that because we're U2, that makes us want to do it even more. Because we think that the spirit of the group is so strong that it can use any style and still be U2. From the past and what's being done today we are trying to build a future. William Burroughs said I think, "You cut up the past to find the future". We're at exactly that point at the moment: if we keep our interest awake our music will be alive. Whereas if you're too sure of what you're doing, you come to a dead end.

It's the same thing when you make a film. If you want to control everything it's stillborn. On my last town films I worked by instinct and that's what kept their sould and spirit.

Bono: I'm asking myself a question: when you see advertisements wearing out cinema clichés, should you find a new visual approach for filming things and people, to frame their faces, to capture their emotions?

When I began making films and people said to me, "I like your film because of all those marvellous images", I was proud. These days I say to myself, "Shit, I must have boobed somewhere". Because any image, any beauty is only an instrument for saying something. The only moral code a film-maker can have from now on can no longer be that of an aesthete. It would be better to say something with a horrible image than with an ultra-polished image. I think more and more that the more beautiful the images the more meaningless they are. They are surrounding us.

Bono: People have lost all confidence in images. Same thing in music. The polish of over-produced work ends up as smooth and glossy surface. That's why a large part of this album is improvised. It's just the four members of the group shut in a room playing together taking risks for six weeks.

Do you go into the studio with songs in your head or do they come as you go along?

Edge: We had pieces which might give birth to songs, but which have lost their interest through familiarity: too structured. Musically, we tend not to give in to logic any more. Mystery gives the tempo, the emotion and the setting.

I get the same feeling when I watch my own films. Everything I've done while sticking to the script now seems relatively uninteresting. Whereas everything I've done trusting to chance has merit.

Bono: It's easy to be complacent with oneself about this idea but I think that when you know what you're doing, everything else must be swept away. It's difficult to experience, but we struggle on. You always want to keep your hands on the wheel, you don't want God to drive. Yet all the best U2 songs have been written by accident. And all the worst have been written by us ... Brian (Eno) has just joined us.

Hey! Brian, you've got a big fan on the line.

Brian Eno: I return the compliment. I've seen the beginning of your film, just the first scenes ...

... and then it'll get worse, Brian.

Brian: Not it won't, Wim, no.

Bono: I want to tell Brian what you said about the way you see films now; Wim listens to them just as much as he watches them. *Yes. I remember that during the time we were mixing "The Goalkeepers' Fear of the Penalty" we had one film and four sound-tracks. These days we still have one film and hundreds of soundtracks with an army of sound editors. The image has become secondary in the long process of finishing a film.*

Brian: Do you feel freer in relation to the world of sound like we do in relation to the world of images?

With the sound I think my work is nearer to the truth than

with the image. The only thing that matters is what you have to say, and the sound has more purity than the image.

Bono: The words are the only thing which should be mistrusted more than the image. One of the things we are learning is that sounds have a meaning and that they speak in a way which may be clearer than words. I'm the group's lyricist and I have this incredible responsibility of putting into words what the musicians are expressing. I often feel that I achieve my purpose less when I am too specific, too precise, because there aren't any appropriate words for what I want to say. Do you trust words?

In any case, more than images. I am persuaded that we are getting to an age where you can believe the words much more than the images.

Brian: Isn't it the same for everyone? Isn't it that we end up losing confidence in the media we work on? For you it's images. For me it's music. Because I know how it's made and marketed. And I know how it can be tampered with. Yet I believe in manipulation and special effects, even if I haven't any

arguments to defend them.

Bono: We've spent a crazy time dissecting TV and adverts to make a parody of the chaos they cause. We've done a very critical satire of them in ZOO TV. The irony is that ZOO TV has now been taken over by the advertising world and at the moment there are three or four international campaigns inspired by what we did ... We're now a bit puzzled about authenticity. In musical terms, a gospel chorale would be authentic whereas the German genius of a group like Kraftwerk wouldn't be. It would be considered a synthetic. Whereas, for me, Kraftwerk has just as much soul as the Temptations. The idea of authenticity is more and more difficult to define. What do you think?

Absolutely. I think that "contemporary" is more appropriate. For it indicates a rapport with the forms. Language and style of the moment. Kraftwerk was completely authentic in the '70s because they illustrated the data of the period.

Bono: In any case "authenticity" is a word I can't use anymore because it doesn't mean anything for me any more.

For me it's "reality" which I've crossed off my vocabulary.

Bono: I think that when words present a problem, you don't solve the problem but you stop using them, because if they don't mean anything anymore they're no use any more.

Agreed, throw them out.

Bono: Let's draw up a black list: "original" is a word which can disappear. And what do you think about "working class hero"?

After Communism the word may make a come-back.

Bono: Talking about that, we live on a small island on the edge of Europe, in Ireland. You, in Germany, live right in the middle. We'd like to know your feelings about what's happening, just before your next cob-nut.

Right, I'm just cracking one under the table so you won't hear it.

Bono: Don't be bashful, Wim, we understand!

You can feel Berlin's pulse with a quite distinctive sharpness at the moment. There's a sense of a huge migration beginning to move. Suddenly an incredible number of Russians, Poles and Czechs are becoming our new neighbours. That frightens quite a few people. Racism is reappearing and with it fascism. Fear of seeing their wealth appropriated by others.

Bono: That's doubtless because the situation in Berlin is more fluid than anywhere else in Europe. People want to recreate rules, systems and classes, so as to separate themselves from each other. Berlin has always been a place in the front line.

That's why I live here; there's a smell of truth in the air here. There's no other city like it.

Brian: Truth is another of those words, Wim.

Okay, okay, scrub it.

Bono: I'm for truth. Brian is against it. I'll agree to a small "t". But about the reappearance of racism and fascism in Berlin, we think that the cure is close to the poison. In the '30s the Dadaists were one of the great antidotes to Fascism. If they were crushed and left Germany, it's because they represented a threat to one of the least revealed aspects of Fascism; its virility, its sexuality. They took the piss out of the Fascist devil by opening his flies and ridiculing his claimed erection. That's what sprang to my mind after a few jars. Humour, as a weapon, is one of the most important legacies of the Dadaists. I think that humour is evidence of freedom. The fact that everyone in Europe and the States has become completely hysterical in the face of the race riots in Germany is very interesting. I'm not trying to avoid the problem but if you look at the statistics, there are probably more racist attacks and murders in France and England than in Germany. Once again it's this problem of perception which is destroying Germany's image, in Europe and within its borders. The positive side is that the Germans have reacted en masse. Whereas in France and England racists are only perceived as one of the negative aspects of society, and people couldn't give a damn.

Yes, the Germans have been in total shock and that's the best thing that's happened these last two years. They find themselves confronted by the image everyone still has of them.

Brian: Have you never made violent films?

Not the slightest desire, and, anyway, I wouldn't know how to do it.

Bono: Something crazy happened to us with Edge and my wife, Ali, in Berlin. We were coming out of the Scorsese film *Goodfellas*. While we were waiting for our car in front of the cinema, a fellow came out of an alley with a small pistol and fired at the ground. The film had sort of anaesthetized us. I think Edge dropped a "What a bastard" at the time. I looked at the fellow. Hard. Then we got in the car, drove a little way, stuffed down a pizza. Then, when we'd half finished, my wife asked if the fellow hadn't aimed at us. Suddenly we felt sick. The funniest thing was that we were so unimpressed that the fellow with his weapon was embarrassed to the point of going back into his alley. You can now assess the effect of violent films; they sort of immunise you against violence.

I think that films are in fact images which our subconscious can't control. Films can't accommodate violence without exploiting it. Same thing with sex. Films are incapable of

capturing what can really happen between a man and a woman. The problem lies in the fact that you reproduce and transform into images the act of love, which seems to be contradictory with the act itself.

Bono: What I particularly enjoyed in *Wings of Desire* and *Faraway, So Close!* was that they dared broach the subject of paradise as a let-out. Both films weren't scared to talk about the possibility of another dimension, whether you call it God or something else. Because it's one of the last great taboos. The other day I saw written on a wall "*God is dead. So's Nietzche.*" That amused me. The other fairly exciting subject is these attempts people make to understand their spirituality better. That brings on loads of guilt and weird ideas.

Six years after Wings of Desire *I thought it was important to again take up the idea of angels in Berlin with* Faraway, So Close!. *To take the spiritual element more seriously because it's so urgent.*

Edge: Okay. Wim, we ought to get back to the grindstone. We really like the feeling which comes out of your film. For the songs, be frank, if it doesn't work, don't use them. We won't be annoyed. We're already pleased you asked us.

Okay, I ought to get back to the editing table too. As soon as I've listened to the songs a bit better, I'll call you back. Have

you got a title for your album?

U2: Just a working title for the moment: *Zooropa*. That country born of the imagination.

Good luck, I'll keep my fingers crossed.

U2: God bless, Wim.

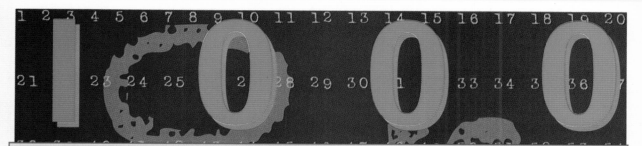

U2's show designer Peter "Willie" Williams has been keeping personal journals and notebooks since he was

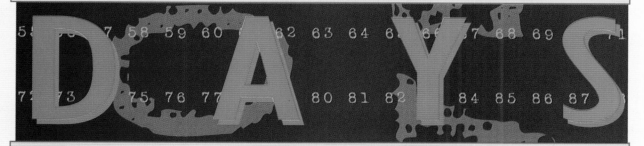

15 years old. With some persuasion, he has allowed *Propaganda* to take a peek at some of the more memorable

recent entries. They document his view of the 1,000-day journey from Dublin on St Patrick's Day 1991 to

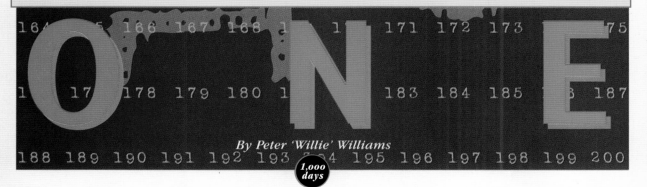

the final Zoo TV show in Tokyo in December 1993. The Polaroids are his too. In this issue – part one. Read on:

By Peter 'Willie' Williams

1,000 days

17 March 91

DUBLIN. Being here after so long away does have that "strange yet familiar" quality. I'm over for a few informal meetings with the band, to start the head-scratching about how to present U2 live this time round. Really great to see everyone again, and being St Patrick's Day everyone was in party-mode, which was fun. The new material is quite extraordinary and another departure. If "God Part II" was the exit ramp, then this stuff is a thousand miles further down that particular freeway of noise. Favourite tracks were called "Ultraviolet" and "69".

Peter 'Willie' Williams beside one of the destined Trabbies, this painted in a motif by the artist Keith Haring

20 March 91

CAMBRIDGE. Home again with a headful of thoughts & ideas. Listening to the band talk it's clear that this album tour will be of a different league to all previous. Bono talked again about using video in a more integrated way, which will tie in perfectly with the kind of thing I'd like to do. He had this phrase "Zoo TV", after the U.S. free-form radio format, and there's a new song called "Zoo Station". They've also brought a Trabant car back from Berlin and are enjoying photographing each other in it.

16 May 91

ROTTERDAM. Over in Holland to see Gloria Estefan's video system and some Philips gear. Jake Kennedy & Steve Iredale (U2 production team) are with me, as is half the music industry it seems. The three of us have talked over lots of ideas, and there does seem to be a general desire to cut the mooring ropes with sanity. Most encouraging. Wondering if I could make the entire lighting system out of recycled Trabants We could carry them on a car transporter.

1 June 91

BIRMINGHAM. Went to see Light & Sound Design to show them my drawings of "Trabant as giant light" and see if they were up for taking on such a lunatic project. I had the engineering department crying laughing over the idea, but they seem very keen to be involved.

14 June 91

DUBLIN. So this was the big one. Today I presented the band with two ideas on paper. One being the "video stage", with a whole pile of big video monitors scattered about the place, and the other being the "Trabant stage", with a dozen of the little cars flown all over the building. I was so concerned that the Trabi idea might sound very stupid when presented formally in the office that last night I went to see Bono & Edge separately on the quiet, to ease them into the idea ahead of time. Both ideas were well received, but as always, there's a request for more.

22 July 91

BIRMINGHAM. The first Trabi arrived in Birmingham and the warehouse staff are looking at me strangely. It's fawn and brown, with a "Captain Birdseye" sticker in Norwegian stuck in the back window. Perfect.

16 August 91

BIRMINGHAM. Felt a bit like Dr Frankenstein this week, overseeing the birth of my creation, but it did finally rise from the dead. The Trabi has been gutted, fitted out with lights, strobes & all, with a suitable paint-job. It looks great, and I now know for sure that this is going to work. Took lots of video footage to show the lads.

13 November 91

DUBLIN. And so ends the week from hell. After eight weeks of commuting to Dublin we finally make some decisions. The big problem has been deciding which ideas to throw out, this thing could go in so many different directions. The tour will be called the "ZOO TV tour", and we are going the whole hog – to take the Trabant system, AND an entire miniature TV station on the road.

25 November 91

DUBLIN. Heard Christmas carols on Grafton St this morning. Total panic has set in now that people realise the first show is only three months away. Final decisions still to be made on exactly which video wall system to use, but mercifully Jake has taken on all the practicalities of that process. My current major concern is getting a start on making the video imagery. Catherine Owens has recommended a New York video-maker called Mark Pellington, and I got in touch with Brian Eno today, who seems keen to be involved. Freddie Mercury died of Aids today.

3 December 91

DUBLIN. Closer. Bono's very up about everything just now, which gets you through a lot. They're rehearsing like mad down at the Factory, with a meeting every ten minutes. They were doing "So Cruel" today, and Joe had it turned up to eleven so you could swim about in the sound.

10 December 91

LONDON. Went to see Archaos tonight, the French punk circus. Adam and Edge came over to see it too as we would like to get them involved in the outdoor show. Their show is phenomenal. Fast and dangerous, with motorbikes and trucks and fire and noise and all the strangest mutants you've ever seen doing bizarre things. Kind of *"Mad Max* meets *Night of the Living Dead"*.

13 January 92

DUBLIN. An influx of new faces gives a sense of impending action. Mark Pellington is here, we did a shoot with Bono for Zoo Station, where Bono as The Fly gave a performance like Hannibal Lechter doing an Elvis impersonation. Carol Dodds and Monica Caston are here too. They will be running the video system during the shows, and having seen what we're intending to do I think are still in shock.

1 February 92

DUBLIN. We have 27 days till the first show, so spent the week lashed to an edit suite at Windmill Lane. We got a huge amount done. Burning crosses for Bullet, Martin Luther King speeches, the extraordinary text sequence for The Fly – can't wait to see it all on the big screen.

10 February 92

NEW YORK. It's so bloody cold here I can't believe it. Made the sequence for "One" with Mark Pellington. It went well – David Wojnarowiez's buffaloes made it in there too. The slow-mo buffaloes really work.

Key sound man Joe O'Herlihy

28 February 92

LAKELAND, FLORIDA. So, here we are. Months of angst and a million meetings later and finally we are on the verge of show-day. Been a wild week here. Wild, but not too bad, given that production rehearsals are always hell. As show day has drawn nearer, I've found that the distance I can walk between questions has diminished. Two weeks ago I could get about 20 yards before someone asked me a question about

Joe, Bono & Willie

some aspect of the production. Today it was down to about three feet – I had to run from place to place or I'd never get there. The back end fell off one of the Trabants, which does not bode well for their durability. We did a full run-through tonight which was far and away the best yet. It's really starting to look good. Eno's here and he's been very helpful. Annie Leibowitz is taking pictures of everything. It's so busy. Exhilarating though. I've had some extraordinary dreams this week. Plummeting Trabants, exploding Vidiwalls, wild. It's been a wild journey getting here – and we haven't even started yet.

29 February 92

LAKELAND. First show. What a riot. It. felt like this little arena would explode tonight, and I was concentrating so hard on so many things for me the gig seemed to last about ten minutes. My lasting memory will be the look on Larry's face as he headed down the catwalk to the B-stage, with punters inches away from his legs. I think "Oh Fuck" just about sums up.

12 March 92

HARTFORD. During "Desire" Bono announced from the stage "Taste is the Enemy of Art". In his mirrorball suit and silver platforms I guess he speaks with some authority. Reviews have been generally ecstatic, with the exception of one reviewer whose vibe was "How could U2 do this to themselves?" Edge was saying today that he's surprised there hasn't been more of that, but generally people seem to be coping with U2's self-destruction very well. We're a long way from Red Rocks right now.

1000 DAYS OF ZOO TV PART ONE, ISSUE 19

20 March 92

BOSTON – MEADOWLANDS – NEW YORK. Three big ones in a row. Boston was St Patrick's Day – major party. I think there were more people outside the building than inside. David Wojnarowicz came to the New Jersey gig. It was wonderful to meet him. Bono dedicated "One" to him. Madison Square Garden was nothing short of a triumph really. The entire music industry was there – Peter Gabriel, Bruce Springsteen, et al. My personal highlight was getting Phil Joanou's wedding video footage into "Desire". He got married to Kate Hyman last night at the Elvis chapel in Las Vegas. Thing was the couple only met the night before in the aftershow hospitality area of the Meadowlands Zoo TV show. They met, and an hour later flew to Vegas to tie the knot. Such is the power of television.

27 March 92

TONIGHT'S gig was hilarious. Joe got the stage phone going today, so after "Real Thing" Bono ordered 10,000 pizzas from the stage. The guy on the other end was freaked, so Bono says, "Bring as many as you can by 10.30pm". Sure enough, a guy in a classic white "delivery boy" outfit arrived with a huge trolley of pizzas and Tim Lamb (stage manager) ushered him out into the crowd to "distribute" them. We could see close-ups of this poor guy on the video screen, and the desperate look on his face when he realised he was being sacrificed to 10,000 over-excited punters going for free pizza. The crowd descended on him and a tidal wave of pizza boxes shot up into the air. Pizza Frisbees were flying all over the building. Messy, but very funny. Never did see the delivery boy again.

29 March 92

CHICAGO. Long meeting with the band today, and with Fisher Park the design team who are starting work on the outdoor version of the Zoo stage. The question is how to

Willie with dancer Morleigh Steinberg

re-package this incredible vibe so it will work in a stadium. Looks like the answer is going to be very large.

22 April 92

VANCOUVER. Day off. To celebrate the end of this first leg of the tour, there was a boat trip round the waterways of Vancouver's spectacular harbour. Everyone was on board, the band, the truck drivers, The Pixies. With the sun in the sky & a bar on board it was blissful. Looking at the staggering beauty of it all we began to unwind a little at last. We've made it through this mad dash across north America, and the show is being acclaimed as a mile stone in rock history, etc, etc. Now we just have to make it work in Europe.

7 May 92

PARIS. Disappointing gig tonight, to be honest. I think the practicalities of getting this massive amount of equipment up and running in Europe was distracting us from concentrating on the gig itself. Mind you, the audience loved it – nobody went home in disgust.

12 May 92

LYON. Good show, though the pre-London nerves are starting to kick in. How can we make the show bigger, faster, hipper, funnier. All this and the stadium show to design in our spare time. The French translation of "The Fly" text did look pretty cool.

15 May 92

SAN SEBASTIAN. Stonking gig last night. These Spaniards are a riot This is a beautiful place. Old, crumbling, sea side, Basque. Paul McGuinness confessed that he used to come here a lot, in a former life when he used to be an Ecclesiastical tour guide for a company called Pilgrim Air, who brought parties of Irish Old Folks on trips to great shrines of Europe. Hard to picture him doing it, I have to say.

Any time, anywhere, any amount

1,000 days

26 May 92

MUNICH. Greatest moment of tonight's gig was the raising of the mirror-ball Trabi right before the show. It's out in the audience, and gets hoisted out of the way just as "Be My Baby" the intro tape starts. As it slowly rose into the air, the punters started throwing things at it – mainly plastic beer mugs. After a minute or so there was all manner of shit just raining down on the poor Trabi, with huge cheers every time anything landed right in it. It was good-natured and very funny – their way of saying, "Thanks, but really we've seen all the Trabis we ever want to see".

29 May 92

FRANKFURT. Spent an hour organising the fireproofing of the fake-fur covered Trabant in case it spontaneously combusts in London and then, of all things, trying to get the suspension repaired on the Keith Haring Trabi, which is falling apart.

Before the show, we did a video shoot with Bono. He was delivering one-liners to camera, dressed as The Fly, which we can slice up and use in the show somewhere. The first ten

Willie with Gavin Friday

minutes were quite serious, then it just got funnier and funnier as the one-liners got increasingly absurd. It eventually dissolved into abject lunacy with Bono announcing things like "ZOO T.V. – a load of old Bollocks". We were just rolling with laughter & consequently the gig that followed was one of the best we've done to date. I'm sure we'll never use any of that footage, but it was worth every moment.

1 June 92

BIRMINGHAM. And so to Britain. We did Earl's Court last night and Birmingham tonight. I'm dead beat but the shows went really well which is a relief. And there was much rejoicing.

8 June 92

There was a big article in *Q* magazine, which said that the personnel on the ZOO TV tour fall loosely into two camps; those who push flight-cases and those who carry faxes. Brilliant observation.

11 June 92

STOCKHOLM. Well, tonight was the one. It was the night when I stopped during the gig and thought to myself, "This is the high point of my career." The entire gig from the Globe in Stockholm was broadcast live to just one person's house

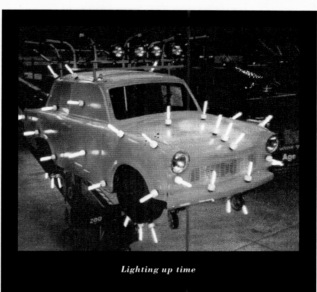

Lighting up time

– that of Mr John Harris of Nottingham, England. He won an MTV competition, so got the private broadcast. His small living room was piled high with TVs and of course everybody from the whole street was in there. There was also a camera at their end, sending pictures back to us, so at various points during the show, the living room in Nottingham would appear on the stage video walls. Bono would speak to them, and they would reply. Of course by 10p.m. everyone at the Nottingham end was blind drunk, which made it all the more entertaining. Technologically it was flawless too, which was pretty astounding.

So later on, Benny and Bjorn – the guys from Abba – appear. We have U2 and Abba performing "Dancing Queen" beneath the mirrorball Trabant, being broadcast live from a giant spherical building in Sweden to one terraced house in Nottingham. I rest my case.

17 June 92

SHEFFIELD. My home town – I grew up here. Good gig too, and before "Still Haven't Found" Bono gave a brief speech, saying, "Let's hear it for 'Mr ZOO TV' – Willie the home-boy." Sheffield gave me a standing ovation, which was very surreal, but fair made me glow.

19 June 92

MANCHESTER. The indoor tour ended with this special gig – a "Stop Sellafield" protest event. Kraftwerk played which was a real treat, with BAD II and the extraordinary Public Enemy. The production crew worked miracles getting all the bands on and off stage in such a tight schedule and the gig went well, with just one exception. The computer that

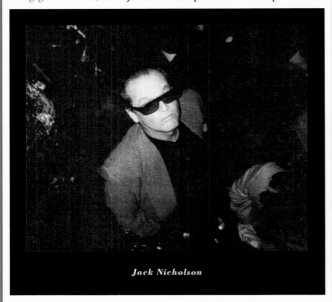

Jack Nicholson

controls all the Trabant movements went berserk, so some of the cars were on auto-pilot, making moves all by themselves. Rock & roll meets "Herbie rides again".

12 July 92

SAN FRANCISCO. Preparations for the outdoor tour continue, and its still a giant bag of loose bits. It has a name now the "Outside Broadcast". It's been a very long haul getting the final design together. There's a lot of people involved and the inevitable conflict between Art and Budget has been a long one and at times a ferocious one. Mark Fisher & Jonathan Park from London have been taking overall responsibility for the outdoor stage's structural design, though as with all things U2, there are many voices involved in the final item. U2's production managers Steve Iredale and Jake Kennedy have been trying to make it all practical enough to tour and I am somewhere between these two camps, and the band of course, who will no doubt have plenty to say when they see the final construction. When drawings on paper become giant pieces of metal.

24 July 92

HERSHEY, PA. Production build and technical set-up have been happening here in this little stadium-in-a-theme-park for the past week. Last night a wind-storm destroyed the biggest video screen, which didn't help. I thought the sound system was going to blow over at one point. There's just SO MUCH stuff everywhere, and redesign suggestions are coming

in thick and fast. The production team and the design team are at the point of declaring war on each other, and I've never seen so many trucks in my entire life.

31 July 92

HERSHEY. Today confirmed my growing suspicion that this is in fact the Twilight Zone. We're staying in the Hotel Hershey – an upmarket family hotel, which is pretty much a vision of Hell. Families everywhere in Mickey Mouse ears, "showband" entertainment in the bar. It's extremely surreal, especially when you see our roadcrew barging through with toolboxes and Trabant parts. The band arrive tomorrow and we're not even close to having the whole system up. We're making progress, but it's painfully slow.

Willie with Kevin Godley

3 August 92

HERSHEY. What a long, long day, but at least we have a plan. The band have been worried about making the show intelligent enough to justify the scale of the thing. In Bono's words "the stage is fantastically impressive for all the wrong reasons". The production team and design team are each recommending that the other be fired. I, as ever, remain somewhere between all factions.

25 August 92

PITTSBURGH. Long days, but at least things become more positive. Doing some shows and getting ecstatic reviews helps. Bono's anxiety is turning into optimism and excitement, though the question of how to sort out the stage roof remains. Fortunately, the design and production teams have at last made up their differences, and the general consensus is just to throw the roof away.

8 September 92

DETROIT. We flew here after the Toronto gig. It's my Birthday, so Edge said for me to get in the car with him &

188

U2 THE BEST OF PROPAGANDA

1,000 days

Bono at the airport. I thought we were going to the hotel, but I get out to find we're at an unbelievable seedy sports bar. "We could have gone somewhere flash," he says, "but I felt this was just more you." So it was beer and chicken wings till 4am & they bought me a T-shirt bearing the inscription "Just Do Me". That's what friends are for.

25 September 92

ATLANTA. In the fabulous brand new Georgia Dome they have a computer that controls the house lights for the building. This computer malfunctioned and some of the houselights wouldn't go out when the show started. Rocko (stage manager) & his hammer sorted that right out.

10 October 92

TAMPA, FL. Wild show. Bono was in psycho-Norman mode. The heat and humidity sent him out into the stratosphere. A very tall, excited punter leapt onto the B-stage during "Running to Standstill" and stood over one of the pyrotechnic bombs that was just about to go off. Bono grabbed hold of her, threw her to the ground and leapt on top of her as it exploded. They were both unhurt, but I imagine that'll fuel fantasies for the rest of her life.

17 October 92

DALLAS. Big TV shoot at Texas Stadium. Went great, the band played a blinder. I was here all night getting all the additional gear ready. A stage-hand told me that the country with the shortest male life-expectancy is Chad, with 38 years. Bummer.

3 November 92

VANCOUVER. Election day. TVs were on in the catering room so we were getting the results in all day. It was so exciting – everyone was in there watching & waiting, as Clinton gradually became President. We were running news

Willie with D.J. Paul Oakenfold who was to appear later on the Zoo TV tour in Europe and Down Under

updates on the giant message boards on stage to keep the audience updated. The California result that gave Clinton victory came in just before Public Enemy went on stage. I had the great thrill of announcing to a packed BC Place

'Macnas' Theatre Co. who appeared on the Zooropa trip

stadium that the US had a new President. The place went berserk – even up here in Canada they're glad to see the back of Bush. Gave me a cheap thrill anyway.

14 November 92

ANAHEIM, CA. Our 100th concert, and it's at Disneyland, which seems appropriate. In Vegas we held a tour "Oscars" ceremony giving awards to the tour's great performers. Nominations, prizes, "and the winner is", categories such as "Excess baggage of the year", "Tour bimbo", "International diplomat", etc. Great fun.

15 November 92

LOS ANGELES. Quote Robert Hilburn, *L.A. Times*, "Zoo TV is the yardstick by which all other stadium shows will be measured."

25 November 92

MEXICO CITY. Four shows here with absolutely the wildest audiences I have ever seen in my life. Even eclipsing the Italians and Spaniards. The energy level is beyond comprehension – people bring banners and set fire to them in the crowd. Life on the edge. Spent time with Bono & Adam talking about the next step, which is to take Zoo TV back to Europe. "Zooropa" they want to call the tour.
The last show was a riot, with lots of fun extras, including Bono doing a spontaneous a cappella rap version of "We Will Rock You". We even got Edge to do Van Diemen's Land which was a bit of a rocker from the locker. So that's it, we go home for Christmas now then dream it all up again for Europe.

1,000 days

OF ZOO TV PART TWO

IN THE LAST ISSUE WE BEGAN A PEEK THROUGH SOME OF THE MORE MEMORABLE RECENT

ENTRIES OF U2'S SHOW DESIGNER WILLIE WILLIAMS' PERSONAL JOURNALS AND NOTEBOOKS.

THEY DOCUMENT HIS VIEW OF THE 1,000 DAY JOURNEY FROM DUBLIN ON ST PATRICK'S DAY

1991 TO THE FINAL ZOO TV SHOW IN TOKYO IN DEMBER 1993. THE JOURNAL CONTINUES –

FROM THE START OF ZOOROPA TO THE END OF ZOO TV IN JAPAN. READ ON.

By Willie Williams

4 February 93

NEW YORK. In a nightclub, I saw a woman at the bar write a question onto a napkin – "What did the first Punk Rock girl wear to your school?". I'm definitely going to put that into the next edit of "The Fly" text.

22 March 93

DUBLIN. Eighteen months on and were still in Windmill Lane editing "The Fly". The band have decided they'll try to release a whole new album. Why does nothing surprise me anymore?

8 April 93

DUBLIN. Foot to the floor. The band are recording non-stop. We are in Windmill Lane making video footage by the mile. We have all five edit suites going. Mark Neale is in a translation frenzy, Maurice Linnane is working with blood, the EBN guys are up in the Avid suite working with bombs and drummer boys and I made a little singing cosmonaut today who's very sweet.

21 April 93

CARDINGTON. Construction time again in a giant old airship hangar, somewhere in the middle of England. The stage is up and the new video walls are HUGE. They're like small buildings. We have replaced all last year's projection screens with video walls because of the daylight problem in Europe. They look so much cooler. Like Jake Kennedy said, "It's like the old screens ran on gas, but these are electric." The band are going to love it.

8 May 93

ROTTERDAM. We actually did (nearly) a full run-through this evening. Went pretty well. The star of the show was Bono's new encore character. It will replace the mirrorball-man/preacher character from the American show. We spent the afternoon in the dressing room trying to suss out quite who this character is. He's called "Mr Gold" on account of his tasteful gold suit and platforms. The voice is kind of doddery English eccentric, sort of Laurence Olivier meets Quentin Crisp, and there's a whole host of other feelings in there. Joel Gray, *Clockwork Orange*, the gameshow host from hell. He's the devil, basically. Its really very peculiar, funny and disturbing at the same time.

9 May 93

ROTTERDAM. Opening night. It went well too. The band did really well, and the technical end of things was quite astonishing really, given that most of this ridiculously enormous new video wall system was in cardboard boxes two weeks ago. Of course Bono's new character stole the show. He's been christened "MacPhisto" and there's been the addition of a little pair of red velvet horns, which appeared at he very last moment. White face and red lipstick. First encore, "Desire" was one of those great moments where you know something that the audience (and the enormous amount of press people) don't.

Out he comes, and you can feel 50,000 people go "What the fuck?" The absolute crowning glory was that it stayed dry all night until the encore break when the heavens opened, so MacPhisto made his first entrance in a raging downpour under a sky full of thunder and lightning. It looked like *Faust* meets *Apocalypse Now*. Great first night. And there was much rejoicing.

18 May 93

OVIEDO. It's in Northern Spain. We arrived here yesterday after a 12-hour drive from Lisbon. It was a night off with no load-in the following day which, let's face it, is asking for trouble. Oviedo is a very small, picturesque, ancient town, so the arrival of 200 road-crew with cabin fever was pretty scary. The crew practically filled the town so wherever you went you'd run into yet more well-oiled people speaking English very loudly and wearing U2 gear. Legend has it that lighting crew member Andy Kitchen woke up at 9 o'clock this morning and found himself in the park wearing only a T-shirt. Another triumph for international diplomacy.

27 May 93

BRUSSELS. On the way here, the caterers' bus broke down so we stopped to rescue them at about 5am on some autobahn somewhere. Its a glamorous life. The Edge gave me a copy of the *Zooropa* album today, which is finally complete. I slipped away and listened to it from cover to cover. Bono says, "It's not a rock album – I don't know what it is," but they all seem very positive about it. I asked what they would do with their spare time now and Adam says, "We could always start on the next album."

30 May 93

FRANKFURT. And so to Germany. We have spent a lot of time discussing and considering whether some of the video sequences in the show might be a little too close to the bone here – particularly the brief swastika sequence in "Bullet". As they appear Bono shouts "We must never let this happen again!" in the local language. We were concerned that it might be misunderstood, but oddly, the vibe I get from the German audiences is that after 50 years of foreigners muttering "don' mention the war" jokes, it's a relief to have someone come in and mention it very loudly, very directly and say, "Look we don't blame you for this, but it happened and we must all make sure it doesn't happen again."

6 June 93

STUTTGART. Meeting with the band tonight. It's the first proper meeting we've had in ages, as finishing the album has taken up every spare moment. It was just the four band members, myself Monica Caston and Maurice Linnane (*Zooropa* video directors). We took a few hours to go through a video tape, sort out any problems and talk about ideas for starting to work in the some of the new material. Bono says, "We've been absent for the past month, but even so, this is already head and shoulders above the American show." Yes!!!

15 June 93

BERLIN. So we're in Berlin. The gig – the Olympic Stadium – is so over the top it's hysterical. This is where Hitler did his "Achtung baby", Leni Reifenstahl made movies and Jesse Owens was snubbed and did his Black Power salute. This whole building reeks of megalomania. Just the architecture makes you want to rush out and annex a few small countries.

Presenting Zoo TV in this setting may well prove to be the peak of the Zooropa tour.

As it happened, the biggest excitement of the night was the police coming to arrest Joe O'Herlihy, sound engineer, for breaching the very stringent local sound levels. The "Sound Police", who had surrounded the stadium with their decibel meters, decided that as soon as the show was over, our Joe was bound for the slammer. Fortunately, a bit of fancy footwork and a few manoeuvres in the dark ensured that by the time the stadium lights came up, Mr O had already escaped from Colditz, and was happily drinking gin and tonics on the band's plane bound for Dublin.

26 June 93

PARIS. I took half an hour out of my daily routine to watch The Velvet Underground. It's an incredible thought that the last time they did a show, some of the U2 crew hadn't been born. They played all the hits, "Heroine", "Sweet Jane", "All Tomorrow's Parties". Sounded great.

U2 THE BEST OF PROPAGANDA

3 July 93

VERONA. Italy is such a wild place for U2 shows. The audiences are so, shall we say, enthusiastic. After the first of the two shows here was another "Riggers Arms" party. It's been a long haul since Rotterdam, so everybody was really ready to cut loose. Macnas from Galway did their own performance of "Mysterious Ways", complete with Youth, (the 300lb truck driver) bellydancing. The Riggers built a bar, a stage and a maze outside. Naturally, nobody left until it got light.

12 July 93

TURIN. "There is no more disturbing a consequence of the electronic and graphic revolution than this: that the world as given to us through television seems natural, not bizarre" – Neil Postman, Amusing Ourselves to Death.

18 July 93

BOLOGNA. And it's hot. Tonight MacPhisto phoned Benito Craxi, one of Italy's most famous and most corrupt politicians. The whole crowd started to chant "Benito, Benito, Fuck You, Fuck You!"

24 July 93

BUDAPEST. Monsoon. It rained so hard that the audience were doing synchronised swimming during "With or Without You". The saddest thing was watching a close up of The Edge during Ultraviolet – he was singing and playing guitar so he didn't have a free hand to wipe the drops of rainwater off the end of his nose. Talk about suffering for your art.

1,000 days

3 August 93

NIJMEGEN. We did the live-link to Sarajevo during the show, which we've been doing every show for about a month now. It's so powerful, some nights it's hard to carry on afterwards, but going into "Bad" helps. What makes it so powerful is that essentially its really bad television – just a static head shot, none of the cuts, edits or theme tunes that make T.V. news easier to deal with. Tonight there was a Dutch woman in Sarajevo who knew her son was at the U2 gig here in Holland. She hadn't seen or heard from him for three years, but she got to speak to him from the video screens. Devastating really.

11 August 93

LONDON. Wembley Stadium, and not wishing to be cowardly the band put four new numbers in the set for the opening night.

"Numb", "Babyface", "Zooropa" and "Stay". Let us say some worked better than others, but a lighter moment came in "Babyface". The audience member with the video camera jumped on top of Bono, pushed him to the floor, sat on him and shot close-ups of his crotch for the big screens. The crowd always loves a cheap thrill and Bono was laughing so hard he could hardly finish the song.

14 August 93

LEEDS. Eighty-two thousand people came to tonight's show, which is a record for a non-festival U2 show. And they looked beautiful.

20 August 93

LONDON. Salman Rushdie was at the show tonight. Onstage,

with MacPhisto. A man in hiding standing in front of 72,000 people. Luckily there were no armed Muslim fundamentalists in the audience.

28 August 93

DUBLIN. To finish this leg of the tour here might have been asking for trouble, but this time it was great. The show went out live all over the world on radio, but still no major dramas. Next stop Australia.

8 November 93

MELBOURNE. Two years later and we're still in production rehearsals. We had the whole band out at the mix position in the middle of the night watching the new video sequences for "Crashed Car" and "Lemon". Just ten shows to go, and we're still putting new stuff in.

11 November 93

MELBOURNE. The Edge came out with a great one-liner this morning. "Zoo TV brings you the very latest in Hardware, Software and Men's Wear". I've been laughing about that all day.

27 November 93

SYDNEY. The final hurdle, the last global telecast, and we won. It's been a very long day, but what went out on TV was spectacular. I spent half the day with Bono & Edge working on final details and the other half with Allen Branton (TV lighting consultant), looking at video tapes, angles, colours, etc. Adam made a triumphant return, after being too ill to perform last night, so everyone was much relieved. Adam's bass tech, Stuart, had to understudy last night, and in Bono's words was "pretty cool for a guy who's shitting himself". It was a great show tonight. After the show, we sat in the dressing room all night looking at the video tapes, hooting and hollering. Laughing at each other's mistakes but with an overall air of mutual backslapping. When we got into watching it for the second time, the various band guests began to leave, clearly bored senseless at our self-indulgent "home movies". Now we can go to New Zealand and have some fun.

4 December 93

AUCKLAND. The gig here – Western Springs – is surrounded with houses. People had built little grandstands in their gardens and were charging admission for friends to come watch the gig. We sent Libby Wilson (promoter staff) up to one house with a mobile phone, and MacPhisto telephoned them from the stage to congratulate them on their entrepreneurial spirit.

9 December 93

TOKYO. The Tokyo Dome has to be the worst-sounding building on the planet, and Japanese audiences are traditionally quite reserved, which didn't make for a great night. We survived.

in really. Great show, made more so by having about a million guests on the mix position. Madonna came, with her entire touring party, Terence Trent D'Arby came with all his people, plus this group of leather-clad mature gentlemen with big hair, who turned out to be Deep Purple.

Consequently it was a real party both onstage and out front, and really quite moving to think this is the last time we'd see this show, with all its great moments. The text-overload of "The Fly", the endless buffaloes in "One", the apocalypse of "Bullet" into "Running to Standstill" and that magical segue into the opening of "Streets", plus of course Mr MacPhisto's last stand, though somehow I'm not sure we've seen the last of him.

After the show, there was much rejoicing, of course, tinged with a mixture of sadness and relief. We are across the finish line, impossible to take in – rather like the last day of school, where you know nothing will ever be the same again, but at the same time this is just a day like any other, so it's hard to appreciate.

Lots of goodbyes and thankyous, and then the final splitting up of this massive ball of energy that was Zoo TV. Everyone goes home on aeroplanes literally all over the world. On to new places, new projects. I didn't go to bed, it would have seemed inappropriate.

THE PICKING OF MELON

THESE DAYS NO ONE SAYS YOU CAN'T DANCE TO U2. THE PROOF IS IN THE MELON. OVER THE NEXT TWO PAGES *PROPAGANDA* TALKS TO TWO OF THE KEY PLAYERS IN THE EMERGENCE OF THE NEW CD OF U2 DANCE REMIXES.

AT ISLAND RECORDS in London, the head of A&R, Nick Angel, was responsible for commissioning a range of remix specialists over two years to work their magic on U2 tracks. Andrew Mueller, a regular writer for England's *Melody Maker* and *Time Out* magazines, got Nick to talk him through the new release. And the name that occurs most in the list of remixers on *Melon* is Paul Oakenfold. Over the page Cole Moreton talks to him about dance music and U2.

1. Lemon
(The Perfecto Mix)
remixed by Paul
Oakenfold and Steve
Osborne
Produced by Flood, Brian
Eno, and The Edge
(P) 1993 Polygram
International Music BV

2. Salomé
(Zooromancer Remix)
remixed by Pete Heller
and Terry Farley for Boys
Own Productions
Engineer Gary Wilkinson
Produced by Paul Barrett
and U2
(P) 1992 Island
Records Ltd

3. Numb
(Gimme Some More
Dignity Mix)
remixed by Rollo and
Rob D
Additional vocals Joy
Malcolm
Engineer Goerts B
Produced by Flood, Brian
Eno, and The Edge
(P) 1995 Polygram
International Music BV

4. Mysterious Ways
(The Perfecto Mix)
remixed by Paul
Oakenfold and Steve
Osborne
Produced by Daniel
Lanois with Brian Eno
(P) 1991 Island
Records Ltd

5. Stay
(Underdog Mix)
Remixed by Underdog for
Bite It/Unmanageable
Artists
Mixed at Monroe Studios,
London
Mix Engineer Roger
Benou
Produced by Flood, Brian
Eno, and The Edge
1995 Polygram
International Music BV

6. Numb
(The Soul Assassins Mix)
Remixed by the Soul
Assassins
Produced by Flood, Brian
Eno, and The Edge
(P) 1995 Polygram
International Music BV

7. Mysterious Ways
Remixed by Massive
Attack
Produced by Daniel
Lanois with Brian Eno
(P) 1995 Polygram
International Music BV

**8. Even Better Than The
Real Thing**
(The Perfecto Mix)
Remixed by Paul
Oakenfold and Steve
Osborne
Produced by Steve
Lillywhite with Brian Eno
and Daniel Lanois
(P) 1992 Island Records
Ltd

9. Lemon
(Bad Yard Club Mix)
Remixed by David
Morales for Def Mix
Productions
Engineer David Sussman
Keyboard programming
Satoshi Tomii for Def Mix
Productions and Peter
"Ski" Schwartz
Percussion David
Morales
Produced by Flood, Brian
Eno, and The Edge
1993 Polygram
International Music BV

Music U2 Words Bono
(except "Numb" —
The Edge)
Executive Producer
Nick Angel.

Strange to think that only three years ago the idea of an album of remixes of U2 songs would have seemed so unlikely. But *Melon* turns out to be a fine companion piece to *Achtung Baby* and *Zooropa*, nine selections from the two albums worked into eminently danceable shapes by an assortment of painfully hip names. And lurking at the centre of the operation was Nick Angel, Head A&R at Island Records, who took time off plotting the success of The Cranberries, Pulp and The Stereo MCs, to coordinate the remix magic on U2.

"I think the original way it came about", he remembers, "was that Bono was quoted somewhere as saying that nobody dances to U2 ... which I know from knowing Paul Oakenfold, is not really true. Even in the Baleario days they were actually playing U2 records. "And the whole nature of *Achtung Baby* was for U2 to get experimental, to change people's perception of what to think of U2 and a small part of that was to see whether other people could interpret their stuff in a way that people could dance to U2."

Oakenfold, whose version of "Mysterious Ways", "Even Better Than the Real Thing" and "Lemon" feature on *Melon*, was the first person thus approached but, surprisingly, what he came up with was not as adventurous as the band had hoped. Nick told him to take a few liberties, which he did.

"The band really liked it and from there the idea that we could have remixes done really snowballed."

Having recast "Mysterious Ways" as something resembling the snarling offspring of Primal Scream's seminal crossover classic "Loaded", Oakenfold then set about souping up "Even Better Than the Real Thing" to memorable effect, the "Take me higher" refrain wryly recalling the gospel influences of "Rattle and Hum" while simultaneously tapping into the unfettered hedonism of European club culture.

"I'm not sure the band like it a first," remembers Nick. "I think they thought it was a bit cheesy. I remember the Edge phoning and saying that he wasn't sure that the guitar was in time with the base line and

all that sort of stuff, and they weren't sure that it wasn't all a little bit disco. But then they heard it in a club – I think they may have even taken it to a club in Italy and played it – and they heard it over a huge sound system and they watched the crowd and realised that, you know, whether the guitar was perfectly in time or whether the drum beat was a bit cheesy in their mind was absolutely irrelevant. It was just a really big club record."

Suddenly U2, best-known rock band in the world, were in the strange position of having a Number One dance record and being on the front cover of hip dance-music titles like *Mixmag Update*. Island decided to release the remix as a single.

"At one stage I thought we were going to have two versions in the Top 40, but the remix ended up being a bigger single than the album version. U2 were making hip dance records."

With ZOO TV underway, Paul Oakenfold warming up the concert crowds with dance anthems, rap acts on the support bill and U2 throwing their music into different lights through innovative staging and lighting work, the experimentation continued in the studios of some of the world's sharpest producers. Unsurprisingly the idea emerged of an entire set of U2 remixes by different producers.

"Of course when *Zooropa* arrived", recalls Nick, "there were three or four tracks that were stone bonker obvious for doing remix versions of."

He then set about trying to match the tracks with the right remixers. "We did a real dark hip-hop mix of 'Numb' with DJ Muggs of Cypress Hill, which I think is one of the best ones we've done, and at the time I was utterly convinced was potentially a really big record in its own right. It was the first time I'd heard a remix that genuinely took one band into a completely different genre without it being half-arsed. This was a genuine hip-hop record. Cypress Hill's record company in America were very into the idea of trying to push it as a genuine club record for a while, but it was eventually decided not to press ahead with it.

"There would have been quite a nice symmetry to it as *Zooropa* was knocked off the American Number One by Cypress Hill's album just at the time I wanted to go to American radio with Cypress Hill's

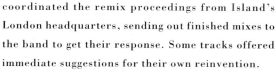

version of 'Numb'." This malevolent masterpiece duly made the cut. Another, perhaps because the remixers interpreted their brief a shade liberally, didn't.

"I thought we could get a slightly more trancey, hypnotic version of 'Numb', which is what we got from Rollo's 'Dignity' mix, which is on the CD."

By this stage the idea for a full-blown remix album, perhaps along the line of The Cure's winningly irreverent *Mixed Up*, was gathering pace.

"I wanted to do 'Crashed Car' with Trent Reznor of Nine Inch Nails, who was quite interested in doing it. Nine Inch Nails were at the time finishing up with Flood, who'd worked on both the U2 albums, and Trent was up for it, but couldn't do it in the time frame."

While the band and U2's management travelled around the world with ZOO TV, Nick Angel coordinated the remix proceedings from Island's London headquarters, sending out finished mixes to the band to get their response. Some tracks offered immediate suggestions for their own reinvention.

Still further names were mooted. Leftfield were keen to have a crack at something. There was even talk of asking Dr Dre to rework "Angel Of Harlem", a prospect with extraordinary possibilities for maverick greatness or baffling ignominy. Then there was more talk about whether this wasn't all starting to get a bit much.

"The idea started wavering," says Nick. "We'd had a lot of high-density U2 for a while and there was talk of a simulcast on MTV and VH-1, talk of another album called *Zoogaloo*, which was going to be other people interpreting U2 songs, and it all just suddenly seemed we were in danger of overstating our case, I think."

And so the remixes they had accumulated seemed destined to be occasionally ladled out to film soundtracks and benefit albums and the like – it seemed a touch crass and pointless to release them for sale so long after the event – when the band came up with the bright idea of putting out a remix CD free to readers of *Propaganda*. This of course is a solution not without quandaries of its own: the limited print run will turn *Melon* into an instant collector's item, leaving determined non-subscriber fans with appreciable holes in their finances.

"I should think it will do. As a by-product of the fact that there are limited numbers of it, it will be coveted. And yes there's a concern about that, but I don't know how you can legislate against that. If you don't make many available, you're right, the people who can't get it by fair means will get it through foul.

"I'm sure it will be massively bootlegged. I think it's just one of those things you have to accept. Otherwise you'd have to print a million copies, and people would be wondering what you're doing flogging remixes a year and a half later. This is a way that the people who love U2 enough to want to be subscribing to *Propaganda* can get a copy for nothing."

> **THIS IS A WAY THAT THE PEOPLE WHO LOVE U2 ENOUGH TO WANT TO BE SUBSCRIBING TO PROPAGANDA CAN GET A COPY FOR NOTHING.**

THE PICKING OF MELON, ISSUE 21

PAUL OAKENFOLD

KNOWS HOW TO MAKE YOU MOVE. HE'S THE
CLUBLAND GURU WHOSE SPARKLING
PERFECTO REMIXES TRANSFORMED SONGS
FROM *"ACHTUNG BABY"* AND *"ZOOROPA"* INTO
GLOBAL DANCEFLOOR FAVOURITES – THREE OF
WHICH YOU'LL FIND ON "MELON". HE WAS
ALSO ONE OF THE MEN BEHIND THE
TURNTABLES KEEPING CROWDS HAPPY ON THE
ZOOROPA TOUR. COLE MORETON MET HIM.

It's four in the afternoon – the crack of dawn for the pale-faced inhabitants of clubland. DJ Paul Oakenfold is in the recording studio, about to remix somebody else's song. By the time he's finished, there might not be much of the original left.

"People don't have a clue what the remixer or the producer does," says Oakenfold, who'll try out the new mix on the turntables of a London club later that night. But record companies know the power o£ his magic. "You can take an old band and give it new life. A new market. Or you can take a totally unknown band and break them, by giving the mix to someone like David Morales or ourselves."

Paul and partner Steve Osborne made their name with clean, clubby Perfecto remixes of songs by rock bands Happy Mondays, Stone Roses and Primal Scream. They were natural choices when U2 came to think about remixing their own material.

"When we were first asked to remix 'Mysterious Ways' in 1991 we didn't change that much," says Oakenfold. "Then the record company came back and said, 'No, take it all the way. Don't hold back'. So we stamped our mark on it."

Employed because of their massive experience about what will work on the dancefloor, they always insist on a free hand to remove or replace anything that won't work. "The overall structure needs to be changed. You need an intro, a break and an outro. We give songs more of a club structure, with a build, a drop, highs and lows."

Live drums are the first thing to go. "Almost all dance records feature drum machines, and it's that perfect beat that people are familiar with. Live drums can be doing lots of mad fills and going off all over the place and it doesn't really work. Bass lines have to be tough, or they're changed. Larry and Adam are

> **"WHEN WE WERE FIRST ASKED TO REMIX 'MYSTERIOUS WAYS' IN 1991 WE DIDN'T CHANGE THAT MUCH," SAYS OAKENFOLD. "THEN THE RECORD COMPANY CAME BACK AND SAID, 'NO, TAKE IT ALL THE WAY. DON'T HOLD BACK.' SO WE STAMPED OUR MARK ON IT."**

not really on many of the remixes that we do."

Edge's guitar work is often trimmed too. "Clubs are not that keen on guitars, so we will either lose them or take a riff from the overall guitar part and arrange something around it. Then I change any other instrumentation I don't like – anything from a keyboard line upwards."

Oakenfold started DJing in small bars 12 years ago. These days he headlines at world-famous dance venues like Heaven in London and the Hacienda in Manchester – and begins 1995 with a six-week tour of clubs in Asia, the Middle East and Europe. He released two remix albums last year, volume five in the *Journeys By DJ* series on JDJ Records and *Bust A Groove* on Music of Life. Completely changing the music of the biggest rock and roll band in the world held no fear for him.

"It's like a chef knows the ingredients that work for a cake. I'm on the frontline every week. I know the arrangements and structures that work. I knew when we were doing 'Mysterious Ways' that it wouldn't be a huge club record because it's a down-tempo tune and they never really do that well in clubs. But I knew it would still be a credible record because I used hip-hop loops and other right ingredients."

Soon after that first mix he was DJing in Dublin when the invitation came to meet the band in the studio. "I was really nervous, thinking 'Fucking hell, I'm gonna meet U2 here, what am I gonna say?' Suddenly I was sitting in the studio being asked what I thought of this and that as they jammed on a tune, and I was thinking 'What's going on here? They're asking me?' Then I just sat back and thought, 'Well, I do know what I'm doing'. We got on very well. What appealed to me was that although they're a huge band they were very open-minded. They listened."

Oakenfold and Osborne are fussy about who they work with – when we met they'd just turned down Guns and Roses, Seal and the Rolling Stones. But U2 had something special. "Bono is a rock vocalist, but he's got soul. Edge delivers good clean hooks. I knew I could take that and put on a powerful organ line, a really good dance riff, or female backing vocals that would make the crowds put their hands in the air. I knew I could make people dance to their records."

Which is exactly what he did with "Even Better Than The Real Thing" in 1992, virtually re-recorded at 126 beats per minute because "that's just the tempo that works".

"I liked the line that Bono had, 'Take me higher', and thought a female R&B vocalist sitting behind him would give it a lot more depth. I tried out the dub version at the club Ministry of Sound in London and it went down a storm."

The other Perfecto mix on your free CD is "Lemon", which was apparently more difficult to do because of the loose structure of the song. "We needed a strong riff, and Steve came up with one that became an established riff in the clubs. We built the whole thing around that."

For the Zooropa tour Oakenfold had a special DJ console built with three turntables, DAT machines, CD and cassette players. "We didn't have a brief, as such, but people were standing around a long time so I wanted to create an atmosphere that was happy and excited, get them ready to see the band. I would play classics from Bob Marley to the Rolling Stones, some Hip Hop – that always works well with a rock crowd – and new dance tunes that I knew would become commercial hits down the line. When we travelled the world I would go to local record shops and find out what the big tunes and the happening bands were and incorporate them into the set." In Ireland that included the national football team's World Cup song.

The soundtrack to the film *Once Upon A Time in America* was a big favourite. "A lot of clubby tunes wouldn't cut through on a big sound system, so we wanted records that sounded really big and powerful."

Dance music has dominated the charts – at least in Europe – since 1987, and the club network is a powerful new alternative to the traditionally rock-led music industry. Critics claimed U2 were attempting to buy credibility with this new young club-land audience by hiring the likes of Oakenfold. He disagrees. "Why would they need to buy credibility? They are huge. *Zooropa* was a credible album to me because they had the balls to change. In my opinion they just wanted the best people for the job, and we fitted the bill because we're one of the few remix teams that can work with bands and songs."

Oakenfold is a qualified chef, and would like to go into the kitchen full-time when the heat of the clubs gets too much. But the next step for he and Osborne is to put their own band together.

"It's easier to deal with other people's material because they're delivering the song. I can give you the music, make an arrangement and paint a different picture, but you need a song. I could go and make some more DJ albums that will be big club records but I want to do something with more depth, and for that you need songs."

"I KNEW I COULD MAKE THE CROWDS PUT THEIR HANDS IN THE AIR. I KNEW I COULD MAKE PEOPLE DANCE TO U2'S RECORDS."

IF YOUR Go DRO

AS WE REPORTED IN AN EARLIER ISSUE, AT LAST YEAR'S GRAMMY AWARDS IN NEW YORK, BONO

PRESENTED FRANK SINATRA WITH A SPECIAL AWARD AND DELIVERED IT WITH A SPECIAL SPEECH.

BUT THERE'S MORE, IT WASN'T THE FIRST NIGHT THE TWO HAD MET. EVER HEAR ABOUT THE TIME

WHEN BONO WOKE UP IN FRANK SINATRA'S PLACE

WITH A FEELING OF MYSTERIOUS WETNESS

ABOUT HIS PERSON? READ ON ... BONO'S

STARSTRUCK TOO AND FRANK'S

THE STAR.

nna OP A NAME

i'm still starstruck, it doesn't wear off... frank sinatra gave me a solid gold cartier pasha watch with sapphires and an inscription... to bono with thanks FRANCIS A SINATRA... WATER RESISTANT... i'm not gonna get over this... Frank likes me... hell i've hung out with him, drunk at his bar, eaten at his table, watched a movie at his place... in his own screening room... dig that asshole... i usually drink j.d. straight up without ice, it's a tennessee sipping whiskey, so why did i go and blow it by ordering ginger ale... "jack and ginger" a "girls drink"... FRANK looks at me with my two earrings and for the first time in my life i felt effeminate... i drank quickly to compensate and worse i mixed my drinks... over dinner (mexican not italian) we drink tequila in huge fishbowl glasses, never drink anything bigger than your head i thought as FRANK pushed his nose up against the glass like it was a hall of mirrors...

later asleep on the snowwhite of FRANK and BARBARA's screening room sofa i had a real fright and woke up to wetness, a damp sensation between my legs... hmm... dreams of dean martin gave way to panic... first thought: i've pissed myself. second: don't tell anyone. third: don't move they'll see the stain... yellow on white. fourth: make a plan... and so i sat in my shame for twenty minutes, mute, waiting for the movie to end, wondering as to how i would explain this... this... irish defeat to italy.. . this sign that what was once just verbal incontinence has matured... and grown to conclusive proof that i don't belong there/here. i am a jerk. i am a tourist. i am back in my cot age 4... before i knew how to fail — mama – i've pissed myself... again.

well i hadn't, i'd spilt my drink. i was drunk, high on him, a shrinking shadow boxing dwarf following in his footsteps... badly... STARSTRUCK.. . "what now my love? now that it's over?" i went back to the hotel... (turn left on frank sinatra boulevard). i would never drink in the company of the great man again... i would never be asked to. wrong, twice.

NOTE: IF YOUR'E GONNA DROP ONE, DROP A BIG ONE... A NAME... A NAME TO HANG ON YOUR WALL. EPISODE NO.1. december 93, u2 had just got back from TOKYO, the capital of ZOO tv, it was all over... i felt wonderful. i felt like shit. my TV had been turned off... it was christmas.. . there was a parcel from FRANK a large parcel... i opened it. . a PAINTING, a painting by FRANK SINATRA and a note... "you mentioned the jazz vibes in this piece well it's called JAZZ and we'd like you to have it. yours Frank and Barbara" this is getting silly... there is a SANTA CLAUS and he's Italian... (opera, Fellini, food, wine, Positano, the sexy end of religion, football, now grace and generosity?)

... heroes are supposed to let you down... but here i am blown away by this 78-year-old saloon singer and his royal family... starstruck.. a skunk on theoutskirts of las vegas with my very own Frank Sinatra, last seen in his very own living room, on the edge of his very own desert, in palm springs... THE PAINTING, a luminous piece as complex as its title, as its author... circles closed yet interlocking, like glass stains on a beermat.. circles with the diameter of a horn... Miles Davis... Buddy Rich... rhythm... the desert... they're all in there

... on yellow... to keep it mad... fly yourself to the moon!

EPISODE NO. 2 MARCH 1. i'm not alcoholic i'm Irish, i don't drink to get drunk do i? i drink because i like the taste don't i? so why am i drunk? i'm drunk because Frank has just fixed me another stiffy that's why! jack daniels this time straight up and in a pint glass.

it's the "Grammys" and i've been asked to present the boss of bosses a life achievement award... a speech... i know i'm not match fit but of course i say yes.

and now i'm in NEW YORK CITY and so nervous i am deaf and cannot speak

... two choices: BLUFF or concentrate on the job at hand. i do both and end up with a rambling wordy tribute with no full-stops or commas... that might explain how i felt about the man who invented pop music... and puncture the schmaltz... a little...

anyway we're in FS's dressing room (the manager's suite) where the small talk is never small, Jan talking to Susan Reynolds, Frank's pa and patron saint and Ali (my wife and mine). Paul McGuinness (U2's manager) asks Frank about the pin on his lapel... "it's the legion of honour... highest civilian award... given by the president..." "which one?" enquires paul... "oh i don't know... some old guy... i think it was lincoln..." cool... do you have to be american to get one? i think to myself... already feeling my legs go...

next up the award for best alternative album u2 are nominated for this... better get ready... what's the point... we're never gonna win that... that belongs to the smashing pumpkins, one of the few noisy bands to transcend the turgid old-fashioned format they've chosen... you have to go downstairs you might win... what's there to be embarrassed about... you've been no.1 on alternative/college radio for 10 years now... it's the most important thing to you... tell them... it's your job to use your position... abuse it even... tell them you're not mainstream you're slipstream... tell them... you'll make it more fun... that you'll try to be better than the last lot... tell them you're mainstream but not of it and you'll do your best to fuck it up... TELL THEM YOU KNOW FRANK... tell the children... so i did.

the speechifying below wasn't heard in the uk so loud is the word fuck over there but Frank heard it and Frank liked it... so here it is:

Frank never did like rock'n'roll. And he's not crazy about guys wearing earrings either, but hey, he doesn't hold it against me and anyway the feelings not mutual.

rock'n'roll people love Frank Sinatra because Frank Sinatra has got what we want... swagger and ATTITUDE... HE'S BIG ON ATTITUDE... SERIOUS ATTITUDE... BAD ATTITUDE... Frank's THE CHAIRMAN OF THE BAD.

rock'n'roll plays at being tough, but this guy's... well he's the boss of bosses. The man. The Big Bang of Pop. I'M NOT GONNA MESS WITH HIM; ARE YOU?

who is this guy that every swinging city in america wants to claim as their own?. this painter who lives in the desert, this first-rate first-take actor, this singer who makes other men poets, boxing clever with every word, talking like america... fast... straight up... in headlines... comin' thru with the big schtick, the aside, the quiet compliment... good cop/bad cop in the same breath.

you know the story because it's your story... Frank walks like america, COCKSURE...

it's 1945... the US cavalry are trying to get out of Europe, but they never really do. They are part of another kind of invasion. A.F.R. American Forces Radio, broadcasting a music that will curl the stiff upper lip of England and the rest of the world paving the way for rock'n'roll with jazz, Duke Ellington, the

big band, Tommy Dorsey, and right out in front, FRANK SINATRA... his voice tight as a fist, opening at the end of a bar not on the beat, over it... playing with it, splitting it... like a jazz man, like Miles Davis... turning on the right phrase in the right song, which is where he lives, where he lets go, and where he reveals himself... his songs are his home and he lets you in... but you know... to sing like that, you gotta have lost a couple o' fights... to know tenderness and romance like that... you have had to have had your heart broken.

people say Frank hasn't talked to the press... they want to know how he is, what's on his mind... but y'know, Sinatra is out there more nights than most punk bands... selling his story through the songs, telling and articulate in the choice of those songs... private thoughts on a public address system... generous

... this is the conundrum of Frank Sinatra left and right brain hardly talking, boxer and painter, actor and singer, lover and father... troubleshooter and troublemaker, bandman and loner, the champ who would rather show you his scars than his medals... he may be putty in Barbara's hands but I'm not gonna mess with him, are you?

LADIES AND GENTLEMEN, ARE YOU READY TO WELCOME A MAN HEAVIER THAN THE EMPIRE STATE, MORE CONNECTED THAN THE TWIN TOWERS, AS RECOGNISABLE AS THE STATUE OF LIBERTY... and LIVING PROOF THAT GOD IS A CATHOLIC... will you welcome THE KING OF NEW YORK CITY... FRANCIS... ALBERT... SINATRA.

This is one of a series of essays on being a fan to be found in *idle worship: how pop empowers the weak, rewards the faithful and succours the needy* edited by Chris Roberts (HarperCollins UK, £5.99)

When U2 became the biggest band in the world in the eighties, somehow, maybe by accident, they also became one of the most serious. ZOO TV and the nineties U2 shattered that image. So are they funny or serious or what? Bill Flanagan, Editor of *Musician*, who spent two years travelling in the ZOO to write his book *U2 At The End of The World,* discusses this vexed issue.

THEY'RE NOT VERY

I once met an American tourist in Ireland who said she had been having tea in a hotel restaurant when U2 came in and sat at the table behind her. She and her friend could not believe how funny the four of them were – they traded jokes, quips and can-you-top-this punchlines. "They were like a comedy team," she said. "I alwas thought they were serious!"

I can't tell you how many times I've heard similar things from people who only know U2 through the mass media. I met U2 in 1980 and kept in touch with them over the years since. Three years ago they agreed to let me follow them around and write a book about their music and the whole wild circus that revolves around it. If I knew the band pretty well before, I got to know them very well while travelling in buses, planes and automobiles from Mexico to Tokyo, Italy to Australia. When people ask me about all the time I spent with U2, I usually say, "Well I remember a lot of great music and I remember laughing all the time."

The great music people accept, but a lot of folks raise their eyebrows when I say how funny Adam, Bono, Edge and Larry are. Maybe because I knew U2 as people I knew them through the media, I bring a knowledge of their humour to anything I read or write about them. People who see them only through the eyes of journalists may miss that. While one can never underestimate a critic's ability to not get a joke, there must be something in the way U2 operate that keeps their humour from coming through when the tape recorder is turned on and the notepads are out.

The band may be at the disadvantages of people coming at them with serious preconceptions; if someone walks in and starts asking you to explain art, love and God, it's hard to say, "That reminds me of a funny story…" U2 probably also pay the price of restricting most of their interviews to quick sessions in an office or studio. (There's a good reason for that – if they spent as much time doing interviews as the press would like, they'd never have time to make any music.) Reporters don't get the chance to observe the sort of "Hard Days Night" scene that I witnessed in a limousine with U2 heading to the Los Angeles airport:

In the car Bono struggles to get the TV to change channels but it stays stuck on one of those half-hour self-help commercials. Finally in exasperation, Bono says, "Edge, you're the scientist, can you get this to work?" Edge leans over and tries to change the station. Each time he does, it clicks back to the self-help ad. This is very strange. Edge gets down and fiddles with the switches with the furrow-browed dedication of a Louis Pasteur

FUNNY, ARE THEY?

at his Bunsen burner, oblivious as Bono to the fact that Larry is sitting with a remote control by his leg, clicking the channel back each time Edge tries to change it.

At last they give up and accept the infotainment. "Too bad you can't get cable in a car," Larry says. Then he asks if anyone else has seen the Fishing Channel. "Lots of talk about rods and hooks and the one that got away."

Bono says, "I prefer the 'rides bikes, likes boats and lives with the same girlfriend for twelve years' channel."

Larry groans and rolls his eyes. Edge asks what they are talking about. Larry explains that Bono's recapping the thumbnail description of him in the new *Vogue* cover story on U2. Once again a journalist who was given access to the whole band went home and wrote a story that was chock-full of Bono, had a few wise parables from the Edge, and devoted Adam and Larry roughly the same number of words that go on the back of a bubblegum card. Bono says euphemistically, "She painted Larry in bold strokes."

Adam smiles and says to the sullen Mullen, "At least you're not the one she called 'handsome in an ugly way.'"

One of the funniest things U2 do in their conversation with each other is put on voices and play-act different characters. They sometimes kid each other by adopting 'Spinal Tap' poses.

An outsider who walks into the middle of this can come away thinking that these guys really ARE spoiled rock stars (though their parodies are so broad that the outsider would have to be lacking any sense of humour himself.) Here's a scene that took place during the recording of *Zooropa*, when Larry was interrupted in the lavatory by a summons back to his drums:

Larry strolls in in a cocky mood, "What's so important you had to interrupt a perfectly good crap?"

"We need you to do some drumming," Bono answers.

Larry says, "Call my manager."

"We sent a letter to Mr Paul McGuinness," Edge says, "requesting your services to play some drums."

"It's the song we were playing last night," Bono says. "Apparently you did a tremendous job but the rest of us ..."

Adam says, "Amazingly enough YOU were fine."

"We face a problem we have faced in the past," Bono explains. "The song has no chorus."

"Aha!" Larry says.

Generally Adam is the quickest with a quip, which may be part of why Adam has a looser image than the other three. Bono's humour is missed by those who assume that everything he says has the weight of philosophy behind it – and miss his gift for leg-pulling at an Olympic level. Edge's jokes are so deadpan that they fly over some heads. Larry probably has the biggest obstacle to overcome in getting his wit across, because Larry's humour usually comes out in the classic Ralph Kramden slow-burn of the straightman whose patience has been stretched past the breaking point by the nuts around him. Larry phoned me after reading my book in manuscript and said, "You make it look like I'm angry all the time." I said "That's silly, Larry, I do not." He said, "Let me read you a list of some of your descriptions of me: 'Larry fumes, Larry burns, Larry shouts, Larry sneers, Larry comes in boiling, Larry says angrily, Larry's pissed, Larry got upset, Larry was mad …"

I had to admit Larry had a point. What I had not considered and I dare say what even other band members who read the book might not have noticed – is that if you know Larry you know that his 'This is the last straw' persona is a running joke. But objective readers would not realize this; they'd just figure Larry was always in a bad mood. Heck, one time – toward the end of the Zoo TV tour – Larry greeted me by saying, "Three more weeks of seeing your ugly face!" Of course he was joking (Wasn't he?).

There is one other reason why U2 have gotten an undeserved reputation as Serious Men. While they are not stuffy, they are very kind. Most humour pokes fun at someone or something. U2 can do hilarious riffs on any number of silly people they encounter

in their professional lives. Between Bono's impressions, Edge's one-liners, and Adam's bon mots, they skewer a wide range of showbiz hustlers and sleazy hypocrites. But while U2 are happy to publicly poke fun at themselves and their own vanities (to their detriment if journalists don't get the joke), they are very sensitive about hurting the feelings of even a deserved target with an offhand crack on TV or in a magazine.

My deal with U2 was that I'd let them read my book about them before publication so that they could correct, object or argue – but I had full control of what I decided to keep or change. There are probably things in the book that are annoying to the band members, moments they were sorry I was around to record. I wondered how hard they would lobby me to change those bits. To my surprise none of them asked for any of that to be cut. Adam said, "Well there's some things in there that I'm sorry you wrote but I understood the groundrules so fair enough." What Adam did ask me to change was a funny joke he made at the expense of someone who is not famous. Bono was the same way – he was very concerned with hurting the feelings of people who might have been a little bit silly, or behaved in a way that invited teasing, but felt did not deserve to be mocked in print. That became the pattern for Edge, Larry and Paul McGuinness too. They didn't mind what

I said about them – they wanted to spare the feelings of others. If that meant that their own wit might not come through, that was to them a fair trade.

I didn't always agree to the changes U2 wanted – in some places I left their wise-guy jokes at the expense of silly people. But I thought it was remarkable that they were so willing to publicly kid themselves and so bothered by the thought of publicly teasing someone else. I realized then that as great as their sense of humour is, their sense of humanity is even better.

ABOUT THE BAND'S FUTURE DIRECTION.

'My drumming career has always been based on a complete lack of Expertise'

LARRY MULLEN JNR COULD NEVER BE DESCRIBED AS A GREAT FAN OF THE "ROCK INTERVIEW". HE USUALLY LEAVES THAT TO THE OTHER THREE, BUT HE DID

CUNNINGHAM, LARRY RECALLED THE BIRTH OF U2 IN THE MULLEN FAMILY KITCHEN, REFLECTED ON HIS UNUSUAL PEDIGREE AS A MUSICIAN AND WONDERED A LITTLE

RECENTLY AGREE TO TALK WITH THE SPECIALIST DRUMMING MAGAZINE RHYTHM. IN A CANDID CONVERSATION WITH MARK

After more than a decade at the height of commercial and critical success with ground-breaking albums such as *War*, *The Joshua Tree*, *Achtung Baby* and *Zooropa*, it is hard to believe that U2's epic journey to success began when 15-year-old Larry Mullen Jr pinned a "Musician Wanted" ad on the noticeboard at Mount Temple Comprehensive school in Dublin. Nineteen years later the band is arguably the most talked about and revered on the planet.

As the chameleon-like quartet enjoys a well-earned sabbatical from the limelight, Larry recalls those early days when the fledgeling U2 rehearsed in his parents' kitchen. "We'd all had some form of interest in music and there were about six or seven of us, plus a couple of friends, jamming away with no real direction. The idea was to see who could and couldn't play, as normally happens with new bands. The thing that was most interesting about the meeting was that Edge (then plain Dave Evans) and his brother, Dick, who later played with The Virgin Prunes, had built their own very funky looking electric guitar, which didn't work very well. Everything else was borrowed or didn't work, and it was pretty chaotic."

It was the following day, they figured out who was going to be in the band. "It was down to who had the loudest voice and the most money," explains Larry, tongue firmly in cheek.

"I saved up my cash from mowing lawns to buy my first drum kit; Edge attempted to build guitars and Adam already had a bass. But Bono was slightly in dire straits and we wanted him to play guitar, although he insisted on singing. Now we know why – because he didn't have to buy or move any equipment."

Larry is quick to destroy several well-documented myths that have gone down as "facts" in the U2 history books; one of which concerns the band's original name. "At the first rehearsals people were referring to the band as Larry Mullen's Band, for want of a better name. We never played under that name but I think it was done to protect my ego at that stage, because we had rehearsed at my house and when Bono came in he could sing better than me, looked better and was just that bit older. He basically shot my chance of becoming the leader of the band." It has also been cast in literary stone that a Bay City Rollers cover was a regular feature of their early set. "That was bullshit – we only did it once for a laugh. Very early on we started writing our own material, albeit badly. It wasn't until much later, in 1978–79, that we had some idea of musical direction. The band had gone through a whole lot of changes and it wasn't a proper working band until '78 or '79.

Growing up in the mid seventies, Larry's staple musical diet consisted of glam-rock greats, like The Sweet, T-Rex, Roxy Music, Slade and Gary Glitter, whose two-drummer band fascinated the Dublin lad. "I just knew that this was something I wanted to do. If you listen back to a lot of that music as far as beat is concerned, it was so 'on' and rhythmic in a very simple way. I also loved Bowie – rhythmically he was so advanced, and that's why Ziggy Stardust and a lot of that seventies stuff still stands up today. At the other end of the scale there were Steely Dan, Bruce Springsteen and Yes, but I knew nothing about them, even though my sister would bring those albums into the house. Glam rock was certainly the foundation of my influences and I used to take out a pair of drumsticks and hit things along to the records."

U2 producer Brian Eno has said that he thought many aspects of Larry's distinctive drumming style and sense of rhythm had their origins in his experiences as a young marching band drummer. Larry agrees: "Yeah, certainly some of it did. I'm very interested in Irish traditional music and rhythm and that's really where I come from. I have played in a lot of military style bands and at some point I think it crossed over into U2. If you listen to the first three or four albums you can spot the influence. One of the things I find when I listen back is that my playing was very simple, kind of inventive at times, but at other times it didn't have a lot of rhythmic qualities.

"When you're playing with two guys like a bass player and a guitarist, there are a lot of spaces to fill. A good example of that was The Police, where they filled those gaps in quite a sophisticated way compared to U2. We were rhythmically unsophisticated, and a lot of that came from the fact that when I was playing in military bands there were other people covering all those different areas. You had percussionists, another drummer and three or four bass instruments, and there was confusion over who exactly should be providing the beat.

"For me in military bands I was providing a form of rhythm but not necessarily the 4/4 beat, and it was only after we started working with Danny (Daniel Lanois) that I started to understand what the position of a drummer in a band was. I know it sounds strange but we don't have a rock 'n' roll tradition in Ireland and when you're 15 or 16 and starting out in a band, like I was, it's hard for a drummer to instinctively know what to do in that role. Do you provide a musical element or just a beat? It was a dilemma and I notice it now when I listen to some of our early records. I suppose it's the challenge for drummers to both provide the beat and be inventive, all at once. In traditional Irish music, where they play bodhrans, it's rarely on the 4/4, it's always on the off-beat and other instruments like spoons and bones provide the 4/4. So I guess those things have had a huge influence on me."

These influences do not come any stronger than on the U2 classics "Sunday Bloody Sunday" and "Pride (In the Name of Love)", the latter exhibiting some of the most electrifying snare fills in rock's 40-year history. "When it came to recording 'Pride' for the *Unforgettable Fire* album, Danny was able to pick up from me that I had some interesting ideas but there was a slight lack of focus. My kick drum technique was then, as it is now, completely underdeveloped and I never got a chance to practise and learn like most people would. In the marching bands, I only used a snare and when I first got a it, I never learned how to properly use all the elements together.

"So I went and listened to a basic demo of 'Pride' and tried to play a beat just using the kick and snare. But I couldn't get the kick to do what I wanted, so I got a floor tom down and did what I'd done in the past, which was if I couldn't physically do what was necessary, I'd find another way around it. I couldn't do what most most people would consider a normal beat for the song, so I chose alternatives. Those snare rolls were originally very straight, until Bono told me it didn't sound right. So I spent a couple of hours trying things out until I came up with the build-ups and accents you hear. If I'd had the knowledge I would have done something completely different, but I don't think it would have been half as interesting. You give up something to get something else, and my drumming career has always been based on a complete lack of expertise!"

Despite Larry's razor-sharp self-criticism, there is no doubt that his unique approach is highly effective in the context of U2's music. "I've never thought of myself as U2's drummer but rather a contributor to the overall sound. I'm still learning about rhythm and over the last year since U2 have taken some time off, I've been working with a couple of guys in America. It's shown me how professional drummers really play, because I really want to know. I don't necessarily want to emulate them but I certainly want to know how it's done."

Keen to improve his craft, Larry practises whenever time permits at his North Dublin home. In fact wherever in the world he roams, a set of electronic drums is not far away for the occasional honing of paradiddles and other rudiments. "I have some exercises I go through, although I don't do it as often as I should. But I try and keep my hand in as often as possible. As I said my kick drum technique leaves a lot to be desired, but the time comes when you think 'Hey, I really want to be able to do this shit!' I won't stop doing all the other things but it's getting a little embarrassing now to ignore it!"

It is clear from talking to Larry that the musical traditions of his home-land run thick in his veins and he is not averse to dabbling with that most famous of Irish percussion instruments, the bodhran. "I played one on the last two U2 albums and also on the new Nanci Griffith record (which also features his remixing talents), although I don't play it in the traditional way. I play it with mallets or my hands or any way I can because, again, it's not something I learned to play properly. But it's a great versatile instrument that's underrated. That and the tabla are my favourite items of percussion.

The kit on which Larry began his career was, he says, "a bit of a nightmare". Made by a Taiwanese toy company, it was a mother of pearl ensemble of odd-sizes including a 19 1/2" kick drum that Larry had to cover himself with calf hide, due to the absence of off-the-shelf skins. "I persevered with it for quite few years and, like an old friend, I was sorry to see it go ," he remembers.

These days with considerably more punts in his pocket, Larry has been able to improve his set-up and regularly used up to three kits in the studio. "My main kit is a Yamaha Studio kit with a 22" kick, one mounted rack tom, a floor drum on the left and right, a Brady 13" snare, Yamaha or Ludwig piccolos and a selection of Paiste cymbals. There is also a monitoring system around that set-up. I also have a Yamaha cocktail-type kit with an 18" kick, a couple of toms and another Brady snare, but without any monitoring. In addition, Edge has an old Slingerland kit that is always thrown up in one corner for me to play if necessary. Then there are various percussion instruments, but the volume affects Brian (Eno) these days so I have to find the kit that's furthest away to avoid upsetting him!"

For a real live drummer with an "organic" approach, it is surprising how warmly Larry has embraced experimentation with drum samples, loops and machines. Although this use of technology began to infiltrate the band's music as early as 1984 ("Bad") and progressed with spectacular effect on "God Part 2" (from *Rattle and Hum*), it was not until *Achtung Baby* and *Zooropa* that it became an integral part of their sonic make-up. Vital to this process has been co-producer and engineer Flood. "It evolved quite slowly and gave me a chance to understand what was going to happen by the time we got to make *Achtung Baby* because we were using a lot of machinery by then and we were able to strike a good balance. Flood has a vast knowledge of how studios work and the use of electronics, as his work with Nine Inch Nails and Depeche Mode demonstrates.

"My relationship with Flood has always been about taking basic ideas and making them special, using the technology available in the studio. As far as playing with samples and things like that is concerned, a lot of that is done during the putting together of a song. There might be some sort of a pulse or rhythmic idea that's been used in constructing the melody, and when we get to playing on that, it will be a question of maybe emphasising more of the machinery and using less of the real drums. I believe the future will see more of a marriage between rock 'n' roll and technology. That is definitely the way forward. For me, it's not like I'm coming from a position of strength where I can say 'Hey, I know better'. I'm open to anything that will make it sound better. Machines do that, so I'm perfectly happy with that marriage.

"I actually get off on playing alongside machines and it has certainly improved my playing a hundredfold. There may have been a bit of resistance in the beginning because I think the expectations for what would happen between machine and drummer were very high.

"When you actually work through it, you find that it's not about one or the other, it's about the marriage of both elements to create a musical atmosphere in which the best work can come out. However it has to be an equal marriage, otherwise it's disastrous. There are some producers who prefer not to use drummers, letting the machines take over and concentrating on the 'musicians' but it's important to strike a balance." There are one or two bands around at the moment, including the rather excellent Doppelgangers, who are marketing themselves as U2 copycats.

To change the mood of our conversation I ask Larry if he finds this flatering or should they go away and get a life? For the first time in their brilliant career, U2's members find themselves with time on their hands to catch up with their personal lives. "We are all individually out in the world, doing whatever we need to do to get ourselves in a frame of mind whereby we can get back together at some point and make a great record. One of the mistakes we made between *Rattle and Hum* and *Achtung Baby* was that we didn't give ourselves enough time to get back into listening to music and being musical. The whole process of *The Joshua Tree* and *Rattle and Hum* was so difficult that we kind of hibernated for a while, and when we regrouped, we didn't have any new ideas. But this time around we are going to keep our hand in to make sure we don't repeat our mistakes."

How the hell do you follow an album like *Zooropa* and a multi-media extravaganza tour like Zoo TV? "To be honest, I don't think you ever can follow something like that and I don't think I ever would want to.

"On a musical level, I still don't believe U2 has reached its peak and there are a lot of things for us to do. I look forward to that challenge and without that goal there is no point in continuing. But I don't want us to repeat anything we've done before and instead of improving on *Zooropa* and the tour, I think we should do something different, although

there's no telling what it will be like. I'd like to think that whatever happens will be better not bigger."

Does Larry think that there is a danger of the band's apparent obsession with unpredictability eventually compromising its music? "Musically, I think U2 is unpredictable but I don't think it's contrived, it's just a fact of life. We've never been proficient enough to be regular and have always worked in an ad hoc way, experimenting with different producers, and I don't think that will change. Surely that can only enhance the music and not take away from it?"

Finally, I ask Larry what it is that makes U2 so special? "Whatever it is, it has nothing to do with the four individuals, but what happens when we get together and the music we make as a collective unit. The band's greatest strength is that there are no boundaries, there are no limits. You can't get any bigger, we have been able to achieve everything, for the most part on our own terms.

"That's the most satisfying thing for us." ∞

A version of this article originally appeared in Rhythm Magazine...

213

All Pass
Present

IT IS LATE JULY, A WEDNESDAY. DUBLIN IS HOT.

THE MEMBERS OF U2 AND THE MEMBERS OF BRIAN ENO ARE IN A RECORDING STUDIO ON THE RIVERSIDE, WITH A

PROMISE TO FINISH MAKING THEIR JOINT ALBUM IN THREE DAYS. AFTER THAT THE MEMBERS OF U2 GO OFF ON THEIR

HOLIDAYS AND THE MEMBERS OF BRIAN ENO START TO FINISH THE MUSIC OF WHAT WILL BE *YOUR BLUE ROOM – MUSIC*

12am
Bono and Edge were at the studio late last night and they are first in this morning. Edge is playing a synthesizer in the studio, writing a theme, so he says, for the new James Bond film. Such is the purple patch that U2 are in at present that while they have only three days to finish off their soundtrack album, Edge is writing a different piece which will not be on the album at all. Bono is wandering around the premises, allegedly in search of a missing chord. Edge gave it to him last night but he has lost it already. "We've got till Saturday," says the guitarist. "But we've got a few nuts to crack yet."

12.30pm Bono is excited with the material that U2 and Eno have come up with. He tries to operate an intimidatingly big tape-machine in a bid to find the latest version of "Your Blue Room" which they have written for a film that the legendary Italian director Michelangelo Antonioni started and their long-time cinematic collaborator Wim Wenders is helping to finish. The track is for a love-scene, an erotic scene, explains Bono, chuckling at the idea of Wim Wenders directing it.
Edge arrives, wondering where "that TV scene of the alcoholic talking to the priest" is. They're writing music for it. It's a scene from a new Phil Joanou film – the man who directed "Rattle and Hum".
Brian Eno, fifth member of the burgeoning group of musicians

making this record, is sitting in front of a sophisticated Apple Mac computer and manipulating scanned images of the band into something that could become an album cover. "There are a number of Brian Enos," explains Bono. "This is the art-work Brian Eno."

On two noticeboards in the room are scrawled lines of song-titles, most of which will have been changed before the album is released. At the foot of one board reads the slogan. "Make the Music of the Future You Want To Live In."

Tokyo Drift
Ito Okashi
Davidoff
Antartica
Fleet Click
Plot 180
Tokyo Glacier (Fact)
Slow Star (Time)
Always Forever

The early signs confirm the earlier ones: it was Japan at the end of the Zoo Tour which is where this record was conceived.
"For whatever reason, Tokyo seems to be the home of this record," says Bono. "Arriving there at the end of the Zoo TV tour it became clear to us that this was actually the capital of Zoo TV."

engers
and Correct

FOR FILMS 4. EXCEPT OF COURSE IT WON'T BE. BUT THAT WAS THEN AND THIS IS NOW. IN

BETWEEN THE PASSENGERS ARRIVED WITH *ORIGINAL SOUNDTRACKS VOLUME 1.*

THIS IS THE STORY OF THAT DAY IN THAT STUDIO.

"In Tokyo, you don't feel you are in the present tense. You feel as if you have stepped into the future."

He pauses, recalling those final days of the ZOO TV tour at the end of 1994. "It's not all good but it is definitely not boring. I went to bed hardly at all. I just couldn't sleep, there was just so much going on outside. We spent a lot of time in this area called ShunShuku and Electric City where you have these 25–50 foot neon signs in blue gold, flashing messages and huge hoardings advertising manga movies or cartoons."

Looking back it seems to the singer that Tokyo was like a "waking dream", the strange mix of the Yakuza – the Japanese mafia – sliding around in bullet-proof Rolls Royces, mixed in with the mundane humility and unending politeness of everyday folk in the city. "We had to keep escaping our minders because the promoter wants to take care of you and doesn't want you to get into the dodgy area of town. So we'd slip out of the back door and disappear into the night just to meet people."

So, in a strange, slightly surreal way, this latest U2-driven project was born in Tokyo, where the band felt like they had slipped into the 21st Century or into Ridley Scott's *Bladerunner*.

"Something went off in my head," says Bono. When the bits came to ground, some of them landed on Passengers. "Tokyo opened the next chapter for us," he adds.

It was a year later that the band were in the studio in West London, experimenting with Brian Eno on abstract ideas and sound-track possibilities. With videos of old movies and cartoons playing on the monitors, something clicked.

"We would stick these videos on and play to them with the sound turned down and the thing that came out to me was the sound of where we had been the year previously ..."

"In Tokyo, you don't feel you are in the present tense. You feel as if you have stepped into the future."

1.15pm Bono is waxing enthusiastic about the experimental noises coming out of the speakers as he plays back some of the new material. At this stage, three months before official release, it has some of the strangest sounds and most jagged noisescapes that U2 have ever featured in. The plastic soundscapes of "Zooropa" have been warped even further back into the future.

"A song doesn't have to have a centre," says Bono. "In dance music it is the rhythm that is the centre. We are making music for movies and we're trying to pull that off without seeing the picture."

Edge expands a little: "Often things are set up as instrumentals but at some point they just seem to turn into songs, which I think is lovely myself." The beautiful moving piece that is "Your Blue Room" is playing back at full volume. Eno is yelling at the keyboard. Bono is yelling on the couch.

2pm Bono explains how he impersonated his dad Bob Hewson, impersonating an opera singer in the bath to lay down the operatic tenor vocal for "Miss Sarajevo". He had been approached by Pavarotti to write him a song. Bono replied that, while he felt this a great honour, unfortunately he had no time at present. Pavarotti was undaunted. And he had God on his side. He said that he had spoken to the angels and that Bono would be writing him a song and also singing at his autumn charity concert in Italy. Bono said that okay he could write him a song but he was definitely not coming to Modena – there was just too much going on, not least recording an album with Brian Eno.

Luciano Pavarotti cannot even spell the word "No". To cut a long story short, a deal was brokered. Pavarotti would sing the tenor part on "Miss Sarajevo" and Edge, Bono and Eno would play a couple of songs at Luciano's charity gig in September.

"It's a beautiful song," says Bono. "Quite elusive and sometimes I think it overpowers us. Sometimes it's a breeze that blows in one window and out the other without you noticing."

3.30pm A piece of music presently called "One Finger Piano" – later "Beach Sequence" – is playing and everyone is listening to make comments. It is written for a scene in the Antonioni/Wenders film where John Malkovich is on the beach by a swing. It opens with birdsong and the one finger is Bono's. The singer is murmuring a single vocal line: "Time... shoots on by" repeated over and over.

Adam arrives though a window, with Anton Corbijn. They have been doing photos out at Adam's place. Edge asks Brian what's happening next. Brian is lost in his computer screen.

4pm Howie B arrives from another studio in Dublin where he has been up all night mixing tracks at U2-Eno's suggestion. Bono met him recently performing at The Kitchen and promptly recruited him to the cause of the new album. "Let me show you this Elvis poem I've got," says Bono. "I

wonder if you can do anything with this."

Bono reads it rap style and Howie B gets into the groove and can barely be restrained from moving all over the floor. "Fuckin Mad," says Howie B in his thick Glaswegian accent. "I've got some stuff here from last night, Edge was fuckin wild."

Howie B plays the track back to Bono and Eno, listens too, while still making the front of the album on his computer. As the music plays Howie B is bending and blowing like a devout Jew on acid at the Wailing Wall. Bono is also

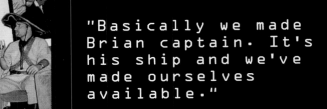

"Basically we made Brian captain. It's his ship and we've made ourselves available."

grooving, thinking the "trip" fits the mood of the record. Howie B is alarmed at a rogue click but Eno reckons he can get rid of it. "Thank fuck for that," says Howie B.

"We better go after that *Bladerunner* soundtrack," says Bono, "that one would fit perfectly."

It's a bit long but that's no problem: "It'll fade into something else," says Howie B, "It'll fade into any fucker." Bono says it is perfect Million Dollar Hotel material, a scene he describes where a train is arriving at an airport. "It's got a bit of Hawaiian style," says Howie B.

"Nineties Hawaiian style," says Adam, who is as pleased as Bono with what Howie B has come up with and they send him off with the Elvis poem. Meanwhile the search is on for something called After The Jungle, or at least a version of this that everyone liked – and approved – last week. "We could do another version," someone says.

"We don't want ninety four fucking mixes to choose from," says Eno, throwing his hands up in the air in mock theatrical horror.

Eno has a different kind of role on this recording than in other U2 records. Adam explains: "As we let the chemistry of the sessions develop we put Brian in the role of choosing the material and deciding to what extent it needed finishing. We were really working under Brian's instruction so when we had those pieces identified we then brought up the rear with melodies and other ideas ... the chemistry has been a different one to a normal U2 record."

"Basically we made Brian captain," chimes Bono. "It's his ship and we've made ourselves available."

Then a qualification: "At the same time it's not that simple, because we're a band with a very strong identity and strong ideas about what we want to do – so inevitably some songs, for instance, have appeared, which were not part of the original plan."

But it's worked well: "It's not a U2 record, it's a U2-Brian

Eno record so it's much better," says the singer.

Anton Corbijn, the band's favourite photographer who is over to do a shoot for the record's release, wanders over to Eno's screen to see how he is "ruining" another of his photos. "What we need," says Anton, "is to get to the stage where we have the picture and then make the music fit the picture."

4.45pm A track called "Tokyo Drowning" is being rubbed off the main white board, no longer featuring in the future of U2, the future of Brian Eno, maybe the future of anything. It has been played twice to the general lack of enthusiasm of the Passengers and it has been found wanting.

A track called "Davidoff" goes the same way: "Can we say the same for this old stodge?" asks Eno, not particularly mincing his words.

"Tokyo Drift" metamorphoses into "Different Kind of Blue", a memorable song with the refrain, *"With twilight breaking thru, It's a different kind of blue."* It's a low key, laid-back number, riding on a smooth bass line but Captain Eno is characteristically unsentimental in his judgement: "I have to say, I think it's a weak track ..."

Bono: "I disagree, I really like it ..."

Edge: "It's got that lazy, lounge lizard feel, the only phrase I can think of."

Bono: "I like that lounge lizard thing."

The comments go round the room. Adam can live with it, Larry is less sure, wondering how it will fit in the context of the whole album. Bono wants it played again. This time round there is a slightly stronger feeling that it is not quite there but that it is only missing something special from being something special.

Captain Eno would be happy to lose it but concedes that if it had a more "inter–planetary" feel (Bono's phrase) then it could work. "A Different Kind of Blue" has hovered within an inch of the studio floor but has miraculously survived.

"Right, let's listen to 'Miss Sarajevo'," says Eno. "Which one do you want," asks Bono, "No Pav, Fake Pav, or Italian Pav." They go for fake Pav but the search for the Pav is to take the best part of two hours.

Bono explains that the lyrical idea behind "Miss Sarajevo" invokes – and maybe undoes – the spirit of the book of Ecclesiastes, a "time for everything under heaven". But is there a time to finish this album?

Everyone leaves the green room for the recording studio to hear the track on a different system. The opinions continue, getting more mixed as they go. "It may seem a bit lazy," explains Larry, "But we've been in here quite a while now and we're getting a bit tired."

And as this is the playback, it's down to everyone's opinions: "It's much more directive when we're actually recording."

It's time for a break. Anton and a camera beckons.

6.15pm While the set is prepared for the photo-shoot, Adam talks about the creation of the record, a process he has enjoyed immensely.

It was last February that the potential of the ad-hoc recordings seemed to become clear.

"We looked at the tracks and said, yes, they have potential but we don't want to get bogged down into a long project so let's look at the tracks where we can most quickly realise the potential."

It was not going to be the next U2 album at this point? "The idea had always been for some kind of collaboration depending on the material that came out of it – but we were never quite sure what form that would take. Once we thought of it as a soundtrack then it looked like a record that was a collaboration between the five of us."

Propaganda: "Are there times when you've thought, that track would fit on the next U2 record, let's keep it."

"In a minor sense: some songs that look like they're going to take a lot of time to finish, we've said we'll put them on the backburner and those things may turn up but it depends on how much new material we generate.

"At the moment we've already generated about ten ideas for a new U2 record but it will be a long time before the character of the new U2 record will be decided."

Propaganda: "Is there a different attitude in making a record like this one ?"

"Certainly, the attitude going into this has been, well it doesn't have to be anything, we can make it up as we go

"None of us in U2 want to make music that you can eat to. We want to make music that you can have sex to. Dinner party music is never going to be our thing."

along; we found some songs along the way and we found some instrumental pieces."

A huge day-glo orange painting has been erected in one corner of the first floor of the studio complex: the scene shows a tower block, atop with Japanese hoardings, under a royal blue sky, with helicopters flying at the side and a cartoon mermaid sitting on one wing. Within minutes, for some reason, Edge is walking around in a tweed suit, plus-fours, brogues, a floppy golf cap and looking for all the world like a pre-WWII golfer. Not to be outdone Adam is entirely got up as an airline pilot in dark blue suit, cap, shirt and tie. Brian Eno is decked out as a chef, Larry as a biker and Bono as a bizarre Mexican revolutionary, huge-bullet-belt slung round his waist and all hidden under a monster sombrero.

"I have no idea what the idea is," says Larry, speaking for the entire cast. Eventually all five members of U2-Eno are lined up on the set and only Anton Corbijn knows what he is up to. He begins shooting. And shooting. The photo-session goes on for days and days. Bono changes into an Hawaiian shirt-clad holidaymaker look. Then all five members change into chef-wear and depart from the studio complex to walk down to the Liffey where Anton has a further scene in his head. There is a certain surreal authenticity to the scene: drinkers in one of the pubs lean out of the window and shout "Beef Curry and Egg Fried Rice", unaware at just who they are making their mock orders. The photos, apparently, come to nothing but it's a good way to work up an appetite and by the time everyone troops back to the studio supper is being served.

9.30pm Howie B is back again with some more mixes, and everyone is listening in to the lost version of "Miss Sarajevo" that the engineers have found. The scene continues as before but this time Edge, for one, feels like they are closing in on the object of their hunt, that the end game for the Passengers beckons: "We were a million miles away earlier on today but now it feels like it's getting there." For another two hours the Passengers listen to tracks and argue their merits.

11.30pm Bono, loungin' on a settee while the others continue to play-back; talks about *Original Soundtracks*. There's a lot of air and space on some of the more ambient material, almost reminiscent of *Boy*. The singer jumps at the word "space".
"Space, see that's the hardest thing of all," he enthuses. "That's one of the reasons we picked up on Howie B because his mixes have a lot of space in them. Density seems to be the thing of the eighties but air is of the nineties." He too has found the concept of making music for films liberating – even when the films don't exist. "Soundtracks are a great place to experiment, to find sounds and musical ideas that are not pinned to traditional song-structure ideas," he explains. "Even people like Ennio Morricone formed little experimental groups from which they would make discoveries and then bring them back to their mainstream."
"Before we did *Achtung Baby*, myself and Edge worked on 'Clockwork Orange' and you start to see things in different perspectives: you can formalise those ideas later but there is an excitement in the raw when you first make them so we decided to put out a record that was like that." He explains that some of the songs from the West Side studio sessions in November 94 have "sprouted" and "turned into songs" which will not be on the Passengers work but on the next U2 record. That, he says is going to be "a rock record": "This," he adds, with a wink, "Is just getting the art out of our system."

Propaganda: "So what kind of album does he think *Original Soundtracks* is ?"
"We've always wanted to make what you might describe as a blue record, an ambient record, an atmospheric record."
"People listen to records for a reason, there's a function. Even though often musicians don't like to believe this, people play their records at certain practical times – like going out or going on a long drive – and U2 hasn't yet made an 'after

"It's probably best to view Passengers as a completly separate project but it has been great fun and it has meant that we've done creative work this year to get ourselves in shape for the next U2 project. It's been an adventure for us."

midnight' record. I thought it would be nice to have such a thing in our collection."
It's pretty late-night as we speak, after a hard-days work in the studio. But Bono is not tired yet, indeed he is warming to his theme.
"None of us in U2 want to make music that you can eat to," he says. "We want to make music that you can have sex to. Dinner party music is never going to be our thing ..."
"It's a chill-out record in club-scene terminology. We'll make the record spikey towards the end so that people can take it off, they won't be able to fall asleep to this."

12pm While some U2 fans may find this record an experiment too far. others, says Bono, will find it an exciting new departure.
"Our audience has proved to be very elastic over the years and *Zooropa* certainly pushed it. There are very few guitars on *Zooropa* and we used a lot of very plastic sounds and video-arcade noises."
"This record is going even further but it is connecting with what is going on in club-culture where people are tired of safe dance rhythms and easy tunes. They are looking to be poked a little as well as seduced."
Which is what he fancies a little of just now himself, getting up and inviting all and sundry to The Kitchen for a little late-night club action. Does this man never tire? Edge meanwhile has gone off to do some photography with Anton, Larry is watching telly and the last word on this day and this record is left to Adam.
"We're going to put out the record and see how people react to it .
"It's probably best to view it (Passengers) as a completely separate project but it has been great fun and it has meant that we've done creative work this year to get ourselves in shape for the next U2 project.
"It's been an adventure for us." ∞

BILL GRAHAM 1951–1996

Bill Graham shouldn't simply be remembered as the man who "discovered" U2. For one thing, the band's early history is too complex to credit just one person for such a historic find. But there's another reason for avoiding this simplistic tag. Bill Graham's influence stretches far beyond his association with this one group.

In his 19 years as a senior writer for Ireland's Hot Press magazine, Bill exercised his immense intellect over subjects as diverse as religion, folk music, philosophy, jazz, conspiracy theories and the connection between African music and Irish traditional styles. Bill's colleagues and the many musicians he encouraged over the years often called him a "head" – a powerful source of knowledge, a formidable transmitter of ideas. He was also a much-loved person. This was illustrated by Hot Press' decision to put his picture on the cover of their commemorative issue following his death.

Bill was important to U2 in that he could explain many of the artistic feelings that the fledgling band could barely put into words. He became fascinated by the community that had evolved around U2 and the Virgin Prunes – a clique that called itself Lypton Village. Bill recognised the value of this scene when he visited the bands at Willows House, the Prunes' hang-out in February 1979. Over a series of Hot Press features, Bill detailed the rich exchange of ideas that went on in this suburban stretch of Dublin; the fabulous nicknames like Bono, Gavin Friday and The Edge; the Village's sense of ritual and ridicule and the way that the two bands often bounced ideas off each other. Importantly, Bill also protected the acts from their more naive outpourings. He wasn't simply a journalist – he had decided to nurture both groups at this critical stage, to allow them to stay unique.

"We didn't know what rock and roll was," Bono remembers, "and he thought that was great. He was determined to stop us finding out. So he'd fill our heads with other ideas. He was very sensitive to The Village – that whole scene – and relationships, Guggi was becoming a painter and Gavin was getting into all kinds of arty stuff and Brecht. He thought this was amazing.

"He was the first person outside of our little scene that believed in us. He wasn't so much a critic as a kind of catalyst or visionary. We didn't know what Dada was. So he told us. We'd be putting on some daft performance art at the top of Grafton Street with a step-ladder and a pneumatic drill – it was naff, but he saw the little bit of great that was in it."

Bill's next move was to find a manager who could give U2 a chance to matter beyond Dublin. Again, this degree of foresight is astonishing, given the fact that the band was at such an early stage. But already, Bill was talking about them succeeding "internationally". He recommended the job to an old friend from Trinity College Dublin, Paul McGuinness. Paul would later admit that "he made the most important introduction of my life".

One of Bill's trademarks was his ability to find an individual's interests, and to develop the value in these traits by passing on books, cuttings, records, or even introducing a completely new circle of friends. U2 also benefitted from this touch. Bill admired Edge's unusual guitar sound, and encouraged him to listen to surf tunes and Country Joe And The Fish records. He also passed on Love albums – helping to foster the band's bright, chiming style.

Photo: Colin Henry, Courtesy of Hot Press

Bill wrote two books on the band. Another Time, Another Place (Mandarin) is a history of U2's infancy, putting their ideas into the context of contemporary Irish society. The Complete Guide To The Music Of U2 (Omnibus) is a highly insightful song-by-song guide. But he was essentially a print journalist, and it was in the pages of Hot Press that Bill's sparkling ideas were best appreciated. Better still was a personal conversation with the man, when he'd go rifling off into a seemingly unconnected series of themes, that would all make magnificent sense, several hours – and several pints of stout – later. Bono remembers such sessions with fondness. "You'd be pebble-dashed with words and ideas by this great tuba voice. It was a whole brass section late at night. I don't know what he was – a wild orchid of a man. Amazing."

Bill died suddenly and painlessly of a suspected heart attack on May 11 at the home he shared with his mother. At the funeral service in the Church Of The Assumption in Howth, Bono sang Leonard Cohen's "Tower Of Song" while Gavin Friday chose to perform Bob Dylan's "Death Is Not The End". There were additional musical tributes from Maire Brennan of Clannad, accordion player Sharon Shannon and Simon Carmody of The Golden Horde.

Dublin's musical community has experienced a huge sense of loss. This sadness is only offset by the happy memories of those who've been touched by Bill's spirit.

"In a funny way, he didn't live in his body." Bono muses. "His brain was just too full. It was sort of inevitable – something had to give. But I'll miss that brain, I really will."

Stuart Bailie

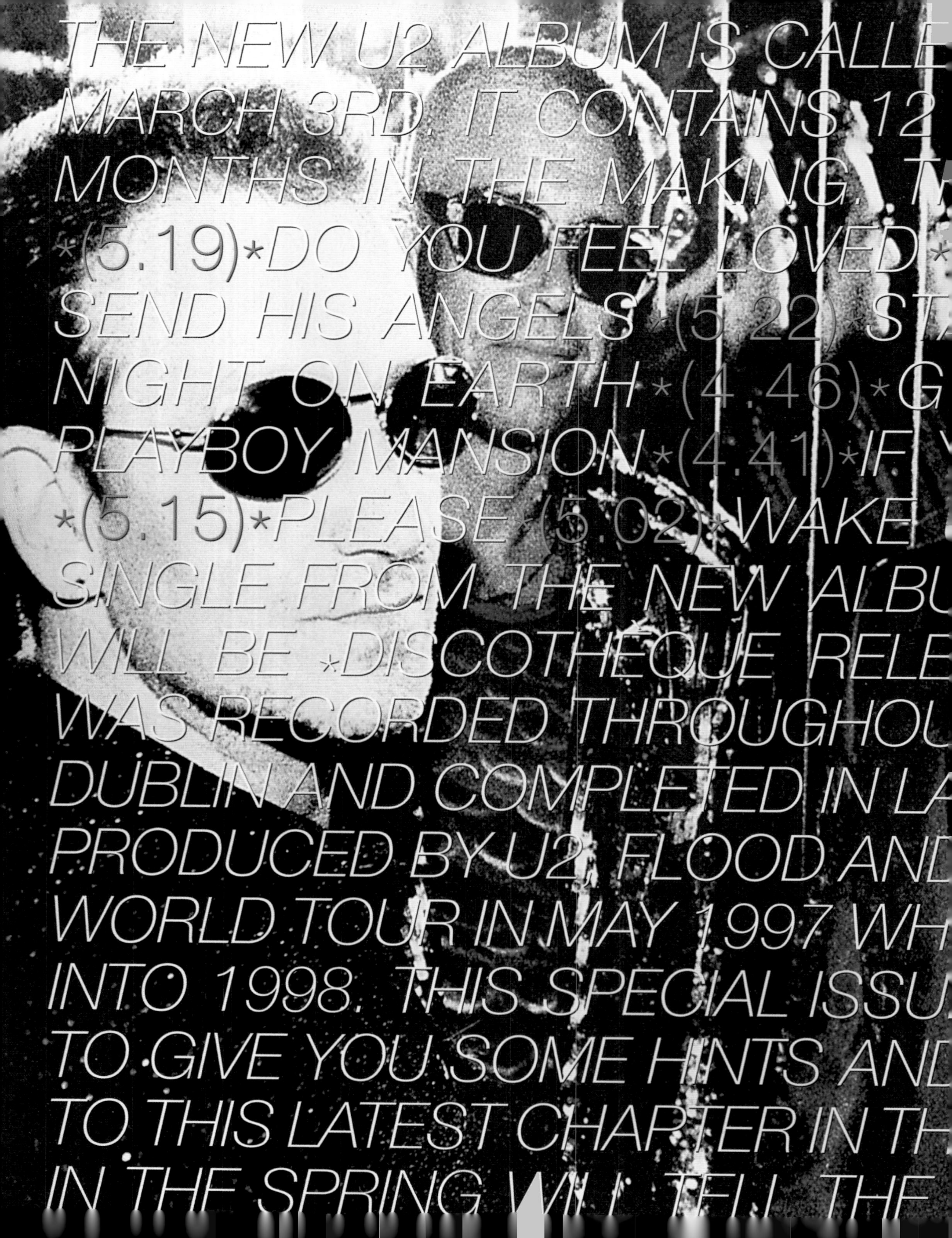

THE NEW U2 ALBUM IS CALLE
MARCH 3RD. IT CONTAINS 12
MONTHS IN THE MAKING. T
*(5.19)*DO YOU FEEL LOVED*
SEND HIS ANGELS*(5.22)*ST
NIGHT ON EARTH*(4.46)*G
PLAYBOY MANSION*(4.41)*IF Y
*(5.15)*PLEASE*(5.02)*WAKE
SINGLE FROM THE NEW ALBU
WILL BE *DISCOTHEQUE REL
WAS RECORDED THROUGHOU
DUBLIN AND COMPLETED IN LA
PRODUCED BY U2, FLOOD AND
WORLD TOUR IN MAY 1997 WH
INTO 1998. THIS SPECIAL ISSU
TO GIVE YOU SOME HINTS AND
TO THIS LATEST CHAPTER IN T
IN THE SPRING WILL TELL THE

POP. IT WILL BE RELEASED ON

EW SONGS AND HAS BEEN 12

SONGS ARE DISCOTHEQUE

07) MOFO *(5.47)* F GOD WILL

RING AT THE SUN *(4.37)* LAST

NE *(4.27)* MIAMI *(4.53)* THE

OU WEAR THAT VELVET DRESS

P DEADMAN *(4.52)* THE FIRST

IS CALLED DISCOTHEQUE. IT

SED ON FEBRUARY 10TH. POP

1996 AT HANOVER STUDIOS IN

NOVEMBER. THE ALBUM WAS

HOWIE B. U2 WILL BEGIN A NEW

H IS LIKELY TO CONTINUE WELL

OF PROPAGANDA IS INTENDED

CLUES IN WORDS AND IMAGES

STORY OF U2. OUR NEXT ISSUE

GGER STORY.

For us a song isn't a static thing – in the way that some people might write five or six songs. We'll take one song and put it through five or six moods. The same song – a speed metal song – could end up a ballad. We do have a rough idea of what we are doing, which is to take all the ideas in the air musically speaking – pop, trance, hardcore, hip-hop, metal, rock, whatever – and to try and make a record that acknowledges where we live musically, the sort of music that we ourselves get off on. It was inevitable that Pop would have a lot of different and disparate influences – the trick is trying to make it sound like it's from the same people.

Bono

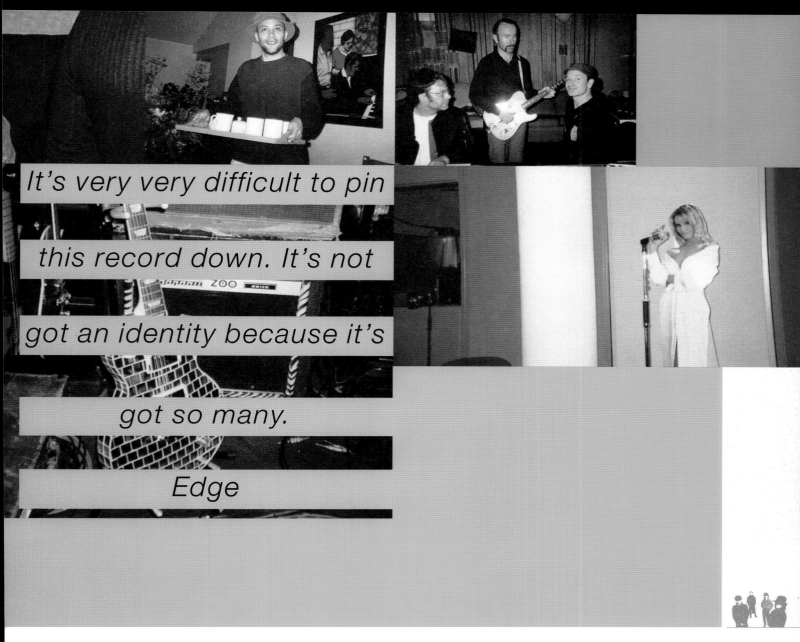

It's very very difficult to pin this record down. It's not got an identity because it's got so many.

Edge

you're not the only one starin' at the sun

afraid of what you'd find if you stepped back inside

I'm not sucking my thumb I'm staring at the sun

not the only one who's happy to go blind

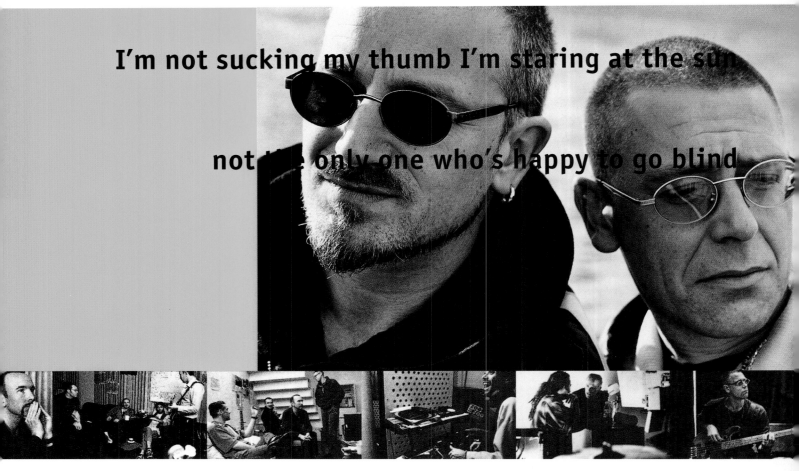

When people pick out The Joshua Tree, what they mean is why don't you make something as accessible as that. And that's not our job, it's never the job of a rock and roll band, if people want just melodic music there are other places they can go ... occasionally you make a record like that and there are songs on POP that are great in that respect but that's not our reason to be. There is a clear deal that we have with people who buy our records and that is, here's a shitload of money, you won't have to worry about where you're going to buy your shoes or what food is on the table ... but in return all we want is you to be fucking brave and a bit brilliant. I think that's the deal. The day we bow down to commercial pressure or sell ourselves out – by that I mean don't do the work that we actually want to do – will be a very sad day.
Bono

Each song is its own little world, that's what this record is going to be like I think. If "God will Send his Angels" is like a Temptations song – something like that would not normally find itself on the same record as a hardcore rocking song like "Last Night on Earth". Then "Velvet Dress" is like a lounge classic while "Holy Joe" – b-side of "Discotheque" – is a garage tune. "Do You Feel Love" is like a dance song and "Gone" is a guitar song, a rock guitar song.
Bono

WAKE UP WAKE UP DEAD MAN
WAKE UP WAKE UP DEAD MAN

Twenty One Years of Pop Music

WHEN THE BAND THAT BECAME THE BAND THAT BECAME U2 PLAYED THEIR FIRST EVER CONCERT ON A SCHOOL STAGE IN 1976, **NEIL McCORMICK** WAS THERE AND IT CHANGED HIS LIFE. TODAY HE IS A CRITIC WRITING FOR BRITAIN'S DAILY TELEGRAPH NEWSPAPER. BUT HE REMAINS A FAN OF THE BAND FORMED BY HIS CLASSMATES. HERE HE MUSES ON THE JOURNEY FROM PETER FRAMPTON COVERS TO POP.

BY ITS VERY NATURE POP – stemming as it does from the word popular – should be a transient, ephemeral thing. Yet it is one of the undoubted paradoxes of life that often it is the most ephemeral things stick in your mind the longest.

I can still vividly recall the first pop concert I ever attended. It was in the gymnasium of Mount Temple school, Dublin, back in 1976, when I was 15 years old. It was the middle of the day, all the lights were on, and the familiar smell of rotten sneakers and stale sweat filled the room. Most of the school was there, milling about with end of term excitement, paying little attention to official proceedings. Five friends strode out onto a rickety stage constructed of several shoved together tables, for the first ever performance by their group, Feedback. Their leader, Paul Hewson, struck a chord on his guitar and, I swear, a jolt ran through the room.

'POP: a musical of general appeal, especially among young people that originated as a distinct genre in the 1950s. It is generally characterised by a heavy rhythmic element and the use of electrical amplification.'
– Collins English Dictionary

It's probable that few of the kids there had seen a live electric hand before, and as they launched into an enthusiastic version of Peter Frampton's "Show Me The Way" the place exploded. I was utterly awe-struck. I stood transfixed in front of that stage, feeling those electric guitars and pounding drums ripping right through me, watching Paul as he stopped playing his guitar, grabbed onto the mike stand and yelled "I want you! Show me the way!"

Even the song title seems strangely pertinent. For in that moment was the beginning of something that brought me to where I am now, writing about popular music for the *Daily Telegraph* having mis-spent my youth in pursuit of my own rock dreams. And it took four members of that teenage group to where they are now, standing at the very summit of the big rock candy mountain, having just released their eagerly awaited tenth album. Paul Hewson, of course, is better known to the world by his teen nickname Bono. The musicians who shared table-space with him were Dave Evans (The Edge); Adam Clayton, Larry Mullen and Dick Evans (Dave's older brother). The group later began writing their own material and changed their name to The Hype. And then, after Dick left, they became U2. I suspect you may have heard of them.

Some years later, I told Bono that concert changed my life. He could only concur. It changed his life too.
"There was, from the very start, the evidence of a spark," he told me. "When I heard that D-chord, I got some kick ... It was like starting up a motorbike ... And the audience went wild! And I think we might as well forget the actual piece 'cause that wasn't important ..." (cue embarrassed laughter) "... but, it was the first thing I ever sang well. That was a very special concert, that was one of the best concerts of our lives ... And we built ourselves around that spark. I'll tell you, it was like four blind kids

U2 still haven't found what they're looking for ... U2 are dancing to a new pied piper ... Last Night on Earth – the Edge's guitar is in excelsis. – *Yorkshire E Press*

Five friends strode out onto a rickety stage constructed of several shoved together tables, for the first ever performance by their group, Feedback. Their leader struck a chord on his guitar and, I swear, a jolt ran through the room

blustering away and there was the evidence of just a little light in the corner and we started to work towards that. Getting to grips with our instruments, getting to grips with performance. And the light was getting clearer. Right now it's like standing in the daylight as far as I'm concerned. Looking around me, I've grown up. I mean you're talking about when we formed. You're talking about fifteen year olds."

Looking around me, I've grown up. He made that remark in December, 1980, sitting up late one night in a London flat after an exhilarating concert at the Marquee. He was twenty years old. I was nineteen. As it turned out, much to our surprise, we all still had a lot more growing up to do.

U2 have done theirs in public. I have often had the rather disconcerting experience of being in somebody's house only to be confronted by a picture of my classmates, perhaps pinned to a bedroom wall. I have to stop myself asking, "How do you know them?" Everybody knows them. Over the course of two decades, U2 became the most popular rock band in the world. They have sold over 70 million albums and gained a reputation as rock's premiere live act, making the transition from Mount Temple gymnasium to Wembley Stadium seem almost effortless. And they have done so creating music of undeniable integrity, passion and creativity, crossing the two most essential but usually mutually exclusive schools of rock: street (they have the post-punk emotional credibility of Bruce Springsteen or Oasis) and art (their modernist meshing of influences from other genres demonstrates the adventurousness of Roxy Music or David Bowie).

From their shining 1981 debut album "Boy", an evocative portrait of spiritually troubled adolescence; through the rousing and anthemic "War" (1983); the rough-house American roots stylings of "The Joshua Tree' (1987) to the dark-spirited, post-modern European ironies of "Achtung Baby!" (1991), U2's music has continually embraced change, never resting on a proven commercial formula. But one aspect of the group has remained reassuringly constant. Their personnel. In an ego-driven profession where splits and line-up changes are a routine hazard, U2 are a rare example of a group that have stuck together all their lives.
Their intense loyalty to one another is reflected in their attitude to those around them, the members of their organisation (who are always treated as colleagues, not employees) and their many lifelong friends (Gavin Friday, who grew up on Bono's street and forged his own art-pop career, remains Bono's intellectual sparring-partner). And in a union remarkable by any standards, let alone those in the fickle world of showbusiness, Bono is married to Alison Stuart, his childhood sweetheart, another former Mount

227

TWENTY ONE YEARS OF POP MUSIC, ISSUE 26

This isn't a dance album ... Whether Pop is the sound of Bono and the boys running scared in the face of rave's young gunslingers, or U2 running to stay ahead of the pack, hardly matters ... they're still running ... – Jewish Chronicle

Temple pupil (mind you, those of us who went to school with the gorgeous and feisty Mrs Hewson have no trouble comprehending the longevity of this particular relationship). The couple have two daughters (and as Bono comments on the laddish behaviour prevalent in so many contemporary British rock groups: "Liking a drink and being able to take care of yourself doesn't make you a hard man. To be a father – now that's hard.").

It is these enduring relationships that Bono credits (often and effusively) with keeping U2 in touch with the same core values that first inspired them. "The classic rock and roll star disease, is being surrounded by people who agree with you," he observes. "It gets harder and harder to work with a bunch of people who are your equals and who don't always agree with you. Especially if you've known them a long time. I see people as they go through life getting rid of arguments, shedding friends, every year, till they're left with just one or two people who agree with them. But 1 always think you're as good as the arguments you get. I like to be around a row."

So let me share with you a slightly esoteric argument that Bono and 1 have been having for years. I have always preferred the genre description "pop" to the rather more narrow "rock", since it has an openness that allows it to embrace a multitude of elements from the world of popular culture. He would have none of it. U2 were always a rock group. Until now. Taking on board the influence of Bjork producer and ambient experimenter Howie-B, U2's new album embraces the hip-hop techniques of modern dance (drawing a hitherto unsuspected grooviness out of Adam and Larry's rhythm section), crossed with the Edge's searing guitar rock and all hung around songs of melodic width, emotional depth and intellectual wit. It is an extraordinary record of glittering surfaces and dark undercurrents. And they have called it, quite simply (and perhaps with just a hint of irony), "Pop". "I thought pop was a term of abuse," Bono recently confessed to me. "It seemed sort of insulting and lightweight. I didn't realise how cool it was. Because some of the best music does have a lightweight quality, it has a kind of oxygen in it, which is not to say it's emotionally shallow. We've had to get the brightly coloured wrapping paper right, because what's underneath is not so sweet.

He has apparently been swayed by a multiplicitous dictionary definition of pop that he loves to drag out. "Let me see now ... Pox," he laughs, flicking through the pages of an enormous volume hauled from his bookshelves. "Practice. Pram. Prant. Prang. God, all my words are here! Pratfall. Preach. Prayer rug. Hold on, Fill past it. Here we go. Pop: To make or cause to make a light; sharp explosive sound. Isn't that great?" But it doesn't stop there. He proceeds to rattle on through a dozen or more definitions, as varied as "taking a drug in pill form" to "a flavoured non alcoholic beverage".

His new-found enthusiasm for the notion of 'pop' centres on his realisation that it is a word capable of reflecting his own voluminous excitement with life. Bono is a remarkably vibrant individual. Even as a schoolboy he had that most indefinable of qualities – charisma. And he has it in abundance now, as if he's somehow expanded to fill the dimensions of his larger-than-life existence. I can remember him in the earliest days, stomping around the rehearsal room, urging his fellow hand members to play and almost trying to suck the music out of their instruments. He is still fuelled by that same energy and desire, driven by restless intellect and spirit.

His conversation shoots off down unexpected alleyways. Discussing one of the albums stand-out tracks, "Mofo", a wailing techno-blues for an absent mother, he'll suddenly launch into an animated flight of fancy. "We should have called it 'Oedipussy'," he declares, laughing. "Maybe I could sing it hanging from a giant umbilical cord." There is, however, darkness lurking behind the humour. Bono's mother died when he was 14 years old, and he has long recognised that this was a defining moment in his life, pushing him in two directions at once: towards his profound faith in God and towards rock and roll.

The prevailing wisdom is that the devil has all the best tunes. Yet three members of U2 (Bono, Edge and Larry) have been devout Christians since their teens. Although they avoid preaching or crusading, their spiritual faith infuses their music. It could even

What, you may well ask, has happened to U2 ... The only song that really comes up to the "Pop" title is "Staring at the Sun" – *Midweek* be argued that the tension between their Christian values and the very primal, sexual and usually hedonistic nature of their chosen art form lies at the very heart of U2's creativity. As Bono sings on "Mofo", he has been "Lookin' for to save my soul / Lookin' for to fill that GOD shaped hole".

"Everyone's got one," he says. "Some are blacker and wider than others. It goes right back to the blues, it's what first makes you want to shout at God, when you've been abandoned or someone's been taken away from you. And I don't think you ever fill it, not completely. You can fill it up with time, by living a full life, but if you're silent enough, you can still hear the hissing." Lightening the mood, he starts to sing, to a familiar Bruce Springsteen tune, "Everybody's got a hungry hole."

Some might imagine that faith would be enough to fill that hole. Yet several tracks on "Pop" suggest Bono might be experiencing a crisis in this department. On songs like "If God Will Send His Angels", "Please", a stunningly ironic paean to the values of quick-fix capitalism entitled "The Playboy Mansion" and the album's emotionally raw closing track "Wake Up Dead Man" he seems to be searching in vain for evidence of the hand of God amidst the chaos and injustice of worldly life (Jesus, were you just around the corner? / Did You think to try and warn her? / Or are you working on something new? / If there's an order in all of this disorder / Is it like a tape recorder? / Can we rewind it just once more?).

"Belief and confusion are not mutually exclusive," Bono insists. "I think belief gives you a direction in the confusion. But you don't see the full picture. That's the point. That's what faith is. You can't see it."

Which brings us back to another argument we've been having ever since we first met. Between faith and faithlessness. I am an atheist and he's a believer and sometimes the gulf of mutual incomprehension that lies between these opposing points of view seems more than even friendship can compensate for.

It's funny, 'cause I really have grown to like the word pop, says Bono. I didn't realise how cool it was. It was the skinny boys who insisted it was rock and roll. It's the grown-ups who called it pop music. And now we've all grown up.

"It's a hard thing to explain to another person," he says (though it does not seem to stop him trying). "It hasn't happened to you, so why should you believe it? I was just lucky, I just saw that there was logic in the universe, I could see it in everything, by just looking around me. When I was a kid I could see it in flowers, or in a beautiful woman, or in the sound of strings, the sound of an electric guitar, just life. Life had a real beauty to it. I looked around and I saw it. It comes back to instinct. You're a writer, you know about instinct. Faith is just up the street, if not next door neighbours. Faith and instinct. But you can't just rely on it. I'm sure you question your atheism, just as I question faith. You have to beat it up. You have to pummel it to make sure that it can withstand it, to make sure you can trust it."

"Pop" demonstrates that, whatever doubts Bono may be expressing about his faith, U2's instincts are very much intact. "It's funny, 'cause I really have grown to like the word pop," Bono admits now. "I just didn't realise how cool it was. It was the skinny boys who insisted it was all rock and roll. It's the grown-ups who called it pop music. And now we've all grown up."

Ah, it's that grown up business again. But Bono has proof that pop is a grown up word. "Look," he laughs, hauling out his dictionary once more. "There's another definition for pop here: An informal word for father. That's pretty grown up, you have to admit."

For "Pop" is one of the bands darkest, most anguished records, and, killer single "Discotheque" aside, one of their hardest to digest. It's also a rock album. Reports of their conversion to techno, trip hop or anything else have been greatly exaggerated ... There's plenty that jumps out even on a first listen "If God Will Send His Angels", the chorus of "Staring at the Sun", where the ever morphing Edge turns into George Harrison ... *The List*

The U2 and Oasis Mutual Admiration Society

BONO CALLS IT A "SCI-FI GOSPEL SHOW". LIAM OF OASIS IS "MAD FOR IT". WHEN "THE WORLD'S GREATEST BAND AND THE WORLD'S NEXT BEST BAND" – NOEL`S WORDS – MET UP IN SAN FRANCISCO ON THE POP MART TOUR **NEIL McCORMICK** WAS THERE TO WATCH THE FIREWORKS AND TALK TO THE MAIN PLAYERS IN EACH BAND ABOUT WHY THEY LIKE EACH OTHER SO MUCH. ALONG THE WAY HE EVEN GETS BONO TO EXPLAIN WHAT POPMART IS ALL ABOUT... SORT OF.

IT IS A NIGHT NEITHER I, nor any of the participants, will forget in a hurry. U2 had just played the first of two dates in Oakland Stadium, San Francisco, and a small group of diehards, fired up on alcohol and adrenalin, were still toasting the success of the Irish superstars' PopMart show. At four a.m. in the almost deserted Tosca Cafe, while an ancient jukebox cranked out Caruso, Bono clambered on to the bar and delivered a magnificent, drunken rendition of "O Sole Mio". Oasis singer Liam Gallagher perched precariously on a barstool beneath him, a grin of disbelief pasted across his face. His brother, Noel Gallagher, leaned against a wall, bottle of beer in hand, eyes half-closed, smiling with the satisfaction of the cat who got the cream. "You know what POP stands for?" he joked, later. "Paddys on the Piss!" There are those in the British press who would probably suggest other acronyms for the word Pop; like Pretentious Overblown Pastiche or Posers Out to Pasture. Elements of the British media – along with a majority of British rock bands – have long displayed a sneering and supercilious attitude to the Irish group. During the course of the PopMart tour, newspapers have seized on reports of cancelled shows with undisguised glee – backed by the kind of research that gives journalism a bad name. Conveniently glossing over legitimate reasons for the cancellation of two U2 dates; ignoring the addition of extra shows due to increased demand and finding no room in their stories for the fact that receipts of $130 million have already made this U2's most successful tour ever, the *Guardian, Independent, Daily Star, Daily Express* and *Observer* have (mis)informed their readers PopMart is becoming FlopMart. "If Hubris has a sound," scoffed the *Observer*, "it is the hiss of air leaking out of the giant inflatable olive that is key prop on the world's most expensive rock tour." "U2 are feeling the cool wind of rejection for the first time", gloated the *Guardian*.

> I come from the position that 50,000 people gathered together might not be wrong. In fact, if they're gathered together at one of our gigs, I'm tempted to think they might be right! Bono.

Finding these apparent underachievers playing to 50,000 admirers with Oasis as their support band, it seems safe to conclude reports of the demise of U2 have been greatly exaggerated. Surveying the elegant circular stadium from a glass walled office high up behind the stage, U2's manager Paul McGuinness is in bullish form. "We're two months into a world tour and we've already sold two million tickets," he declares. "And I confidently expect to sell over five million before we finish next year." Dressed in a white boxing robe, like a fighter preparing to defend his title, Bono wanders agitatedly around the dressing room before the show. "I just wonder why they don't want us to win?" he says of his critics in the British media. "I feel it's an old public school thing. We're the outsiders being dragged through the bushes. We're the ruddy Irish boys getting a kicking."

Before you start speculating that U2's frontman is entering an advanced stage of superstar paranoia. I should mention that he makes these observations with a provocative grin playing on his lips. He is, in fact, philosophical about the negative press. "The term stadium rock is a term of abuse," he remarks, "but it's a bogus term. It's a bit like pub rock, which is a term of abuse for hands who won't ever play outside of pubs and generally play the blues badly and drink a lot of beer. But not all groups that play in pubs are pub rockers. We can play anywhere we want. It just happens that we have the magic wand to turn these large open spaces into something else." He's on a roll now, bobbing and weaving like a genuine world heavyweight. "I think the media have a problem with respecting 50,000 people. They have a problem with popularity and mass appeal. Well, I come from the position that 50,000 people gathered together might not be wrong." He laughs at his paraphrasing of the legendary Elvis Presley publicity line. "In fact, if they're gathered together at one of our gigs, I'm tempted to think they might be right!"

Oasis take the stage at dusk. In their own country, the boys of Britpop have played to the largest audiences ever gathered in one place, but here in America they are a sideshow rather than the main event. The stadium is still filling with U2's

followers as the five-piece, augmented by a keyboard player, blast through a rocking, no nonsense set. It is the first real gig they have played in 10 months, and they clearly revel in this opportunity to strut their stuff. Liam's singing is impossibly balanced between passion and nonchalance, while Noel's incendiary lead guitar cuts through the crowd's indifference, bringing people to their feet for a climactic, cataclysmic "Champagne Supernova". And astonishingly, Oasis, so used to being revered on their own terms, play the part of understudies with grace and humility, thanking U2 and the audience for the opportunity to perform. "If me mam could see me now," crows Liam, "She'd say 'you done good, lad, you done good'." "I love stadium gigs," Noel declares afterwards, backstage, eyes burning with excitement. "There's just so many people. How many bands can do this? How many?" He looks defiant; as he proposes a topsy-turvy theory of their status in the rock world. "U2 and Oasis are the underground and everybody else is the mainstream. Cause they're all afraid to be big. They're afraid of success!"

U2's manager declares himself suitably impressed with the leading challengers for the unofficial title of Greatest Rock Group In The World. "You can't help but admire their appetite and style," says McGuinness. He nonetheless holds reservations about how Oasis might take their live show to the next level. "Not many groups can play stadiums. You have to embrace the size, which requires a degree of theatrics. For some reason, a whole generation of groups have turned their back on the theatrical side of rock, which I find disappointing."

It is not an accusation that can be levelled at his own charges. Rather, they have gone beyond theatre. The PopMart show is genuinely spectacular, appealing on every conceivable level: artistic, intellectual; emotional, visual and musical. The band play beneath an arch of glittering neon, before an enormous video wall alive with inventive pop art imagery. A guitar solo is delivered to a mind-bending psychedelic display, spread across 700 square metres of screen. The group arrive for encores inside their own glitterball UFO. The show has constant momentum and is delivered on a scale that makes the full moon, suspended in a cloudless sky, look like just another part of the lighting rig. Yet, most impressively of all, there is room for personality, improvisation and intimacy. U2 transcend the problem of physical distance with the generosity of their performance. Bono reaches out to audiences with the exposed humanity of a genuinely great stage performer – albeit one who is employing all the resources the modern world can provide. In an attempt to encapsulate this mixture of the emotional and technological, Bono calls it a "sci-fi gospel show".

It is certainly the most impressive multi-media pop event since, well the last U2 tour.

Liam and Noel stood at the mixing desk, watching the show wide eyed. Never regarded as the most articulate of people, Liam nonetheless has a distinctive way of expressing himself. "This is the first time I've seen U2," he declares. "Now I understand! It's phwoarghghghgh!" He shakes his head in disbelief, and makes a second attempt at verbalising his enthusiasm. "Fuckin' mad, man. Mad!"

U2 and Oasis have formed something of a mutual admiration society. Backstage after the show, Adam Clayton emerges from a refreshing shower decked out in Manchester City blues. "It's very humble of them and very humbling for us to have them play with us," admits Bono. "They're a great group and it's a great moment. And they've been so supportive of us. You get the feeling the Gallaghers could call round into a few houses and sort them out on this U2 soap opera that's going on!" Liam Gallagher, who appears to have made an early assault on the backstage supplies of alcohol, hijacks the sound system. "You gotta listen to this," he insists. "This is fuckin' great!" It is the new Oasis album, fresh from the studio. The music booms from the speakers, at once recognizable, yet, if anything fuller, fatter, even more impressive than before. Liam clutches Bono by the shoulders, singing the lyrics of every song directly into his face, Bono – immediately catching hold of a succession of instantly memorable choruses – sings along. The Edge nods his head approvingly. "People say Oasis songs are obvious, but the way the melodies relate to the chords is quite unusual," he observes. "You get the feeling you have heard the songs before, but they still surprise you." "There's a genius in pulling the obvious from the air," observes Bono, as Liam lurches around the room, lost in the moment, singing along with a new Oasis track, "Stand By Me". Only Noel Gallagher would have the gall to write a song with the same title as one of the world's best loved classics. And, right now, only Oasis could carry it off, and make it sound even more classic than the original. "There's a great joy there ... the joy of pop music is the momentum of the music as it changes, as it morphs into different styles and its success as it carries these groups and these people, surfing, just flying along, that's what pop is," says Bono. Liam, the pop star of the moment, strikingly handsome, moving with the animal grace of some magnificent simian creature, spreads his arms wide and sings, "Stand by me, nobody know-ow-ows, the way it's gonna be ..."

A small crowd of backstage revellers – including Winona Ryder and her new beau from Green Day, singers Lisa M and Lisa B, producers Howie B (no relation!), Nellee Hooper and Hal Wilner – watch in open admiration, applauding this astonishing private performance. Liam tunes them all out, eager only to lock Bono into this private world of music. Noel sits on a sofa and takes it all in, a perpetual, secret smile playing on his lips. "There's a joy in success," Bono insists. "It's a joy you find in club culture, in black music. From Soul II Soul putting out their t-shirts, getting their own culture going. Beastie Boys, Wu Tang Clan ... Oasis. Noel Gallagher is taking care of business. It doesn't take away from the soul of what we do. In fact, it helps because there's a sort of fabric of lies around white alternative music. This is what people won't own up to: does everyone want to be in a great group and take it as far as they can? Yes! And anyone who tells you otherwise, they're not telling you the truth. People will take it as far as they can. Some people don't have whatever it needs to go to this level. Well that's fine. But don't spank us 'cause we can! Because we're obviously not bending over. And no one could accuse Oasis of bending over. We're independent spirits, you know?"

Bono is clearly baffled – perhaps even a little bit hurt – by the negative press surrounding the PopMart tour. "It's not like we're a crap group who are going through the motions and then running back to our fish farms," he declares. "We're doing our best work now. Everyone kind of recognises that. If there is a criticism you could level at us it is for over reaching. The Rolling Stones go out with a big snake over their head, no one's asking them what that means. We go out with it giant olive and we've got to explain the concept behind it!"

'U2 and Oasis are the underground and everybody else is the mainstream. 'Cause they're all afraid of success!'
Noel Gallagher

The show has constant momentum and is delivered on a scale that makes the full moon, suspended in a cloudless sky, look like just another part of the lighting rig.

The olive. There it is. That might be the root of the critical problems with the PopMart tour. No matter how hard Bono tries, he knows he is never going to be able to explain the giant olive that perches on top of a giant stick, towering over the stage while U2 play songs of faith and doubt, of passion and reflection, of love and war. Three chords, the truth ... and an olive on top? Perhaps it is the suggestion of frivolity that critics find hard to comprehend. How can U2 – a group who grapple with the big issues, writing songs that struggle to find meaning in the chaos of life at the fag end of the 20th Century – carry with them as a symbol of their new direction something as meaningless as a giant inflatable olive. "We're trying to be honest about the size of the group, the scale of the event and the fact that it is a commercial enterprise," says Bono, taking a deep breath and – against his better instincts – trying to explain the thinking behind the PopMart concept. "And we're

drawing on, or piggy backing, an entire philosophy that came with the word pop. We're in a commercial world and there's artists like Warhol, and new pop artists like Keith Haring, people who wanted to be part of the real world, they didn't want to be on a gallery wall, they wanted to make prints and make it accessible. Warhol was one of those people who, rather than trying to dodge the contradictions of his situation as an artist working in the commercial world, he actually enjoyed it, mined it, drew from it. He embraced the contradictions. There's freedom in that. Freedom for us to get away with these songs, which are spiky, and bitter and there's a brokenness to them.

"You just wouldn't get away with them unless you surrounded yourself with neon and cosmic glitter. This is the Nineties! It's a decade that, in my experience so far, is like this great party and its hangover. And that's what we've put on the record. It starts out like YEAH! and it's left you the next morning with a blinding headache and moments of clarity. And I think there's something in facing that, in facing the other side of the party. Because no one can live that life without it turning in on you and getting shallow." So let me see if I've got this right. The olive represents freedom. And it also symbolizes a decade of excess. The night before the millennium after. Well, blame it on the late hour, blame it on the champagne, beer and wine flowing backstage, but this seems to make sense. Sort of. But what about the forty foot lemon beneath the giant olive? "You've got to have a lemon," says Bono. "A vodka and tonic without the lemon is just not the same thing."

Rounding up the stragglers backstage, Bono announces a visit to Tosca's, which is being kept open for the band. It is a favourite venue of his, a bohemian writer's enclave, once a haunt of Charles Bukowski, Sam Shepherd and Tom Waits (Bono's brother named his Dublin restaurant in honour of Tosca and their father's life long love for opera). The last few diehards pile into a minibus. Noel, pressed next to Bono, clutches the singer's knee as he enthuses about U2 songs he admires. A diligent student of other bands, he displays an impressive knowledge of subtle lyrical twists and musical phrases. And then, with startling synchronicity, the minibus radio, tuned to a late night station, begins to play U2's hit, "One".

"This is the greatest song every written!" yells Noel. And he and Liam begin to sing it at the top of their voices. Bono, swept away by their exuberance, joins in. And as we roll down a San Francisco highway, long after midnight, three of the world's greatest rock stars treat us to an impassioned, impromptu rendition of a song of unity and brotherly love. "We are one," they sing, "but we're not the same, we've got carry each other, carry each other ..."

As the track comes to an end, Bono laughs and hugs Noel's shoulders. "Bands won't admit they like you, right, and you're the greatest band in the world," declares Noel. "And the only band that will actually come out and admit that is the next greatest band in the world!"

'CLICK.

THE VIEW MASTER WHEEL TURNS AGAIN. DAY BY DAY YOU HEAR THE CLICK OF THE WHEEL. CLICK. THE EIFFEL TOWER. CLICK. ST. PETER'S IN ROME. CLICK. THE 170,000 ITALIANS. CLICK BLOWN-UP BUILDINGS IN SARAJEVO. CLICK. A GREEK ISLAND. CLICK. THE HOLY LAND. CLICK. THE GOLDEN GATE BRIDGE. CLICK. DOWNTOWN DETROIT. CLICK. FRENCH SPEAKING CANADA. CLICK. CROWDS OF UNRULY MANCHESTER UNITED SUPPORTERS IN HOLLAND. CLICK ...

PHOTOGRAPHY BY WILLIE WILLIAMS

INSIDE POPMART

AND SO IT GOES ON ...'
FROM ROTTERDAM IN JULY TO RIO DE
JANEIRO IN JANUARY, THE FINAL
EXTRACTS FROM THE WILLIE DIARY
OFFER A UNIQUE TOUR-INSIDER
ACCOUNT OF THE POPMART JOURNEY
WRITTEN BY THE BAND'S LIGHTING
DIRECTOR AND SHOW DESIGNER,
WILLIE WILLIAMS.

'CLICK.

THURSDAY JULY 18TH 1997

Rotterdam and we are back to work. It never ceases to amaze me how easy it becomes to switch back and forth between work mode and play mode. After a week off everyone is much rested, but now we are back together again it's like we never left. Same faces, same environment. Except of course that we are thousands of miles from our last gig and in a different continent, but such things are of little real consequence when you're on a rock & roll tour.

The stage loaded in to the Feynoord Stadium in Rotterdam a couple of days ago. This is where we debuted the Zooropa tour, so it is very much home territory. Mr MacPhisto was born in the dressing room here. Not being a band to shy away from a high pressure challenge, U2 have opted to open the European tour with a live TV broadcast being fed to the whole of Europe. Consequently we are here with a whole pile of additional cameras, lights, mobile recording trucks, etc. Tonight was a full rehearsal run through, which was pretty uneventful. After the run through the band stayed to play "Please" through a couple of times more, to shoot some close-ups which aren't possible during an actual show. There may be a video clip to be had out of this.

So tomorrow we start again, giving PopMart to the Dutch. This European leg will be a wild ride – shows here have such a different vibe to America. It's all so civilised over there, with rows of seats and popcorn stands. The Euro crowd are nowhere near as organized and the resulting energy level is often way higher. The only potential set back is that the weather looks like it could be pretty awful. Not that this has ever held U2 back before now. Say a couple of prayers and remember Red Rocks.

FRIDAY JULY 19TH

So, it rained. It rained a lot, all day, but in the end it didn't hurt us too much. The audience here in Rotterdam were so up for it that nothing was going to hold them back. From the minute Skunk Anansie opened the evening's proceedings (in the rain) it was clear this was an unstoppable crowd. As mercy would have it, the rain stopped the minute U2 set foot on stage and the show took flight. The stadium in Rotterdam is built on land-fill, so when many thousands of people jump up and down at the same time the pitch really starts to bounce, like a sprung dance floor. It was might exciting watching the entire massive construction swaying to and fro. Four songs from the show were broadcast on live television all over Europe – "Please", "Streets", the "Lemon" sequence, "Discotheque", "Velvet Dress" and part of "With Or Without You". OK, that's five and a half songs. Live broadcasting is always a nerve wracking affair, because any screw-ups go out on air, but then that's the whole point. What you see on TV is genuinely what was happening in the stadium. Mercifully, tonight it all went very well. "Please" I think was given its finest looking performance to date – I love it when that happens.

songs from the show were broadcast on live television all over Europe – "Please", "Streets", the "Lemon" sequence, "Discotheque", "Velvet Dress" and part of "With Or Without You". OK, that's five and a half songs.

SATURDAY JULY 20TH

Rotterdam show number two, which seemed a much more relaxed affair now that the whole BBC TV crew has left us. It's just the band and the audience, for a private show. Great show too, with an unforgettable karaoke moment. The most famous song, internationally, by any Dutch band ever has to be "Radar Love" by Golden Earring. Yesterday we had talked about getting The Edge to do a karaoke version by way of tribute, but there were a couple of potential problems with the song. For starters, it was recorded an awfully long time ago, so you have to wonder if the younger audience members would know it, and in any case the song is nearly six minutes long, doesn't have a sing-a-long chorus, starts with a minute long guitar solo and has a three minute drum solo in the middle. It would be a brave man indeed who would attempt such a feat in public. Photographer Anton Corbijn, who is Dutch, assured us that this would be no problem and that the crowd would love it. This was encouraging, but all the same, you couldn't help but wonder what would happen on the night. In short, it was a sensation. Bono and The Edge finished their beautiful, delicate rendition of "Staring at the Sun", then up on the video screen comes "Radar Love", with its Dutchly familiar opening guitar chords. The audience were stunned into silence for a moment then when they realised what was happening, quite simply, they went berserk. The entire stadium joined as one and sang every single note in unison. Very loudly. It was such a fantastic moment of national unity that it was all Edge could do to not laugh out loud. And to think we worried about whether it would go down OK ...

FRIDAY JULY 25TH

Belgium. Werchter festival site – the scene of many early U2 appearances. It was also a home coming for much of the PopMart production – "Stage Co.", the staging company providing all the tower technology holding the stage together, is from Belgium, our gigantic video screen was built here in Belgium and the band's stage clothes were designed by Walter Van Beirendonck, another Belgian. Consequently we have more than a few Belgians on tour with us, who were all enjoying being home. A good show too, despite being a bit of a mud-bath.

SATURDAY JULY 26TH

Germany. Koln. Load in day. I went down to the venue to tweak some of the show's video elements with video director Monica Caston. I wanted to try a couple of new ideas for the "Mysterious Ways" visuals, and it's always good to make the most of the available time. I got to the mix position booth on the field to find that the front-of-house crew were having a spontaneous toga party in there, utilizing a consignment of large towels and red wine which had appeared from sources unknown. Suddenly this seemed a far better idea than reassembling video sequences, so that particular task was put off for a couple of hours and I'm sure looks much better as a result. It certainly did at the time, anyway.

SUNDAY JULY 27TH

The Koln show gave new meaning to the phrase "Staring at the Sun". The gig was at a disused airfield (the Germans have such romantic venues), facing directly West into a large patch of open ground. Consequently the sun shone straight onto the stage all day, including during the performance of our German opening band "Der Fantastichen Vier". I doubt that they could see anything past the first two rows. The sun had just about crept below the horizon when U2 took the stage and PopMart made its German debut. My favourite moment came during "End of the World" where The Edge strolled way way out to the end of the stage right catwalk whilst Bono was heading right out to the end of the b-stage. This put the two of them about 150 feet apart, with a sea of audience in between them. Seeing Bono and Edge singing to each other, playing off each other over the heads of the crowd was oddly exhilarating and something I'd not seen before. The Edge sang "Daydream Believer" for the Karaoke spot, which is the first time we've aired it in Europe. The German crowd seemed to know the song just as well as American audiences did, and one wonders if there are any countries at all in the world where The Monkees didn't have hits ... and why this should be.

TUESDAY JULY 29TH

Leipzig is a city in former East Germany, and despite the Wall being long down, it retains much of that character (for better and for worse). Over the past few years there has been a massive drive to turn Leipzig into a fully functional Western business city, so the joke is that its national bird is the Crane ... because literally dozens and dozens of building cranes fill the horizon as more and more "modern" buildings are erected as fast as finance will allow. I have to say the result is (at best) weird, or (at worst) about as ugly as you can imagine. I'm sure life must have been pretty awful here under the old regime, but you can't help but feel at least the city would have had some authenticity about it then, as opposed to this modern and convenient nothingness.
The "venue" we were playing was a car park outside of an old stadium. One wonders why we weren't playing the show inside the stadium, but ours is not to reason why; the parking-lot-as-music-venue tradition seems to have very deep roots in German live performance. Perhaps the phrase "rock and roll" inadvertently translates as "pay and display". The only thing I can't fathom is, where do they put all the cars whilst the gig is going on?

WEDNESDAY JULY 30TH

Travel day from Leipzig to Mannheim, so we go from one rock and roll capital to another. I went down to the gig in the evening to work on a couple of songs with Bruce Ramus (lighting director) and Monica Caston (video director). We are looking at the Last Night On Earth/End Of The World section, as I think, visually it needs some tidying up. Part of the solution came from Dave Neugebauer, PopMart's chief video engineer, who was working on a test pattern. He had this extraordinarily moving pattern up and running on the screen and before Monica could cover my eyes I spotted it and of course wanted to put it in the show.

THURSDAY JULY 31ST

Spent the morning looking at some of the recent press clippings. The reviews from the European shows have been almost unanimous in their over-the-top praise, which is most heartening. Today was show day in Mannheim. Another German car park masquerading as a rock venue. Just a field, actually, with a great view of the stage from the nearby freeway. After a gorgeous day yesterday it rained all day. Despite rain on previous days on the PopMart tour, U2 had not actually played in the rain so far. Tonight it rained for every single moment of the show, start to finish, but it didn't spoil the show. Great show, with another great crowd, brought together in unison by The Edge's rendition of ... "Singin' in the Rain". Of course.

SATURDAY AUGUST 2ND

Show day, Gothenburg. The first of four sold out shows in Scandinavia, which should be a fun run. Amazing shape, this stadium and a particularly attractive sight when completely full of punters, as it was tonight. This was the stadium we should have played in on the Joshua Tree tour, but it was out of commission, having been damaged by intense audience bouncing at a Bruce Springsteen gig. We ended up playing a "car park" type site by the docks, so as the band played there were enormous freight vessels floating by in the background. Anyhow, the newly mended stadium can now withstand the shocks, which was just as well, as there was an enormous amount of audience bouncing at this show too. Amazing to see a stadium sized crowd almost solely composed of blonde heads!

MONDAY AUGUST 25TH
"When the rain comes ...". A very wet show tonight, at Parken stadium in Copenhagen. I know it's a cliché, but it really didn't dampen the enthusiasm of the audience – groups of people were being extremely creative with rolls of plastic sheeting, in ways I never seen before (cue for a song, "There ain't nothing like a Dane"). Helena Christiansen came down to the show, and hosted a party for the band afterwards, so despite the rain it was a fun night all round.

FRIDAY AUGUST 8TH
The Edge's birthday, and a gorgeous day it was too. We all were taken out for a boat ride through a set of waterways around a 12th century town, about an hour outside of Helsinki. It was a gloriously tranquil afternoon, which sequed neatly into a mellow birthday dinner in this ancient little place. There was, to some extent, the taking of alcohol, so not entirely unpredictably the room turned to songs and speeches. People calling upon one another to tell their story of "the first time I met The Edge ...". This is pretty much a U2 custom, and given that most people have a birthday every year, you'd think that you'd hear the same stories over and over. Oddly though, there are always new tales, new songs and new laughs. Selective memory? Creative remembrance? Narrative embroidery? I don't know what causes this phenomenon, but the results are inevitably hilarious.

SATURDAY AUGUST 9TH
Show Day Olympic Stadium, Helsinki. What a night this turned out to be. This past couple of weeks the show has hit a new peak, but tonight was the crowning glory. U2 have only played in Finland once before – 15 years ago at a festival – so the people here were more than ready for them. They were an absolutely spectacular audience and this could well have been the best show of the tour so far. It's sometimes hard to compare one show with another, because so much changes from night to night. Depending on the audience, the nature of the building and so forth different parts of each show have their own charm, so choosing one above another is a bit like choosing a favourite child. Some nights though, you just get on a 100% energy roll and the gig becomes a beast unstoppable, and tonight was one of those nights.

MONDAY AUGUST 11TH
Load-in day in Warsaw. We took the opportunity to look around the town this afternoon. Buoyed on by the Gothenburg experience a couple of us headed for the Botanical Gardens, which not only proved to be beautiful, but also to house "the best restaurant in Poland". Having come all this way, it seemed rude not to go in, so we had dinner there. Now, it has to be said, if you're in search of haute cuisine, you wouldn't necessarily make Poland your first stop, but this restaurant ("Belvedere") really is exceptional. It's located in a huge glass house full of tropical plants and looks out over a lawn and trees, sun going down, piano player going at it – you get the picture. What a glorious night, with conversation turning to cyclic spirituality and astro physics, as it so often does where road crews are involved.

TUESDAY AUGUST 12TH

Show Day Hippodrome, Warsaw. It's hard to describe tonight's show in any meaningful way as it was so emotional and so extraordinary – U2 have never been to Poland, so an enormous number of people came to this show. The band had to delay show time by fifteen or twenty minutes, as there was still such a high volume of people entering the park. In the end an announcement was made asking everyone to move over to try and let more people in. It was jammed full of people, and a very loud and enthusiastic lot they were too. Once we got started, the show was like holding on to a firework. The high point of the show was New Year's Day. It's a little-known fact that the song was written about the Polish Solidarity movement, Lech Walesa and his wife, and a few other abstract angles. This has become a point in the show where we turn off our gigantic video screen to let the music do the talking, but for this show only Bono had asked if we could find some pictures of our man Lech, of the solidarity banners, marches, etc. Now, we've all heard the crowds roar, but it was the depth of emotion in the deafening cheer that went up which was so disabling. Looking around the mix-position where I was watching from, crew, management, tour staff, everyone was transfixed by this enormous moment of communal empathy, national pride, celebration and joy. The pictures on the screen dissolved one into the next, moments of this country's victorious history, and deafening cheer after deafening cheer went up. It was moving almost to the point of tears, to think about what this country was like when that song was written, how much these people had seen, how much they were sharing in that field, in those pictures, in that song – and they didn't come down for the rest of the night. I know it's only rock and roll, but I'll remember that one for the rest of my life.

WEDNESDAY AUGUST 13TH

And so to Prague, another city new to U2. Beautiful place too, one of the most exquisite cities in Europe and another place witnessing enormous change. These former Eastern Bloc capitals have a strange atmosphere to them in the summer, when they are groaning under the weight of so many tourists. Like Poland, it's cheap here (for foreigners), so the floodgates open, producing a very weird cultural mix. Against a backdrop of archaic public transport and fantastically over the top architecture (the Catholic Church really never embraced minimalism as a design concept), you get this flourishing "freedom" manifested in the form of tourism, alongside the invasion of every corporate multi-national company imaginable. (Local reaction seems to be divided between resentment and an odd kind of pride – in Poland I bought one of those "scenes of Warsaw" type postcards, featuring eight sights of the city, which included pictures of the Cathedral, the Chopin monument, various museums and palaces – and their first McDonald's!).

As tourists and businesses arrive with cash, there's an equal number of entrepreneurs, chancers, black marketeers (and of course the Mob) ready to rally round and take it off them. This is only to be expected, but being a perpetual traveller the thing I find most curious is that be it Auckland, Scotland or Prague the tourists are accompanied by exactly the same kind of tourist activities. There's the portrait painters, scenic artists, hair braiders, boards of silver jewellery on black velvet, 'human statue' performance artists, those particularly stupid giant multicolored jester's hats with bells on, ceramic flute sellers, pan handlers and always, always a fucking Peruvian pan-pipe-and-drums band. I've seen all this stuff in every capital city of the world and you wonder if someone's franchising the stuff, or if there was just a memo put out a few years ago. There can't be any musicians left in Peru at this stage. Coming to a city as stunningly beautiful as Prague, you can't help but wish you could have seen it before the flocks of handi-cams and Spice Girls t-shirts arrived. But then, let's not kid ourselves, even ten years ago it must have been pretty brutal here. Memories of East Germany in the 70's are all it takes to make you drop the lofty nostalgia. Rather tourists than secret police. And after all, we are here to bring the good people of the Czech Republic our "sci-fi disco supermarket", so who am I to whine about the consumer invasion?!

THURSDAY AUGUST 14TH

Show Day Strahov, Prague. U2's first live meeting with the good people of Prague turned out to be another great event. They turned up in droves and were most enthusiastic – I haven't seen that many bouncing Czechs since I worked with Beverley Craven. This venue is enormous, like a stadium, only bigger. Apparently it was used for a lot of military displays, as a make-shift prison camp, etc., which always gives a place a certain edge. After the show, a thunderstorm broke. We were back at this hotel, close to the river and the wild energy of the storm brought out an extraordinary primal response. Out we went, into the street, onto the bridge in rain so heavy it was like standing under a shower head. Every few seconds, lightning lit up the ancient buildings and statues with horror movie shadows as the deafening thunder made us jump & shriek with laughter. We ran about, jumping in puddles, kicking water at each other, hooting and hollering with the ecstatic release. It's a wonder were weren't jailed.

INSIDE POPMART, ISSUE 28/29

MONDAY AUGUST 18TH

Gig in Nurnburg in Germany, on the very field where Hitler held his rallies. The whole stone tribune where he made his speeches is still there – live from "Triumph of the Will", straight out of every photo you ever saw. Chilling. Talk about vibe off the place – the stone is alive with it. In front and to one side of this hideous monument sits the PopMart stage. A giant Lemon now stands in front of where Hitler stirred a nation to violence. Here, right here where I'm standing, is where it all went on. To watch "Bullet the Blue Sky" with its "cathedral of light" searchlight beams heading off into the night sky – the original of which happened in this very field ... thoughts run wild. A giant stuffed olive stands proudly above where tanks and troops once saluted Nazi Leaders. Thank God the world turned out this way. Surrealism may not be much of a weapon, but in this instance it became part of a celebration. Very heavy place. Apparently, they don't know what to do with it, given its enormous historical significance. You can understand the hesitation to destroy it, but on the other hand what could it ever become, other than a shrine for shaven headed morons? One suggestion was to turn it into a shopping mall. Can you imagine? I'm saying they should just level the place and have done with it.

WEDNESDAY AUGUST 20TH

Show day in Hannover, at the Expo site. We flew in from Nurnburg this afternoon, arrived late at the venue and flew straight onto London after the gig. Consequently, our feet barely touched the ground. Good gig though. Bono said he felt like U2 had connected with the German audience (at all of the German shows on this leg) in a much more emotional way than they ever had before. He seemed very encouraged, and rightly so. There was something of a knees-up on the plane going back to London. The flying lemon was rocking. Much as we've had a good time in continental Europe, there is always an indescribable thrill (and relief) about going back to a country where you speak the language. It was a long journey, as we landed at Luton airport, an hour's drive from London. However, patience was rewarded, as we arrived at the hotel to find they had laid on trayfuls of bacon and egg sandwiches. Now you know you're in England.

FRIDAY AUGUST 22ND/SATURDAY AUGUST 23RD

Wembley stadium, in swinging London. Not unreasonably, some shows on a tour are seen as the "big" shows. Not to belittle any of the other cities involved, but some places just have that vibe. Wembley is one of them. The other side of this coin is that it's rare that a band (any band) will pull off their greatest performances under this kind of pressure. If you want to see a band play a truly stellar gig, it's usually best to see them somewhere on a par with the civic centre in Vladivostok. The other thing about London, particularly Wembley, is that its audiences tend to be somewhat cooler and more reserved than places which see fewer shows. At best you might call it the "come on impress me" syndrome, at worst it's quite simply the band verses the audience. U2 have always done well in the past, but Wembley certainly hasn't been the scene of any of the greatest U2 shows in history. The past two nights have changed all that. London took PopMart to its heart with absolutely no holds barred. Larry said of the first night that the audience reaction was so warm, so enthusiastic and so energetic that it took him half the gig to get over the amazement of it. For reasons best known to themselves, the majority of the British press have been consistently mean towards U2 all year, but these gigs just rocked. Two sold out Wembleys and we all just loved it. Might even come back one day!

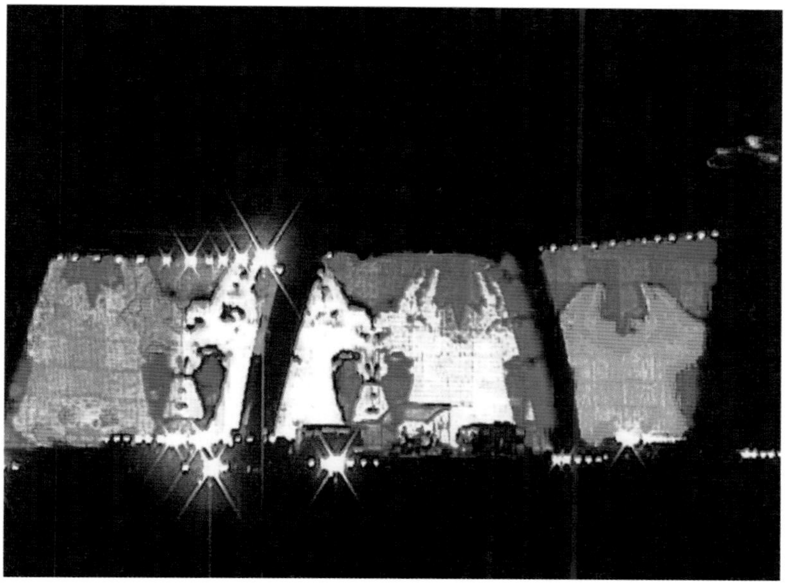

TUESDAY AUGUST 26TH

U2 play Belfast for the first time in ten years, it's the biggest concert ever held in Northern Ireland, and the IRA cease-fire is six weeks old. It's hard to know what to say, as much of the poignancy of the evening is better left unspoken. Suffice it to say that this was a very rowdy gig, with a boisterous audience composed of people from all sides of the political debate. For two hours, politics were put aside and music ruled. As Bono said at the airport on arrival, "we haven't come to bring peace, we've come to make a lot of noise". Mind you, The Edge couldn't help but introduce his karaoke moment thus ... "This song is not a rebel song ..." (much audience cheering) "... actually, it's an Elvis Presley song" and dedicated it to all involved in the Peace process. The song? "We can't go on together, with suspicious minds".

THURSDAY AUGUST 28TH

So we open the papers this morning to find this rather baffling assault on U2 from George Harrison of all people. Speaking, one can only presume, from the "Sunshine Home For The Bewildered", our George denounced U2 as talentless, having carved out their career solely on the strength of "ego, money and big hats". It was such a bizarre thing to read that you couldn't really be annoyed. It was just ... well, sad, really. The Edge was heard to say it sounded like something his dad would have said many moons ago. Tonight was a show at Roundhay Park in Leeds, up in Yorkshire in the North of England. Always a great crowd, always a great show. "Cast" supported and faced the Yorkshire fans in the absolute pouring rain, who responded by making mud slides and keeping warm by means of human pyramids and communal hugs. Fortunately (for us, anyway) the rain stopped before U2 went on, and the celebration commenced. The natural bowl shape of this venue makes for an implausibly intimate atmosphere – I remember the same on the Zoo TV tour – and it gave the show a lovely feeling. One of the animated sequences in the show's screen footage had its homecoming tonight. The bizarre and naively violent shopping cartoon, which we call 'MultiMart', features characters who speak with deep Yorkshire accents. Having seen this in stadiums all over America and Europe it was very funny to see it "at home". I thought the audience would love it, but apparently most of them thought we'd made it specially for that night. After several good natured, if pointed, comments to the audience about George Harrison throughout the show, Bono has us all rolling laughing during "Mysterious Ways". He managed to intertwine with the melody of the song snatches of "My Sweet Lord" and "Something in the way she moves". I still can't imagine what brought on the George Harrison attack, but with a good dose of humour the band certainly got their own back.

"This song is not a rebel song ...' (much audience cheering) '... actually, it's an Elvis Presley song'"

SATURDAY AUGUST 30TH
Dublin Show One. The great homecoming, and if there was ever any doubt as to how U2 would be received in Dublin, it was laid to rest tonight. The show was like having a bath in the communal spirit of this city. All inside the venue were there for the party, almost wallowing in the occasion, the uplifting celebration and not a little pride on the part of the audience that their lads had conquered the world yet again, and brought it home on a silver platter. The audience sang, they roared, they laughed. Great great vibe. Even a private joke, as The Edge sings "what could be the Irish national anthem come November" – a song called "All Kinds of Everything", which won the kitschfest Eurovision Song Contest in the mid-eighteenth century, sung by a child star called Dana, who is now a grown woman and running for the presidency of Ireland.
After the show, what else but a "Rigger's Arms" party down at the "Kitchen" club in town, where we laugh, dance and celebrate some more. Bed late, hearing unsettling rumours of Princess Diana in a car crash.

SUNDAY AUGUST 31ST

Dublin, second showday. Waking to find a world in shock at the news of the death of Princess Diana after the car crash in Paris. Disbelief & non-comprehension. Dead? How could that be possible. Thoughts run all over the place. Grace Kelly, Marilyn Monroe, what now for the Royals, the end of the 20th century, the most famous woman in the world dead in the hands of those who made her famous, kiss me kill me, when am I going to wake up out of this, a million dollars for a kiss and a nickel for your soul, surely this isn't happening … It was happening all right. Our group meet up at various points during the day and the biggest shock of all is how shocked we are. I don't know what's going on, but it's certainly greater than the sum of its parts. Lots of phone calls. Universal disbelief. Even in Ireland, hardly a Royalist stronghold, this woman was loved because she was the Robin Hood, she took on the Great British Establishment and won. Ireland is in mourning and Britain just doesn't know what to do with itself.

The night's show was equally great as yesterday's, with a tribute to Diana in the form of "MLK" coming almost at the end of the performance. The audience were clearly relieved to acknowledge communally that this has been a day unlike any other. This is going to be a very strange week.

TUESDAY SEPTEMBER 2ND

Edinburgh showday, and the longest day in living memory. The spectre of Diana permeates all things, with anger and blame surfacing and being variously apportioned to the paparazzi, the royal family, the driver, the hotel, etc, etc. Britain is setting up camp in central London, abandoning its routines, leaving normal life behind to make pilgrimages to the books of condolence and makeshift shrines at various sites. The volume of flowers outside Kensington Palace is humbling to the point of tears.

Rock and roll is full of long days, but this was unique even for us, in that we landed in FIVE countries in the space of one day. Lunch in Dublin, by plane to Edinburgh for the show, leaving immediately after to head for the MTV awards. We leave Scotland on Air-Lemon, stopping twice to refuel in Iceland and Canada, before landing in New York. Met at Newark airport by a fleet of cars, though a dust-pan-and-brush might have been more appropriate. The private plane is comfortable, but doesn't have the fuel capacity of a 747, so it takes a while to cross the Atlantic. Evening rehearsal for the MTV awards at Radio City Music Hall. Dog tired. To bed in New York City. Didn't we wake up in Dublin and do a show in Scotland? Princess Diana looks at us from every direction, in every country we go to. I think it must be Wednesday by now.

THURSDAY SEPTEMBER 4TH

Waking in New York, on the day of the MTV video music awards. U2 are to perform "Please" live on the show. Now, U2 have never performed at an awards show like this before, so it was something of a new challenge. The "game show" aesthetic of the staging and the lack of time due to high number of bands makes it more of a hit and run affair than one would like, but we were treated very well. It helped that many of the technical people involved are old friends (the lighting designer for the show is Allen Branton who worked with us on the ZooTV Sydney shoot) so they already had a good sense of what will and won't work for U2. We had just a few hours to try to turn a game show into a suitably atmospheric performance setting for "Please", so it was all hands on deck. By the end of rehearsal, it was looking vaguely promising, but come the appointed hour, it is live live live, so you can never be sure.

Camera, action, and off we go. U2 perform, the song ends and …yes … we head for the cars, head for the airport and get back on the plane, bound for France. Can't stop to chat, we've got a show to do in Paris.

FRIDAY SEPTEMBER 5TH

Friday? I guess it is. Depends which time zone you're looking at. Back on the plane, another long long overnight flight, but this one is a time for partying. We managed to grab a tape of the MTV awards' performance as we fled from Radio City, and have been watching it on the plane. Unbelievably, it seems to be OK – actually pretty damn good. I mean if it was a video clip of your own that you were making, you'd bin it and shoot the director, but for live TV, in a multiple band awards show, it's verging on the miraculous. So, to Paris. Again, via Canada and Rekjavick, but hey, I haven't been to Iceland in over 24 hours, so I was long overdue a visit. Into the Paris hotel, not sure what time it is or who I am. It might even be tomorrow, and I might even be you, but as long as there's a hot bath and clean sheets I'll fake it till show time.

SATURDAY SEPTEMBER 6TH

Paris, Parc des Princes. This morning a few of us made the pilgrimage down to the Pont de l'Alma, where Princess Diana's car crash happened. Across the English Channel, London had come to a standstill for the funeral so it seemed the least we could do. There's a grassy slope by the underpass, and a convenient "eternal flame" monument, which had become a shrine to the princess. There were a lot of people there and the piles of floral tributes had reached shoulder height. The oddest thing of all though was to see a large crowd be so silent, so quiet. Just milling about, reading the notes and cards. Very moving.

Consequently, a lot of mixed feelings at the show, but it was a very good night none the less. We played "MLK" tribute again, before "One" and here too you could feel the appreciation of the audience. Diana certainly crossed boundaries.

MONDAY SEPTEMBER 8TH

Floating up and down the River Seine after midnight, on a boat that used to belong to Winston Churchill, the moon above, the great illuminated buildings of Paris to either side ... Notre Dame, Eiffel Tower, Ile de la Cite ... touring's hell, I tell you.

THURSDAY SEPTEMBER 11TH

Lisbon showday. Audiences in this part of the world are notoriously rowdy, but tonight was special, even by their own standards. This stadium – the Alvalade – has been refurbished somewhat since U2s last visit. It's a large, enclosed bowl-like structure with wonderful acoustics, which enhance the already deafening singing of the audience. Such a great feeling to hear an audience like this – you feel like you're surfing on the waves of joy that they produce. Mid-show I was overcome by a desire to be out amongst it all, so made my way up to the back row, the top of the highest bleacher seats in the whole place. It was such a fun journey – not easy to make fast progress, but being surrounded by such a jubilant pack of people you weren't bothered about getting anywhere in a hurry, it was enough to just soak it up. I managed to soak up a good deal of other things too – beer, sweat and probably more besides – but crowds like this are what it's all about. Such a high.

SATURDAY SEPTEMBER 13TH

Barcelona Olympic Stadium. Another beautiful stadium, in a city of beautiful buildings. I've been off on the Gaudi trail for the past couple of days. Park Guell, Sagrada Familia and various houses. Gaudi was such an extraordinary architect, made all the more remarkable given the period of time when he was working. With Picasso, Miro and all, Bono remarked that there's a sense of surrealism built into the bones of this culture. It's a fabulous looking city. The Sagrada Familia – Gaudi's Cathedral – is the most remarkable of all. Like a huge Gothic edifice busy morphing into a surrealist birthday cake. Pop coloured ceramics, giant statues of assorted sea creatures hanging off the exterior faces, broken wine bottle mosaics, text woven into the walls, columns topped with baskets of fruit. And it's a house of God! The photographs in the museum show Gaudi explaining what he was doing to the various bishops, etc. The other men in the pictures are wearing straw boaters and blazers and the women are in floor length black dresses with bussles, (it was 1896).

I'd love to have been at that meeting. Can you imagine? ... "so, your excellency, what I'm going for is this kind of wedding-cake-on-acid feel, with big stone frogs and there's going to be these giant pink bobbly bits on the top ..."

MONDAY SEPTEMBER 15TH

Montpellier, in the glorious South of France. There was a time many years ago, when U2 tours appeared to be organised specifically in order to follow the Winter around the planet. We'd do Scandinavia in January, Canada in November, etc. Even the videos in those days seemed to require either a monsoon or a snow storm. Fortunately those days seem to be behind us, and we find ourselves in the middle of a run of gorgeous climates. We'll have a couple of days here, so all are hoping to chill out for a while. The end of this leg of the tour is now firmly in our sights, and once you can see a break coming, an odd kind of tiredness begins to set in. Like your body knows there may be a chance to slow down, so starts making early appointments.

THURSDAY SEPTEMBER 18TH

O.K., here comes Italy, hold on to your hats. U2 shows in this country have always been extraordinary, as far back as I can remember. Playing tents or car-parks, they have the most intense atmospheres imaginable. Today we get to play in Rome. (Not a tent, not a car park, but at an airport, which makes a change). There's only one road in and out of the venue, which makes for the kind of situations our security team have nightmares over. There are a total of five security people travelling with the PopMart tour. One travels with the advance crew party, liaising with the building management and giving instructions to the 200–250 local security people and stewards at the venue. The rules laid down are simple. No one gets hurt and the audience must be treated with respect. Sometimes firmly and with respect, but always remembering that "these people pay our wages". Without the ticket-buying audience, none of this would be possible. This a fact which U2 have always been very aware of.

The remaining four security guys travel with the band. As well as overseeing crowd control during the show, their responsibilities include dealing with all the necessary vehicles to get the band and management personnel (about 25 people) into and out of the building. On days like today, this may take a good deal of strategy. It's not a question of the band wanting to avoid contact with the fans, in situations like today there's a real concern for safety – both the band's and the audience's. With an attendance of 60,000 today and only one way in and out of the area, things could get out of hand too easily. There will usually be a police escort laid on to help get the vehicles through, but given some of the. legendary Italian police escorts of the Zoo TV tour, there's no guarantee that this will be any more of a help than it is a hindrance.

SATURDAY SEPTEMBER 20TH

Reggio Emilia, Italy. The show in Rome turned out to be a great event, but compared to today it was just a warm up. A totally accurate figure remains unconfirmed, but it seems certain that in excess of 170,000 people attended tonight's U2 concert in Reggio Emilia. This, according to our rock trivia experts, puts it in the record books as the highest ever attendance for a paying audience at a one-act concert – i.e. if you don't count festivals and free gigs, this was the largest one night stand in the history of rock. As Larry would say, "not bad for a bunch of Paddies". Flying into Reggio that afternoon, Rob the pilot of the Air Lemon plane had obtained permission to fly over the concert site. This he did (circling three times!) at the astonishingly low attitude of 900 feet. The audience (already vast at 4pm) guessed it was the band's plane – not least on account of the lemon & shopping trolley logo painted on the tail fin – and there was much mutual rejoicing. The view from the cockpit was one to remember. This was a BIG venue.

By show time, the people were packed in so solidly it required a team of sherpas with pack-mutes to get to the mixing desk booth out in the field. However, the crowd was extremely good natured despite its vast proportions, and we prepared to rock.

As night fell the scale of the event could only be judged by the sea of lighters held aloft (the singular benefit of playing in cultures where smoking is compulsory by law). It was the most beautiful sight ... the endless sea of dancing flames. Quite a night ... and the parking lot traffic was still thick by the time we left at 4am!!

SUNDAY SEPTEMBER 21ST

Slept late and got up just in time to make the lobby call for our flight to Sarajevo. Only knowing the place by hearing its name on news bulletins makes the whole episode a tad surreal – seeing an airport TV monitor bearing the words "check in for flight 284 Sarajevo" only strikes you as odd when you see it and realise you've never see the word Sarajevo in an airport before. We flew at 8pm, so we made our descent into Bosnia after nightfall. This added even more gravitas to the situation – being struck by just simple things, like seeing the lack of streetlights and how many illuminated windows had no curtains. The whole crew was on board the aeroplane and the communal mood was taking on an increasingly nervous edge. Sombre, almost. As you leave the airport the first thing you pass is a huge cemetery. By night, the light of many candles could be seen flickering in the surrounding darkness – a reminder of how very recent so many of the graves are. Our journey continued, and gradually a silence fell over the bus, as we all looked out of the windows at the passing landscape. Close to the airport many of the buildings are residential tower blocks. The (again mostly uncurtained) windows lit up the night, but every other tower block was entirely dark, blacked out. Peering through the window you could see why – they were just burned out shells of buildings.

I've never heard a road crew so quiet in my life as we rolled on into town. This juxtaposition of normal life and devastation became the ongoing motif as we drove on. Domesticity meets CNN live. Even arriving at our destination – the newly refurbished Holiday Inn – you couldn't fail to be moved by seeing, right across the street, a huge burned out tower block with a gigantic hole in its side, clearly made by something substantially larger than a bullet. Even the Holiday Inn is pock marked with bullet holes. Out front, in the lobby and most noticeably right above the bed head in the room of one of our camera operators. We certainly ain't in Kansas anymore.

By the time we got in and settled it was approaching midnight on a Sunday night, but we had to go out. You couldn't arrive in a place as disturbing and exhilarating as this and just go to bed. So a few of us set out and walk along the street towards the old town. It's cold compared to where we have just come from, and the darkness adds to the Wintry vibe. Despite the day and the hour, there were a lot of people on the streets and the mood seemed very buoyant. Young people, well dressed, out and about. We followed the main stream and ended up in the old town. Again the visual contradictions are massive to the point of disorientation. A completely blown out shop unit sits next door to a shop selling vacuum cleaners and TVs. People sit drinking in a bar on an alleyway where all else lies in charred ruins. You recognise streets and buildings from news reports, and just a little way away you can make out the hills which were alive with snipers only a year or so ago.

Reminders of this recent history are everywhere, of course – bullet holes in every wall, mortar craters in every sidewalk. But not all of the monuments are so destructive. It seems local artists are making reminders of their own, even if they seem a little macabre to us newcomers. Around the city are these 3' high sculptures of a "flash", like a Roy Lichtenstein Pop Art explosion. Also, I saw some mortar craters filled in with a kind of red plastic or vinyl, permanently set into the pavement like a blood splatter. I'm not. sure what these represent exactly, but clearly they are tributes or monuments of some kind.

"As night fell the scale of the event could only be judged by the sea of lighters held aloft (the singular benefit of playing in cultures where smoking is compulsory by law)."

SUNDAY SEPTEMBER 21ST

Myself and Bruce and Lynno from the lighting crew found a little snack bar place which seemed pretty lively and entertained the locals by trying to order food. Just as we were about to bite into our food, all the lights went out. Major power failure. The whole street went black and silent, only interrupted by the odd passing car. It added a certain minimalist ambience for half an hour or so. Moving on we found a basement bar which was just jumping. Having been frisked for weapons on the door, we went on in, to find some of our tour crew in there – notably Kurt, Smasher, Chris and Klass from the Belgian video screen crew. It was great – a simple basement room with a bar and very loud music, so it was beer and eventually talking to the locals. The place was close to closing, but the Belgians had made friends with some of the clientele who were headed on elsewhere, so I tagged along.

The next bar (another basement) was a quarter of the size, but equally loud, playing James Brown, R&B and more, with a young crowd who were pleased to talk to us. A guy called Dan was telling me that he grew up here, but in '92 moved away to London and then to Croatia because of the war.. He had come back to Sarajevo because he wanted to see U2 and today was the first day he had been here in five years. He was constantly being greeted with delight by people who were obviously old friends, and a real party atmosphere took over the place. I met another guy who said he was the singer in a band who were on the bill at the U2 show. He was really excited about the whole thing too – everybody was – and you begin to understand what this show represents for the city. "the beginning of the new Sarajevo" one guy said.

In search of food, we took to the street again, and it really seemed that the whole city was so upbeat. Dan was telling us that this is like the atmosphere was in Sarajevo before the war, and he was clearly quite emotional about it all. We walked across an area of open ground and he told us this was where many people died & pointed out the hills where the snipers used to be. We walked along the streets past the functioning shops with the blackened shells of devastated buildings in between. Dan was giving a running commentary as we walked, though I'm not sure if he was really talking to me, or to himself. "The house I grew up in was right there. That building used to be a shoe factory, this was an expensive restaurant, that one was a supermarket ... and I can't remember what used to be just here ..." The look on his face told his story more poignantly than the words coming out of his mouth. It's beyond my comprehension, what regular people in this city have been through. Yet for those that remain, life goes on, in all its glorious ordinariness.

MONDAY SEPTEMBER 22ND

Sarajevo, set up day. It might have been the mind-expanding evening I had last night, or it might just have been the combination of junk food, espresso & Bosnian beer, but despite going to bed at 5am, I found myself awake at 8.30 with "Zooropa" going round my head. I haven't thought about that song for ages, but this is the city of Zooropa if ever there was one. Zoo-nited Nations. Opening the curtains was revelation number one for the day. It was a clear, crisp, blue sky morning, and now I could see clearly what was hidden by the darkness last night. A ring of hills circles the city, and sitting within this bowl, the cityscape is devastated. Tower blocks which looked reasonably intact last night were now seen to be blown apart – the lower floors often still functioning and inhabited whilst the floors above were in ruins, or just not there at all. The tower block opposite the Holiday Inn, which had seemed so shocking with its large hole in the side, was just a ruin. If we thought our side was bad, the side facing away from our hotel was facing the hills, and looked like a piece of Swiss cheese. The ring of hills made the city so vulnerable, and everywhere you look you can see the results of months and months of shells, mortars, bombs and bullets. Buildings like this one just look like they've been used for target practice. We had word that the trucks would be delayed in their arrival by several hours, so I strolled out into the town and spent much of the day taking it all in. It would take a more proficient writer than I to describe in any meaningful way what the place is like, but I hope this sketch conveys something. In short, it looks like there was a war here, which one day stopped and everyone just carried on with their lives.

Wandering the streets, shops & markets, you see people rebuilding their lives some with more success than others, but the city is clean, and there is remarkably little evidence of poverty. Hiking up into the hills a little way and looking down over the city provided a moment which was sobering and amusing. Near to us were the old hillside cottages, all very rustic and overgrown (though often still badly damaged), then the modern cityscape stretch wide, with its half ruined buildings and then more green hills behind. In the middle of all of this, just peeping up into view you could see the top of our yellow arch – the PopMart stage, sticking out above the top of the stadium. It was so funny to see it there, so alien, so out of place. A symbol of hope? An omen of an impending capitalist invasion? The sign of a good time tomorrow night? Who knows? But one thing is certain, despite the countless buildings which are entirely gone, or reduced to rubble, the people of Sarajevo are working hard to get back to some kind of normality, and in many ways it seems to be working. The streets are full of people, the cafes and bars are packed and the mood is up. You begin to understand why this U2 show is such an important event for them – this isn't a charity show, this isn't a benefit gig, it's just a regular "big rock show", like they have in ordinary cities in countries where there aren't wars. Cities like the one Sarajevo is attempting to become once again. In a way we could never have imagined, the arrival of our arch is one tiny sign that the return to normality is underway.

TUESDAY SEPTEMBER 23RD

Sarajevo, showday. Sarajevo hosted the Winter Olympics in 1984, and one of the sporting venues was this stadium in which U2 are playing. The stadium itself is in remarkably good condition – nice curving grandstands, lush green playing field and so forth. The same cannot be said of the Zetra Ice Arena next door, which we are using for dressing rooms, offices, catering and so forth. This is the arena where Torville and Dean won their gold medal skating to "Bolero", but now it looks like ... well it looks like a bomb's hit it. The top half of its modern tubular metal structure is twisted into a surreal crow's nest of girders and practically all the windows are missing or covered with plastic. However, inside it's reasonably functional, if a tad Spartan. The offices were used by the army until one month ago, and all the walls are covered in the graffiti of their farewell notes and poems. Another surprising use for the arena was to house around 3,000 fans for the night after the show. Clearly a good many of the audience were not going to be able to get home after the show, so the battered arena's basement was to be used as a huge dormitory.

Other unique events of the day included the running of the first passenger trains since the war. A train full of U2 fans came to Sarajevo from Mostar, and another from Maglaj. The railway system has been potentially functional since last year, but no trains have run because the Muslims and Croats haven't been able to agree on who's going to run them. People came from all over Bosnia and other former Yugoslav republics, in the greatest movement of civilians across this country in years. Special buses brought fans from Zagreb, Ljubljana and even Bosnia's Serb Republic, from where at least 500 fans made a rare journey across the ethnic boundary line into the Moslem-Croat Federation. Even the requirement of Slovenian visas was suspended for the day – one might have expected some cynicism toward the concert from some quarters; but you really felt that the whole country was responding positively to our being there.

Come show time, the atmosphere in the stadium was like the Cup Final meets Christmas morning. One entire grandstand was filled with uniformed troops – not there as a safety measure, but there because they wanted to have a good time. They were singing, dancing and having a high old time, it was quite touching. Like old newsreel footage of the troops coming home and dancing in the street.

The highlight had to be the first live appearance of all five "Passengers" for the tour's first performance of "Miss Sarajevo". Brian Eno was at the show and joined the band on the b-stage to provide some backing vocals and operate the antique wind-up gramophone which was substituting for Luciano Pavarotti.

After the show, as the crowd was leaving a rather curious but very moving scenario occurred. The troops were waiting in the grandstand whilst the bulk of the audience filed out, and somehow spontaneously the crowd began to applaud the troops. This turned into a big cheering standing ovation, and when it was over the soldiers applauded the crowd in return. Beautiful moment.

THURSDAY SEPTEMBER 25TH

Day off. Crete, the morning after. Last night got completely out of hand, and I'm just now trying to piece together the various shreds of memory I have left. We arrived in Crete and found ourselves staying in what is basically paradise – a large coastal resort hotel with chalets by the clearest blue sea you ever saw, with beaches, palm trees, hills, little rocky paths everywhere, the whole bit. Clearly, it's going to be a great few days here. Today was also the birthday of Bess from Principle Management, so later in the evening, The Edge invited us all over to his place to celebrate, because he was so amused to find that his chalet/room had not one, but two swimming pools. It had an outdoor pool and, yes, a fair sized indoor pool and whole spa set up, making it, he said, the most over-the-top accommodation of his entire career.

Now, I don't know whether it was the beauty of the place, or the realisation that the end of this leg of the tour is so close, or some psychological reaction to the massive contrast between here and Bosnia, or maybe it was just the moonlight and the moment with a birthday thrown in, but something in us ignited and we declared "party time" of the highest order. The bar was raided, the tunes were cranked up and into the pool(s) everyone went in various states of dress and undress. The Edge found himself hosting Crete's very first Aqua-Disco and we made the most of it. In the pool, singing, yelling, dancing. We did "Go West", we did "YMCA" and birthday girl Bess performed the whole of "Born Slippy" on the side of the pool.

Everyone piled in. Madness. Dancing on the treadmill. Ice-cube fights in the steam room. Building a make-shift bar on the edge of the pool. Making candle sculptures to float in the water. Aching from hours of water aerobics, and laughing, laughing, laughing. Couldn't find the way back to my room. After an hour wandering about little paths, peering at chalet numbers, hopping fences and climbing over rocks I knew I was utterly, hopelessly lost. Nice night for it, mind. Still had the mobile phone, so called a friend in California who had a tour itinerary, so he could give me the hotel reception number here. I called reception and they sent out a little Greek porter to find me and lead me to my room. I've no idea how anyone else got home.

FRIDAY SEPTEMBER 26TH

The town of Thessaloniki in Greece is having a cultural festival and today's PopMart show is part of it. The venue was on the docks, with a row of huge industrial cranes making a fabulous additional backdrop behind the stage. The gig was sold out and absolutely jammed, so the city had decided to put up video screens in parks and squares around the town to relay the gig to the people who couldn't get in. The truck drivers made me laugh. They've spent the past week driving through war zones to get from Italy to Sarajevo then out and around to the middle of Greece. From here the trucks are going by ferry to Israel, and the ferry leaves from this very dock, so they were talking about the gruelling 500 yard drive they were facing tonight. They certainly deserve the break.

TUESDAY SEPTEMBER 30TH

After three whole days off in our Cretan paradise, going back to work comes as something of a shock to the system, but Bono's excitement about going to Israel was infectious enough to provide the required energy for all of us. He said that Israel is a place he has always wanted to visit, ever since he was a kid, so to come for the first time with this show was a perfect way to finish this part of the tour.

So, we conclude this European leg and we certainly finished on a high. One of the greatest things about this section of the tour has been seeing U2 play in countries they haven't visited before. The crowds have been so big and so receptive. Going back to North America will be a change of pace – in many ways it will be a lot more straightforward than this past few weeks. We'll be indoors too, in the huge covered all-weather stadiums that the U.S. specialises in, which will make life easier. Europe is certainly a more difficult place to tour, less predictable, not to mention all the language and currency issues. It has to be said that this past leg has had about as tough a touring schedule as I can imagine, but you know, there have been some extraordinary moments. This tour and the energy of these crowds I won't forget for a long time yet.

WEDNESDAY OCTOBER 1ST

Do not disturb.

SATURDAY OCTOBER 25TH

Toronto. Load in day. So back to school. Everyone returns, having just had an experience in practical relativity – three weeks on tour seems like forever, whereas three weeks off seems like a long weekend. Still, everyone's back and in fantastic form. The crew all look so clean – fresh haircuts and laundered clothes. Some time off has helped everyone get back on their feet.

This North American leg consists of shows in what the Americans call "Domes", which are 50,000+ seater stadiums covered by a big inflatable roof. This huge white barrage balloon-like thing covers the entire building, and is inflated by a constant flow of air. This means that all the doorways to the outside world have to be either revolving doors or airlocks, otherwise the roof would deflate and collapse. Bit of a weird concept, but it means sporting events can carry on year round. As it happens, the SkyDome in Toronto is a bit of an exception in that it has a solid, retractable roof, but the principle of it being a covered stadium remains the same.

Having just come from months of shows in open air stadiums, airports, ploughed fields and German car parks, the experience of putting up the stage indoors was ecstatic – if a little disorientating. It was a bit like the feeling you get when you come home after a fortnight's camping. Suddenly you notice all the little home comforts you took for granted before you went away, but now they suddenly seem utterly luxurious – carpet under your feet, a roof over your head, solid walls and running water. We were practically skipping around the place. The crew were loving it – English speaking local crew, prompt Fed-Ex delivery, 24 hour stores. Western decadence certainly has its practical applications.

The only slight hitch was that due to plagues of frogs in the Atlantic, the shipping of all the touring equipment was delayed 24 hours. The band were due to spend today rehearsing (not having played a note in three weeks), but were denied the opportunity as the stage wasn't ready. Let's hope they haven't forgotten too much.

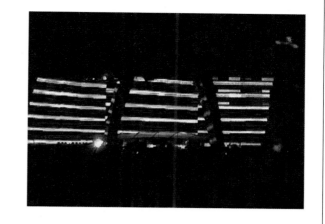

"The building was so small that it inspired Bono to jump off the stage and run round the entire audience during I Will Follow."

SUNDAY OCTOBER 26TH
Toronto SkyDome show #1. Hee hee ... I guess it's like riding a bike. When you do a show like this often enough, you never really forget how it goes. Except sometimes you remember the cue or the chord just a split second after it should have happened.
This made for a very loose show all round, but that was no bad thing – it was a good deal more spontaneous and actually more fun than a lot of shows we've done. We all had a good time. I'd been a little concerned that the seated venues and non-Italian audiences would mean that the energy-level of the crowd would be lower than we'd got used to in Europe. However, I hadn't taken into account the effect of having a roof over our heads, which made the crowd noise deafening. It was all really very exciting, and in a moment it was like we'd never been away. Edge played "Sunday Bloody Sunday" again, as he did in Sarajevo. It was very well received, as you'd expect, so I hope it becomes a regular item.

WEDNESDAY OCTOBER 29TH
Managed to get out to see a great Keith Haring exhibition at the art museum in Toronto this morning, before getting on the plane to Minneapolis. It was a great exhibition, including a lot of his personal artifacts, notes, sketches, trash. He had such strong direction so early in life, and being exactly of our generation his teenage influences were very similar to ours. On the way into the museum, Bono, half jokingly, had said that one key influence picked up in his "Jesus Freak" period must have been the simple line-drawing illustrations from the (then very hip and alternative) "Good News Bible". Sure enough, in one of the case of Haring's personal stuff, was a pile of 70's hip-religious material made into collages, including "One Way" stickers, including the line drawings, "chick" cartoon booklets, etc. There was some great work in the show – so vibrant, so instant and so totally Pop. Joy and anger in equal measure. Aftershow runner on to Detroit.

FRIDAY OCTOBER 31ST
Pontiac Silverdome. This is the third time U2 have played this venue – and also the next one, Montreal Olympic Stadium. We did these places on the Joshua Tree tour with a one-armed singer. All seems lost in the mists of time at this point. I shot some of the show using a "PXL-2000" camera, which is the fully functioning kiddies' toy video camera made by Fisher Price at the end of the 80's. They record onto a regular audio cassette and make fantastically grainy black and white pictures. They don't make them any more, which has elevated these little cameras to cult status, with their own web pages, etc. They have about 40 lines of resolution (less than 10% of TV quality), but it makes for interesting pictures. Our screen is so pixilated anyway, that the two seemed made for each other. Some of what I shot was beautiful, in an abstract art kind of a way, but unless you knew what the pictures were supposed to be you'd never guess. It was fun, but not remotely usable.
Larry's birthday today, so he was ceremonially toasted and caked, as one would expect, including a cake delivery to the b-stage at the beginning of "Discotheque". Frankly, I was amazed that the cake didn't end up in the audience, but through a miracle of self restraint the thing survived to be eaten later

SATURDAY NOVEMBER 1ST
Surprise news of the day was to learn that Bill Berry, R.E.M.'s drummer, is leaving the band. It's funny, because on the plane only yesterday we were talking about bands splitting up and what a tragedy it is that The Smiths and The Clash no longer exist. The Edge was saying that people wouldn't believe how hard it becomes to keep a band together. U2 have survived, but it would only have taken a different set of circumstances and they might not have. Who was it that said being in a band is like being married but you didn't get to have sex? Steve Tyler? I forget.
Today we hear about Bill leaving R.E.M. – an event in their camp with equal significance to Larry leaving U2 – and you see how right Edge is. Bill's departure is a great surprise, but understandable given his near-death experience with a brain haemorrhage on their '95 tour. That would certainly give a man cause to reflect.
Whilst U2 spent half the night in a diner in downtown Detroit, I had an early one in preparation for what looks like being a particularly full on week. They were shooting a video for "If God Will Send His Angels" with Phil Joanou. Nice to see him again, he always adds a rush of positive energy to any situation. As for me, it was cocoa in bed with a good book and lights out early. Rock & Roll, eh?

"The Lemon had stopped revolving in a position where it would be impossible for the band to get out of it."

SUNDAY NOVEMBER 2ND

Montreal Olympic Stadium ... and back to Europe. Everyone was a bit blurred this morning, having been shooting in the diner till 5 or 6am. Still, everyone said it had gone well, so all were happy. We went on to Montreal, which is the home of the PopMart screen. The Montreal based "Smartvision" built all of the electronics for the screen and developed the LED video technology which made it possible. The gig was sold out and packed to the rafters with extremely noisy people. It was a good night, after which we did a runner from the gig straight onto a plane bound for The Netherlands. The reason for this eccentric behaviour was that the band are to appear live on the European MTV awards in Rotterdam on Thursday. A curse of itineraries had us flying from Europe to New York to play the US MTV awards, and now we do the reverse journey. Fortunately we managed to score a fantastic plane for the trip – a full sized 747, decked out in shockingly decadent oil-company-executive comfort. There were only about 30 of us on the thing, so we had plenty of room to sprawl and crash out. Big fuel tanks. No stops en route. Who'd have imagined how grateful one could become for such seemingly trivial things? It'll be tomorrow night by the time we get there.

TUESDAY NOVEMBER 4TH
Click. The View Master wheel turns again. Do you remember those "View Master" toys? A set of binocular-type lenses, with a cardboard wheel of "stereo" visual images that slips in. You click the lever on the side and the picture changes. The starter wheel that came with the machine would always be a "scenes of the world" kind of deal, showing famous landmarks of our planet. I've long thought that my life is much the same. Day by day you hear the click of the wheel. Click. The Eiffel Tower. Click. St. Peter's in Rome. Click. 170,000 Italians. Click. Blown up buildings in Sarajevo. Click. A Greek Island Click. The Holy Land. Click. The Golden Gate Bridge. Click. Downtown Detroit. Click. French speaking Canada. Click. Crowds of unruly Manchester United supporters in Holland. Click ... and so it goes on. View Master life, showing this series of seemingly random images – except you're actually in them. Little wonder we're all becoming very strange people. Click ... the European MTV awards rehearsal, at the Ahoy in Rotterdam. Haven't been here since LoveTown, which was a staggering eight years ago. How many clicks of the View Master wheel must that be? The stage set is hilarious – kind of a Jacques Cousteau in Space vibe, including giant clubs of day-glo sea weed behind the drum kit – but it takes colours well and looks great on the TV. U2 arrived to sound check & rehearse, and it was all surprisingly straight forward. Highlight of the day was seeing the Spice Girls rehearsal, which took the concept of post-modern entertainment to dizzying new heights. We're well into Morecambe and Wise territory here. There's another rehearsal day tomorrow, for all the other bands, but fortunately we don't need to be here, so may get some sleep.

THURSDAY NOVEMBER 6TH
Going live. The European MTV awards. These events are so surreal, not least because in the backstage compound every other person you see has a famous face. The place is just crawling with celebrities, and dozens of other people you know from previous tours and previous lifetimes. U2 had the dubious honour of opening this show – first performance of the night, and actually it was the perfect thing to do, playing "Pop Muzik / MoFo" which is the opening of the PopMart show. We'd spent much of the day hanging around at the venue waiting to do the final run-through, so by the time show time came around we were more than ready to get on with it. The band did pretty much their regular entrance – the walk in through the crowd, and it translated well on the TV. Into the song and it really looked OK, and the TV sound was stunning. Before you know it, it's all over and you're left wondering what hit you. Everyone was happy with the performance and after that, the advantage of going first becomes apparent – you can sit and watch everybody else knowing your part is over. There were a lot of great acts on the bill – Bjork, Skunk Anansie, Aerosmith, the bizarre combination of Blackstreet and Slash, and of course the Spice Girls, who excelled. Not quite sure what at, but they certainly made their mark. Fun Lovin' Criminals were around too, and it was great to see them again. They're really on a roll now, having just scored "Best New Band" at the Q awards this week. U2 won the MTV award for "Best Live Band" which was gratifying. "Live is where we live" says Larry. Well, that's certainly true in 1997.
Once cleared we did a runner to the airport, to get back on our stupidly big aeroplane to fly back to St. Louis to carry on with the North American tour (where am I again). When we were leaving the venue we saw the Spice Girls leaving at the same time. On the way to the airport we were being followed by a fleet of limos full of people with big hair, which we assumed must be them. At the airport, across the tarmac from our 747 was a small jet. We headed for our plane and the fleet of limos went to the jet. The members of U2 hadn't arrived yet, so the crew thought how funny it would be to invite the Spice Girls over for a pre-take off party. We thought it would be a laugh to have U2 arrive and find the Spice Girls on their plane. So, in the absence of a volunteer from the studio audience, I ran across the tarmac to invite the Spicers over. Having composed a good opening one-liner, I heroically sprinted up the stairs of their aeroplane ... and found myself looking at Aerosmith. "Ah ... erm ... doors armed and cross-checked", I mutter, before fleeing in a fit of embarrassment.

FRIDAY NOVEMBER 7TH
zzzzzzzzzzz...

SATURDAY NOVEMBER 8TH
Woke up to discover that it is show day in St. Louis, home of another famous arch, the "Gateway to the West". And what an arch it is – a huge silver job, spanning the Mississippi, glistening in the early morning sunshine. Meanwhile, our own arch (the "Gateway to the Mall") was spanning Larry's drum kit, as ever. The new venue here, the Trans World Dome, is truly colossal. You only realise how big these places are when you see how they dwarf our stage which is not a small item itself.
Triumph of the day was finally sorting out the video sequences for "Last Night on Earth". The song starts with the rather strange and naively violent cartoon sequence, "MultiMart", but thereafter I had never been 100% happy with the structure of the visuals. After months of occasional tweaking, we finally nailed it this afternoon. Only took us 67 shows – not bad!

...pretending to be Phil on stage with a movie camera shooting U2.

MONDAY NOVEMBER 10TH

We commuted to Tampa to do the show there today. We play outdoors for the first time on this leg and of course it rains. To do November shows outdoors, even in Florida, certainly wasn't the brightest idea of the year. The video screen suffers the most. Our screen is the first of its type in the world. We conceived it, designed it and built it, and are in effect touring a giant prototype. As with all such prototypes there is an element of experimentation and some risk involved. In almost all respects, the screen has performed far better than we dared hope. Its resolution, clarity, brightness, its ease of deployment, its colour and quite simply its beauty have way surpassed our expectations. Overall, there's no question of the magnitude of the screen's triumph, but some elements were bound to prove problematic, and the Achilles heel has been moisture. Oddly, one of its great benefits – the fact that the screen emits no heat and requires no cooling system like other video systems – makes the moisture problem worse, as heat would help the moisture evaporate. Consequently, it takes a lot of work from our Belgian screen crew to keep up the level of required maintenance. In the past they have even resorted to scaling the back of it with hair dryers to help it dry out. At this point in the tour, most of these problems are solved, but the rain/humidity combo of a day like today will still bring on Belgian headaches.

FRIDAY NOVEMBER 14TH

Show day Miami. U2's meteorological curse continued true to form today, after a week of glorious weather in Miami, the storm broke and deluged over Joe Robbie Stadium. Fortunately this was prior to the show, but even so it makes it a hard day's work for all involved. The Belgians are hating life again. Tonight's show was an odd one. Despite being in the home of a U2 song, the audience seemed a little reserved. Might have just seemed that way with us not having a roof, after a couple of weeks indoors, or perhaps the fact it was still 85 degrees and 100% humidity when the band went on, but the crowd did seem a bit puddingy. Party afterwards at the Marlin Hotel, owned by Chris Blackwell. Chris founded Island Records many moons ago and has been with U2 for their entire recording career. This month he's decided to leave the company, so it's very much the end of an era and the party was a nice way for the band to acknowledge his part in U2's Life. A good night, but not an early one ...

SUNDAY NOVEMBER 23RD

San Antonio show day. Tonight's show was an emotional one, due to the news of Michael Hutchence's suicide in Australia. It was hard to take in as it seemed so unlikely and so pointless. During the show, Bono paid tribute to him a couple of times. It was particularly hard for Bono as they'd been friends, and he was clearly upset by the whole ordeal.

WEDNESDAY NOVEMBER 26TH

Atlanta show day. Swung by the R.E.M. office in the morning. Bertis Downs met us there and we left laden with swag and product. Such generous folks. Breakfast at "Guaranteed", Michael Stipe's veggie diner, then on to the Georgia Dome. It was a pretty straightforward day. Catherine Owens was in from New York which was a treat, and by nightfall our many guests began to arrive. Stipe came, with Mike Mills and Bertis (Bono entwined a snatch of "Shiny Happy People" into "Discotheque", by way of tribute).

Howard Finster – a local folk artist, whose angel appears in the show – had some people come down, though Howard himself declined the invitation. He's 81 years old now, so road trips are tough, but his grandson Michael came along, who's also a folk artist producing a good quantity of work. Today was Michael Hutchence's funeral, so Bono paid tribute again, noting that given the time difference the funeral was happening at the same time as the gig. It's been hard for him, but the audience's warm response to Bono's words has been helpful. After the show, Michael Stipe threw a party at an Athens restaurant, "Mumbo Jumbo" which was a lot of fun. I'll be sorry to leave here, but I get the feeling we'll see these people again soon enough.

258

U2 THE BEST OF PROPAGANDA

THURSDAY NOVEMBER 27TH

Thanksgiving. Atlanta. Thanksgiving has no resonance for the Europeans on the tour, but "being the day that's in it", as the Irish say, we decided to have a dinner anyway. The U.S. citizens amongst us appreciated it, and hey, any excuse for a party. After a nice turkey dinner we all headed to a local Irish bar. Sitting with Joe O'Herlihy, the bar tender comes over and in a broad Cork accent says "are you Joe?", "er ... yes", "I used to work for your cousin..." It's a global mafia, I tell you.

FRIDAY NOVEMBER 28TH

A long, long day today. We got up in Atlanta & boarded a plane for Houston, where we did a show at the Alamo Dome. All the T.V. crew arrived too, director David Mallet, lighting consultant Allen Branton, and their team. After the show we all boarded the Lemon Air plane and headed for Mexico City, which is where this TV broadcast is going to be. It was a lengthy flight to do in the middle of the night, and we got in to Mexico City about 3 or 4am. Despite the lateness of our arrival, there were fans waiting at the airport, who'd brought flags, banners, T-shirts etc. We got into our cars and buses, and set off into town. These kids proceeded to chase us down the freeway, hanging out of the windows, waving banners, screaming, taking photographs ... it looks like this is going to be quite a week.

MONDAY DECEMBER 1ST

December already. Advent and all. Down here in Mexico City the rather lo-tech but utterly charming Christmas decorations are going up at a pace. In our hotel there's a charming note which says "we recommend you stay indoors when the pollution index level is too high. Please contact the concierge for today's pollution index reading." Amongst the street billboards advertising local and international products, there are ones advertising oxygen. A stylishly dressed model with flowing hair and that post-produced flawless dental smile has a demeanor of rapturous joy as she holds up her "industrial chic" plastic oxygen mask, connected to a rather scientific looking green cylinder. William Gibson where are you? It was a long day at the gig. The band came in to soundcheck both for the live sound and the recorded sound going to the broadcast truck. They then rehearsed for a couple of hours to allow us to view all the new camera positions and re-light them accordingly. Our only major problem was that our colossal video screen proved to be way too bright for the new cameras. With a regular screen "turning down the brightness" would be simple enough, but this being the first of its kind it was a little tricky.

Making a show look good on TV is an entirely different discipline to making it great for the stadium viewer, so some compromises to the existing show are inevitable. Fortunately all the players involved here have been around the block so many times now that we all understand the common goal. Myself and Allen were in the truck looking at sixteen video monitors – one for each of the TV cameras, whilst Bruce and the lighting team and Monica and the video screen team were out in the field making it happen. It was exciting to see the show from all of these new angles. At 5.30am we called it a night and sleep-walked onto our Mexican shuttle bus to take us back to the hotel. Our driver was an enthusiastic non-English speaking chap who got very excited when we reached the stadium gates and found them chained up, with the night watchman long gone. ("...and then depression set in...") Fortunately no major tour ever travels without a sturdy pair of oversized industrial bolt-cutters, so we were soon on our way home ...

WEDNESDAY DECEMBER 3RD

Mexico City. Two nights at the Autodromo, the second of which (tonight) went out on live television to most of the planet. Mercifully, we won. The show was great and the shoot was great too. This stage production looks like it was made for television – I think it's because despite being huge it is a very simple design -just an arch and a line, really. All were pleased and in which is now becoming a tradition, we all jammed into the band's dressing room to watch the tape playback. We cheered at our favourite moments and pointed fingers and laughed at each other's greatest mistakes of the night. Back to the crew hotel we watch the sun rise through the viscous pollution which hangs over Mexico City. So there it is, it's printed, PopMart is on video tape and just two shows to go before our Christmas holidays. Any excuse for a party.

WEDNESDAY DECEMBER 11TH

Seattle load-in day, after which we held a "Rigger's Arms" party, in order to host the 1997 PopMart Crew Awards ceremony. It is something of a tradition on long rock tours to honour those amongst us for their triumphs, failures, lapses of good judgement and lapses of consciousness. We held the event in a local pool hall, which turned out to be a great idea. After an hour or two's socialising (i.e. heavy drinking) we had reached a suitable frame of mind for the event. A couple of weeks ago, ballot forms with nominations were issued to all tour personnel, outlining all the award categories and requesting nominations and votes. The results were announced and presented with trophies made by Monica Caston our video director. Sam O'Sullivan, Larry's drum-tech arrived with a snare and cymbal so with Pete the Greek on CD samples they made up the orchestra. Oh how we laughed. Opening envelopes, nominations, and the winner is... for "Excess Baggage of the Year" (wardrobe dept.), "Rookie of the Year" (Mona from the catering dept.), "Fashion Statement of the Year" (sound tech, Jo Ravitch in a Heidi wig), "Party Animal of the Year" (a backline dept/wardrobe dept tie) and climaxing with the highly coveted "Biggest Fuck Up of the Year" (the Lemon not opening in Oslo).

FRIDAY DECEMBER 12TH

The last day of school – show day in Seattle. On arrival at the gig, I noticed that the steel crew had erected a twelve foot tall Christmas tree – 100 feet up in the air on top of the Arch, complete with flashing lights. Very slick. The show was a party of course. For reasons which never quite became apparent, Bono shaved his head, so when he pulled his hood off during the middle of "MoFo" there was an audible gasp from the audience. And from the crew for that matter. Pranks were running high. Bono's muscleman character for "Real Thing" was joined by an extra half dozen bald and muscled Bono clones, and his cheek to cheek dance partner in "Velvet Dress" turned out to be one of our riggers in a wig and lingerie. As Bono said, "that's the thing about road crews ... you can't live with them and you can't live without them." Well, we'll all be living without each other for the next six weeks, as we break for Christmas, and dispense with 1997. Quite a year that was ...

MONDAY FEBRUARY 9TH

Rio de Janeiro, rehearsal day. Was awoken this morning by the throng of fans outside the hotel howling ... een-nuh naaaaim oh luuuuurve – at the tops of their voices. Well, at least they're keen. Down to the venue once more to get to grips with being back to work and to try to remember just how a PopMart show goes. The band showed up and we did a fairly respectable run through, given that it's still 30 degrees in the middle of the night.

TUESDAY JANUARY 27TH

Show day, Rio de Janeiro. I ended up travelling to the gig in a helicopter with Bono & Edge (as you do). This was an out-of-body experience on many levels, not least because Rio is so beautiful to see from the air – the water inlets that double the number of beaches as the land folds back on itself, the blue blue ocean, white sand. As if this wasn't extraordinary enough, our pilot decided to give us a treat by circling Corcovado and giving us a close up view of the huge statue of Christ the Redeemer which looks down from the highest point in Rio. We hovered in front, eyeball to eyeball with Jesus, Like a soundcheck for judgment day. Hovering above his head, with the whole of the city spread out far below, I did have to give myself a reality check. Just another dull day with a couple of rock stars in a chopper over Rio.
A last minute addition to the show was a group of fifty drummers from a local Samba club which Bono had visited a couple of nights ago. He & Edge had what might loosely be described as a rehearsal of "Desire", and before we knew where we were it was show time.
The gig was wild. I knew we were in for a treat when even the appearance of the giant revolving football in the opening video sequence drove the crowd into hysteria. (They're pretty big on footy down here ...) As soon as the band arrived on stage, our mix position compound completely filled with people. All over the gear, up the camera tower, everywhere. I set about clearing out the intruders from at least inside covered area, and was slinging people out left right & centre. Unfortunately, in my enthusiasm I also threw out Bruce's translator for the followspot operators, and the director from MTV, but these were desperate times.
Although enthusiastic to the point of being crazed, the crowd were extremely good natured – polite almost. Our security had cleared the whole area within about 15 minutes and from that point we just surfed on the energy all night.

SATURDAY JANUARY 31ST

Two shows at the Morumb Stadium in Sao Paolo, and the place just rocked. Rio is the jewel in the tourism crown, but Sao Paolo with its 25 million inhabitants is where the guts of the nation seems to be. The capacity of the stadium is 75,000, but unofficially they reckon to have got 95,000 in tonight, the second show night. It reminded me a lot of the first time U2 played in Madrid, at Real Madrid stadium on the Joshua Tree Tour. You couldn't move in the place. Midway through the gig, Susie Smith and I took a hike way up into the top bleacher of seats to bathe in the joy of it all. We also bathed in a good deal of the sweat of it all, but it was worth the trek. Susie says to me "This is what it's really all about – everything else we deal with is just details.' The good people of Brazil have waited a long time for U2 to come and were singing their hearts out up there.

SUNDAY FEBRUARY 1ST

Travel day, Sao Paolo to Buenos Aires. My anniversary: I have been working on the PopMart project for exactly two years today. Touring does take huge chunks out of your life. Not to mention that we are all six years older than we were when we started the Zoo TV tour, but let's not even start that train of thought.

THURSDAY FEBRUARY 5TH

Buenos Aires, opening night. At the very end of the show, the band were joined on stage by Los Madres de Plaza de Mayo. The women who have lost children to the country's past military regimes. They are a group who, despite the granting of an amnesty for Argentina's war criminals, continue to campaign that those who tortured and murdered their offspring be brought to justice. Bono spoke as an introduction about every country having its ghosts and the need to find a way to face them and lay them to rest, then the band played "Mothers Of The Disappeared" for the first and only time since the "Rattle & Hum" shoot in Arizona over ten years ago. The Mothers came on stage, doing their circling walk back and forth, and the result was about the most moving thing I've ever seen on a rock stage. It was one of those ideas that really could have gone either way, but the obvious empathy of the audience towards these women made it an unforgettable moment. They were practically silent for the whole song, then began jumping up and down chanting, EL QUE NO SALTAR, ES MILITAR (if you don't jump, you're military), being an anti army slogan. The whole place was jumping in support of the Mothers, and continued to do so even as we drove out of the stadium when the gig was over.

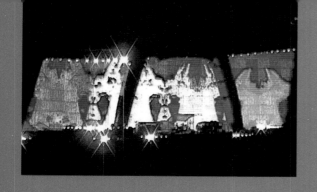

"I ended up travelling to the gig in a helicopter with Bono & Edge – as you do."

MONDAY FEBRUARY 9TH
I woke to find myself in Chile. Chilly it is not, as it is basking in a most pleasantly Mediterranean climate. The countryside around us does look very Portuguese. Our hotel is new, as are most of the buildings we have seen. I'll have to ask what the story is, but it does appear that they completely started again when they'd sorted out their 1970's dictatorship issues. Sitting in the hotel's club lounge, I have a comfy couch, a glass of chilled white wine and a nice view of the Andes. Click. There goes the View Master again.

TUESDAY FEBRUARY 17TH
Perth. Show day. The venue here in Perth is like a gig only smaller. The Super Dome holds just 17,000 and our stage pretty much filled the place even before the punters came in. Tonight's gig was, well, quiet. Compared to 70,000 mad Chileans, 17,000 respectable Perthians couldn't hope to reproduce the volume of audience noise to which we've become accustomed. The building was so small that it inspired Bono to jump off the stage and run round the entire audience during "I Will Follow". He can be a funny chap sometimes. Anyhow, the audience seemed to have a good time, so we left just feeling glad to be here and not in an aeroplane.

FRIDAY FEBRUARY 27TH
Sydney Football Stadium. Some sort of homecoming ... So many memories lurk in the air of this venue. This is where we did the global telecast of Zoo TV, and so is the venue to which that show seems most closely tied. ZooTV Live From Sydney. It was a great show, despite the curse of Fred Nile. Who? The very Reverend Fred Nile, who's some high up Protestant church guy in Sydney & our friendly local bigot. Being a charitable soul and violently anti-gay, every year at Mardi Gras he gets his congregation together to pray for rain – no kidding. The guy does a rain-dance before God, asking that the parade will be a wash-out. He obviously has a strong connection with the Almighty, but his timing was a little off. After a week of blazing sunshine, the heavens opened tonight and we copped all of Fred Nile's rain, Well, rather tonight than tomorrow. Bono made mention of it: whatever the weather's like tomorrow, he said, don't ever let Fred Nile rain on your parade. Crowd loved it.
Video director Monica Caston got into the spirit of Mardi Gras with a couple of spontaneous additions of her own. We have had a couple of Ken (as in Barbie) dolls on tour with us for five years now. Ken & Ken did most of Zoo TV and also did the R.E.M. tour, sitting out at the mix position every night. Over the years they have been dressed up in various different outfits and have become part of the furniture of touring. (Incidentally, when we did some shows with Pearl Jam in '93, they arrived with a Ken doll of their own, so we are obviously not alone in experiencing this phenomenon). Monica got out a camera and made a video sequence of Ken & Ken at Mardi Gras which she put into the visuals for "Real Thing" (Ken & Ken, 50 foot high!). Also, in the pre-Lemon encore break, she re-edited the sequence of Leigh Bowery, the huge transvestite belly dancer. There is one little clip we took out of the original Leigh Bowery video sequence on grounds of good taste. Old Leigh (an Australian himself, I should mention) spins around in his very scanty garment and lifts up his leg, in a reverse kick towards the camera. This is extremely revealing and frankly gives the viewer way more information than most would care to have. In honour of Mardi Gras, Monica not only put this little clip back in, but she looped it, so it repeated over & over about six times. We were dying. Crowd loved it.

261

INSIDE POPMART. ISSUE 28/29

THURSDAY MARCH 5TH

Tokyo. Survived the journey from Sydney, dozed a lot & watched the Bond movie *Tomorrow Never Dies*. I'd never imagined in a million years that I'd ever feel a personal affinity with James Bond, so I had to smile watching him get chauffeured from A to B having tickets and gadgets thrust at him by total strangers in unlikely situations – there are similarities. Nick Welch always said he thought of Bruce & I when he was watching *Mission Impossible* – two groovy dudes running all over the world with Powerbooks. Except not quite so many people have been killed on our tour. And their Powerbooks worked. Got into Tokyo Narita airport at 6am, finding a refreshingly crisp morning waiting for me, along with a little Japanese man, old enough to be my grandfather, who seemed intent on prostrating himself before me when I identified myself as the owner of the name on the large, printed, laminated sign he was holding (Mr. Bond?). He took my baggage trolley from me, bowed deeply (again) and handed me a package containing a hand gun, one billion Yen in used notes and a sonic key to the small thermonuclear device I had brought with me. Prease to Forrow he said smiling, and led me to his vehicle – a sleek black number, with massage vibrators built into the seat backs.

WEDNESDAY MARCH 11TH

Show day, Osaka Dome. Another good show tonight, with another surprisingly responsive audience. By Japanese standards, anyway. The Lemon gave us another fright, as it is getting old and cranky after its global sojourn. It's doubtful that any lemon in history has made such an epic pilgrimage as this one – around the world, across continents, over the Andes, through rain, snow and blazing sun ... plus it's 40 foot high and composed largely of glass, which gives it some excuse to feel at least a little fragile these days. Tonight the Lemon took off as usual on its nightly journey from discreet repose to centre-stadium stardom, revolving as it went, with the band hidden inside it. About half way down its track it ceased to revolve, though carried on with its forward motion. Hmm. We watch and wait. Knowing more about 40 foot Lemons than most, I was aware that this particular moment of eccentricity had the potential to be more spectacular than any before it – the Lemon had stopped revolving in a position where it would be impossible for the band to get out of it. During its two previous moments of madness, Oslo and Sydney, the band were able to climb back out of the Lemon out of view of the public and so carry on with the show as if nothing had happened. Not so tonight, this was the big one and I could already envisage the pick-axes coming out to smash through the mirrored egg-shell and perhaps the band being lowered on ropes to the stage below. Come on, I prayed, get the back-up system going. And all this in a heartbeat ... a brief jolt and the Lemon resumed its revolving, as if nothing had happened, carried on its journey, opened flawlessly and let the band descend as graciously as on any other night. Close call – it's high time we retired this particular piece of fruit.

FRIDAY MARCH 13TH

Friday the 13th – the second one this year, and coincidentally, another major travel day as was the last one. Today's (& yesterday's) journey was the longest we will undertake on the whole tour, being about 10,000 miles. We flew from Osaka to Singapore, then to Johannesburg and on to Cape Town – a total of about 21 hours in the air. You know what, though, it wasn't so bad.
It was long. It was boring. It was fine. It was also the last journey I shall do with this group of people, as I am making my own way from here to Johannesburg next week. Thank you and good night.

MONDAY MARCH 16TH

Show day, Cape Town. I keep feeling that I should go and do and see lots of things whilst I'm here, but frankly I can't really see it happening. I don't know whether it's the end of tour shaggedness, or the fabulous weather, or the joy of this ludicrous haven which is the Mount Nelson Hotel, but I seem to be casting my lot in with the lolling by the pool under willow trees crowd. Fair enough.
The show was good, if a little strange in parts due to Phil Joanou doing a spot of filming. Phil of course was the director of the "Rattle & Hum" movie, who gained further notoriety on the Zoo TV tour by flying to Vegas after the U2 show in New Jersey to marry a woman he had met an hour previously at the aftershow parry. They flew back to New York the following day, bringing their Elvis Chapel wedding video with them, which we played on the video screens during the show that same night in Madison Square Garden. The tour lasted longer than the marriage, but it was still quite an extraordinary sequence of events. Now, six years later, Phil is working on his next movie which is a story based on his own life. Steven Dorff is playing Phil Joanou, and tonight Phil shot a sequence recreating the above episode. A couple of days ago they'd been to Vegas to re-shoot a version of the wedding video, and this we showed on the PopMart screen during "Mysterious Ways" in tonight's show. Also during the show Phil was on stage with a movie camera shooting footage of Steven Dorff, pretending to be Phil on stage with a movie camera shooting U2 ... confused? We certainly were, and the audience was absolutely baffled. I'm sure it'll all make sense in the final edit. Or not.

THURSDAY MARCH 19TH

I stayed in the crew hotel for the couple of nights prior to the Jo'Burg gig, so I could spend some time with all of these people whom I would not see again for who knows how long. Tonight was lampies night out and the whole lighting crew invaded a traditional African restaurant. They invited me along to sample such delights as crocodile steaks, and wildebeest casserole – when in Rome, and all that. Going to bed in the hotel I could still feel the gentle rocking of the train ...

FRIDAY MARCH 20TH

The final load in, as PopMart gets constructed for the very last time. Tomorrow's show is being broadcast on TV throughout South Africa in honour of Human Rights Day, so I went down to the venue to make sure all was well – though in truth I would have gone down anyway, just to hang out, chat to folks and be amongst it all. It was a beautiful day, so spirits were high and load in was finished relatively early. Most of the crew spent the night in the hotel bar, like a night in at home, and an informal party developed. Much talk about "what are you doing after this?", "what's your next project?", etc. Some folks go right out on Janet Jackson next week, the lucky sound guys get to join the Travis Tritt tour whilst others are asking around to see which tours are going out this year. A good number of people are staying on in South Africa for a holiday – much talk of safaris and so forth, but I'm off home. Beautiful though this country is, there's only one place that I really want to be just now. The hotel kept the bar open for us, so it was a late night, but a lot of fun and a chance to feel some kind of closure with a lot of the people we've been travelling with for the past year.

SATURDAY MARCH 21ST

Show day, Johannesburg. Once more with feeling. Final shows of a tour can go in any direction because so much expectation is weighted on them. In this case, U2's decision to go live on TV for the last show gave a different focus to proceedings, as we actually had to think about what we were doing, rather than being on auto-pilot. Still we did manage to get a few last night pranks together, including turning the Lemon into a cocktail party. When it opened, the band appeared with their backs to the audience, amid balloons and streamers holding large fruity beverages, apparently oblivious to the 50,000 people waiting to be entertained. The audience were a little bemused, but we thought it was funny. Song by song we went through the show, each one being seen for the last time in its current incarnation. All went well and the band added 40 to close the show. Thank you and good night. Lots of mutual hugs and thanks as the crew wade into the final load out. A few of us, myself, Bruce, Monica, Sharon and various other passers by ended up in the dressing room being force fed champagne and generally wallowing in the relief of having crossed the winning line. The rest of the night was very low key. I had a feeling it might be, as the conclusion of this tour has had a slightly odd mood to it. I think it's a lot to do with the fact that in many ways this tour (certainly when compared to previous ones) has been a real struggle. Having come through and won there's as much a feeling of relief as anything.

TUESDAY MARCH 24TH

The first day of the rest of my life. Completely out of it for the most part. Don was around which was nice, but I can't imagine that I could have been very good company. By 4pm I had gone nose down into the duvet and my brief nap extended to a dead sleep till about 10pm. On waking of course I was ready to rock.

The club was packed and jostling my way through the crowd I bump into ... Michael Stipe. I knew R.E.M. were in town, but I was going to leave it a couple of days before getting in touch. He greeted me like a long lost friend and was telling me all his news, about the songs, the studio, the ideas, the plans for the future. You see, the carousel never stops turning, but for once in my life I feel like I've got time for a decent break before getting on the next ride ...

The United
Nations of Pop

IN SEPTEMBER BONO, AS A SPOKESMAN FOR THE JUBILEE 200 CAMPAIGN TO CANCEL THE DEBTS OF THE WORLD'S POOREST COUNTRIES, WAS INVITED TO ADDRESS THE GENERAL ASSEMBLY OF THE UNITED NATIONS IN NEW YORK. POP STARS DO NOT DO THIS VERY OFTEN AND BONO WAS ACUTELY AWARE OF THE ODDITY OF THE OCCASION. HIS SPEECH COINCIDED WITH THE LAUNCH OF NET AID, A PROJECT WHICH WAS ALSO ENDORSED BY BILL CLINTON, TONY BLAIR, NELSON MANDELA AND KOFI ANNAN. WITH POLITICAL LEADERS WORLDWIDE SCRATCHING THEIR HEADS AND WONDERING WHY TO PARTY ON NEW YEAR'S EVE – BONO GAVE THEM A REASON WHY. HERE, WE REPRODUCE HIS SPEECH.

When rock stars speak out on political issues I get nervous, and I am one. When musicians open their mouth to do anything but sing, I generally put my wallet in my boot and yet music, more than anything has kept my conscience. It's the noise that keeps me awake, stops me falling asleep in the comfort of this wild freedom some of us are enjoying on the eve of the 21st Century.

I'm involved with Net Aid because Net Aid supports the Jubilee 2000 campaign to cancel third world debt. Plus there are some of us who want to see Live Aid through. In the 80s, I was a proud part of the spoiled generation who brought you Live Aid, Band Aid, We Are The World, all that stuff. It was an amazing thing, that moment in time where Bob Geldof said, "fuck" on TV and led a bunch of pop stars to raise $200 million for famine relief in Africa. I was so proud of it. We walked around thinking we had cracked it. Musicians, we could do what the politicians couldn't – $200 million!

Then I learned that Africa spends $200 million every week servicing its debt to the West. It's time now to write off the unpayable debt of the world's poorest nations because for every $1 sent in Government Aid to these countries, $9 is sent back in loan servicing. What they're repaying a lot of the time are old loans made to dodgy dictators and cracked despots a couple of generations ago. It's inefficient, it's barbaric and it's preventing the developing countries from joining the world stage. These countries have a lot to offer in terms of growth and new trade but they can't even get to the starting line. In Jubilee 2000 we want to take the energy that's going into New Year's Eve '99 and the millennium celebrations and give it a meaningful goal. It's complicated. But don't let anyone tell you it's "too complicated." Some very smart people are involved. The politicians have already done some work on debt reduction. They have the script – they just need some prompting from you to go the whole way. As well as politicians and economists, churchmen of every persuasion have come on board the debt cancellation bus; from Pope John Paul to the Dalai Lama. Jews, Muslims, Christians. Mohammed Ali is going to go back in the ring if it doesn't happen. This is the kind of broad coalition that brought about the end of apartheid or slavery. And that's no exaggeration – this is 'economic slavery' whose abolition we are now talking about.

Potentially this is a fresh start for a billion people. Now that's a reason to party and a real reason to celebrate New Year's Eve '99. As for tonight, you have shown your support by being here. What you should do now is stay informed, write to your politician, sign a petition, make yourself heard.

Bono addresses the general assembly of the United Nations in New York, September 1999

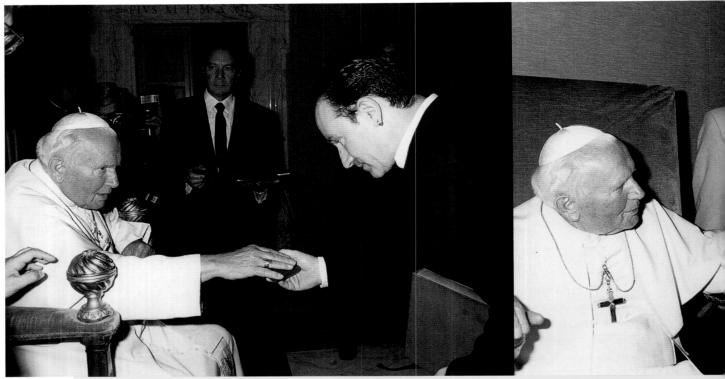

Bono was amongst a delegation of musicians, economists and church activists to meet Pope John Paul II in Rome in late September.

EXACTLY 100 DAYS BEFORE THE MILLENNIUM, Bono, Bob Geldof and Quincy Jones led a high-profile delegation of musicians, economists and church activists to meet Pope John Paul II in Rome in Late September. The Pope was among the first to call for the turn of the Millennium to be marked as a year of Jubilee in which the unpayable debts of the poorest countries in the world were cancelled by the richest. No-one had doubted his commitment to the cause – but members of the delegation were impressed by the moral strength and willpower of the Pope, whom Bono promptly christened the "first funky pontiff." "You're a great showman as well as a great holy man," he told the Pope, before the showman took the singer's fly-shades, tried them on for size, and decided to keep them for future use. "The Pope's run off with my sunglasses," he joked after the meeting.

Funky Pontiff Legs It With Singer's Goggles

Bono said he was aware that the Pope was not in the best of health and was grateful that he had made the effort to meet the delegation. "You could see what a struggle it was for him and yet he made it seem so easy to hang out with a bunch of economists and pop stars. I don't know how you could turn such a man down, and I don't think Bill Clinton wants to turn this man down, or Tony Blair, or Gerhard Schroeder." Bono has met all three politicians on behalf of the Jubilee 2000 Campaign in recent months. He added that the Pope had agreed to ask leaders of the richest countries to meet again and take further the issue of debt cancellation. The Pope said that cancelling the debt was essential to fight poverty. "I appeal to all persons involved, and in particular to the most powerful nations, to prevent the jubilee passing by without decisive steps towards a definitive solution to the debt problem."

"Why the difficulty in providing funds needed even for the already agreed initiatives? It's

the poor who pay the cost of indecision and delay," Bob Geldof, Live Aid organiser in the mid-eighties and drawn into the drop-the-debt movement by Bono, said. "Were the spirit of this frail old man mirrored in a practical way by our political leaders then the final push of political will to eradicate this unnecessary tragedy would be easily achieved. And I liked his shoes."

Bono suggested that the Pope's red-brown Gucci's may well have been fakes bought in Poland. "To have that grace, to be so light with such a heavy issue weighing on his mind was something I'll remember always," the U2 singer continued. "And it is a heavy issue that, at the end of the 20th century, there are over a billion people in dire circumstances, and people of my generation are tired of throwing pennies at the problem."

"They want to be part of a bigger idea, to effect the structure of this economy, and this is the biggest and best idea that any of us have heard to deal with such a problem on such a scale." The American producer Quincy Jones, who was also part of the delegation, said: "We're talking about humanity. This man is not in the greatest of health right now, but he put every inch of fortitude and spirit into being involved in the project because he feels the same, if not more so, as we all do."

"I don't think I've been this impressed since meeting Duke Ellington, Frank Sinatra and Stravinsky, but this was in a whole other realm."

Latino jazz star Willie Colon said the Western economies could afford to wipe out the debts of their poorer neighbours: "It would take $6 billion to educate everyone in the Third World, and in America they spent $8 billion a year on cosmetics. It would take $9 billion to bring electricity and water to everyone that needs it, and in Europe and America we spent $17 billion on dog food."

"It really is a shame. It's not gonna cost us anything, we're not gonna feel it, and it's the right thing to do." Delegation members received a medal from the Pope as they left. "What did you get yours for?" Bob Geldof asked Bono, "Mine's for geography."

267

THE RECORD YOU HAVEN'T HEARD YET

IF IT ALMOST CERTAINLY won't be this year then it will definitely be next year. It has no name, no running order and no release date but it's safe to say that a new U2 album is being made even as you read these words. In fact, despite talk of well-earned rests and long breaks, the band, according to Adam, went back into the studio just six weeks after returning home from the PopMart tour. "We didn't want to lose the momentum that the touring had produced," he explained, in a break from recording to keep Propaganda readers up to speed.

"We wanted to write songs while the material that we had generated on the road was still fresh in the mind." So from the summer of '98, the band have been in and out of the studio in Dublin, developing material partly conceived on tour and partly written since.

THEY'VE BEEN RECORDING ON AND OFF FOR OVER A YEAR. WITHIN A YEAR WE'LL KNOW ALL ABOUT IT. (PROBABLY.) MEANTIME, ADAM CLAYTON OFFERS A FEW CLUES TO WHAT U2 ARE UP TO IN THE STUDIO.

A year on, there have been, inevitably, many interruptions. Brian Eno and Daniel Lanois on board, they got some speed up in the autumn and there was even talk of a second millennium release date – but then came the decision to release the first volume of the Greatest Hits album which begat the Sweetest Thing single, which begat a video, which begat a promotional schedule ... which begat some perspective.

This year, however, Eno and Lanois have been a more constant presence as the raw material from touring and the late autumn '98 demo sessions have been developed. By late spring, Adam reported that the band were working with 'about 20 pieces of music and trying to reduce them to fifteen.' One plan was to complete the bulk of recording by late summer.

'THERE IS A GREAT DEAL OF JOY IN THE STUDIO; IT SEEMS EFFORTLESS AT TIMES'

Bono, unsurprisingly, was sounding upbeat about the atmosphere in the studio, when asked about the recording during an on-line interview for the Jubilee 2000 Campaign. "We're kinda running after it at the moment which is a good sign," he said.

"It's usually the other way round. It's the sound of four people playing in a room, four people who have spent most of their lives together, but feeling like it's the first time. It feels really fresh to me."
The theme of "four people playing music" was common to Adam's upbeat report on recording. "It's not a difficult process, in fact it's been very pleasant," he said, sounding almost surprised. "Everyone is in good form, Larry is playing great, as is Edge, and Bono is coming up with some great melodies. I have to say there is a great deal of joy in the studio; it seems effortless at times."

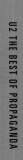

But after all these years, he also knows that U2 albums are rarely born painlessly. He has no doubt that it, "will inevitably come down to hard graft and putting in the hours – but to date the inspiration for this record has come much more easily than last time."

And the band have taken a different approach to recording than they did last time round. With "Pop", he explained, "we set out to try and mould the music into many different things." In contrast, this time they are "trying to preserve the recording of the band as a unit", U2's music from "Achtung Baby" has been such a critical success not least because it has signalled a band who have been successful with one kind of music, making a successful transition to a new mode, without abandoning the former. As the creative community that is U2 grows older, Adams points out that, "it's one thing grabbing the music, it's another to find your place in that music when you are artists like ourselves with a certain maturity." "There is some soul-searching as we embark on a new record, it's what any artist is trying to do." What they try not to forget when they are recording is to aim to "continually redefine yourself through the music."

'THE MOST UNIQUE MUSIC WE MAKE AS U2 IS WITH THE FOUR OF US PLAYING INSTRUMENTS IN A ROOM TOGETHER'

"You know that you have been successful with one kind of music in the past but you don't want to repeat yourself ... With 'Pop' we were happy to allow programmers and mixers to go off with material and come back with mixes, stamping their mark on the music ... and that was a record we are all immensely proud of, the only record we could have made at the time. But the principle we're working with this time is that the most unique music we make as U2 is with the four of us playing instruments in a room together."

So, after two decades of making songs, how does the process work today?

"We come to the table with certain songs and ideas but Brian and Danny have an input which allows us to do things that just the four of us could not do. They are really the conscience of the band: we are always trying to do things that are hard for us but they are always trying to make us do things that we find easy!"

Eno, who has been producing U2 since "The Unforgettable Fire" in 1984, emphasises the importance of "time-investment". He is constantly asking if the band are investing too much time in one track when another, which might have had far less time spent on it, may have far more potential. "It can be a strong argument and offers us a lot of possibilities in the studio."

But the flame of optimism and self-belief, at the heart of U2 since they first met, appears to burn no less brightly two decades on. The new U2 record, whenever it arrives, will be the best they could possibly make, perhaps the best they've ever made. "I'd like to think," concludes Adam, "That we are making the greatest U2 record we've ever made. Bono already does think that! But I'd say that we have still to go through a lot of heartache and pain, we have still to feel the real pressure of deadlines."

PROPAGANDA

SUMMER 2000 - SUMMER 2002

10 November 1999: Bono models with Naomi Campbell for the Millennium Issue of British Vogue. Photo: Mario Testino

under construction

You want to know what is happening with the new U2 album. We want to know what is happening with the U2 album. Only four men have the answer – and one of them is The Edge.

Interview: Martin Wroe
Additional reporting: Jim Carroll

Right here and right now, there is only ONE thing we want to talk to The Edge about. Yes, we do want to know about The Million Dollar Hotel and we do want to know about what music he is listening to at present but, more pertinently, we want to know about the new U2 album, slowly cooking over a stove which Brian Eno and Daniel Lanois are tending in Dublin's docklands.

When Propoganda sits down with The Edge to have a cup of tea, he's quite chipper. "There is a good chance that this could be our best record yet, it's all in the next couple of months.'

It has taken a while, hasn't it?
We could probably have had an album finished last year and had it out before the end of the year but I don't think it would have been as good a record. I'm really happy we stuck at it. When I wake up in the morning I'm really excited at what we're creating – which is not to say it's easy, but there is some great stuff going on.

How would you describe the album-to-be?
I would say it is very much a band record, it's us playing together, very simple, perhaps back to like our first few records with guitar, bass, drums, maybe some keyboards but not that much – I might have done a couple of different guitars on some tracks but still very simple. It's in the face of the way technology is pushing music forward. Rather than go in that direction, this is an attempt to bring it back to what a band does best. I'm a huge fan of dance music, but we have an expertise, something special that no-one else can do. And that's where our focus is.

So these back to basics rumours we have been hearing are true then?
It's a very simple record. This place is really a kind of glorified songwriting workshop, a rehearsal room that we've added recording equipment to. Consequently, the emphasis is not so much on the sonics but more on the nuts and bolts of the material, the ideas that go into it. We can either keep working here and find a way of bringing them alive sonically, of else we might even look at recording some of them elsewhere. But most of the effort has gone into the material.

It sounds like you have rediscovered a lust for rock & roll?
We certainly haven't given up our interest in exploring the fringe of what the band is capable of and what a band can mean today, but for the moment, we are interested in exploring what actually it is to be in a band, in the face of where music is being pushed by technology. There is stuff you just can't do with samplers and drum machines – there are certain feels and sounds that only a band can produce. Previous to this, we would have been excited at exploring the outer limits of where the band could go as a band, and still hold the centre. Now we're happy to explore what that centre is all about, the band itself, what that can do. There is a certain kind of vitality and immediacy, an impact that music can have when it is chopped back to its primary colours.

Any tracks which stand out at this stage?
"Stuck In A Moment (Which You Can't Get Out Of)" is very strong because it's so unusual: it's like an incredible pop song, but done by us and done our way so it sounds like a U2 song but it's incredibly melodic and also has this gospel aspect. Another track called "Home" is going to be a stand-out, very uplifting and beautiful. There's a tune called "Elevation" which has an almost hip-hop groove – but being played by us doesn't sound like anything out there.

Have you been digging out many unused gems from before for this record?
[Laughs] I suppose I am the archaeologist, I will find the rough mix from four months ago that has the classic drum fill on it. Generally I can find it, these are the things you tick off in your subconscious – "That's classic, whatever happens that is going to make the album" – and when you find that, you keep your hands on it. The subconscious is weird, if you really are consumed by something, it will keep working and sometimes it will get the answer. It tends to happen when you're really in it – and that's the way its been for the last six months.

It's clear that when it comes to songwriting, it's a combination of the four members. Has this continued on the new record?
Oh yes, there is no demarcation. Like yesterday, Larry was sitting down and going through this tune that we had pretty much left to one side most of last year and hadn't really thought about. It was just this very atmospheric two minutes that we had, which we thought might be a little interlude. And suddenly he goes, "Wow I think this could go somewhere else..." and hums this melody

>>

>> line, which was actually very cool. So we tried that, we hummed it into a cassette player, I've worked on it and it's ended up being the centre piece of the music on this new song. Larry might only do that twice on a record, but they might be some of the most important steps. That happens the other way too: there might be a drumbeat I have in my head that I'll hum to Larry, and he goes off and develops it – and hey presto, we have some other angle on a song.

Despite this democracy, I assume each member has a certain role?
Well, my role has developed into probably instigator of musical ideas, putting forward chord progressions or whatever could go towards making a U2 song. That said, it's always a surprise when you see what happens to them; what ones fly and what ones don't.
At times I felt sorry for Bono – at different moments he would have loved to be in a studio with us, but happened to be on a plane going to some meeting. Mostly it worked out okay, because the rest of us have a hell of a lot of work to do on our own. I felt I benefited hugely from having the amount of time that I did to work on music, on chord progressions and guitar ideas. He didn't have as much time as he might want to work on the lyrics but we've no gun at our heads and when this next deadline comes along, if we're not happy, we can always put it off a little longer. I'd say the benefits of Bono not being around for certain periods have outweighed the negatives – we've made good use of the breaks. That said, if there was more than one person scattered then we would not have a record at all.'

Did many ideas destined for the new album end up finding space on the *Million Dollar Hotel* soundtrack?
Wim had already earmarked "The First Time" from the *Zooropa* record as something he wanted in the film and it seemed like a mutually beneficial situation to allow "The

Ground Beneath Her Feet" to go onto the soundtrack – since it was already pretty much finished, it was perfect. There's also a tune called "Stateless", which again was one we felt was a beautiful tune but that might not make the U2 record. So when Bono was starting to put the soundtrack together, he asked whether they could go on the soundtrack record. It seemed like the perfect thing to do with them, because they weren't going to make the U2 album. The only one that was in any doubt was "The Ground Beneath Her Feet", but we already had so many great ballads that it seemed like we didn't really need another one.

An American college band – Mnemonic – released a cover version of "The Ground..." on their website before your version had even been aired on radio...
They've released their version of our song before we've released our version of our song? That's very funny, some kind of a first but it's great, I love that stuff. The internet should be welcomed with open arms because technology has always been good for music. Whatever shape it's come in – cassettes, or CDs – music has benefited. The record companies should stop being so scared of it and get into it: the truth is that people are interested in great music along with great artwork, great pressings – great quality – and while the market for proper CDs will always be there, that doesn't mean people won't download music from websites. There will be additional forms of distribution which can be instigated by the record companies or the owners of the copyright.
In fact I heard of a great idea – Project Nigel, I think it was called – where music on the net would be encoded with some sort of watermark, so that whenever it was transferred on the net someone would have to pay a tiny amount of money to the copyright holder. That would make every person on the net a possible music outlet; far from trying to stop people compiling their own websites for music, it would turn it around, and everyone out there who's into music could put together compilations. It would cost a few pence to send them to your friends or to download them and everyone is served – the musicians get something out of it, the record companies who own the copyright get something out of it and people get the freedom to do what they want. I think that's creative, turning what people see as a negative into a positive.

There's talk of a tour next spring, isn't there?
I was just looking through a Japanese magazine at some shots of the Chili Peppers on the road and my heart did sink! But I'm always somewhat daunted at touring, it's not unusual for me. I can't conceive doing the stadium show in a more impressive way than Zoo TV and PopMart, they were purpose-built ways of doing those big shows, so in some ways I feel we've done the stadium thing. We've achieved that when a lot of bands were saying it couldn't be done.

So we can expect something a bit different next time found?
It will be a little bit less of a big deal in every sense and I'm looking forward to that – simply because the workload last time was astonishing. We had fantastic designers and great people to help us, but basically we oversaw everything, and it was too ambitious given the amount of time we had to do it in. I imagine we'll start smaller, try and keep more options open about where the tour is going. Perhaps we won't tie ourselves into a set period of time. That said, I looked at the concert film the other week and it was great!

What does The Edge in 2000 feel there is left to achieve?
As a songwriter and guitar player there's a lot more I have to learn, and also for U2. Whatever we have, I have no idea how it works, but I do recognise that it is unique and special. When we're on it, there's no-one like us and I'd love to see that continue. There are challenges along the way – like how are we going to do it in ten years time, when we're all nearly fifty! How will we be able to keep doing what we're doing? I don't know all the answers to that one yet!

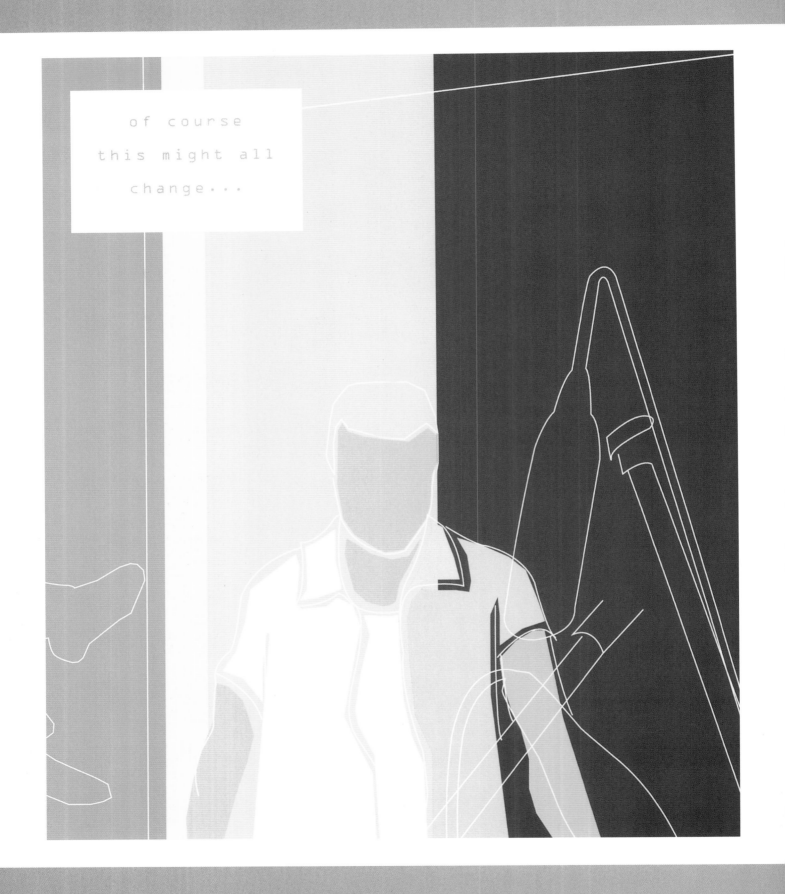

A fly-on-the-wall glimpse of life in the studio ... MARTIN WROE watches U2 assemble the new album and offers to make the tea while ANJA GRABERT takes the shots

Bongolese, as Daniel Lanois calls it, is coming through the loudspeakers in a recording studio on the riverside in Dublin where a new U2 album is being born. The tune is a new one, the words and phrases random, with the occasional explicable line emerging, but there is no doubt who the musicians are. The song is called "Home" ... at the moment.

"'Dampening down the soul ...' was that?" asks Lanois of Edge. "I like that." Both have notebooks in hand but as they try to decipher the taped language of the singer, each is transcribing a different lyric.

"'You compensate for common sense with moonlight...'?" says Edge, smiling at a line he enjoys. He asks the engineer to stop the tape. It is February, there are only two full months of recording left before the point when U2 want to have the new record finished if it is to have an autumn release date. The album has been in the making since the end of the PopMart tour but it was never the intention to rush things: in between band-members have had soundtracks to make, campaigns to back, children to give birth to and life to catch up on. But now it feels like the end-game is approaching.

"Sometimes," says Edge, "when you are making a record you sense that there is some magic going on. And at the moment with this one, that sense is there a lot."

Bono will be back in a moment, he has gone across to the offices of Principle Management to receive an award on camera from MTV for his work with Jubilee 2000. It is mid-evening, and after eight hours in the studio, Adam and Larry have departed, leaving Edge and Lanois discussing how many "definites" they have for the new album and how many "maybes".

There's a large whiteboard hung on the studio wall. On the left-hand side, the band have listed twelve tracks, followed by boxes with ticks inside them – big or small – indicating the progress of lyric, arrangement, recording and so on. On the right hand side of the board is another list, with another eight songs. Surely not a double album?

"The songs on the left are those that are favourites for the album," explains Edge "The songs on the right are those that are fighting for a place on the album." As he says this he suddenly remembers another track presumably from another list that is fighting to be remembered to get on a whiteboard to get on the album. "Peace on Earth," he says to Lanois. "Danny, we've forgotten to put up Peace on Earth."

"That's true," says Lanois. "But you know, we might only need nine great songs to make a great album." The names of the songs are working titles and may well be entirely different by the autumn, but for the record, the column on the right reads: "Original of the Species"; "Stuck in a Moment"; "Elevation"; "Kite"; "Yesterday and Tomorrow"; "Sometime"; "Home"; "In A Little While"; "The Sun", "The Moon and The Stars"; and "Wild Honey".

The column on the left features "When I Look at the World"; "Beautiful Day"; "Jubilee"; "Bulldozer"; "Love and Peace (soul)"; "Stranded and Grace". "Wow!" says Lanois, scribbling in his notebook as the tape rolls again. "'Lonely soul'."

"No, that wasn't 'Lonely Soul'," says the guitarist "That's 'Morning' he's singing." Even if they can't agree on an interpretation between them, the duo transcribe what they believe are the words corresponding to the sound of Bono's voice and try to develop the phrasing, to improve the way they scan.

'You need round sounds in the vocals,' explains Edge. 'Song lyrics are distinct from poetry, you've got to capitalise on the vowel sound in the song.'

Lanois has been in the studio for a few days, the latest of several visits. Brian Eno hasn't been here for a few weeks but he will be back soon and is listening to the latest material every week.

"It's probably as well they haven't been here the whole time, they might have lost their reason at this point!" explains Edge. 'It's given us a chance to work on the songs on our own so when they come back in we play them stuff and they get inspired and that keeps the energy up.'

Bono arrives back, looking exhausted. He didn't enjoy the video-link but now he has his songs to think about and Danny hands him a sheet of their translation work. Only he really knows what he's singing. Within minutes he is tapping away on the keyboards of his recently recovered lap-top, using Lanois' notes as a prompt to fashion a finished lyric from the work in progress. While Edge suggests ways of musically re-editing "Home" to the engineer, Bono is lost in song-world, mouthing phrases while one hand raps to indicate progress.

"The songs keep cell-dividing," he says. "You take a musical idea to what you hope is a transcendental point, but maybe it doesn't get there. Then you have to go back and take it in a new direction which means I have to keep reworking my lyrical ideas. I've got about twenty sets of lyrics," he adds with a laugh. "And we've got about forty songs."

The phone goes and he has to leave the room to take it.

"I thought we agreed Clinton couldn't ring before ten pm," says Edge to Lanois, in mock-anger "We're trying to make an album here!" Lanois grins, they've been here before.

"It can get a bit surreal here sometimes," adds Edge. "Sammy came down one day making a halo-shape above his head and it turned out it was the Vatican for Bono. Just what you need, the Pope interrupting the overdubs."

Still, the absence of Larry, Adam and now Bono is an opportunity not to be missed. While no-one else is looking Edge wanders across to the whiteboard, studies it for a moment or two and then deftly rubs out "In A Little While" from its proud position on the left, transferring it to the right. He writes "Peace on Earth" into the now vacant place on the left. Of course, this might all change.

building the new U2

Guess what? They're back. And they mean business.
MARTIN WROE took notes

three and a half years ... in brief. A smash hit single with "The Sweetest Thing"; several million sales of a greatest hits album; a global campaign to cancel the debts of the world's poorest countries; a film soundtrack for **"The Million Dollar Hotel"**; eighteen months in the studio and forty new songs. Which came down to eleven. Which spawned a worldwide hit in Beautiful Day. And finally, the eleventh U2 studio album in two decades – on your radio, in your CD player, hell ... everywhere.

Larry, Edge, Adam and Bono are here again, and guess what? With a worldwide tour starting in Miami in March, they're planning to stay around for some time.

Always good to keep busy, don't you think?

PART ONE – THE FACTS, THE FIGURES

"All That You Can't Leave Behind" hit No 1 in 32 countries worldwide. In the US, the album produced record opening week sales for U2, with 428,000 copies. U2's last album sold 347,000 copies in its opening week in the US.

The album topped charts in Australia, Austria, Belgium, Brazil, Colombia, Denmark, Finland, France, Germany, Iceland, Ireland, Israel, Italy, Mexico, Netherlands, New Zealand, Norway, Portugal, Slovenia, Spain and the UK.

In the UK it was U2's eight No 1 album – the only group in chart history with more are The Beatles (13), The Rolling Stones (10), Abba and Queen (9 each), while Led Zeppelin also have eight.
"All That You Can't Leave Behind" sold 164,000 copies in its first week on sale in the UK – **"POP"** did 152,000 and the **"Best of 1980–1990"** sold 140,000 copies.

PART TWO – LET'S MAKE A MOVIE …

Charles de Gaulle airport, Paris. Midway through an ecstatic live performance of "Beautiful Day", a jumbo jet roars out from behind U2 and into the sky over their heads. The band, naturally, just play. "They were incredibly brave to go through with that," says Jonas Akerlund, Swedish director of the "Beautiful Day" video. "I feared for their lives, risking everything in the cause of art." Akerlund is one of the hottest properties in the game; recent work includes promos for Madonna ("Music"), Moby ("Porcelain") and the dearly departed Smashing Pumpkins ("Try") – he's probably best known, however, for Madonna's Grammy winning "Ray of Light" video and The Prodigy's rather controversial "Smack My Bitch Up".

"I always knew that I wanted to do a performance-based video with U2, they've done so many memorable videos but I can't remember them performing as a band in such a way before." The 34-year-old may be at a psychological advantage to other directors, owing to his pedigree as a musician in several rather, ahem, loud Swedish bands. Artists like Metallica and Marilyn Manson still rave over cult legends Bathory, in which he played drums. The man has been listening to U2 since they began, but only met them when he visited their Dublin studios in late spring of this year. If he was impressed with the new material, well … nothing was finished.

It wasn't until July that "Beautiful Day" had become the first single and, following a successful photo shoot with U2 regular Anton Corbijn, the strikingly modernist architecture of Paris' Charles de Gaulle airport identified itself as a perfect video location. Akerlund knew that he wanted to put an element of surprise in the video because "the song surprises you, the way it really kicks in, this big contrast between verse and chorus."

The two days of filming, though, were less than beautiful, hovering on the borders of a bureaucratic nightmare. "There was so much red-tape," he recalls. "It was a mess at times. All shoots have dramas, yes – but this had more than most."

Not surprising really, when you elect to shoot the band on carpets, on a runway – between two other runways – with planes landing and taking off every two minutes. Then there's the singer of course, invited to mischief-make around the

arrival and departure lounges while Akerlund kept him in focus with a (hidden) long lens. "We had a sort of plan for Bono, like we gave him some fake money to give out to people, but generally he was improvising most of the time," he explains. "He feels like an actor to me."

The finished results are already a classic of sorts, and its creator has no doubts that U2's new music will score with fans worldwide. "We have a phrase in Swedish, 'to age with beauty', and I feel this is a band who will do this. They are a 'man band' and that is strong – for me the only band in the world like that. They are going to be as influential with this new album as they have been in their career so far."

And are you going to argue with him?

PART THREE – A WALK ACROSS THE ROOFTOPS ...

You go away for a couple of years, then you come back and there's four thousand people waiting for you, lining the River Liffey. U2's first live rooftop appearance since the last one – 1987, Los Angeles, "Million Dollar Hotel" – almost stopped the traffic again, this time in their own town.

Late September, the band showed up atop their own hotel, The Clarence, and performed "Beautiful Day" and "Elevation" for BBC TV's legendary **Top Of The Pops**. It was the first time they had performed live for the show in 17 years.

"The last time we played on a roof

they threw us off," said Edge. "This time it's our own roof, so they can't touch us." Fans, piled onto adjacent buildings and lining the Liffey, cheered and danced as the band played – and half-way through Bono requested a pair of scissors to cut down the waist-high curtain around the balcony railings of the roof-top garden. Anyone there will tell you it was an afternoon to remember.

To mark the elpee release, the band have conducted a series of live performances in cities and countries on several continents. They followed the Clarence performance with appearances in London, Paris, Madrid and Stockholm ... pausing only to steal the show at the MTV European Video awards along the way (Bono's sheepskin jacket – nice). Amongst the songs they were playing regularly – hinting perhaps at the set list for the tour – were "New York", "Elevation", "Stuck in a Moment" and (of course) "Beautiful Day".

PART FOUR – OH YES, THE SOUND ...

Let's turn to the people in question ...
"It's a very simple record. This place (the studio) is really a kind of glorified songwriting workshop, a rehearsal room that we've added recording equipment to. Consequently, the emphasis is not so much on the sonics but more on the nuts and bolts of the material, the ideas that go into it ... most of the effort has gone into the material."
EDGE

"One of the only problems we've had is that when you put the band in the room with no shenanigans or trickery, they tend to sound a bit like U2."
BONO

"Who would have thought that'd be a problem when we started out?"
LARRY

"Bono's lyrics this time ... in a sense they're less poetic, less romantic and more real. To me they're much more about where he's coming from and what he's dealing with. I think this record has a great tenderness. And I'm sure it addressed the way he feels about the commitment to the band, and to his family, to his children and to Ali."
ADAM

"I was looking for intimacies and conversational kind of stuff. I said to myself, 'This is no time for poetry, in the arch sense of that word. No time for smart arse. People are busy, the beginning of a new century, it's like what's on your mind, what's in your heart, and what have you go in your soul that might make a difference in a day?'"
BONO

"The pressure is to be innovative – to come up with something fresh, exciting,

a new way of looking at things. Especially at this place in the history of music. We've got 50 years of electric guitar behind us, and we've got to be innovative. That's tough. Edge has always managed to do it. Even on this record, he's come up with a few new sounds that are very impressive."
DANIEL LANOIS, CO-PRODUCER

"What gets us to our best moments is a kind of explosive energy, where it kind of all comes together. You can be waiting a long time for that to happen, and that's the frustration sometimes for us. That's the only way we know how ... Nothing is sacred. Nothing is finished, literally, until the CD's in the shop."
EDGE

"I'm a big fan of 'Beautiful Day' – probably because I was instrumental in breaking the back of it, coming up at a certain point with a vocal melody with the Edge. Eno manipulated it to the point where we sounded like a boys' choir. When you get something like that, and it suddenly sounds uplifting, it's one of those little gifts where you think, my God, we've got it!"
DANIEL LANOIS

PART FIVE – THE PACKAGING ...

Adam's grinning about something. Larry's wondering what the hold up is. Edge is lost in the middle distance. Bono's checking his passport. Four travellers, caught with their baggage, midway through the journey. A kind of homecoming? The cover of "All That You Can't Leave Behind". Beautifully simple ... but the simplicity is deceptive.

"It's an image that harks back to 'The Joshua Tree'," explains Steve Averill, of Dublin-based design consultancy Four5One. "U2 love the cyclical nature of what they do, that their albums come in sequences and I think the feeling with this new one is that it marks another departure."
Steve has been designing the sleeves of U2 records since, well, before there were U2 records. With the exception of "Rattle and Hum" – which was done in America because of Paramount Pictures' involvement – he has created the look of every album. Often he will come up with dozens of approaches before the band find what they are looking for. This time, travelling with the band and Anton Corbijn from Dublin to the south of France, they found the final look almost by accident, while on a stopover under the cool, modernist lines of Charles de Gaulle airport.

"We didn't have a lot of time, Anton was shooting on the move, between flights – which gives the photos a sense of journey," Averill says. "And when we came to look at them afterwards, it was interesting, this sense of all four band members stopping to think, 'Where do I go from here?'"
Corbijn's shoot at Charles de Gaulle was so evocative that it also ended up providing the images for the sleeve of the "Beautiful Day" single, and for the booklet accompanying the finished album. Averill, who listened to the album as the band recorded it to glean clues for his own direction, says the look, like the music, is "more simple and organic."

"With U2, the look is like the music, it always comes back to the simple strength of the four of them together."

PART SIX – THE END ... NO, MAKE THAT THE BEGINNING

"We've got eleven songs and we feel they are songs we want to spend a year playing live," says the singer. As for talk of leaving the big stadiums behind, well ... the tour will go smaller, according to Bono – but not that small. "Some people glamourise playing clubs, but we spent most of our early days trying to get out of clubs!"

As Propaganda went to press, the tussle for second single from the album – between "Elevation" and "Stuck In a Moment" – ended with the latter emerging the winner. Maybe "Elevation" will make it as a third single, perhaps before the tour, during which the band will be playing non-stop for six months, doubtless, so rumour has it, completing the first stint with an Irish outdoor show, at Slane Castle in August.

If you are into U2 – and chances are, if you are reading this you must be – don't worry yourself about all that you can't leave behind. The best is all ahead of you.

THIS TIME IT'S PERSONAL

Snapshot **Slane Castle**, Ireland, August 2001. Home at last, writes MICHAEL ROSS

Here are the young men. They are standing on a stage in a field in Meath. To their left is a castle. In front of them is a crowd of 20,000. Some have come to see these young men of whom so much is expected, but most are here to see Irish rock legends Thin Lizzy.

Hedonistic, self-destructive and rudderless, Lizzy represent the past. The four young men, burning with self-belief, represent the future. What they have that makes them special is hard to pin down just yet but has certain visible features. It's ascetic, ecumenical, suburban, fizzing with enthusiasm but also determined in its rejection of received Irish and rock orthodoxies.

Of the four, the singer represents the band's spirit in its most distilled, turbulent and mesmerising form. He has studied other singers – David Bowie, Iggy Pop, Ian Curtis, Howard Devoto, Marc Bolan – and these have fed into what he is doing. But what he is doing is something new, something with a lust for life … But with a big heart, too.

Something spiritual, something that together they are able to tap into. On this Sunday in a field in Meath, they fail to tap into it. Immersed in the recording of their second album, they are badly under-rehearsed. Pale from weeks cloistered in the studio, blinking in the afternoon sun, they stumble through their set.

They're smart enough to know it's substandard, and they resolve never to let it happen again. They never let it happen again. That's the thing about them. They're not just idealistic and bright and diligent: they're extraordinarily determined.

Twenty years later, almost to the day: four middle-aged men are standing on a stage in a field in Meath. To their left is a castle. Much has changed since they were last here, yet perhaps more has remained the same. In front of them is a crowd of over 80,000. All have come to see the four men of whom so much has been expected.

They long ago delivered on any and all expectations. They became the biggest band in the world with "The Joshua Tree". Later, with "Achtung Baby" and the Zoo TV tour, they became the best. Now, a decade on from "Achtung Baby", they are making another triumphant homecoming.

Poetry, wrote the Romanian poet Paul Celan, is both a going out and a sort of homecoming. In borrowing part of Celan's formulation for the title of one of U2's best songs, Bono reinforced the way in which

their work pushes in two directions at once: out into new terrain and home to core values.

U2 have made a life of going out and coming home. Every time one goes out, one returns changed. Every time U2 have gone out they too have returned changed, to a country that itself has changed. A different U2, a different Ireland, a different audience: enough variables to make each homecoming unpredictable.

Since that 1981 appearance at Slane, U2 have become such hardened pros that a dud show is no longer much of a possibility. The question is not whether the show will be good but whether the magic will happen.
When it happens – as it did in 1985 at Croke Park, and at the second 1987 show there – it lifts the experience from merely good to something intimate and dazzling, something one shouldn't have a right to expect from a band. But it's elusive, it either happens or it doesn't, for reasons seemingly beyond even U2's obsessive control.

U2's homecoming at Slane last year happened over two weekends, not one as initially planned, because of unprecedented demand for tickets. The first show sold out in less than an hour, the second show in little more than an hour, a remarkable show of strength by a band so long in existence.
When the Rolling Stones played Slane in 1982, for example, they were at much the same point in their career as U2 are now, 20 years on from their first flush of youth. When the Stones played Slane they were a museum piece, trading almost entirely on past glories, a band with more than a whiff of formaldehyde about it. U2, by contrast, came to Slane this time around with a hit album, and played to largely a new, young audience eager to hear the band's latest work. They came, too, in extraordinarily difficult circumstances, the funeral of Bob Hewson, Bono's father, having taken place the day before the first show.

The magic didn't quite happen at the second show, a week later, but perhaps in part because of the difficult circumstances it happened at that first show, a concert at least as good as U2 have ever played in Ireland.
Not that it was flawless. The gun control visuals that accompanied "Bullet The Blue Sky" on the Elevation tour, for example, clearly aimed at American audiences, had little resonance at Slane. The show flagged a little in the middle, the least assured moment, as it happened, coming with "A Sort of Homecoming", its muted reception suggesting that the crowd mostly stretched back to "The Joshua Tree" but no further.

But the beginning, the end and much in between confirmed U2 as the great live band of their generation, in particular the encores of "One" and "Walk On", the songs' themes of love, friendship, mortality and transcendence fused in a performance of tremendous poignancy.

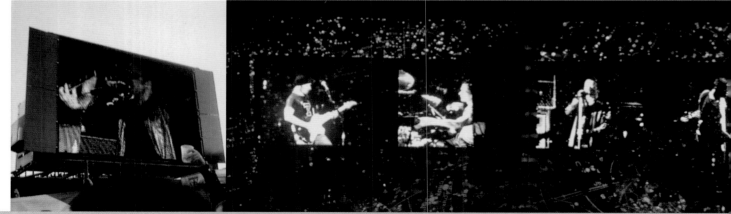

Throughout there were two surprises. One was the way in which the songs from "All You Can't Leave Behind" have grown from the versions on the album, making some of the recorded versions sound like work in progress. Again, "Walk On" was a high point, in its full live form the most articulate expression of U2 as they now stand, unlike the album version, which is frustratingly abbreviated by comparison.

The other surprise was Adam Clayton. He has never played better than he is playing now, and his Zen-like focus and calm, and the way he locks into Larry Mullen's drumming, has given U2 a subtly but powerfully different character.

Also feeding into this is the palpable sense that the band is a finite enterprise. Twenty years ago, around the time they played Slane, U2 experienced a crisis of Christian conscience that nearly ended the band. Thus they have always been aware that it will not go on forever. They got through that and other crises, but now their work is suffused with a sense of the finite, and of realism about themselves, their bond and their differences.

As the staging of "Elevation" reinforced – with its four screens directly over the band showing each member in isolation – they're one but they're not the same. Their great achievement has been to acknowledge that, to grow from boys to men together, to stay faithful to the sense of spirit that has driven them from the start, and despite the finite nature of it all, to keep singing their glorious hallelujahs.

AMNESTY *INTERNATIONAL*

U2 have supported the work of Amnesty International since their earliest days, and frequently used the pages of Propaganda to forward their cause. Here are some examples of campaigns with which they've been involved over the years.

SET THEM FREE

Amnesty International say that one of their most successful methods of securing the release of Prisoners of Conscience is by their consistent letter writing campaign. You can be a genuine help in this campaign, by spending ten minutes writing three letters for the prisoners below. Please help. It does work.

Mohamed Srifi was arrested in 1974 and held until January 1977 when he was tried with 138 others on charges of belonging to an illegal association and plotting against the internal security of the state. All of them were members or former members of three Marxist groups. One hundred and twenty nine defendants, including 39 in absentia, received sentences of between five and 30 years imprisonment. An Amnesty International observer at the trial said that it fell short of international standards of fairness: defendants were not allowed to communicate with their defence lawyers during the hearings nor were they permitted to make statements about torture and ill-treatment they said had occurred in pre-trial detention. Although the prosecution argued that the defendants were planning the violent overthrow of the monarchy, there was no evidence to show that they had ever used or advocated violence.

Defendants had reportedly been held incommunicado before their trial was over a year – far exceeding the limits prescribed by Moroccan law for such detention – and in many cases, subjected to electric shock treatment, beatings and suspension by the hands or feet.

Mohamed Srifi is in Kenitra Central Prison where he is reported to be continuing his studies.

Please write courteous letters appealing for his immediate release to: *His Majesty King Hassan II, Palais Royal, Rabat, Morocco* and *Moulay Mustapha Belarbi Alaqui, Minister of Justice, Palais de la Mamounia, Rabat, Morocco.*

Houmphanh Norasing is a former member of parliament in LAOS who has been held since 1975 for 're-education'. No explanation has been given for Houmphanh Norasing's detention but Amnesty believes that he is being held for disagreeing with government policies and practices. Since 1985 most of the people held in Houah Phanh and other remote north-eastern provinces for 're-education' have been released, but 37 are reportedly still being held. He is thought to be detained near the former Sop Pan detention centre from which, until recently, people held for 're-education' were sent on hard labour assignments. The detention centre has reportedly been dismantled and those still detained are held under the authority of the police in three residence blocks and are given work assignments by the provincial Public Works Department.

AMNESTY INTERNATIONAL

Amnesty International, the worldwide human rights campaigning body, reports that one of its most successful methods of securing the release of Prisoners of Conscience is through their consistent letter writing campaign.

Propaganda readers have been contributing to this campaign from the earliest days of the magazine: in each issue we carry profiles of some prisoners of conscience from different parts of the world. You can help bring pressure to bear on authorities who are imprisoning them unjustly by taking ten minutes to write a couple of letters.

Please help. It does work.

Amnesty report that the pattern of human rights violations around the world has changed and is changing. Long term imprisonment is not the most frequent violation of human rights in some regions of the world. Amnesty has to address a wide range of concerns such as 'disappearances', death penalty cases, extra judicial executions (killings outside the law where no trial has taken place) and unfair trials for political prisoners. The phenomenon of 'disappearances', where people are taken away, usually in the middle of the night, is widespread – it inspired the song Mothers of the Disappeared on The Joshua Tree. Very often such people are never seen again while in other cases their bodies are returned to their families often bearing signs of torture or are dumped by the side of the road. Many graves have been found. Your message can bring liberty to a victim of 'disappearance'. You may prevent an execution. The victims are many. The violations wide-ranging. Every appeal counts.

AYSEI MALKAC

Turkey

Amnesty International is concerned for the safety of journalist Aysei Malkac who went missing in Istanbul on 7th August 1993 and is alleged to have been abducted by government agents.

Aysei, born in 1971 in Tunceli, had been working at the main office of the Kurdish-owned newspaper *OzdurGunden* since May 1993. She was a reporter at the editorial office in Istanbul but on the morning of Saturday, 7th August, she left the office at 10am and has not been seen or heard of since.

During the previous week, the newspaper's office and staff had been under heavy surveillance by the police, patrolling the streets in the neighbourhood and monitoring telephone calls. Reportedly, eye-witnesses claim to have seen her being detained in the street, apparently by plainclothes police officers. They are too afraid to testify publicly.

All efforts by the newspaper and Aysei Malkac's lawyers to establish her whereabouts have been unsuccessful. A detainee who was interrogated in the Anti-Terror Branch at the time Aysei Malkac was detained made a public declaration that he had seen her in police custody on 8th/9th August, but to Amnesty International's knowledge the public prosecutor never took his statement or pursued this important lead.

BACKGROUND

Turkey has a Kurdish ethnic minority which is estimated to number some 10 million people, living mainly in south-eastern Turkey.

Since August 1984, when guerrillas of the Kurdish Worker's Party (PKK) started armed attacks against the security forces, more than 10,000 lives have been lost on both sides and among the civilian population in the context of their fight for an independent Kurdish state.

In mid-March 1993 the PKK declared a unilateral ceasefire, its intention to end the fighting and to enter the democratic process as a political party. Operations by the security forces against the PKK continued. The ceasefire was broken when, on 24th May last year, guerrillas of the PKK ambushed a convoy of soldiers, reportedly travelling unarmed and in civilian clothes. They killed 33 soldiers and two civilians. The security forces responded with large-scale military operations covering the entire region. A state of emergency continues to be in force in 10 provinces in the region and the Emergency Legislation Governor in Diyarbakir has extraordinary powers over three additional provinces.

OZGUR GUNDEM is the only Kurdish-owned daily newspaper in Turkey and has consistently reported human rights violations in the provinces under the State of Emergency in the south-east, where most of Turkey's Kurds live. The State Security Court in Istanbul has been seeking to close the paper permanently on charges of separatist propaganda and praising the outlawed PKK. One ruling for temporary closure has already been given by the State Security Court but has yet to be approved by the Appeal Court. Three other prosecutions are continuing. In the 18 months of its existence, seven of the newspapers' journalists and nine people distributing and selling the newspaper have been murdered.

> **Please write courteous letters to the following:**
>
> Prime Minister, Mrs. Tansu Ciller,
> Office of the Prime Minister,
> Basbakanlik,
> 06573 Ankara,   and/or:
> Turkey.
>
> Minister of Justice,
> Mr. Seyfi Oktay,
> Adalet Bakanligi,
> 06659 Ankara,
> Turkey.

Under the previous government Houmphanh Norasing was a member of Parliament for Saybouli province and a member of the National Consultative Council (NCC). The NCC had been set up in 1973 by the Royal Government of National Union (RGNU), a coalition formed as a result of a peace agreement between communist and non-communist forces previously at war in Laos. In 1975 the RGNU was replaced by the Democratic people's Republic of Laos and the new authorities called all NCC members to a meeting in the town of Viengxai in Houa Phanh province. Some NCC members were allowed to return to the capital, Vientiane, but others were kept in detention in Viengxai until 1977, when they were transferred to another 're-education' camp.

Please send courteous letters appealing for immediate release to: *Premier Kaysone Phomvihan, Vientiane, Laos.*

ACKNOWLEDGEMENTS

Principle Management and Carlton Books would like to thank all contributors to U2: *The Best of Propaganda*, notably Geoff Parkyn, Martin Wroe, Steve Averill, Shaughn McGrath, Paul McGuinness, Sheila Roche, Keryn Kaplan, Trevor Bowen, Susan Hunter, Candida Bottaci, Cecilia Coffey, Avril Slevin, David Toraya, Larry Shire, Peter Grant, Anton Corbijn, Mario Testino, Albert Watson, Mark Allan, Colm Henry, Andrew Macpherson, Andrew Mueller, Willie Williams, Hugh McElveen, Melanie Morris, Derek O'Connor, Jeremy Joseph, John Panaro, Regine Moylett and all other contributors who have helped make *Propaganda* what it has been throughout the years.